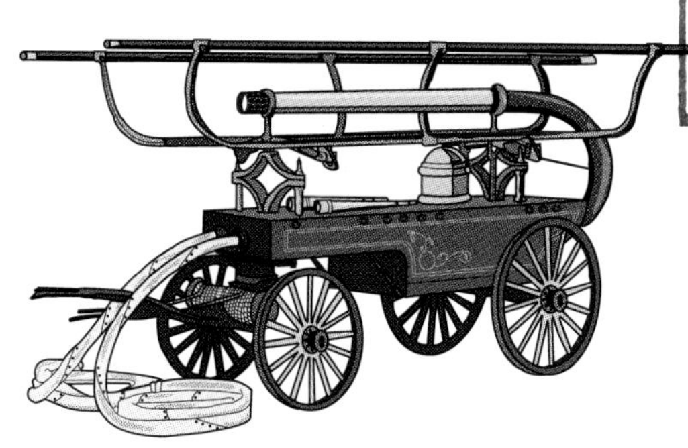

Fire Service ORIENTATION & TERMINOLOGY

Third Edition

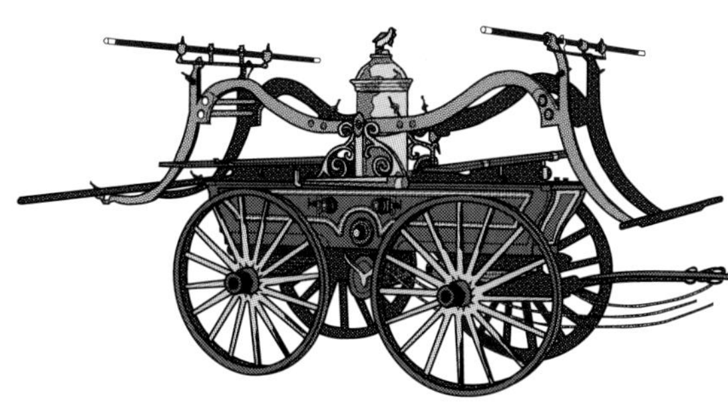

Validated by
The International Fire
Service Training Association

Published by
Fire Protection Publications
Oklahoma State University

Edited by
Michael A. Wieder
Carol M. Smith
Cynthia S. Brakhage

Cover Photo Courtesy of:
Joel Woods, University of Maryland
Fire & Rescue Institute

ISBN 087939-107-3
Library of Congress 93-73664

Third Edition
First Printing, December 1993
Second Printing, February 1995

Printed in the United States of America

Dedication

This manual is dedicated to the members of that unselfish organization of men and women who hold devotion to duty above personal risk, who count on sincerity of service above personal comfort and convenience, who strive unceasingly to find better ways of protecting the lives, homes and property of their fellow citizens from the ravages of fire and other disasters . . . ***The Firefighters of All Nations.***

Dear Firefighter:

The International Fire Service Training Association (IFSTA) is an organization that exists for the purpose of serving firefighters' training needs.Fire Protection Publications is the publisher of IFSTA materials. Fire Protection Publications staff members participate in the National Fire Protection Association, and the International Association of Fire Chiefs.

If you need additional information concerning our organization or assistance with manual orders, contact:

Customer Services
Fire Protection Publications
Oklahoma State University
Stillwater, OK 74078-0118
1 (800) 654-4055

For assistance with training materials, recommended material for inclusion in a manual, or questions on manual content, contact:

Technical Services
Fire Protection Publications
Oklahoma State University
Stillwater, OK 74078-0118
(405) 744-5723

THE INTERNATIONAL FIRE SERVICE TRAINING ASSOCIATION

The International Fire Service Training Association (IFSTA) was established as a "nonprofit educational association of fire fighting personnel who are dedicated to upgrading fire fighting techniques and safety through training." This training association was formed in November 1934, when the Western Actuarial Bureau sponsored a conference in Kansas City, Missouri. The meeting was held to determine how all the agencies interested in publishing fire service training material could coordinate their efforts. Four states were represented at this initial conference. Because the representatives from Oklahoma had done some pioneering in fire training manual development, it was decided that other interested states should join forces with them. This merger made it possible to develop training materials broader in scope than those published by individual agencies. This merger further made possible a reduction in publication costs, because it enabled each state or agency to benefit from the economy of relatively large printing orders. These savings would not be possible if each individual state or department developed and published its own training material.

To carry out the mission of IFSTA, Fire Protection Publications was established as an entity of Oklahoma State University. Fire Protection Publications' primary function is to publish and disseminate training texts as proposed and validated by IFSTA. As a secondary function, Fire Protection Publications researches, acquires, produces, and markets high-quality learning and teaching aids as consistent with IFSTA's mission. The IFSTA Executive Director is officed at Fire Protection Publications.

IFSTA's purpose is to validate training materials for publication, develop training materials for publication, check proposed rough drafts for errors, add new techniques and developments, and delete obsolete and outmoded methods. This work is carried out at the annual Validation Conference.

The IFSTA Validation Conference is held the second full week in July, at Oklahoma State University or in the vicinity. Fire Protection Publications, the IFSTA publisher, establishes the revision schedule for manuals and introduces new manuscripts. Manual committee members are selected for technical input by Fire Protection Publications and the IFSTA Executive Secretary. Committees meet and work at the conference addressing the current standards of the National Fire Protection Association and other standard-making groups as applicable.

Most of the committee members are affiliated with other international fire protection organizations. The Validation Conference brings together individuals from several related and allied fields, such as:

- Key fire department executives and training officers
- Educators from colleges and universities
- Representatives from governmental agencies
- Delegates of firefighter associations and industrial organizations
- Engineers from the fire insurance industry

Committee members are not paid nor are they reimbursed for their expenses by IFSTA or Fire Protection Publications. They come because of commitment to the fire service and its future through training. Being on a committee is prestigious in the fire service community, and committee members are acknowledged leaders in their fields. This unique feature provides a close relationship between the International Fire Service Training Association and other fire protection agencies, which helps to correlate the efforts of all concerned.

IFSTA manuals are now the official teaching texts of most of the states and provinces of North America. Additionally, numerous U.S. and Canadian government agencies as well as other English-speaking countries have officially accepted the IFSTA manuals.

Table of Contents

PREFACE

The third edition of **Fire Service Orientation and Terminology** is written to provide insight for newcomers to the fire service. It will also assist the newcomer with meeting the objectives set forth for the Fire Fighter I level in NFPA 1001, *Standard for Fire Fighter Professional Qualifications*. This manual provides information for new or prospective members on the history, traditions, and organizations of the fire service. There is also an extensive glossary of fire service terminology.

Acknowledgement and special thanks are extended to the members of the validating committee who contributed their time, wisdom, and knowledge to this manual.

Chairman
Robert Noll
Fire Chief
Yukon, OK

Secretary
Bill Hulsey
Drillmaster (Retired)
Broken Arrow, OK

Louis Amabili
Dover, DE

Bob Buell
Alameda, CA

Russ Daly
Lincoln, NE

Nick Duvally
Manhattan Beach, CA

James Hebert
Baton Rouge, LA

Gerald Monigold
Champaign, IL

Charles Page
College Station, TX

Bill Vandevort
Monterey, CA

We would also like to the thank the following individuals and organizations that provided information, photographs, or other assistance toward the completion of this manual.

Oklahoma City Fire Department
  Fire Chief Gary Marrs
  Stations 1, 4, 15, 18, 21, 27, and 33; Maintenance Shop
Stillwater (OK) Fire Department
Edmond (OK) Fire Department
Tulsa (OK) Fire Department
Pennsburg (PA) Fire-Rescue
Harvey Eisner, Tenafly, NJ
Bob Esposito, Pennsburg, PA
Joe Marino, New Britain, CT
Ron Jeffers, New Jersey Metro Fire Photographers Assoc.
Joel Woods, University of Maryland Fire & Rescue Institute
Ron Bogardus, Albany, NY
Emergency One, Inc.
Austin (TX) Fire Department
  Scott Stookey
  Erwin Hadden
Plano (TX) Fire Department
Montgomery County (PA) Fire Academy

East Greenville (PA) Fire Company No. 1
Boulder (CO) Fire Department
Wethersfield (CT) Fire Department
Rocky Hill (CT) Fire Department
Kensington (CT) Fire Department

Gratitude is also extended to the following members of the Fire Protection Publications staff whose contributions made the final publication of this manual possible.

Carl Goodson, Senior Publications Editor
Barbara Adams, Publications Specialist
Marsha Sneed, Publications Specialist
Susan Walker, Instructional Development Coordinator
Don Davis, Publications Production Coordinator
Ann Moffat, Senior Graphic Designer
Desa Porter, Graphic Designer
Lori Williamson, Graphic Designer
Sean Pollard, Graphic Designer
Kimberly Edwards, Photographic Technician
Kayla Moorman, Senior Secretary

Introduction

From a broad perspective, the purpose of the fire service is to protect life and property from the effects of fire and other hazards. This is accomplished by such activities as fire prevention, fire suppression, public fire education, fire investigation, hazardous materials mitigation, and emergency medical services. This list shows that firefighters do much more than just put out fires. Specialized problems, such as hazardous materials and heavy rescue, require extra training to be handled effectively. Emergency medical incidents must now be handled much like a hazardous materials incident.

New firefighters must become acquainted with all of the responsibilities of their job. Firefighters must understand the organizational structure of their department and know how their department interacts with other agencies. It also helps the firefighter to understand some of the history behind his or her occupation.

New firefighters can enter the fire service through any one of several means. They may be hired by one of the career departments that protect larger communities throughout North America. However, the majority of new firefighters are those who join the ranks of the volunteer fire service. Volunteer fire departments protect the major portion of North America. Some may join industrial fire brigades. Regardless of their mode of entry, all firefighters need proper orientation and indoctrination into the field.

PURPOSE AND SCOPE

The purpose of this manual is to acquaint new firefighters with the history, traditions, terminology, organization, and operation of the fire service. In addition, it contains typical job and operation descriptions that should provide insight into the inner workings of the fire service.

This manual will also help the student meet the objectives contained in Section 3-2, **Fire Department Organization** of NFPA 1001, *Standard for Fire Fighter Professional Qualifications*. This will assist candidates for certification to the Fire Fighter I level.

1 Early Traditions And History

Chapter 1
Early Traditions And History

Primitive man's first introduction to fire probably came from fires started by lightning or volcanoes, and these mysterious and powerful forces created many superstitions and myths about fire. One of these myths was that because fire had been created by a supernatural force or being, it would be sacrilegious to allow it to burn out. Man's first use of fire occurred around 500,000 B.C. according to archeologists. When people learned to use fire, the need for keeping it lit became unimportant and its mystic powers declined. People learned that a controlled fire kept them warm, gave them security and light, and served as a focal point for the nightly gathering of the clan. They also learned that an uncontrolled fire could do them physical harm and destroy their property. Recorded in history are many instances where entire villages and cities were destroyed by fire either by accident or as an ancient method of warfare.

EARLY FIRE SERVICES

The earliest known organized firefighters protected the city of Rome. Many great fires destroyed large portions of Rome in 24 B.C. This led Emperor Caesar Augustus to the *familia publica*, a group of 600 servants stationed by the gates of the city for the express purpose of fighting fires. In 6 A.D., after another disastrous fire, Emperor Augustus instituted the Corps of Vigiles, which was to protect Rome for the next 500 years. Rome was divided into districts and protected by about 7,000 vigiles. The Corps was organized by a ranking system of officers and ordinary firefighters — an organization similar to that used by today's larger fire departments. Vigiles were a night patrol of slaves that checked for fires and alerted the town if a fire was discovered. The vigiles, correctly dressed and equipped with buckets and axes, also fought fires and enforced fire prevention. The Corps warned all households that fires could be caused through negligence and instructed occupants to keep water in their rooms. Vigiles also had the authority to dole out summary corporal punishment to offenders.

The First Fire Pump

When was the first fire pump invented? The exact date is unknown. Where people were concentrated in an urban area, the problem of fire became so acute that some methods of fire prevention or fire extinguishment had to be devised. Around 4 B.C., an Alexandrian Greek named Ctesibuis is given credit for inventing a double-force pump known as a *siphona*. This simple device remained the basic mechanical method that operated hand pumps until modern times (Figure 1.1).

A Roman writer who is generally assumed to have lived in the third century B.C. described a fire

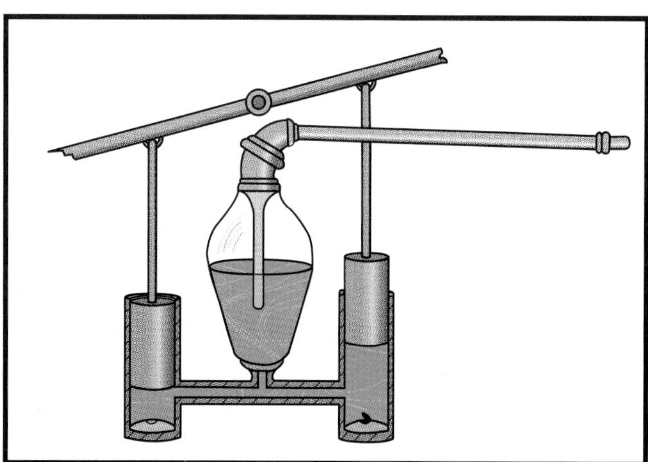

Figure 1.1 The first fire pump was hand operated and used as a double-force pump.

pump that expelled water to a great height. He gave an exact description of the machine, which consisted of two brass cylinders with carefully fitted pistons that sucked water through valves at the base and pushed it through outlet valves into a chamber. As the water rose in the chamber, it compressed the air inside, forcing the water to eject in a steady stream through a pipe and nozzle. The pistons were operated by long handles. It is assumed that the vigiles used these machines. Pieces of these machines have been excavated at many Roman sites.

With the fall of Rome, the vigiles and the fire pump were forgotten in the wilderness of ignorance and superstition of the Dark Ages. With their passing went an organized and well-equipped fire department such as Europe was not to know again for another thousand years.

Extinguishing Techniques

Although people learned early that water was the cheapest, most plentiful, and best agent for extinguishing fire, there were several interesting earlier beliefs and techniques. In Japan, hundreds of people carrying huge fans would line the walls of the palace. They would attempt to fan flying embers away from the palace while the building on fire burned to the ground. In the seventh century, some people believed that ringing church bells in reverse would control large fires. The ringing was not entirely mystical because it served to warn inhabitants that something was amiss. The people would run to the church and be available for fire fighting. This method was later used to call volunteer firefighters, and it persisted in some communities until the twentieth century.

When the Normans conquered England in 1066, one of William the Conqueror's laws of the land required that all fires in the household had to be extinguished at nightfall. The simplest way of extinguishing a fire on the open hearth was to put a metal cover over it and exclude the air. In Norman French, this cover was called a *couvre feu*, which on English tongues became "curfew"; and the evening bell which tolled lights out was known as the curfew bell. It was to toll in parts of England for the next 800 years, long after its original purpose had been forgotten.

Fire Laws And Ordinances

There is no record of any organized fire fighting in the eleventh and twelfth centuries, and large cities and villages continued to be destroyed by fire. The church bells would ring their reverse peals, and the inhabitants would hurry to the outbreak to render what disorganized assistance they could.

Laws and ordinances were passed in an attempt to prevent fires. In 1189, the first lord mayor of London issued the following: Each house should be built of stone, and it should be covered with slate or burnt tile. The dangerous thatched roof was banned. Party walls at least 16 feet (5 m) high and 3 feet (1 m) in breadth were to be provided between places at shared cost to both parties. The citizens were to provide ladders and a barrelful of water before their doors. Fire hooks were to be provided to drag off burning thatch and to hook into the gables or other structural members and pull down the house to create a fire break. Some hooks were large, and horses could be harnessed to them to pull down a building. Some houses were built with an iron ring in the gable into which the fire hook could be inserted (Figure 1.2). The fire hook was an old fire tool dating from Roman times and was used (mostly in Europe) until the twentieth century. The early ladder trucks carried the fire hooks, and the name "hook and ladder truck" evolved from this ancient fire fighting tool.

Causes Of Fire

Some of the main causes of fire in England during the seventeenth century were unsafe chimneys, careless methods of carrying burning sticks or peat from a neighbor's house to relight a fire, and incendiarism. Congestion, thatched roofs, and wooden buildings were probably the greatest fire hazards. Narrow streets allowed quick heat radiation, and the unorganized methods of fighting fire could not prevent the many conflagrations that occurred.

Fires And Fire Protection In Early America

The first settlement in America was almost a failure because of a disastrous fire. The settlement of Jamestown consisted of simple, frail, thatched hovels. The new settlers were unprepared for the cold winters, and their homes were dominated by large fireplaces and chimneys made of wood or

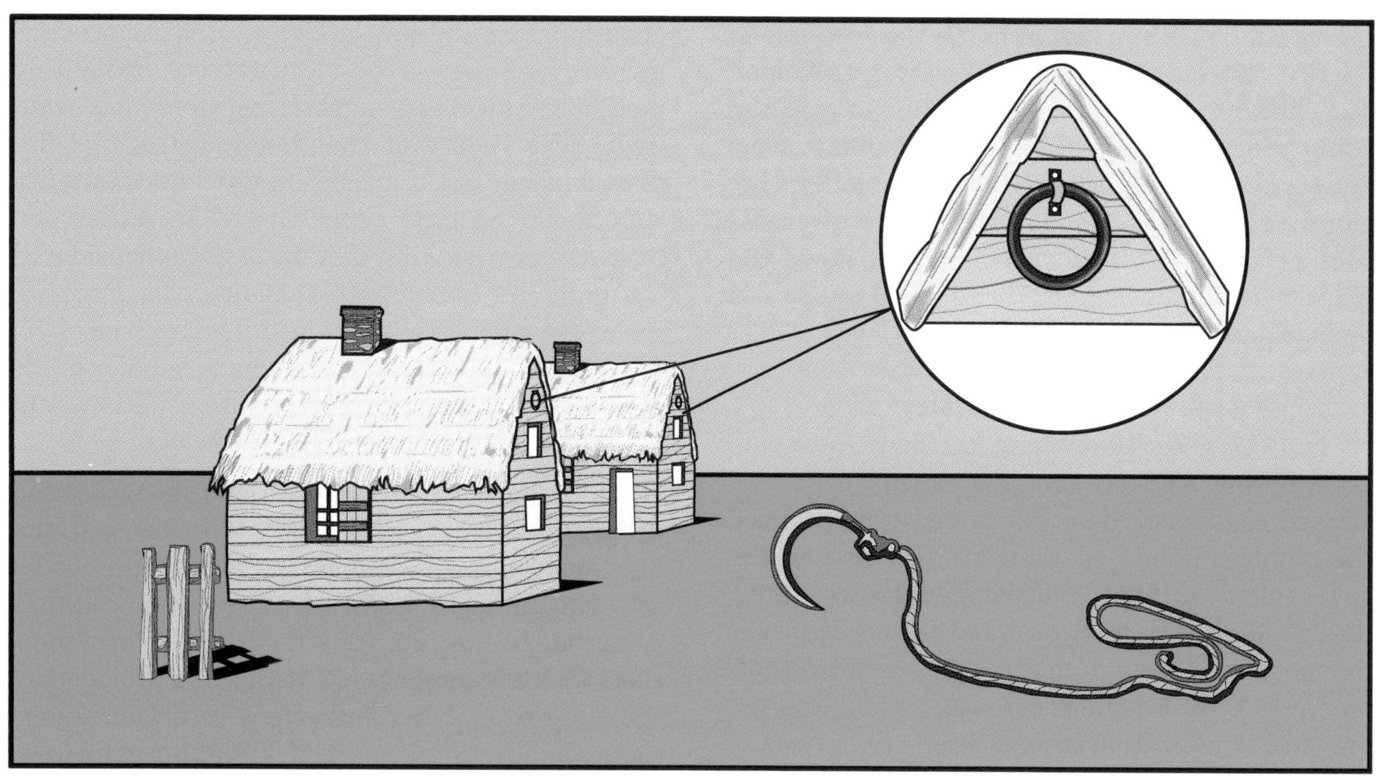

Figure 1.2 Rings, for use with fire hooks, were attached to the buildings' gable.

wooden reeds lined with mortar. The general shape and style resembled the European homes in which they had lived. In 1608, Jamestown had the first recorded big fire in the New World. It burned down every house in the settlement and destroyed wearing apparel and private provisions. Exposure to the severe winter and Indian attacks forced the suffering inhabitants to return to England.

Fire continued to plague the early settlers. Europeans arrived at such a pace that taking care of their immediate needs left little time for town planning. Getting in from the weather was their first concern, and fire protection was hardly given a thought as the towns went aimlessly forward. Organized fire fighting consisted of the town leaders issuing commands and giving authority to pull down houses that would threaten the town. Another form of organized fire protection was the bucket brigade. Village people would form two lines between the water supply and the fire (Figure 1.3).

Figure 1.3 Bucket brigades were formed by men and women to transfer water to the fire.

Men would form one line from the water source to the fire, passing the buckets full of water. Women and children would form another line to pass the empty buckets back to the water supply. This system became ineffective when some mothers began to station their daughters opposite desirable young men in the line. This soon cut down the efficiency of the operation. The problem was solved by placing the lines of people back to back.

First Fire Organization In America

In 1647, Peter Stuyvesant, the new Dutch governor of New Amsterdam (later called New York), arrived from Amsterdam. The new governor stopped the planless habits of the town, reorganized the government, surveyed and mapped the area, drew up a building code, and appointed a group of men as fire masters. Although they had no special authority while a fire was in progress, they did form the first fire organization in America — Surveyors of Buildings. From early evening until dawn these men patrolled the streets carrying wooden noisemakers, called rattlers, to arouse the people in case of fire. They also performed fire prevention work and imposed fines on violators. The people did not always follow the law and some hazards were overlooked, but the tough governor kept the town more fire safe and free from disastrous fires than many other towns in America.

Stuyvesant probably brought the fire protection ideas from his native country, Amsterdam. This was during the Dutch golden age when the wealth of the East Indies poured into Amsterdam, and the merchants built their magnificent tall houses along the canals. Where there is great wealth, the fire risk is generally given serious consideration, and Amsterdam formed a municipal fire brigade.

Britain's First Fire Brigade

The great turning point in fire fighting history occurred in September 1666. The city of London suffered a conflagration that raged for four days and destroyed more than 80 percent of the city. The fire was fought with buckets, hooks and squirts, and some primitive fire engines. The lead and wooden water pipes in the streets served as the water supply. After the fire, officials passed a code of building regulations. The city authorities recommended many new proposals to improve fire fighting methods, but their suggestions were not acted upon. The theory of the "hand of God" in fire disasters had such a hold on citizens' mentality that their thoughts never turned to skilled fire brigades, or when they did, the cost was considered too high. As a result of this fire, the first fire insurance company was formed. The creation of the fire insurance company was to have a major affect on the fire service of Britain, whose traditions and ideas were in turn to spread to America.

If the authorities were cautious about forming proper fire brigades, this was not the case with the hard-headed businessmen who ran the fire insurance companies. These businessmen realized that it was bad business to allow the destruction of their risks with the haphazard fire fighting provided by the authorities. Therefore, they were soon advertising that they had qualified firefighters who were always ready when a fire occurred. Buildings they insured were provided with a fire mark (Figure 1.4). A *fire mark* was the fire insurance company's design on a plaque. The fire mark had to be posted in a prominent place because the fire brigades

Figure 1.4 Insurance companies used fire marks to indicate those buildings that their fire brigade would attempt to extinguish.

would only respond to buildings displaying their company's mark. Thus, Britain had its first organized fire brigades.

Development Of The Fire Engine

In the sixteenth century, syringes were used as fire fighting tools. These syringes were referred to as *fire squirts*, and the larger ones were sometimes mounted on wheels (Figure 1.5). The small syringes were operated by placing the hands on the holding handles midway up the barrel, putting the end of the plunger rod against the chest, and pulling the barrel toward the chest.

It was in the sixteenth century that the writings of the ancients were translated and that fire engines were rediscovered. However, the discovery was not then put to use, and more than a century passed before people began to experiment with fire engines again. Curiously enough, when pumps using the early siphona principle for throwing water were reinvented throughout Europe, they were thought to be a new idea, and each inventor believed the creation unique. By the time fire engines came into use in America, this principle was recognized and understood. The failure of so many of the earliest machines was due more to mechanical imperfection or clumsiness than to error in principle.

The London fire and the competition between the insurance companies' fire brigades hastened the development of the fire engine. The manufacturers also received a boost from Holland. Amsterdam's municipal fire brigades now had 60 fire engines. Its captain, General Jan van der

Figure 1.5 Syringes were used in the 16th century for fire fighting.

Heijden, was an accomplished engineer who invented a new engine. He also invented fire hose (pieces of leather sewn together to form a tube). The cistern no longer needed to be filled by buckets. A close attack with a jet was now possible instead of the impractical long shot of a swivelling gooseneck mounted on the engine. A suction hose and device for drawing water were also invented, but it would be many years before other firefighters realized the value of these fire fighting advancements. Mr. van der Heijden produced a fine book explaining his new machine: *A Description of the Newly Invented and Patented Fire Engines with Flexible Hose, and Their Manner of Extinguishing Fires, by Their Inventor Jan van der Heijden.* The book had many pictures and demonstrated the advantages of the close attack.

Newsham's Engine

By the end of the seventeenth century in England, fire engines were being manufactured by several makers and competition was becoming keen. The best engines at this time appeared to be copies of the Dutch engine. In 1721, Richard Newsham developed an engine that became very popular (Figure 1.6). This mechanical fire apparatus consisted of a rectangular box or tub mounted on wheels. The bucket brigade poured water into the tub while the men on the pump handles supplied the power to produce water pressure. The engine was rugged and practical, and the working parts were beautifully made and balanced.

Newsham was the first to place the long wooden handle bars, known as the "brakes," along the sides of the engine. The brakes were made of oak — smooth, round, and just thick enough to permit a firm grip. Some models had brakes up to 15 feet (5 m) long, extending well beyond the body at both ends. As many as ten men could stand side by side and operate these brakes. The firefighters standing on both sides of the machine worked the brakes up and down like a seesaw, which moved a metal beam that operated the piston pump. A big nozzle or gooseneck, much like the deck gun on modern fire apparatus, was mounted on the engine. The engine

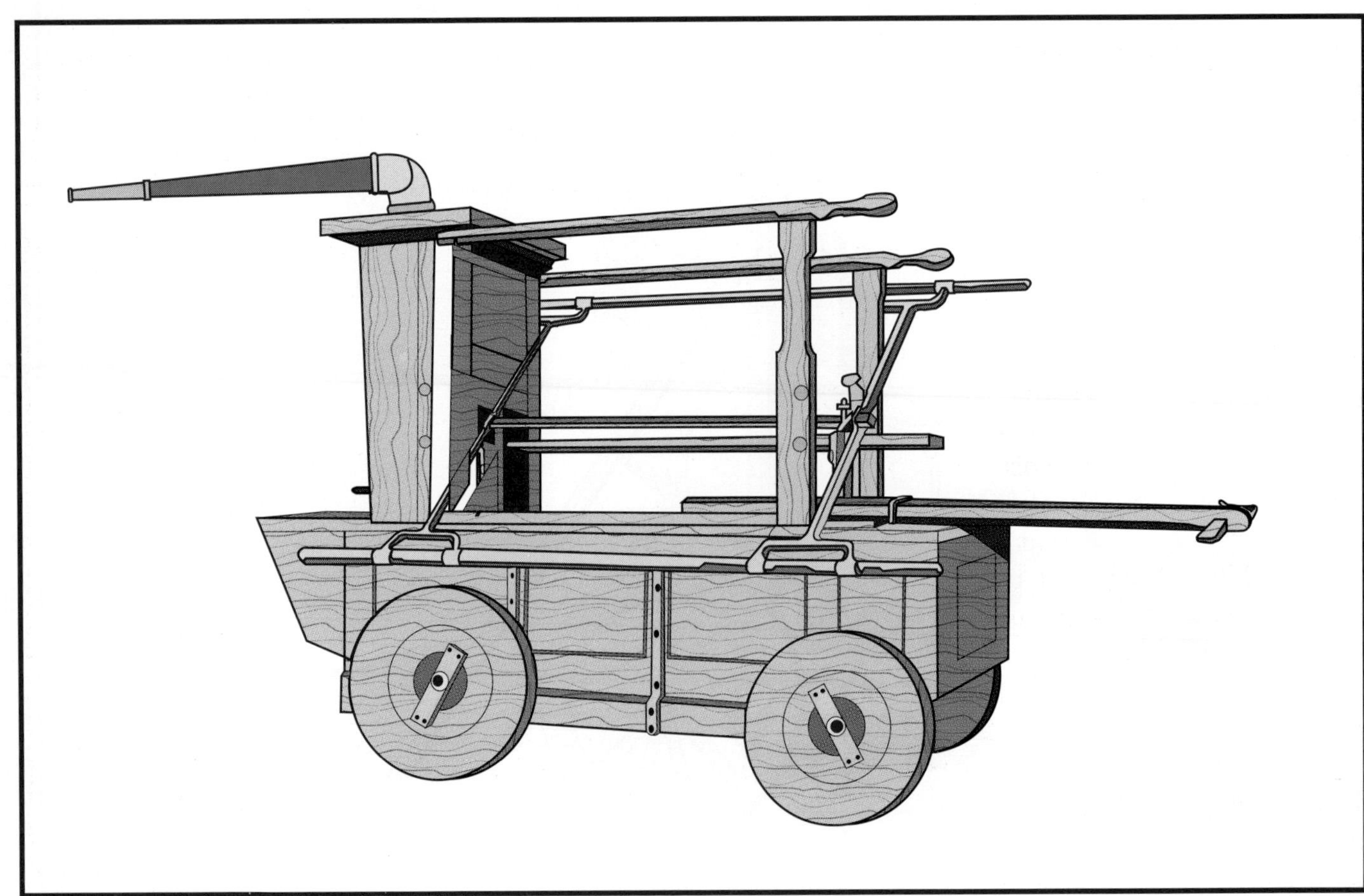

Figure 1.6 The Newsham pumper was one of the first mechanical units to provide pressure for stream development.

was placed in front of the burning building, and the big nozzle shot a stream into the fire; this was a big improvement over men throwing water at the fire. The stream was fairly steady with enough pressure to force water up to a window or roof. Newsham claimed, in his advertising pamphlet, that his engine could send a stream 165 feet (50 m) high.

The Newsham engine was the first hand tub, and many improvements were made as time went on. Engines were produced with bent axles that put the body nearer the ground, making it easier to operate the brakes. Some models had treadles on top, allowing firefighters, while standing, to use their legs to assist in pumping. There were refinements in the swivelling gooseneck, but one of the biggest improvements was the development of the suction hose and a special three-way fitting. This made it possible to fill the tub either by drafting water from a nearby well or reservoir or by using the old bucket brigade method. Many of these sturdy machines are displayed in museums today.

EARLY AMERICAN TRADITIONS

Boston, America's fastest-growing city, was also having fire problems. In 1631, only eight months after it was settled, the city had its first major fire. After the fire, city leaders issued orders that no man should build his chimney with wood or roof his house with thatch. However, this did not solve the problem. Following a disastrous conflagration in 1653, the Bostonian leaders signed a contract with Joseph Jynks to build an apparatus for fire fighting. This was the first mention of any kind of fire apparatus in America, but no description of the engine or record of its construction and delivery exists. American merchants had high praise for an apparatus they had seen at work in London, so in 1676 authorities ordered one. Before the order reached England, Boston suffered another conflagration. The type of apparatus ordered was never described, although it was thought to be a hand-tub type. When it finally arrived in 1678, thirteen men were appointed to keep it in proper repair and ready condition, tow it to fires, and operate the pump. Thomas Atkins was appointed chief engineer, and he and his men were promised pay for their work.

First Fire Societies

MUTUAL FIRE SOCIETY OF BOSTON

In 1717, Boston established America's first fire department. Boston was years ahead in establishing a fire department because the terrible fires made engines, buckets, and other fire equipment vital to its existence. At this time, New York and Philadelphia did not even have one engine in service. In spite of the increased protection, the fear of another conflagration led some of the Boston homeowners to band together, and on September 30, 1718, the first fire society was formed. This was the beginning of the colorful age of the volunteer firefighter who was to play an important role in American history. In that same year, the first, more-advanced fire engine arrived in Boston from England.

The mutual fire societies operated independently and volunteered assistance to the regular Boston firefighters. The limited membership carried a small booklet listing the location of each member's home and place of business. Each member responded to a fire alarm with personal equipment, which consisted of a bucket and a bag bearing the society's emblems, a bed key, and a screwdriver. If the fire was in or near a member's building, members would rush to the scene, make sure all lives were safe, dismantle the bed with their wrenchlike bed keys (Figure 1.7),

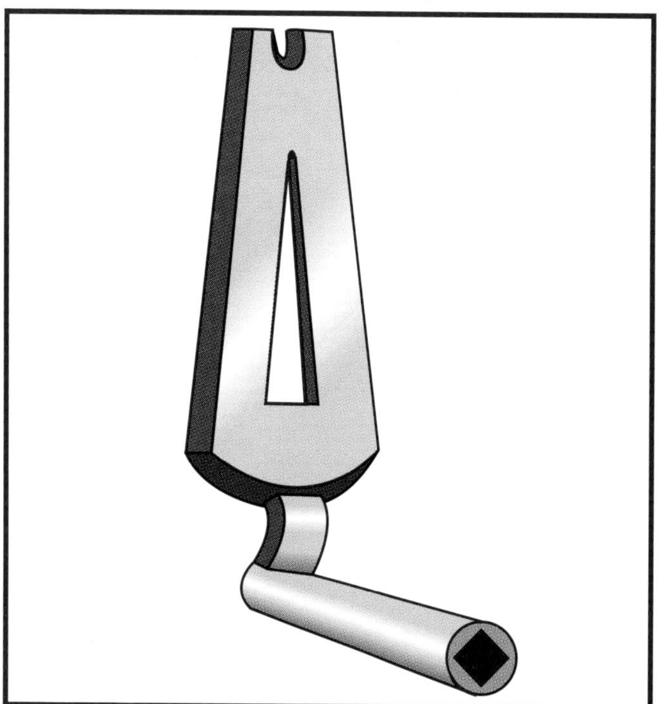

Figure 1.7 A bed was a valuable possession of early colonists; a bed key was used to dismantle the bed during a fire.

fill their bags with the valuables, carry them to safety, and then assist in the fire fighting. After the fire, a member would stand guard against pilfering and admit only recognized members and firefighters for salvage work. The fire societies proved valuable, and within a few years, Boston had several neighborhood clubs that held regular meetings and had rules that fixed fines for nonattendance at fires or meetings.

UNION VOLUNTEER FIRE COMPANY

Benjamin Franklin was born in Boston but moved to Philadelphia where he became a leader in early American fire protection. On February 2, 1735, after returning from a trip to Boston, he wrote an article about fire protection for his newspaper, *The Pennsylvania Gazette.* In the article, he mentioned the Mutual Fire Society of Boston and how this organization was helping fight fires. The following year Franklin and several of his friends organized the first fire organization in Philadelphia, the Union Volunteer Fire Company, patterning it after the Boston Mutual Fire Society (Figure 1.8). In 1752, Franklin and two other businessmen founded the first successful American fire insurance company, the Philadelphia Contributorship for the Insurance of Houses from Loss by Fire. The company's fire mark was called the "hand in hand" because it showed the right hands of four men gripping one another's wrists. Beneath this symbol of unity and strength appeared the number of the insurance policy.

Figure 1.8 In 1736, Benjamin Franklin organized the first fire department in Philadelphia, The Union Volunteer Fire Company.

The use of the American fire mark differed from England's because American insurance societies did not provide fire fighting brigades. The towns had no permanent firefighters, and the American volunteer received no pay. When the alarm sounded, the volunteers dropped their work and responded to their firehouse. In towns where fire marks were used, the insuring company would pay the first company to put water on the fire. Other towns would reward their first-in firefighters with a sum paid out of the town treasury. This incentive is blamed for the competition and fierce rivalry that developed among the volunteers.

NEW YORK VOLUNTEER DEPARTMENT

During America's formative years, the fast-growing city of New York was also forging ahead and showing its ability to get things done. Its leaders were wisely providing money and legislation to increase the personnel of its volunteer fire fighting forces and to keep its fire equipment in good condition. In 1786, the New York City Fire Department was completely reorganized; membership was increased, and districts were created and placed under the leadership of several men. The city had 15 engine companies and 2 hook-and-ladder companies. Thus began the grand and colorful period of the New York volunteer. Every company wanted to be the best, fastest, and the most handsome in the department or its district. The New Yorkers decorated their machines with gleaming metal, used high-gloss paint, and hired well-known artists to execute elaborate paintings. The scenes were usually mythological or patriotic, and many of the scenes still exist in museums. The volunteers also dressed themselves in colorful uniforms for the parades and public contests between companies. The fire department continued to grow and by the 1800s had 25 engines numbered, named, nicknamed, and manned with 10 to 20 men each, depending on the size, the weight, and to some extent, the location of the machine. It also had a chief engineer and six assistant engineers. The companies continued to function on their own while the chiefs did nothing but occasionally inspect the apparatus. This all changed in 1811 when Tommy Franklin became chief engineer and assumed the role of active chief of the entire department, a role never practiced before. Because of his sincere personality and leadership, his role was accepted, and all company foremen hustled to his orders. (The foreman was in charge of a company and was elected to this position by the men of his company.) Franklin's successors had little trouble continuing with the same authority, and for 25 years New York was the only American city to have a fire department under a unified command.

Development Of American Fire Engines

New York imported the first Newsham engines from England in 1731, and Thomas Lote, a New York cooper and boat builder, manufactured the first successful fire engine in America. It was delivered to the city in 1743 and was nicknamed "Old Brass Backs" because of the lavish use of brass on the box of the engine (Figure 1.9).

The competitive spirit of the city's firefighters gave the impetus to develop better and more powerful hand tubs. Soon manufacturers all over this young nation were developing machines. One en-

Figure 1.9 The first fire engine built in the United States was delivered to New York City in 1743 by Thomas Lote.

gine became known as the "coffee mill," a rotary type that operated by a crank on each side of the machine. Another unique rotary engine popularly known as the "cider mill" was worked like the capstan of a ship with the men pushing the bar by walking around the engine (Figure 1.10). Richard Mason built the first successful engine in Philadelphia, and in 1794, Pat Lyon began producing the renowned Philadelphia-style engine (Figure 1.11). This was a powerful, efficient, reliable, double-piston, double-deck, end-stroke engine that is considered by many to have been the best and most successful hand engine developed in this country. Meanwhile, William C. Hunneman of Boston, Massachusetts, was making an excellent end-stroke machine that was small, compact, and easily handled. The Hunneman machine was very serviceable, not only in Boston's narrow streets but also in smaller towns and villages (Figure 1.12).

NEW YORK-STYLE HAND ENGINES

In New York, a style of hand engine was evolving that used Newsham's principle of the side stroke. This type of engine became known as the "New York" style. New York City started replacing its antiquated machines with this new, powerful "gooseneck" engine that was to become New York's most popular engine and the most publicized style of hand engine (Figure 1.13). The gooseneck engine — so named because of the prominent bend in the pipe that protruded from the air chamber — was too heavy and bulky for quick maneuvering and too large for narrow passages. This caused firefighters to experiment with threading a hose instead of a nozzle to the gooseneck pipe and running a line to a strategic point closer to the fire. This method, called *leading hose*, was another big advancement in fire fighting (Figure 1.14). Instead of spotting the engine directly in front of the fire, firefighters could fight fires in narrow streets and alleys. If they wished, they could enter and attack the fire from inside the building. In the beginning, the engines carried a small amount of hose. Leading hose not only led to the development of more powerful engines and improved water systems but also led to the development of the hose wagon company because longer supply and fire fighting lines were needed.

PIANO-TYPE ENGINE

From the gooseneck the more powerful piano-type engine was developed. It was so called because

Figure 1.10 The "cider mill" was powered by firefighters walking around the engine.

Figure 1.11 The Philadelphia-style engine developed in 1794 was an excellent double-piston pump.

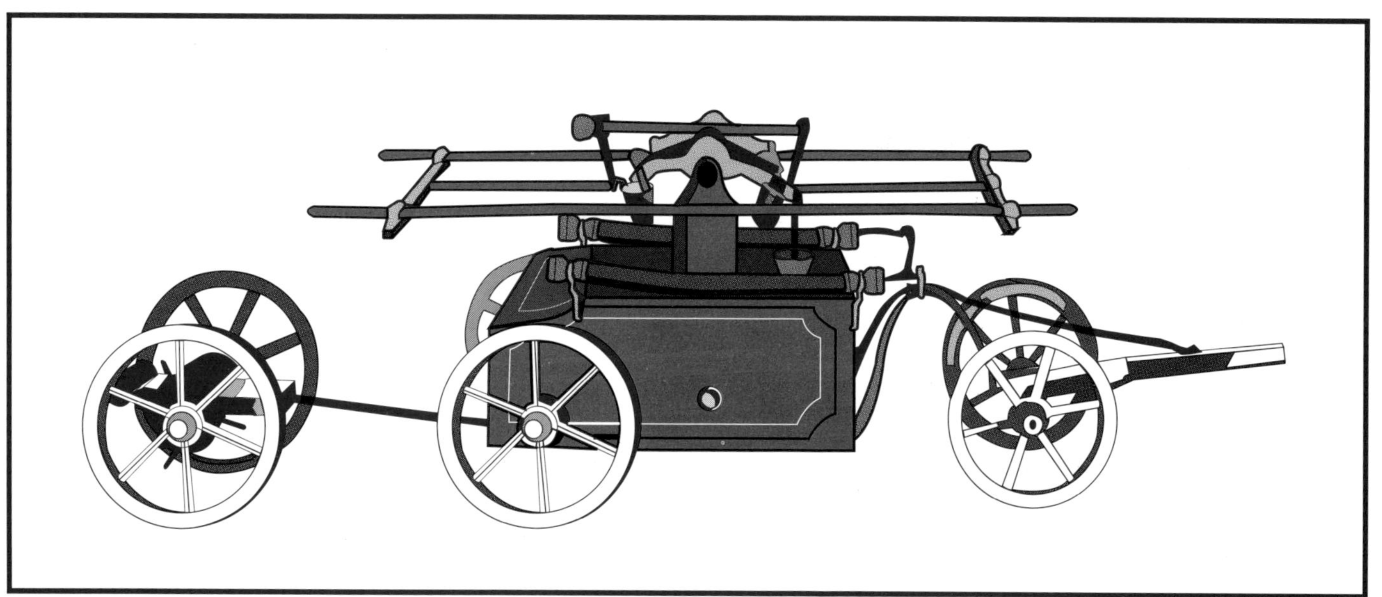

Figure 1.12 The Hunneman hand tub was used extensively in New England because its compact size made it easy to maneuver.

its boxlike body resembled a piano. A development on the piano style was the permanent attachment of the suction hose, which was attached and placed in such a way that it was referred to as a "squirrel tail" (Figure 1.15). Other developments led to a style called the Shanghai (a variation on the Philadelphia style) and another type that had its pump arranged in such a way that men seated on the body could apply their strength in a rowing manner.

IMPROVEMENTS IN HAND ENGINES

As the machines were developed, they became more powerful, bulkier, and heavier. Many of the machines were custom-built with variations in de-

Figure 1.13 The New York-style engine was famous for its gooseneck discharge on top of the machine.

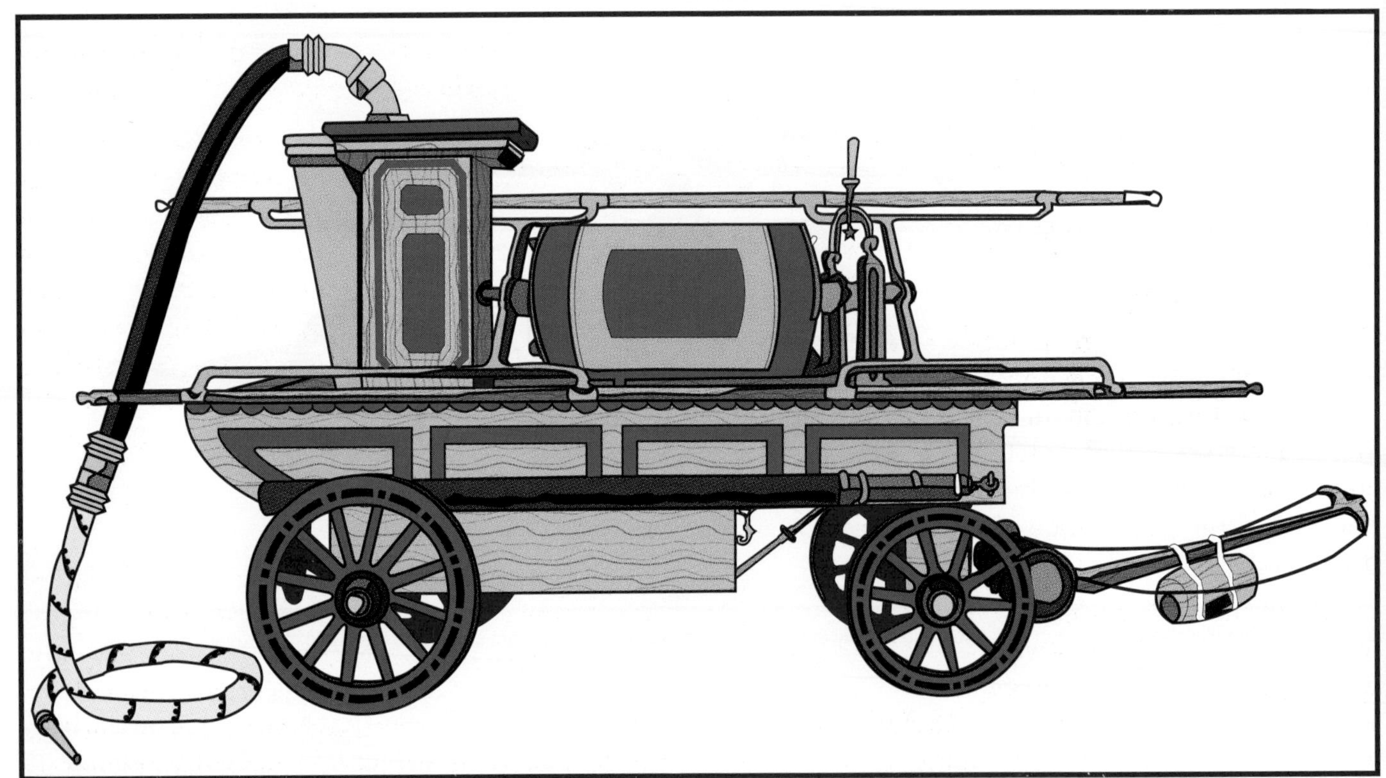

Figure 1.14 From the gooseneck-type engine, early firefighters began to extend their hose. From this practice, leading hose came into use.

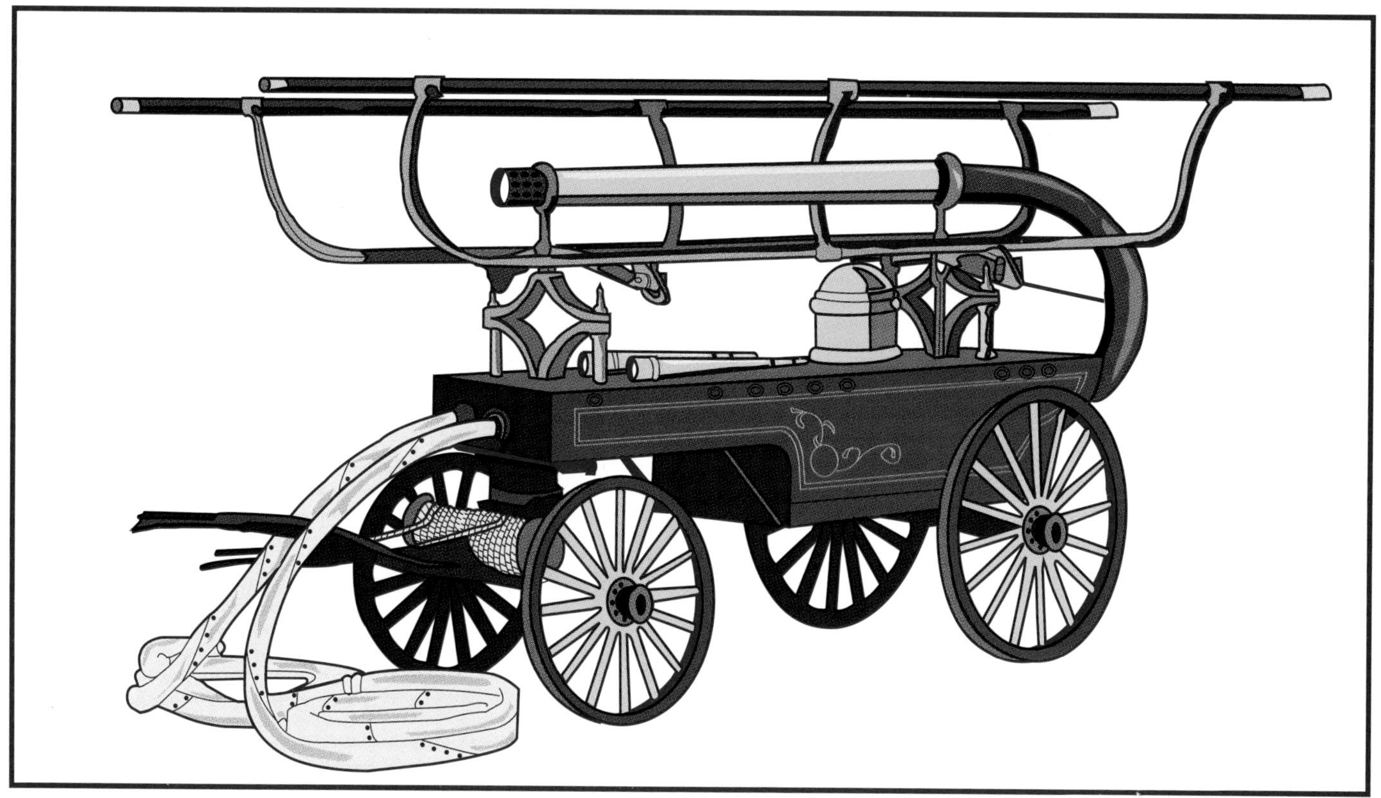

Figure 1.15 The piano-style pumper was distinct because of the preconnected "squirrel-tail" suction hose.

sign, and their power plants were copied and improved upon by other manufacturers. It was fortunate that the suction hose replaced the bucket brigade as a way to get water into the chamber of the engine because all the manpower was needed to work the handles or brakes of the pumping engine. As the hand tubs were improved, the small handles were lengthened until they ran the entire length of the engine, providing room for 15 or more men on each side. Operating these engines usually reduced the crew to exhaustion in a matter of minutes. When one crew was completely worn out, a fresh crew would step in while the first crew rested and had refreshments — some of which came from a brown jug.

Hand engines were normally operated at about 60 strokes a minute. They were sometimes speeded up to 120 strokes a minute, and on one occasion, it was recorded that the men pushed up to 170 strokes a minute. A stroke consisted of a full up-and-down motion of the brakes. At the normal pace, men could last at the brakes for about 10 minutes, but when the engine was being pushed hard, 1 to 3 minutes was all that a man could work. Firefighters frequently suffered painful injuries, such as torn fingers and broken arms, when jumping in to relieve while the engine was being operated at high speed.

Engines were sometimes referred to as having pump cylinders of a certain "class." In different engines, the size of the pump cylinder varied from 5 to 10 inches (125 mm to 250 mm) in diameter; the stroke of the piston rods varied from 8 to 18 inches (200 mm to 450 mm); and the length of the brakes was from 16 to 25 feet (5 m to 8 m). A first-class engine, which would be one with 9- or 10-inch (225 mm or 250 mm) cylinders, would require from 40 to 60 men to haul and operate.

Growth In The Volunteer Fire Service

After the Revolutionary War, the volunteer fire fighting idea spread throughout the country. Veterans returned home and joined a fire company, many of which became veterans' organizations with the engine house as their clubroom. The reward for the first-arriving company changed from pay to pride. Companies became better organized, the men and their equipment were more splendidly decorated, and as a result, rivalries increased. Feelings of exhilaration and self-satisfaction over serving one's community and doing a worthwhile job well became incentive. With all the color and excitement of a volunteer firefighter's life, every company had a long list of young hopefuls waiting for an opening in the limited membership. In the past, many famous Americans, such as George Washington, John Hancock, Alexander Hamilton, Samuel Adams, and Paul Revere, served as volunteers, and now the age of the American volunteer firefighter began.

America was growing, and many changes were taking place in the volunteer fire service. Cities improved building regulations and water systems. Yankee ingenuity was producing bigger and better fire engines to replace the worn-out Newsham engines. Firefighters, cobblers, harness makers, and other enterprising businessmen started making leather hose, fire bell signals, fire fighting tools, and uniforms. Because of the urgent need for more and better protection in the growing cities, nearly all the new equipment and new methods of fire fighting were introduced in Boston, Philadelphia, and New York but were subsequently adopted by the alert smaller towns.

The creation, development, and competitive spirit of the American volunteer firefighter system did several things for the fire service. The zeal to beat rival companies led manufacturers and firefighters to constantly develop new and better machines, equipment, and methods of fire fighting. They practiced fast turnouts to fires, drilled to save time in putting their engines to work, and experimented with the bunking-out system (sleeping at the station). It was also during these early years that firefighters emerged as heroes. Their daring rescues and their heroic stands before the fire were captured in song, verse, and the drawings of Currier and Ives. Soon every young boy in America wanted to be a firefighter when he grew up. The firefighter's exciting and colorful job was one of major interest to the townspeople. In addition to their interest in the fire and its disastrous results, people would gather to watch firefighters in action. The competitive pumping contest would bring cheers and encouragement for local favorites.

Early volunteers were selected carefully and underwent a severe character investigation and trial period before they were accepted by the company. Most of the members were men of means — merchants, manufacturers, and professionals who kept their fire companies as socially exclusive as a private country club. To be a firefighter was to be somebody, and everybody who was anybody usually joined. The volunteers did not labor for money. They expected to endure both cold and hot weather; the hazards of fire, smoke, and falling walls; and physical exhaustion. Every fire was a challenge, and the volunteers gloried in fighting it. The status of belonging to the company, the teamwork, and the pride in the beautiful machine made membership in the company very desirable.

Every member was responsible to the company, the fire department, and the city. The fire department was headed by a chief engineer and his assistants. The man in charge of the company was referred to as the foreman. Expulsion and fines were used to maintain proper discipline, and the men worked under a rigid set of rules. Fines of various amounts were levied for the following:

- Nonattendance at a fire
- Not wearing the badge and fire cap
- Absence from regular meetings or weekly engine washings
- Talking politics
- Profanity
- Intoxication
- Smoking or chewing in the engine house
- Shoving on the engine while on the run
- Failure to return to the house with the engine after a fire

The money collected went into a fund to help keep their equipment in proper shape and to finance picnics, clambakes, dances, banquets, parades, and other social functions.

It was the competitive rivalry with other fire companies that generated the greatest excitement for the volunteer. His engine was the best, and his company was the toughest, the strongest, the smartest, the first to reach the fire, and the most efficient in putting it out. If two companies should happen to meet when responding to a fire, a foot race generally ensued. Nothing stood in the way of the running volunteers and their rigs. When the streets were hazardous, the race too heated, or the only way to pass another company was to take to the smoother sidewalks, they did so, bowling over all pedestrians who got in their way. If the water supply was a long distance from the fire and water had to be relayed by one engine pumping to another, the first engine tried to pump hard enough to deliver more water into the box of the second engine than its crew could pump into the hose leading to the fire. When the box of the second engine began overflowing, this was called being "washed" and was one of the greatest insults an engine crew could receive. When one engine had washed another, the crew would stop pumping to cheer and slap each other on the back while others would saunter down to the washed engine to add a few more verbal insults. Generally, this would result in a few fist fights. In the following days, more fights would break out because the members of the first engine would go around town bragging about the disgrace of the washed company.

As the hand engines improved in power, they increased in size, and enormous numbers of men were needed to operate them. Men pulled the heavy apparatus to the fire and worked the pumps. There were no horses, no steam, and no motors — manpower did it all. The first firefighters to arrive at the fire house took hold of the drag ropes and got the machine rolling. As more men caught up and got a grip on the ropes, they worked up to a dead run with their apparatus. Practice was required at the drag ropes, for if the men were too closely spaced, they were apt to trip themselves into a dangerous pileup while their heavy machine came rumbling on toward them. In spite of practice and prudence, there were ditches, cobblestones, and other obstacles to throw a firefighter off his feet. To see a hand tub coming down the street with 50 men on the ropes, bell ringing, and everyone shouting, was an unforgettable sight (Figure 1.16).

Rowdiness increased when the firefighters not only wanted to be the first to arrive at the fire scene, but also wanted to be the first to put water on the fire. Some resorted to employing a youngster to dash to fires with an empty barrel to put over the nearest fire plug. The youngster would sit innocently upon the barrel until his or her company arrived. These youngsters became known as "plug-uglies," and the battle for fire plugs would sometimes rage while the fire burned unheeded.

A rowdier era developed in the larger cities and by the middle of the nineteenth century it began to spread. It started when the social outcasts and tougher elements in sections of the cities resented not being acceptable for the volunteer life of social prominence, the glorified heroics, and the tough-

Figure 1.16 The larger hand engines could require as many as 50 men to pull them.

ness and manliness of the job. Gangs would wait in alleys and dark streets to pounce upon the alarm-answering firefighters, engaging them in fights, and trying to overturn their apparatus and damage their equipment. The heated rivalries and the troubles they caused did not reach a peak until the cities' growing pains started a deterioration of the volunteer system.

The large number of immigrants escaping famines, political unrest, and depressions in other countries swelled this nation's cities. By 1835, New York City began to assume the proportions of a great metropolis and inherit the problems of all large cities. Fires increased; therefore, the number of fire companies had to be increased. The companies were increasing in size because of the larger machines and the manpower required to operate them. East Side toughs managed to infiltrate the ranks of volunteers and became public nuisances by engaging in drunken brawls, street riots, and dangerous heroics at fires. Efforts by fire department leaders to curtail them were hampered by the political forces at City Hall who supported the gangs because of their friendship and political and voting support.

First Hose Company

The large cities developed a water system using bored-out crude logs that were tapered and fitted together. Every half block or so a wooden plug was inserted into this water system, and this plug was removed to obtain water. From this system came the term *fire plug*. Philadelphia put into service the first successful water system. Philadelphia's volunteers developed a new piece of apparatus, the hose wagon, to take advantage of this new system (Figure 1.17). Hose No. 1, with a limited membership of twenty members, became the first hose company in America. The volunteers designed their hose wagon and paid to have it built. They purchased all the equipment, which included 600 feet (180 m) of hose, nozzles, axes, and candle-burning lanterns. Members of Hose No. 1 also erected a building to house their apparatus. They had an understanding with Engine 1 that they would supply them with water, but once when Engine 1 was late, the hose company connected to the water supply and placed an effective stream of water on the fire. The hose company became popular, and soon other hose companies were established.

Rivalry between hose companies appeared, and when one hose company copied Hose No. 1, the original company attached a bell to its apparatus so that it could be distinguished from the other company. This too was copied, and soon everyone had bells on their fire apparatus. Thus began the alarm signal for apparatus.

Flexible hose had been used since the ancient Greeks used the intestines of oxen. The leather hose invented in Holland was made of the finest cowhide, was sewn together carefully like the leg of a fine boot, and had brass fittings on both ends so that it could be coupled to other hose. When pressure was applied to the hose, water would sometimes burst through the cracks and seams, resulting in a poor water supply at the nozzle. Nevertheless, firefighters realized they had a necessary and effective tool, and improvements were made. The members of Hose No. 1 were an inventive group, and two of its members developed the riveted hose — a great improvement over the leaky sewed hose. This was a big step forward for fire fighting.

During the era of the bucket brigade, water came from wells, ponds, streams, lakes, and cisterns. Most early hand engines were filled by bucket brigades. Some early water systems had such weak pressure that they functioned only as a distribution system for the bucket brigades. The ability to draw or suction water had been known for years, but the American builders and volunteers did not get around to using it until 1819. The New York machines were furnished with suction hose and old machines altered so that they could use them. As the water system improved, the box of the hand engine could receive water from a hydrant. Some would carry a section of hose for this purpose. With the development of its suction ability, the engine started carrying a hard, noncollapsible suction hose to draw water. Water systems kept improving, and some maintained enough pressure to allow a hose company to attach directly to the hydrant and have a good working line. Engines were needed only to maintain pressure for long distances and heights.

THE AGE OF STEAM

The colorful era of the hand machine drew to a close with the development of the steam engine. The development of early steam engines can be

Figure 1.17 When water systems were first developed, hose wagons were developed to make maximum use of the systems.

dated back to 1829 in London. In America, the construction of two workable steam engines in 1840 marked the beginning of the end of the tumultuous days of the huge 80-man volunteer fire company. The New York insurance companies first commissioned Paul Hodge in 1840 to build a steamer. A year later his steamer, which was self-propelled and had a horizontal boiler, was ready to be put to its first test (Figure 1.18). The test for the Hodge engine was successful in that it put a stream of water over the cupola of City Hall. However, it was also a failure because the volunteer firefighters refused to cooperate with the steamer and used trickery to make its performance look poor. The insurance companies were not deceived by the volunteer firefighters, but they realized they were dependent upon these volunteer companies to handle 99 percent of the fire fighting in the city. Eventually, the Hodge engine was sold to power a box factory.

The second steamer was designed by a Swedish engineer, Captain John Ericsson, who later designed the USS Monitor. His prize-winning fire engine was never used because again the volunteers disapproved of the machine. The rejection of these engines was not serious at the time because the hand-operated engines with their multitudes of men could handle the fires that occurred. The situation did become serious when the wild fights

Figure 1.18 The first steamer, built by Paul Hodge in 1841, failed its initial test.

between rival fire companies became so intense that on many occasions a fire would burn uncontrolled.

It was after one of these fights that city authorities in Cincinnati, realizing something must be done, purchased a Latta steam engine (Figure 1.19). The firefighters at first launched a brutal physical attack on the machine until a group of outraged citizens came to the rescue of the steamer. The Latta engine remained at work, and Cincinnati later became the first all-steam fire department in America. In 1853, Cincinnati became the first fully paid fire department. By 1857, St. Louis would also have a fully paid department.

After the acceptance of steam engines at Cincinnati, other cities began purchasing steam engines as rapidly as they became available. As steam became popular, improvements were made. Some of the first steamers were self-propelled, but they were not very successful because they were slow and hard to steer.

Gangs of men pulled the steamer to the fire, but this also proved to be too slow (Figure 1.20). It was soon found that the most efficient way to get a heavy steamer to a fire was to pull it with a team of three powerful horses (Figure 1.21). The use of horses in the fire service brought about the use of dogs. It was discovered that horses would run faster if a dog was leading the way. Dogs would clear the road for the fire apparatus and chase away stray dogs that could scare the horses. Dogs of all types were used for this purpose, but the Dalmatian proved to be the best. Dalmatians seem to have an inherent love for running with horse-drawn carriages. Dalmatians can still be found in many fire stations, where they are used as guard dogs when firefighters are absent.

The problem of how to have the steam engine ready to start pumping when it arrived at the fire was ingeniously solved. The steamer's boiler was

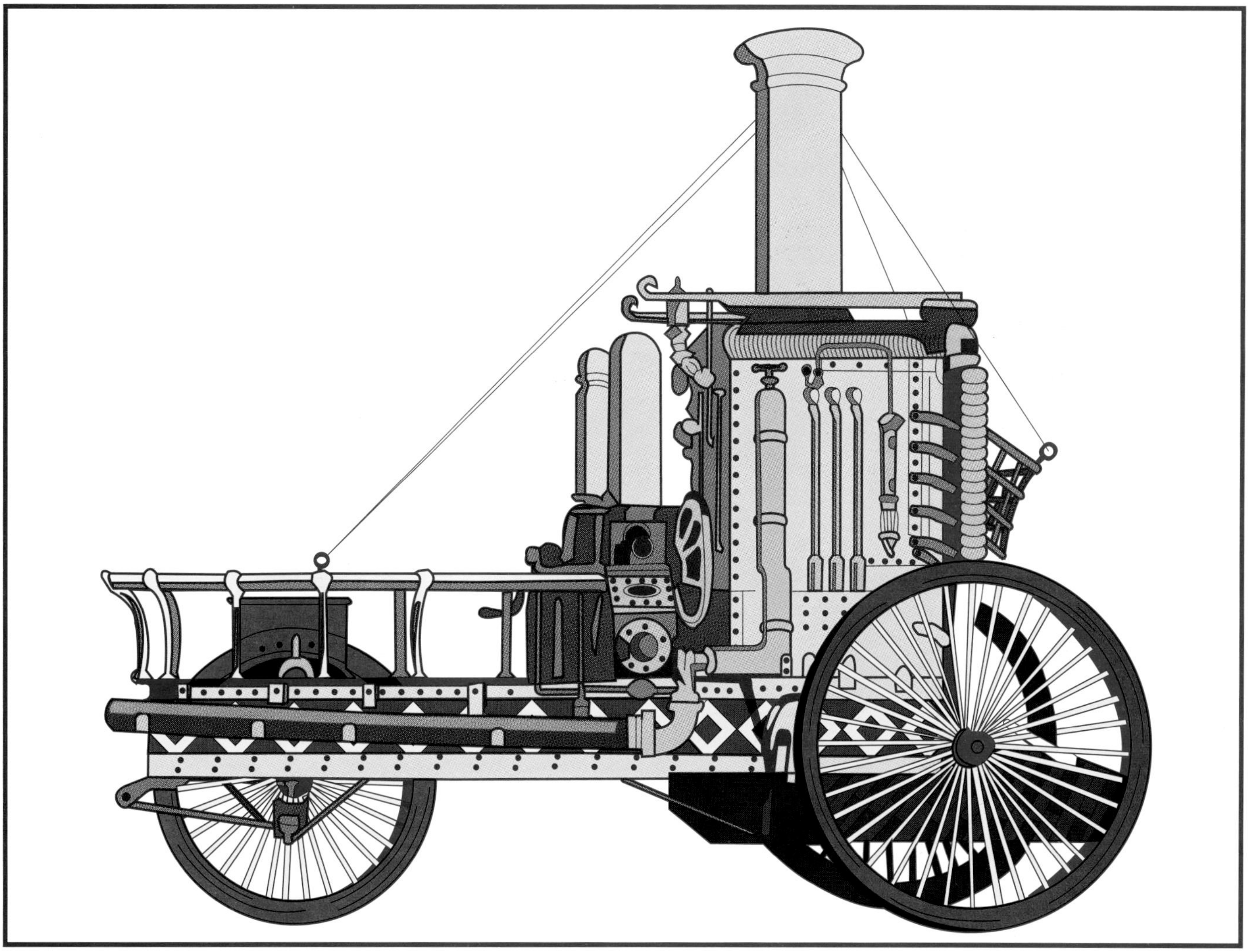

Figure 1.19 The rivalry between volunteer companies led to the purchase of steam engines like the popular Latta.

kept connected to a stationary boiler in the station, and hot water circulated through the steamer's boiler at all times. When an alarm sounded, this connection had to be released before the apparatus rolled. The stoker would ignite a bound pack of matches on a piece of sandpaper attached to the boiler and thrust this blazing torch into the firebox. This ignited a bed of excelsior and about two bushels of pine kindling wood; thus, the stoker usually had a fire going before the steamer had traveled very far. When the steamer arrived at the fire, the stoker would decide whether or not the fire in the firebox was needed. If the building appeared to be involved or flames were visible, he would throw in some cannel coal from his storage bin. This is a hot, quick-burning fuel from England that gave the

Figure 1.20 Early steamers were pulled by hand. *Courtesy of Paul Hanneman.*

Figure 1.21 Due to the heavy weight and lack of manpower, the three-horse team became the method of steamer response.

engineer quick steam. When the hookup was made and the hose laid, the nozzleman would call for water, and the engineer would ease open the throttle. The pistons moved, the flywheel turned, and black smoke flecked with hot sparks spurted up from the stack. Suddenly, the machinery gained speed. The pistons flashed up and down, the flywheel became a blur, and the smoke from the stack stabbed higher. The engineer with his oilcan attended the rhythmic, powerful machine. Meanwhile, the men at the nozzle braced themselves as the water burst out from the hose in a powerful stream.

The horses were unhitched and led away from the steamer because showers of glowing coals could easily burn their hides. The horses would also become unmanageable if they remained harnessed because of the action and vigor the steam engine produced.

The stoker at the engine kept his eye on the supply of cannel coal. If it was a big fire, the supply would soon be exhausted. When the supply became low, the stoker would give a blast on the steamer's whistle — a signal for more coal. A coal wagon would then rush to the steamer, and the driver would toss a couple of gunnysacks of coal to the needy engine. Then he would stand by waiting for the signal of another steamer's whistle.

LADDER TRUCKS AND CHEMICAL ENGINES

Because ladder work and ladder companies did not develop as rapidly as fire engines, one has to speculate on the difficulties of early rescue work. The demand to improve ladders did not occur until the increase of multiple-storied buildings.

Early ladder companies consisted of a group of men whose duties, when the alarm sounded, were to rush to specified locations in the city and retrieve ladders, ropes, hooks, and other equipment stored there. Longer ladders were usually carried by two men, who had spent many hours practicing to avoid the discomforts and injuries that could occur while running with a long ladder. Later, hand-drawn ladder trucks that carried several ladders of different lengths were developed (Figure 1.22). As ladder lengths increased, it became more difficult to steer the long, bulky apparatus down the streets and especially around corners. This was solved by installing a second tillering device on the rear wheels.

Figure 1.22 Hand-drawn ladder trucks were needed to assist in rescue.

Manpower had always raised the 65- or 75-foot (20 m or 23 m) extension ladders. These ladders were extremely heavy and slow to remove from the truck and raise against a building. Because their bases were never secure, these tall ladders were hazardous. Daniel Hayes, a former New York City firefighter and master mechanic on the San Francisco Fire Department, devised a method of attaching the base of the tall ladder to the truck bed and lifting its great weight by mechanical means. The San Francisco firefighters helped him build and experiment with the mechanism. By 1870, they had perfected an apparatus known as the Hayes Aerial, the first aerial ladder truck. The aerial ladder was raised manually by hand cranks. This procedure was succeeded by a set of springs packed in cylinders, then by compressed air, and finally by hydraulic pressure or power from the gasoline truck motor. The ladder truck was further developed to carry several different lengths of ground ladders and assorted equipment, and it soon became the number one lifesaving piece of fire equipment.

Soon after the development of the steamer came the first chemical apparatus, generally a two-horse vehicle. It carried one to four 50-gallon (200 L) tanks of soda (sodium bicarbonate) and a carbonic acid preparation. When the operator mixed these two ingredients, a strong stream was delivered through a ¾-inch (19 mm) or 1-inch (25 mm) hose. The carbonic acid caused a chemical reaction that produced carbon dioxide gas that built up sufficient pressure to expel the water. These small streams were used to extinguish fires in hard-to-get-to places or to extinguish a fire in its beginning phase (Figure 1.23).

The chemical company was sometimes used to run behind the steamers and put out the small fires caused by the boiler sparks. This was a disadvantage because the faster chemical apparatus was intended to be the first at the fire to extinguish it in its early stages. The chemical company probably put out more fires than the steamer, but it was not used much on large fires except to patrol the surrounding areas and put out small fires caused by flying brands.

IMPROVEMENTS AND PROTECTIVE CLOTHING

The steam engine, the chemical apparatus, and the aerial ladder were not the only improvements in the fire service. In the larger cities, bunking out was becoming more popular, and regular shifts of firefighters were being used for this purpose. Horse stalls, which housed the fire equipment, and the firefighters' living quarters caused a change in fire station design. Many stations were two stories with the sleeping quarters on the second floor. Sliding poles were introduced in the 1870s for a quick descent to the apparatus floor. The first poles, which were made of wood, were invented by Daniel Lawler, a New York firefighter.

Standard uniforms were adopted by all the larger departments during the early 1800s. The protective leather fire hat was used as early as 1740, and it evolved to its now-famous shape over

Figure 1.23 The chemical apparatus was the forerunner of units with a booster tank. In many ways, it functioned as the first minipumper.

the next 60 years (Figure 1.24). By 1820, the hat had the front shield that displayed the engine number and firefighter's initials, and the brim had the familiar rear-extended scoop to carry off water and protect the back of the firefighter's neck from falling hot brands. The helmet could also be reversed and the scoop used to protect the face if necessary. Special treatment of the leather made these helmets very durable. Although some are still used, plastic and fiberglass helmets are more commonly used today.

Early protective clothing was made of wool or other natural fibers. This clothing was very heavy, particularly when wet. It also placed a tremendous amount of heat stress on those who wore it. Eventually, rubber coats became the norm. Although they did a better job of keeping the firefighters dry

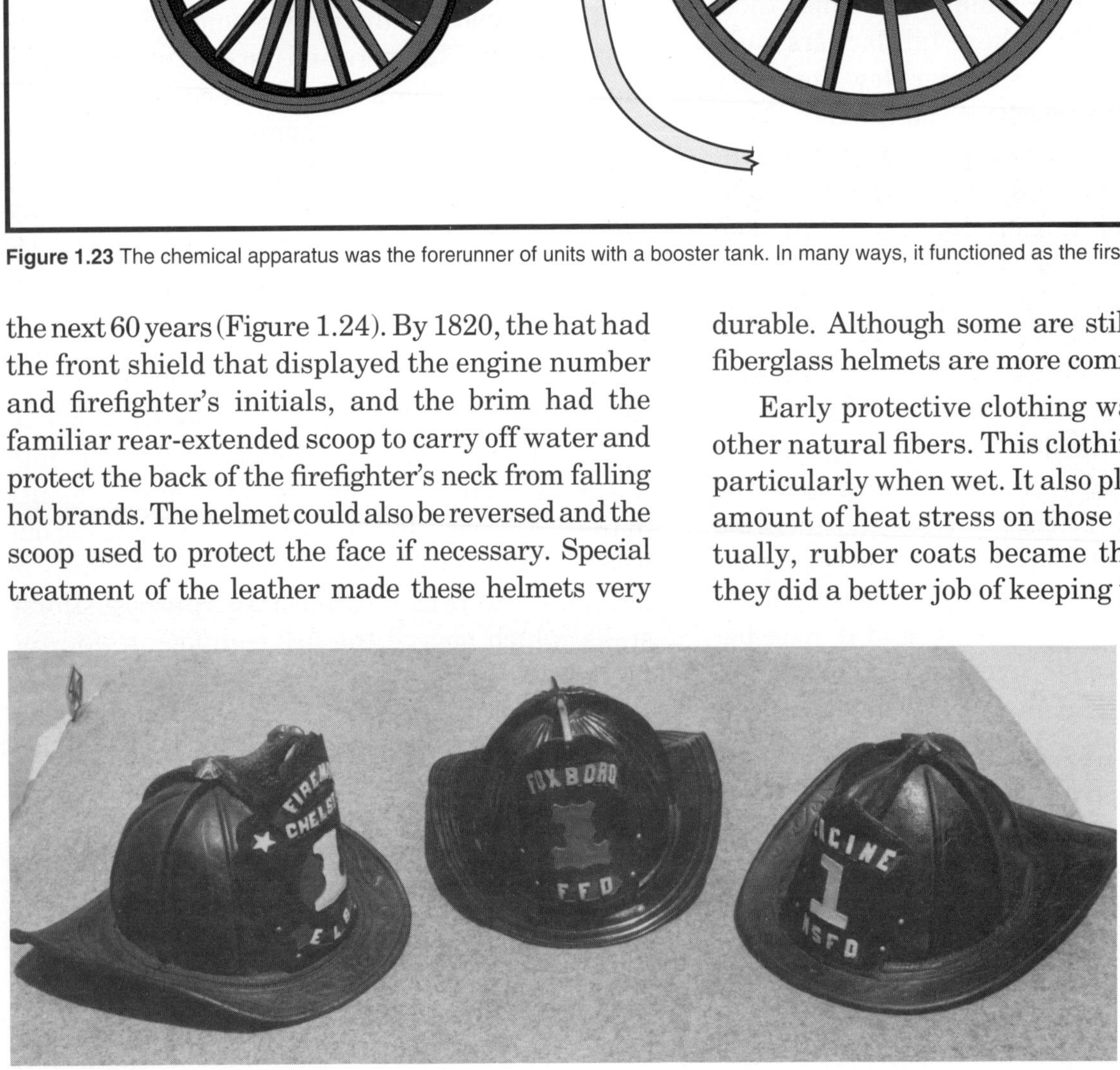

Figure 1.24 Many older helmets were constructed of leather. *Courtesy of Bob Noll.*

beneath the protective clothing, the rubber coats subjected the firefighters to quick fatigue, and the trend reverted back toward woven fibers. For a long time, clothing constructed of heavy cotton duck material was the standard. This material, however, was not very flame resistant. This led to the development of the man-made fibers used in today's protective clothing such as Nomex® fire resistant material and PBI Gold® polybenzimidazole fiber.

GASOLINE POWERED-EQUIPMENT

The beginning of the twentieth century saw a dramatic change in the fire service — the gasoline-powered engine. Eventually, it appeared that steamers and all the other horse-drawn apparatus would go the way of the tub engines. The automobile was becoming a popular mode of travel, and it was only natural that it would soon be adapted to fire fighting. Like the change from hand-operated engines to steam, the transition was gradual because the steamer had finally become the backbone of fire fighting. Tradition and sentimentality had settled in. Firefighters and the public had become attached to their fine horses. They took pride in the speed with which they came out of their stalls for the quick hitch. No sputtering, smelly motor with its lack of soul could take the place of horses for some old-timers.

The gasoline engine replaced horses but did not supersede the steam engine until years later. The advantages of the motor-driven apparatus were recognized, especially when a long-distance fire run was made — a run that would soon tire out horses. At first, engineers were unsuccessful in making a reliable piece of equipment with a shift that would transfer the gasoline engine's power from road gear to pump gear. Failures and breakdowns were frequent enough that many fire chiefs still demanded steam. Many departments compromised between steam and the gasoline engine (Figures 1.25 a and b). They built gasoline-powered tractors on the front of their steamers so that they

Figure 1.25a With the advent of gasoline engines, the steam pumper became motorized. *Courtesy of Joel Woods, University of Maryland Fire and Rescue Institute.*

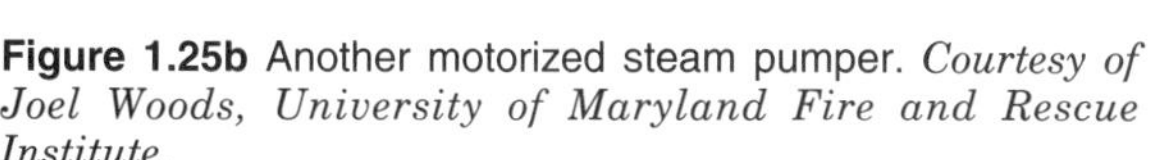

Figure 1.25b Another motorized steam pumper. *Courtesy of Joel Woods, University of Maryland Fire and Rescue Institute.*

could travel to the fire by gasoline power and pump with steam.

Engineering continued to improve, and soon the manufacturers developed reliable and powerful pumps that were driven by the same motor that propelled the vehicle (Figure 1.26). They came in time to replace the motorized steamers as they wore out. The noble and picturesque steamer thus joined the hand pumpers as a museum piece, and today the motor-pumping engine, be it gasoline or diesel, is in universal use.

Today's pumper comes close to being a complete fire department. Powerful pumps have been developed in compact sizes, allowing room for the pumper to carry a large amount of hose. This eliminated the hose wagon. Today's pumper can also carry its own water supply with a small hose reel for putting out smaller fires, eliminating the old chemical wagon. Although it did not eliminate the ladder truck and other specialized equipment, the pumper does carry smaller ladders and some forcible entry tools. On today's apparatus, firefighters carry all the practical tools of the past plus those that have recently come into use.

Today's firefighters, although better equipped and better educated, still face the same dangers as the firefighters of old. The time has not yet arrived that fire does not exist. Although the fire service is staying up with today's progressive advancements, it appears there will always be a need for firefighters as long as people and flammable substances exist.

THE IMPACT OF HISTORIC FIRES ON FIRE PROTECTION IN NORTH AMERICA

History is of no use to us if we do not use it to make the future better. Previously, in this chapter, we have related how fire experiences led to improvments in fire protection. Many of today's improvements in fire protection and code enforcement are the result of tragedies that occurred yesterday. This section examines some of those tragedies.

Although throughout history the United States has seen many conflagrations that destroyed substantial sections of communities (Charleston, South Carolina, burned down four times between 1700 and 1779 alone), no fire is mired in history as much as the Great Chicago Fire of October 9, 1871. As legend has it, Mrs. O'Leary's cow kicked over a kerosene lamp that set fire to the straw in the barn. The resulting fire blackened 2,100 acres, destroyed over 17,000 buildings, left 100,000 people homeless, and killed 250 people. Out of this fire rose a national interest in preventing its repetition. In celebrating its 40th anniversary in 1911, the Fire Marshal's Association of North America sponsored the first Fire Prevention Day on October 9, 1911. In 1920, President Woodrow Wilson declared October 9 as "Fire Prevention Day." Since 1922, the National Fire Protection Association (NFPA) has established Fire Prevention Week around this date. To this day, that week remains the focal point for the exchange of fire prevention information in North America.

Figure 1.26 Eventually, the vehicle's propulsion motor was used to power the fire pump. *Courtesy of Edmond (OK) Fire Department.*

Between the years of 1903 and 1911, there were four major fires that led to the appointment of the NFPA Committee on Safety to Life. These fires were as follows:

- Boyertown, Pennsylvania — Rhoades Opera House (1903, 170 deaths)
- Chicago, Illinois — Iroquois Theater (1903, 602 deaths)
- Collinwood, Ohio — Lakeview Grammar School (1908, 175 deaths)
- New York, New York — Triangle Shirtwaist Factory (1911, 145 deaths)

The work of this committee led to the preparation of standards for the construction of stairways and fire escapes, for fire drills in various occupancies, and for the construction and arrangement of exit facilities for factories, schools, etc., which form the basis of the present code.

In 1937, a fire at the Consolidated School in New London, Texas (294 deaths) pointed out the need for state laws to protect public buildings not subject to municipal ordinance and inspection. In the 1940s there was a string of multiple-death fires in hotels and public buildings that focused national attention on the need for adequate exits and other fire safety features. Among these fires were the following:

- Natchez, Mississippi — The Rhythm Club (1940, 207 deaths)
- Boston, Massachusetts — Coconut Grove Club (1942, 492 deaths)
- Chicago, Illinois — La Salle Hotel (1946, 61 deaths)
- Dubuque, Iowa — Hotel Canfield (1946, 19 deaths)
- Atlanta, Georgia — Winecoff Hotel (1946, 119 deaths)

In particular, the Coconut Grove Fire led to increased research into the use of combustible materials in public spaces. The spread of fire across combustible decorations and furnishings was a major contributor to the magnitude of this fire.

In 1944, 168 people were killed when the Ringling Brothers and Barnum and Bailey Circus tent caught fire in Hartford, Connecticut. This fire led to the development of NFPA 102, *Standard for Assembly Seating, Tents and Membrane Structures.*

Three hospital fires moved hospital administrators and fire prevention officials across the nation to assess the quality of construction and fire protection systems in hospitals. The three hospitals involved were:

- St. Anthony's Hospital in Effingham, Illinois (1949, 74 deaths)
- Mercy Hospital in Davenport, Iowa (1950, 41 deaths)
- Hartford, Connecticut Hospital (1961, 16 deaths)

The Our Lady of Angels Grade School fire in Chicago on December 1, 1958, (95 deaths) probably resulted in the swiftest action in the wake of any major fire since World War II. Within days of the fire, state and local officials throughout the nation ordered fire inspections of schools; and within one year, it was reported that major improvements in life safety had been made in 16,500 schools across the nation.

Fires that have occurred in more recent years continue to influence code development and enforcement and the consciousness of the public about fire hazards. Two high-rise fires in New York City in 1970 led to the adoption of a comprehensive fire code for high-rise buildings in that city. The following fires are still having an effect on life safety code work:

- Beverly Hills Supper Club in Southgate, Kentucky, (1977, 165 deaths)
- MGM Grand Hotel in Las Vegas, Nevada, (1980, 85 deaths)
- Happy Land Social Club in New York City (1990, 87 deaths)
- Hamlet, North Carolina food processing plant (1991, 25 deaths)

Fires without loss of life, such as the 1982 K-Mart warehouse fire in Falls Township, Pennsylvania, have had substantial impact on regulations for the bulk storage and high-rack storage of flammable and combustible goods. Only time will tell whether we have learned enough from the past to prevent similar tragedies from occurring in the future.

Chapter 1
Application And Review Activities

DIRECTIONS

The following activities are designed to help you comprehend and apply the information in Chapter 1 of **Orientation and Terminology**. To receive the maximum learning experience from these activities, it is recommended that you use the following procedure:

1. Read the chapter, underlining or highlighting important terms, topics, and subject matter. Study the photographs and illustrations, and read the captions under each.
2. Review the list of vocabulary words to ensure that you know the chapter-related meaning of each. If you are unsure of the meaning of a vocabulary word, look the word up in a dictionary, and then study its context in the chapter.
3. On a separate sheet of paper, complete all assigned or selected application and review activities before checking your answers.
4. After you have finished, check your answers against those on the pages referenced in parentheses.
5. Correct any incorrect answers, and review material that was answered incorrectly.

VOCABULARY

Be sure that you know the chapter-related meanings of the following terms.

- Conflagration *(6)*
- Corporal punishment *(5)*
- Curtail *(20)*
- Deterioration *(20)*
- Diameter *(17)*
- Heat radiation *(6)*
- Horizontal *(21)*
- Incendiarism *(6)*
- Ingenious *(22)*
- Negligence *(5)*
- Ordinance *(6)*
- Tiller *(24)*
- Treadle *(11)*

APPLICATION OF KNOWLEDGE

1. Research the history of your fire department. Outline the major improvements in apparatus, equipment, and procedures over the life of the department. *(Local protocol)*

2. If you could remedy any one deficiency in today's fire protection/fire service system, what would it be? Why? How would you implement your proposed change? *(Local protocol)*

3. In 1992, a wildland-urban interface fire in Oakland, California, destroyed millions of dollars worth of property. Based on your understanding of the impact of historical fires on today's fire service, what kinds of laws, ordinances, and fire protection equipment do you see as necessary to prevent similar occurrences? Why? *(Local protocol)*

REVIEW ACTIVITIES

1. Explain the origins of our word *curfew*. *(6)*
2. Explain how the hook and ladder truck got its name. *(6)*
3. Explain how the first American fire brigade was formed. *(7 & 8)*
4. Define and explain the function of *fire mark*. *(8)*
5. Trace in outline form the evolution of the fire engine from its beginnings to today's gasoline-powered apparatus. *(9-11; 13-17; 20-27)*
6. Describe the basic operation of a hand-tub fire engine. *(10)*
7. Explain why Boston was the first American city to establish a fire department. *(11)*
8. Describe the American fire mark, and contrast its uses with that used in England. *(12)*
9. Distinguish between mutual fire societies and volunteer departments. *(11 &12)*
10. List in order of establishment the first three American fire societies. *(11-13)*
11. Provide examples of Benjamin Franklin's contributions to the development of an American fire service. *(12)*
12. Describe Richard Mason's Philadelphia-style fire engine. *(14)*
13. Distinguish between a New York-style hand engine and a piano-type engine. *(14)*
14. List ways in which the hand-tub fire engines were improved in the years after the establishment of the first fire societies. *(15-17)*
15. Describe reasons for the growth of American volunteer fire companies after the Revolutionary War. *(17)*
16. List at least six types of infractions for which early volunteers were penalized through fines or expulsion. *(18)*
17. Define and explain the word *washed* as it applies to early volunteer departments. *(19)*
18. Describe events that led to a deterioration of the volunteer system in the early 1800s. *(20)*
19. Explain the origins of the term *fire plug*. *(20)*
20. Describe the operations of Hose No. 1. *(20)*
21. Explain why the first two steam fire engines were rejected failures. *(21)*
22. Name the first all-steam fire department in America. The first fully paid fire department. *(22)*

23. Describe how dogs in general, and Dalmatians in particular, became associated with the fire service. *(22)*

24. Describe the operation of a steam fire engine. *(22-24)*

25. Trace the development of ladder trucks. *(24)*

26. Provide examples of improvements in protective clothing that occurred in the 1800s. *(25)*

27. Explain why — despite the invention of the gasoline-powered engine in the twentieth century — fire departments were reluctant to change from steam to gasoline-powered equipment. *(27)*

28. List advantages of gasoline-powered equipment over steam-powered equipment. *(28)*

29. List four historic fires, and describe their impact on fire protection in North America. *(28 & 29)*

30. Identify 15 of the following in one or two phrases.
    - Bed key *(11)*
    - Boston Mutual Fire Society *(12)*
    - Bucket brigade *(17)*
    - Cannel coal *(23)*
    - Captain John Ericsson *(21)*
    - Cider mill *(14)*
    - Coffee mill *(14)*
    - Corps of Vigiles *(15)*
    - Daniel Hayes *(25)*
    - Daniel Lawler *(25)*
    - Fire hook *(6)*
    - Fire mark *(8)*
    - Fire squirt *(9)*
    - General Jan van der Heijden *(9 & 10)*
    - Gooseneck *(10)*
    - Hand in hand *(12)*
    - Jamestown *(6)*
    - Joseph Jynks *(11)*
    - Latta engine *(22)*
    - Leading hose *(14)*
    - Old Brass Backs *(13)*
    - Pat Lyon *(14)*
    - Paul Hodge *(21)*
    - Peter Stuyvesant *(8)*
    - Plug-uglies *(19)*
    - Rattlers *(8)*
    - Richard Mason *(14)*
    - Richard Newsham *(10)*
    - Squirrel tail *(15)*
    - Surveyors of Buildings *(8)*
    - Thomas Atkins *(11)*
    - Thomas Lote *(13)*
    - Tommy Franklin *(13)*
    - Union Volunteer Fire Company *(12)*
    - Washed *(19)*
    - William C. Hunneman *(14)*
    - Caesar Augustus *(5)*

2
The Fire Service As A Career

Chapter 2
The Fire Service As A Career

Fire fighting is one of the world's most honored but hazardous occupations. It is the duty of every fire department to save lives and to reduce injuries and property losses. By becoming firefighters, people join a profession that is rich in heritage of dedication, unselfish sacrifice, and inspired human action. Firefighters perform no greater service than coming to the aid of others (Figure 2.1). The firefighter's job is not comfortable or easy; it is a profession that exposes an individual to a high level of personal stress and danger. Fire fighting requires a high sense of personal dedication, a genuine desire to help people, and a high level of skill.

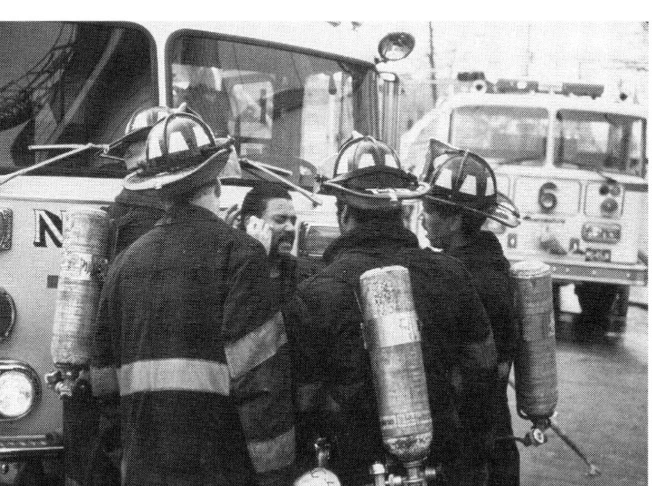

Figure 2.1 Firefighters routinely come to the aid of others, including other firefighters. *Courtesy of Ron Jeffers.*

New firefighters are placed into one of two categories: paid or volunteer. Paid fire departments primarily protect larger towns and cities. Volunteer fire departments are most commonly found in small and rural communities, although volunteers may supplement paid personnel in larger communities. Volunteer fire departments and their firefighters greatly outnumber paid departments and their firefighters. In all, it is estimated that there are over 40,000 fire departments in North America.

Whenever there is a disaster, the fire department is one of the first entities called to the scene. Because it is a disaster, the conditions will not always be favorable. There will be hard, fast work that drains a firefighter's energy and tests his or her endurance. Disasters involve not only fires but incidents such as cave-ins, building collapses, motor vehicle accidents, aircraft crashes, tornadoes, hazardous materials incidents, civil disturbances, rescue operations, explosions, water incidents, and medical emergencies (Figure 2.2). The emergency list is unlimited.

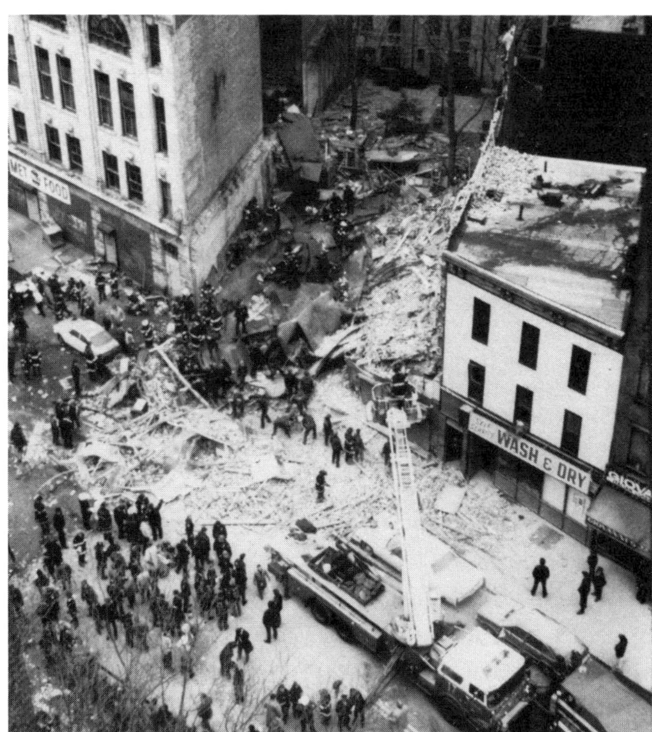

Figure 2.2 In many cases, firefighters operate at nonfire emergencies such as structural collapse incidents. *Courtesy of Harvey Eisner.*

When most people feel that they have an emergency, they think of the fire department first. Firefighters are involved with all types of people and are appreciated by some and scorned by others. Because firefighters are public servants, they are expected to calmly evaluate the problem and bring it to a successful conclusion. As a result of their position, firefighters will come to know sincere thanks, human kindness, misunderstanding, sadness, helplessness, and disappointment. They will see and know unrestricted emotion, destruction, foolishness, pain, and death. From the first time an emergency situation is encountered until the last day of service, firefighters are expected by the public to perform heroically. Firefighters are not extraordinary — they are ordinary people who often find themselves in extraordinary situations. Like other people, firefighters have their limits. Everything cannot be done at once; this fact must be accepted. Any emergency situation requires knowledge, ability, and skill to bring it to a safe conclusion.

There is an old adage that people learn from their mistakes. In the fire service, waiting to learn from mistakes can be fatal. Proper training helps firefighters become proficient in their occupation. However, it is impossible for a firefighter to become completely trained in all areas, because the firefighter's education and training cover such a broad spectrum of subjects. Training is an ongoing process.

RESPONSIBLE BEHAVIORS FOR NEW FIREFIGHTERS

In any profession, adopting a proper attitude is a key factor in an individual's attempt to be successful. Like most occupations, the fire service has its code of ethics and standards of behavior with which compliance is expected. Life in the fire department brings the members close together during working hours. The firefighters eat, live, and share time together while on duty (Figure 2.3). Volunteer firefighters also spend a considerable amount of time together during training, emergency incidents, fund raising, and the like. As a result, these groups tend to establish their own values and norms and make social and labor judgments based on the standards formed. The following suggestions may be important for a successful career in the fire service. These suggestions may also be helpful in providing some basic ideas for a smooth transition into the department.

Figure 2.3 When firefighters are not responding to a call, they spend a lot of time together in the station.

- *Be sincerely interested in and dedicated to the job.* To properly perform in the fire service, firefighters must have a high degree of personal commitment. Selfish interests have no place in the fire service. Only through a group effort can the protection of the public be accomplished. In many cases, such as interior structural fire fighting, free-lancing behavior can be deadly. Cooperation is the key — each person must be willing to work in the position assigned and be dedicated to the performance of the duties of that position.
- *Be loyal to the fire department and to fellow firefighters.* Firefighters make a fire department. Firefighters should understand their department's policies and functions and should be prepared to defend them. To fail to do so is a failure to defend one's self. Firefighters are also representatives of the department, and their dress and actions should be a credit to their department. As individuals, firefighters must develop loyalty to the other members of the department and band together.

- *Be aggressive in the pursuit of all education and training opportunities.* Firefighters are never completely trained. The firefighter's training is an ongoing process that lasts until the individual decides to leave the fire service. There is no such thing as an "overeducated" firefighter. Individuals participating in the fire fighting profession must display a willingness to obtain as much fire education as possible.
- *Guard speech both on and off duty.* As members of the department, firefighters possess information that should not be revealed. This does not mean, however, that firefighters should not discuss the functions, history, and traditions of the fire service with the public. Firefighters should use discretion while discussing information that could have a negative effect on the department, individuals on the department, or other members of the public.
- *Be the type of person who inspires confidence and respect.* Firefighters must strive to be honest, fair, and trustworthy when dealing with fellow firefighters and supervisors. Dependability is a must in the fire service — others rely on it.
- *Be able to accept criticism graciously, and accept praise, honors, and advancement modestly.* There is no such thing as the perfect firefighter. Everyone makes mistakes. Legitimate criticism of mistakes is not something about which to become angry. In fact, it should be welcomed because improvement is the name of the game. With improvement comes honors and advancement; accept these with humility and in a manner that will not alienate others.
- *Ask questions.* If any aspect of the instruction is unclear, ask the supervisor specific questions concerning those areas in which information is incomplete or not understood (Figure 2.4). This is the most effective way for an exchange of information to take place.

TEAMWORK

Teamwork is the smooth working together of individuals to accomplish a task that is important to the total operation. To work together under conditions where the safety of one member is dependent upon the action of another requires teamwork (Figure 2.5). How the emergency is resolved depends upon teamwork.

Figure 2.4 Do not be afraid to ask questions of your superiors.

Figure 2.5 Teamwork is required when raising large ground ladders.

A good team has confidence that comes from belief in each team member and in the team. Studying and drilling as a team develops and nurtures this confidence. The strength of the team is the combined strength of each of those firefighters who compose the team. It is possible to evaluate the strength of a team by evaluating the firefighters. Team spirit is the enthusiasm developed through satisfactory teamwork. The contribution of each member of the team is essential to its proper functioning. This includes all facets of ability, confidence, and spirit. Teamwork is based on the following factors:

- All members must have a common desire for success.
- Each member must contribute to the team.
- Members should know their job function and the job functions of other team members so that they may supplement each other as teammates.
- Members must have two-way communication.
- All members must train together over and over to assure precision and quickness.

SOURCES OF TRAINING

Basically, there are two types of training — classroom study and training drills (Figures 2.6 a and b). Classroom study is the fundamental training for acquiring basic knowledge that can be applied to practical applications. A drill is the practical application of classroom techniques and theories and the rehearsing of pre-incident plans and courses of action. The practices are designed to allow firefighters to rehearse safely until a procedure can be performed without error or hesitation. Many times these practices may be monotonous and tiresome, but they are necessary to perfect the fundamentals and execution of the firefighter's duties. These practices are also an important part of the firefighter's protection and safety. Without firefighter drills, precision and perfection are unobtainable and success is impossible.

Having established the importance of training to the firefighter, it is important to review the sources from which training can be received. Firefighters are not limited to any one of these sources. In fact, firefighters are apt to be more successful if they use more than one of these sources.

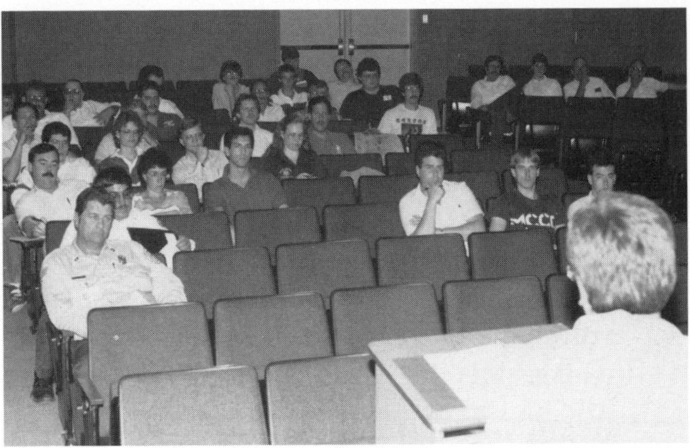

Figure 2.6a Some training must be carried out in a lecture setting.

Figure 2.6b Some tasks, such as working from heights, cannot be duplicated in the classroom.

Departmental Training

In actuality, the majority of a firefighter's training comes from within his or her own fire department. From the paid department perspective, a rookie is hired and immediately placed into the department's recruit academy class. In the training academy, the rookie learns the basics of the job so that he or she may then be assigned to a company. Once in the field, a firefighter faces in-service training the rest of his or her career. In-service training comes in many forms, including individual company training, multicompany training sessions, and members returning to the fire department training academy or division for courses (Figure 2.7). Courses are held to update line personnel on new procedures or equipment and to prepare personnel for promotion.

In larger departments, training activities are coordinated and run through the fire department's

Figure 2.7 Occasionally, firefighters return to the training academy for special classes.

training division. This is an organizational unit that is charged with carrying out the training activities of the department. The person in charge of this entity is usually called the "chief of training." Other personnel, both sworn and civilians, are assigned to the training division as well. Typically, the sworn personnel hold the rank of company officer. Training division personnel are responsible for delivering courses at the academy and coordinating the delivery of company-level training throughout the department.

Small volunteer and paid departments may have only one individual that is assigned the role of training officer. This person has the same responsibilities as the training division in the larger departments. In some cases, particularly in very small volunteer departments, the duties of training officer may be in addition to other responsibilities such as those of an assistant chief.

Volunteer departments have to pattern their training around the lifestyles of their members. Training sessions are often held during the evening or on weekends (Figure 2.8). Volunteer departments generally do not have the luxury of putting new members through the same type of recruit academy as their paid counterparts. However, new members must not be allowed to respond to emergencies until they have adequate training in the types of activities in which they will be expected to perform. According to NFPA 1500, *Standard on Fire Department Occupational Safety and Health Program*, no member (paid or volunteer) may be allowed to actively engage in structural fire fighting until he or she has met the requirements for a Fire Fighter I contained in NFPA 1001, *Standard for Fire Fighter Professional Qualifications*.

Figure 2.8 Volunteers need as much training as career firefighters. *Courtesy of Bob Esposito.*

County And State Fire Training Programs

Many governmental agencies sponsor fire training programs. These training programs may range from occasional seminars to academies with full-time staff and a regular schedule of courses. Training programs are found on the county, parish (Louisiana and Canada), borough (Alaska), and state levels (Figure 2.9).

Figure 2.9 Some counties have their own fire training academies.

County, parish, and borough programs are most commonly found in more populous areas containing large numbers of small fire departments, particularly volunteer departments. These programs provide a wide variety of basic and advanced courses. In many cases, these courses are comparable to those given at the state academies, and certification may be obtained at the local level.

Many state fire training programs operate under a university or educational agency, usually vocational. In other cases, the director of fire training operates under the state fire marshal's office. State fire training agencies may have either a full- or part-time instructional staff. These instructors' responsibilities include assigning and supervising part-time field instructors, developing instructional outlines, developing and producing audiovisual training aids, and monitoring required records.

Many state training agencies have training facilities, and some even provide accommodations in dormitories. Most on-campus courses last a week and cover either a specific subject area or a range of subjects. There are also courses that are offered off campus and usually are taught by state certified part-time instructors.

Community Colleges/Universities

There are hundreds of fire science degree programs throughout North America, most of which are offered by community and junior colleges on either a full- or part-time basis. In most cases, an associate degree is awarded upon successful completion of the program, and some institutions offer a certificate for partial completion. Also offered are a few four-year degree programs with emphasis on fire service management or fire protection engineering and/or technology. Some of the more well-known programs of this type are located at Eastern Kentucky University, Oklahoma State University, University of Maryland, and the University of New Haven. Graduate study programs are available at the University of Maryland and Worcester Polytechnic Institute.

College fire science programs are usually designed to supplement (but not replace) departmental training. The curriculum design for many such programs emphasizes the arts and sciences, with special courses in fire protection subjects beyond the scope of basic fire training programs. A majority of programs emphasize supervisory and management skills along with fire science. These degree programs are designed to prepare individuals for entry into or promotion within the department. A few colleges emphasize engineering and technology courses with their program. These programs prepare the individual to participate in the more technical aspects of the fire prevention field such as fire protection system design, building design considerations, and code enforcement.

National Fire Academy

The National Fire Academy (NFA) is a center for fire protection related education, information, and expertise. The NFA's aim is to improve the professional development of fire service personnel and allied professionals. The academy, which is operated by the United States Fire Administration (USFA), offers a wide variety of courses in the general areas of incident management, fire technology, and fire prevention. These courses are delivered through an on-campus program and an extensive outreach program.

The resident student program consists of courses conducted at the National Emergency Training Center (NETC) in Emmitsburg, Maryland. Students, mainly from the fire service, attend these courses at minimal cost through a stipend program, which covers the cost of tuition, travel, and accommodations in campus dormitories. Most courses are two weeks and are linked so that the student can advance through different levels in a particular subject or develop expertise in a variety of subjects.

The outreach program provides for the delivery of short-term (generally two-day) courses to students in locations all over the United States. The courses are coordinated through state and local training agencies and are concentrated on weekends to allow maximum participation from both career and volunteer fire service personnel.

FIREFIGHTER CERTIFICATION

Certification means to attest authoritatively that an individual has met the qualifications specified in a given standard. The certification of firefighters is important from a liability standpoint. Certification shows that the individual has met the objectives of the applicable standard and should be ready to handle the responsibilities of the job.

The standards that the fire service use to certify firefighters are developed by the National Fire Protection Association (NFPA) and are commonly referred to as the Professional Qualifications Standards (Figure 2.10). These standards are consensus documents that are developed by other members of the fire service. Professional qualifications standards used by the fire service include:

- NFPA 472, *Standard for Professional Competence of Responders to Hazardous Materials Incidents*
- NFPA 1001, *Standard for Fire Fighter Professional Qualifications*
- NFPA 1002, *Standard for Fire Apparatus Driver/Operator Professional Qualifications*
- NFPA 1003, *Standard for Professional Qualifications for Airport Fire Fighters*
- NFPA 1021, *Standard for Fire Officer Professional Qualifications*
- NFPA 1031, *Standard for Professional Qualifications for Fire Inspector*
- NFPA 1033, *Standard for Professional Qualifications for Fire Investigator*
- NFPA 1035, *Standard for Professional Qualifications for Public Fire Educator*
- NFPA 1041, *Standard for Fire Service Instructor Professional Qualifications*
- NFPA 1521, *Standard for Fire Department Safety Officer*

At the time this manual was published, preliminary work was started on two new professional qualifications standards. One standard will address qualifications for wildland firefighters (NFPA 1051 — Proposed), and the other will be for fire service telecommunicators or dispatchers (NFPA 1061 — Proposed). Both standards are anticipated to come on line in the mid-1990s.

These standards provide guidelines for state certification and for local departments to use in setting their goals. Because the standards are minimum requirements, each department will have to adapt and amend the standards to fit the local

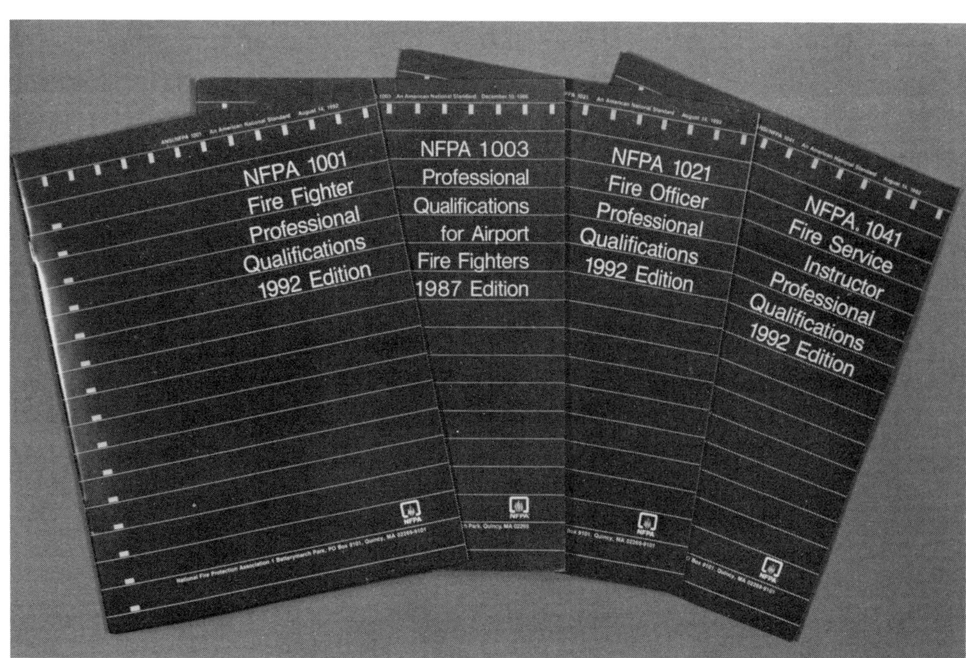

Figure 2.10 NFPA standards are used to develop firefighter certification programs.

situation. In some areas, the national standards may not be adequate to handle the hazards found. Firefighters may need to be trained at a level higher than specified by the standards to cope with local conditions. In such situations, local fire chiefs will determine what to require of their departments and how to effectively apply the standards to provide the best possible fire protection for the citizens.

To become certified to any of these standards, a firefighter must first complete the required training and then pass a certification examination. The certification examination is conducted by an agency accredited to certify firefighters to these standards (Figure 2.11). The two organizations that accredit training agencies to certify firefighters are the National Professional Qualifications Board (sometimes called the NPQB or the Pro Board) and the International Fire Service Accreditation Congress (IFSAC).

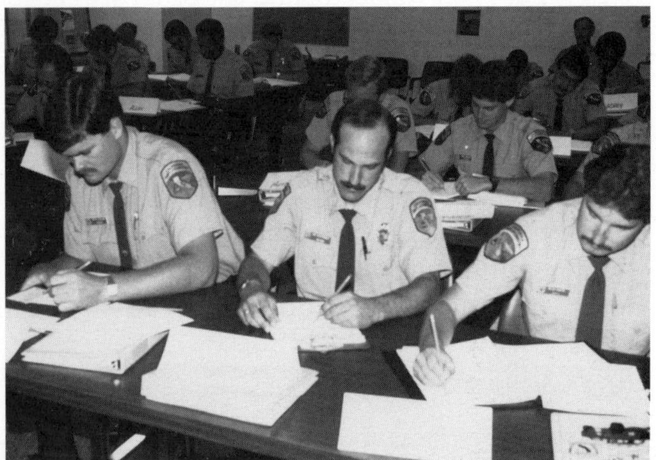

Figure 2.11 Part of the certification exam is a written test.

National Professional Qualifications Board (NPQB)

The National Professional Qualifications Board was an outgrowth of the Joint Council of Fire Service Organizations (discussed in Chapter 3). NPQB was conceived by the Council in 1972 to provide minimum performance standards that can be used to evaluate firefighters' abilities and skills and determine whether they possess the necessary qualifications for that respective level. The NPQB also accredited training agencies that sought to certify firefighters to these standards. In the mid-1980s, the task of developing and maintaining the professional qualifications standards was passed on to the NFPA, and the NPQB concentrated strictly on accreditation of programs. At the time this manual was developed, seventeen agencies were accredited by NPQB to certify firefighters. The NPQB is composed of leaders from some of the organizations that were represented on the Joint Council.

International Fire Service Accreditation Congress (IFSAC)

IFSAC was born after a meeting of the National Association of State Directors of Fire Training and Education in August 1990. IFSAC, which is based at Oklahoma State University (OSU), held its first congressional meeting in February 1991. The purpose of IFSAC is to provide a self-governed system which accredits fire service certification programs. IFSAC consists of three groups of people: Administration, Board of Governors, and the Congress (Figure 2.12). The Administration is the full-time staff at OSU; the Board of Directors is elected by the Congress; and the Congress is composed of representatives of participants in the system. At the time this manual was developed, forty entities had submitted letters of intent to join this system.

Figure 2.12 The basic model of the IFSAC organization.

THE FIREFIGHTER IMAGE

The public view of firefighters is as varied as it is important. People look at firefighters in different ways. Some people consider firefighters as people who sit around all day drinking coffee and watching television. Others view them as those who constantly risk their lives for people and who can do no wrong (Figures 2.13 a and b). Children consider them heroes and often idolize them. Depending on the individual, firefighters can be either all or none of these things. The public's opinion of firefighters constantly changes. New firefighters need to realize that their public image is essential to successfully conduct everyday activities.

Firefighters are often considered the most helpful people in the neighborhood. The qualities that make them firefighters rub off onto their everyday activities and associations. Much is expected of them, and they usually live up to these expectations.

Because of public exposure, firefighters should not indulge in behavior that would lower public opinion of them. If their image depends on doing their job successfully, it makes sense that they should not undertake activities that would interfere with their position. All in all, the position of a firefighter can be summed up as being one in which expectations are high. Firefighters should try to be the type of people of whom their families, the department, and the public can be proud.

PHYSICAL FITNESS

Firefighters must be able to do many things quickly and with little error. At a fire scene, the

Figure 2.13a Some people view career firefighters as people who spend much of their time getting paid to sit.

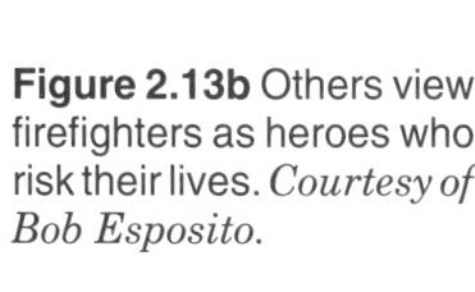

Figure 2.13b Others view firefighters as heroes who risk their lives. *Courtesy of Bob Esposito.*

tasks that need to be accomplished require quick thinking, agility, skill, and speed. The only time that these tasks can be done effectively is when firefighters have the physical ability to perform them. This is why physical conditioning is so important. It is vital that firefighters be in top physical shape, both for individual safety and that of others (Figure 2.14).

Medical and physical requirements are usually high for gaining entrance into a fire department. Oftentimes these requirements are based on NFPA 1582, *Standard on Medical Requirements for Fire Fighters*. Recruits are selected and then put through strenuous training in basic firefighter school. After the initial period, however, most departments decrease their physical condition requirements. It has only been recently that fire departments in general have started increasing their demands concerning fitness. While experience can compensate to a degree for the vigor of youth, there is no excuse for older firefighters to be in poor condition. Lack of fitness endangers the individual, makes the duties more difficult, and decreases the chance of success.

Figure 2.14 Firefighters need to exercise to keep in shape.

Chapter 2
Application And Review Activities

DIRECTIONS

The following activities are designed to help you comprehend and apply the information in Chapter 2 of **Orientation and Terminology**. To receive the maximum learning experience from these activities, it is recommended that you use the following procedure:

1. Read the chapter, underlining or highlighting important terms, topics, and subject matter. Study the photographs and illustrations, and read the captions under each.
2. Review the list of vocabulary words to ensure that you know the chapter-related meaning of each. If you are unsure of the meaning of a vocabulary word, look the word up in a dictionary, and then study its context in the chapter.
3. On a separate sheet of paper, complete all assigned or selected application and review activities before checking your answers.
4. After you have finished, check your answers against those on the pages referenced in parentheses.
5. Correct any incorrect answers, and review material that was answered incorrectly.

VOCABULARY

Be sure that you know the chapter-related meanings of the following terms.

- Accredit *(42)*
- Agility *(44)*
- Authoritative *(41)*
- Certification *(41)*
- Certify *(41)*
- Compensate *(44)*
- Consensus *(41)*
- Conditioning *(44)*
- Curriculum *(40)*
- Preliminary *(41)*
- Telecommunicator *(41)*

APPLICATION OF KNOWLEDGE

1. Describe the training for your department. Where are the training facilities? Who is in charge of departmental training? Does that person also hold other responsibilities within the department? How often do the local firefighters train? Does the department periodically send firefighters away to a larger academy for training? If so, where, how frequently, and for what type of training? *(Local protocol)*

2. Based on your knowledge of the type of incidents to which your department responds, for which NFPA Professional Qualifications Standards have you been certified? For which do you plan to train and become certified? Where do local firefighters go to become certified, and who accredits that training agency to certify firefighters? *(Local protocol)*

3. Firefighters work in very hot conditions, wear heavy equipment that constricts motion, and work under tremendous stress to protect lives and property. Explain, then, why a high level of physical fitness is necessary and can help combat the negative effects of these three factors. *(Local protocol)*

REVIEW ACTIVITIES

1. List the two types of communities in which volunteer firefighters are usually found. *(35)*
2. List at least eight incidents, besides fires, that frequently require firefighter response. *(35)*
3. List the three requirements for a safe conclusion to any emergency. *(36)*
4. Explain why an individualistic, "free-lance" approach to fire fighting can be deadly. *(36)*
5. Discuss the seven desirable behaviors that help new firefighters smoothly integrate themselves into a fire department. *(36)*
6. Name three areas essential to achieving efficient teamwork. *(38)*
7. List and explain the factors that contribute to a smoothly working team. *(38)*
8. State at least two reasons why training is important for firefighters. *(38)*
9. Define and describe the Professional Qualifications Standards. *(39)*
10. Briefly identify each of the following in one or two phrases.
    - NFPA *(41)*
    - NPQB *(42)*
    - IFSAC *(42)*
11. List the names and numbers of the ten Professional Qualifications Standards issued by the NFPA. Mark the ones for which you have been certified. *(41)*
12. Explain why it is very important for firefighters to protect their public image on and off duty. *(43)*
13. Describe at least three negative consequences of poor firefighter physical condition. *(44)*

3
Organizations Related To The Fire Service

Chapter 3
Organizations Related To The Fire Service

During the course of his or her career, a firefighter will be affected by and exposed to many different organizations that are a part of, or related to, the fire service. The purpose of this chapter is to acquaint the reader with trade, federal, state, and local organizations.

TRADE ORGANIZATIONS

Trade organizations relate most directly to the fire service. Historically, trade organizations have arisen from fire service groups with similar interests that band together to unite their cause. Today, many of these organizations serve vital roles in the overall fire protection field. The following section looks at some of the more important fire service trade organizations.

The Joint Council Of National Fire Service Organizations

The original intent and purpose of the Joint Council of National Fire Service Organizations (JCNFSO) was to provide a means whereby national fire service organizations could cooperate in defining and achieving the national goals of the fire service. The Council held its first meeting on August 31 and September 1, 1970, in Williamsburg, Virginia. Originally, the Council was composed of the chief executive officers of the following trade organizations:

- Fire Marshal's Association of North America
- International Association of Arson Investigators
- International Association of Black Professional Firefighters
- International Association of Fire Chiefs
- International Fire Service Training Association
- International Municipal Signal Association
- International Society of Fire Service Instructors
- Metropolitan Chiefs Committee of the International Association of Fire Chiefs
- National Fire Protection Association
- National Volunteer Fire Council

The Council's most outstanding achievement was the establishment of the National Professional Qualifications Board (see Chapter 2). After nearly 20 years of operation, the Joint Council of National Fire Service Organizations voted to disband in August, 1989. There were two principal reasons for its disbandment. One reason was due to a rule change that allowed subordinates to attend meetings in place of the chief executive officers. Another factor was the requirement of a unanimous vote on policy matters. A standing committee of several of the remaining members was formed to handle closing business and to provide assistance in continuing the work of the NPQB.

International Association Of Fire Fighters (IAFF)

The IAFF is a labor organization (union) of permanent, paid firefighters with about 175,000 members. It was formed in 1918 and is affiliated with the AFL-CIO. Membership exists through joint councils, state associations, and chartered locals. Address: 1750 New York Avenue N.W., Washington, DC 20006.

International Association Of Fire Chiefs (IAFC)

Active membership in the IAFC is open to all chief officers of organized public, industrial, or government fire departments. Fire marshals, commissioners, and directors are also included if they are involved in active fire fighting and administrative duties. The association, formed in 1873, is designed to further the professional advancement of the fire service. The IAFC holds an annual conference for the purpose of technical and educational advancement. This conference is held in a different city in North America each year. Address: 1329 18th Street N.W., Washington, DC 20036.

Metropolitan Committee/International Association Of Fire Chiefs (Metro Chiefs)

The Metro Chiefs is a committee of fire chiefs who represent cities that have a population of 200,000 or greater or that have 400 or more paid firefighters. This group concentrates on issues particular to these large departments. Address: 1329 18th Street N.W., Washington, DC 20036.

International Association Of Arson Investigators (IAAI)

Individuals may join the IAAI as active members if they are actively engaged in suppressing arson for a government or private organization. Others may join as associate members if they meet IAAI requirements. The primary function of the association is attacking the arson problem. Address: P.O. Box 600, 25 Newton Street, Marlboro, MA 01752.

International Society Of Fire Service Instructors (ISFSI)

The primary function of the ISFSI is to provide a medium for the exchange of educational ideas and training techniques for the fire service. ISFSI has done much to assist fire service instructors in their quest for improvement. The society was formed in 1960. ISFSI holds its annual Fire Department Instructor's Conference (FDIC) every spring in Cincinnati, Ohio. Address: 20 Main Street, Ashland, MA 01721.

International Association Of Black Professional Fire Fighters (IABPFF)

Since 1970, the IABPFF has been dedicated to assisting black firefighters in areas such as working conditions, advancement, and interracial programs. The association also serves as a liaison between black firefighters throughout the country. Address: 5332 Kershaw Street, Philadelphia, PA 19131.

National Fire Protection Association (NFPA)

The NFPA is an organization concerned with fire safety standards development, technical advisory services, education, research, and other related services. Its members come from the educational and scientific sectors of the fire protection field, both private and public. The NFPA's primary service to the fire protection field is the development of technical consensus standards. NFPA also develops fire training and public fire education materials. The NFPA was organized in 1896. Address: One Batterymarch Park, P.O. Box 9101, Quincy, MA 02269-9101.

Fire Marshal's Association Of North America (FMANA)

FMANA unites those involved in fire prevention and arson investigation and helps its members by correlating activities and exchanging information. The FMANA is open to any fire marshal for a state, town, county, or fire protection district. Organized in 1906, FMANA has its headquarters at the NFPA. Address: One Batterymarch Park, P.O. Box 9101, Quincy, MA 02269-9101.

National Volunteer Fire Council (NVFC)

The NFVC is concerned with the interests of volunteer firefighters. Organized in 1976, it provides a unified position on matters affecting volunteers. Address: Changes every two years with the organization's president.

International Fire Service Training Association (IFSTA)

IFSTA was formed in 1934 to develop training manuals and materials for the fire service. The committees of IFSTA meet each July in Oklahoma to revise and validate selected manuals. After validation, the texts are published by Fire Protection Publications, an extension of Oklahoma State University (Figure 3.1). The publications are used throughout the United States and Canada and in several foreign countries. Address: Oklahoma State University, Stillwater, OK 74078-0118.

International Municipal Signal Association (IMSA)

IMSA's members are municipal signal and communication department heads. IMSA was organized to assist its members with technical knowl-

Figure 3.1 Fire Protection Publications is the home of the International Fire Service Training Association.

edge and information on fire and police alarms and traffic controls. The association was organized in 1896 and has about 3,500 members. Address: P.O. Box 8249, Fort Worth, TX 76112.

Building Officials And Code Administrators International Inc. (BOCA)

BOCA is an organization that provides model codes for city and state adoption. The model codes are for building, mechanical, plumbing, and fire prevention. BOCA also sponsors training, testing, and certification for code administrators and building inspection officials. Address: 4051 W. Flossmoore Rd., Country Club Hills, IL 60477.

International Conference Of Building Officials (ICBO)

ICBO is an organization that provides the Uniform Building Code (UBC) for city and state adoption. The UBC is found mostly in western states and some southern cities. ICBO produces fire codes in conjunction with the Western Fire Chiefs Association. ICBO also sponsors training, testing, and certification for code administrators and building inspection officials. Address: 5360 South Workman Mill Road, Whittier, CA 90601.

Southern Building Code Congress International (SBCCI)

SBCCI is an organization that provides the Standard Building Code for city and state adoption. The SBCCI also has mechanical, plumbing, and fire prevention codes. The SBCCI is found mostly in the southern states. SBCCI also sponsors training, testing, and certification for code administrators and building inspection officials. Address: 900 Montclair Road, Birmingham, AL 35213.

International City Management Association (ICMA)

This is an association of local government executives. Its purposes are to strengthen urban government through quality professional management and to develop and disseminate new approaches by training programs, information services, and publications. Address: 1120 G Street N.W., Washington, DC 20005.

American National Standards Institute (ANSI)

ANSI identifies public requirements for national standards and coordinates voluntary standardization activities of concerned organizations. An example is ANSI Z88.5, *Practices for Respiratory Protection for the Fire Service*. Address: 1430 Broadway, New York, NY 10018.

Underwriters Laboratories Inc. (UL)

The goal of UL is to promote public safety through its scientific investigation of various materials to determine how hazardous the materials are. After testing, the organization then lists and marks the material as having passed its rigorous tests. The nonprofit UL was founded in 1894. Address: 333 Pfingsten Road, Northbrook, IL 60062.

Factory Mutual Research Corporation (FM)

FM conducts research in property loss control, primarily to meet the needs of the Factory Mutual System. The information, however, is available for use by others. Data is gathered by testing, surveys, and studies. Address: 1151 Boston-Providence Turnpike, Norwood, MA 02062.

Insurance Services Office (ISO)

ISO is a voluntary, nonprofit, unincorporated association of insurers. ISO subsidiary, Commercial Risk Services (CRS), evaluates and rates the fire protection in communities throughout the United States. The *Commercial Fire Rating Schedule* and the *Fire Suppression Rating Schedule* are important documents available from CRS. ISO was formed in 1971 by the consolidation of several other insurance services organizations. Address (ISO and CRS): 160 Water Street, New York, NY 10038.

Women In Fire Suppression (WFS)

WFS is a nonprofit support network for fire service women and for women looking for careers in the fire service. Incorporated in 1982, WFS maintains a large resource bank of information on issues relating to women in the fire service. Address: 411 Marathon Avenue, Dayton, OH 45406-4846.

National Association Of State Directors Of Fire Training And Education (NASDFTE)

NASDFTE was organized in 1981 for two purposes: (1) to serve as a representative for state fire training programs at various organizations and agencies whose policies, programs, and decisions have some impact on state programs and (2) to serve as a forum for the enhancement and enrichment of state fire training programs and their managers. Address: Changes each time a new president is elected.

Other Organizations

The following organizations also provide helpful information:

- American Association of Railroads Bureau of Explosives: 1920 L Street N.W., Washington, DC 20036
- American Trucking Association and the National Tank Carriers Inc: 1616 P Street N.W., Washington, DC 20036
- American Red Cross: National Headquarters, Washington, DC 20006
- American Heart Association: A J National Center, 7320 Greenville Avenue, Dallas, TX 75231
- Salvation Army: 799 Bloomfield Avenue, Verona, NJ 07044

FEDERAL ORGANIZATIONS

Because of the national government's concern over the public's safety, numerous federal agencies have been formed to help decrease the number of deaths and injuries caused by fire. These agencies are supported by public funds and are administered by public officials. Some of the more important agencies and their functions will be discussed in this section.

Federal Emergency Management Agency (FEMA)

This agency was formed in 1978 by President Jimmy Carter's third reorganization plan. FEMA gives the President the capability, within a single federal agency, to provide for national needs in preparing for, mitigating, and responding to all types of emergencies. Programs include:

- Fire prevention and control
- Continuity of government
- Strategic stockpiles
- Civil defense
- Federal insurance plans
- Flood plain management
- Dam safety
- Hurricane preparedness
- Earthquake preparedness
- Radiological emergency preparedness

These programs form the foundation on which continuity of civilian government is built and on which authority is exercised in the aftermath of emergencies. The overriding objective is the maximum preservation of life and property in peacetime disasters and in national security emergencies, including attack. Address: 500 C Street, N.W., Washington, DC 20001.

United States Fire Administration (USFA)

The USFA was established by the Federal Fire Prevention and Control Act of 1974 (Public Law 93-498). Its purposes are:

- To reduce the nation's losses from fire through better fire prevention and control
- To supplement existing programs of research, training, and education
- To encourage new, improved programs and activities by state and local governments

The USFA also administers an extensive fire data and analysis program. The USFA and the National Institute of Occupational Safety and Health administer a program concerned with firefighter health and safety. The USFA is headquartered on campus at the National Emergency Training Center in Emmitsburg, Maryland. Address: 16825 S. Seton Avenue, Emmitsburg, MD 21727.

National Fire Academy (NFA)

The NFA was established by the Federal Fire Prevention and Control Act of 1974 (Public Law 93-498). The Academy's purpose is to advance the professional development of fire service personnel and other people engaged in fire prevention and control. The Academy provides programs at the resident facility and in the field through state and local fire training agencies. The NFA offers programs in:

- Organizational and executive development
- Fire service education and public fire education
- Management technology
- Arson mitigation
- Hazardous materials
- Incident command
- Fire prevention

Resident courses are typically two to three weeks and are held on campus at the National Emergency Training Center in Emmitsburg, Maryland. Field courses are typically two-day weekend courses. Its courses meet or exceed the NFPA Professional Qualification Standards and are accredited by the American Council on Education. Address: 16825 S. Seton Avenue, Emmitsburg, MD 21727.

Emergency Management Institute (EMI)

The EMI is authorized under the Civil Defense Act of 1950 to provide training to public sector managers to prepare for, mitigate, respond to, and recover from all types of emergencies. It provides programs in emergency management, technical development, and professional development at the National Emergency Training Center and state emergency management agencies. Address: 16825 S. Seton Avenue, Emmitsburg, MD 21727.

United States Forest Service (USFS)

An arm of the Department of Agriculture, the Forest Service provides fire protection to national forests, grasslands, and nearby private lands across the United States. The Forest Service has equipment, aircraft, personnel, and communications systems to combat large-scale wildland fires. It has research facilities and provides technical and financial assistance to the states. The Forest Service also delivers training, pays the cost of fire fighting, and provides surplus federal equipment. Address: U.S. Forest Service, Department of Agriculture, 14th and Independence Avenue S.W., Washington, DC 20250.

National Institute Of Science And Technology (NIST)

Established in 1901, NIST was formerly known as the National Bureau of Standards (NBS). NIST is under the authority of the U.S. Department of Commerce and is engaged in fire research and tests involving building technology. The Institute fire tests materials and provides the results. A fire research center concerned with advancing fire technology has been established within the NIST. Address: Gaithersburg, MD 20899.

United States Department Of Transportation (US DOT)

The DOT is concerned with public safety on the nation's highways, airways, railways, and coastal waters and also controls interstate petroleum pipelines. The DOT has developed a variety of regulations that control such things as hazardous materials and their shipping containers. DOT subdivisions include the Federal Aviation Administration, U.S. Coast Guard, Materials Transportation Bureau, Federal Highway Administration, Federal

Railroad Administration, and National Highway Traffic Safety Administration (Figure 3.2). Address: 400 Seventh Street S.W., Washington, DC 20210.

Figure 3.2 The Federal Aviation Administration is a subdivision of the Department of Transportation.

Federal Aviation Administration (FAA)

The FAA is concerned with fire protection in all aspects of civil aviation, including aircraft and airports. It also controls the transportation of hazardous materials by air. Address: 800 Independence Avenue S.W., Washington, DC 20591.

United States Coast Guard

The Coast Guard provides on-scene coordinators for spills or emergencies that threaten or reach coastal or navigable waterways or other waterways under Coast Guard jurisdiction (Figure 3.3). The coordinators' authority is similar to that of EPA coordinators. They perform marine rescue and fire fighting operations, although their fire fighting capabilities are limited. Address: 2100 Second Street S.W., Washington, DC 20593.

Figure 3.3 The Coast Guard has limited fire fighting capabilities. *Courtesy of Ron Jeffers.*

Occupational Safety And Health Administration (OSHA)

OSHA was established in 1970 when the Occupational Safety and Health Act became federal law. Its purpose is to guarantee safe working conditions for all. OSHA is part of the Department of Labor, which enforces its regulations. Address: Department of Labor Building, 14th Street and Constitution Avenue N.W., Washington, DC 20210.

OSHA also maintains the following regional offices that should be contacted as the first step in any local inquiry (Figure 3.4):

Region I (CT, MA, ME, NH, RI, VT)
133 Portland Street
Boston, MA 02114

Region II (NJ, NY, PR, VI)
201 Varick Street
New York, NY 10014

Region III (DC, DE, MD, PA, VA, WV)
Gateway Bldg, Suite 2100
3535 Market Street
Philadelphia, PA 19104

Region IV (AL, FL, GA, KY, MS, NC, SC, TN)
1375 Peachtree Street N.E.
Suite 587
Atlanta, GA 30367

Region V (IL, IN, MI, MN, OH, WI)
230 South Dearborn Street
Room 3244
Chicago, IL 60604

Region VI (AR, LA, NM, OK, TX)
525 Griffin Street
Dallas, TX 75202

Region VII (IA, KS, MO, NE)
911 Walnut Street
Room 406
Kansas City, MO 64106

Region VIII (CO, MT, ND, SD, UT, WY)
Federal Building, Room 1576
1961 Stout Street
Denver, CO 80294

Region IX (AZ, CA, HI, NV)
Room 415
71 Stevenson Street
San Francisco, CA 94105

Region X (AK, ID, OR, WA)
Federal Office Building
Room 6003
909 First Avenue
Seattle, WA 98174

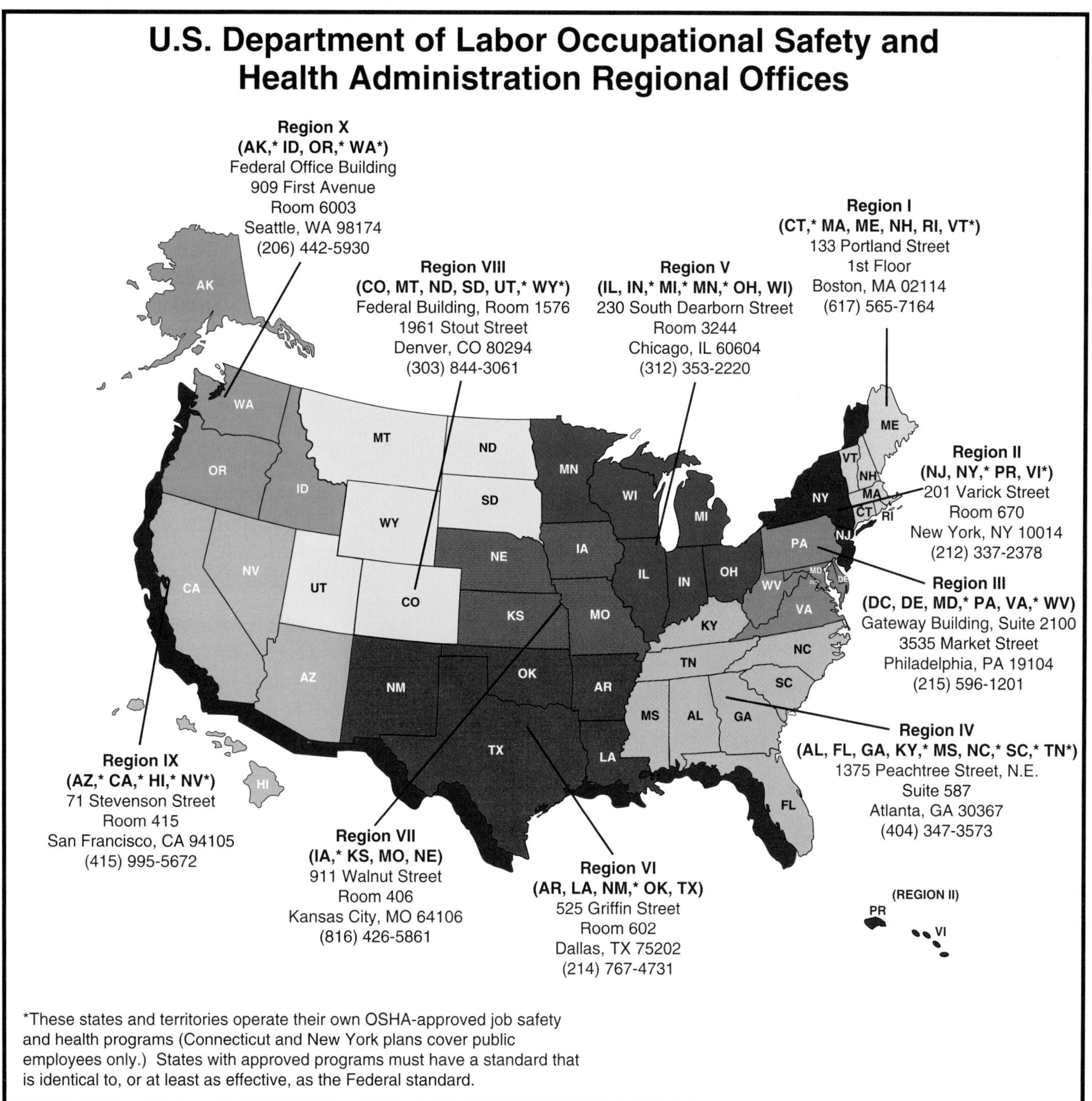

Figure 3.4 This map shows the various OSHA regions.

United States Department Of Labor (DOL)

The Department of Labor is responsible for administering and enforcing the Occupational Safety and Health Act. The DOL compiles national occupational injury and illness data through the Bureau of Labor Statistics. DOL establishes national and regional programs in addition to administration programs. Address: 200 Constitution Avenue N.W., Washington, DC 20001.

National Institute For Occupational Safety And Health (NIOSH)

NIOSH was established within the Department of Health, Education, and Welfare to conduct research and provide educational functions to support OSHA. It also recommends occupational safety and health standards that affect workers. Address: Parklawn Building, 5600 Fishers Lane, Rockville, MD 20852.

Environmental Protection Agency (EPA)

EPA provides an "on-scene coordinator" at oil or hazardous substances spills that threaten or reach inland waters. The coordinator has the authority to ensure that the spill is contained and cleaned up to minimize environmental damage. Address: 401 M Street N.W., Washington, DC 20460.

Nuclear Regulatory Commission (NRC)

The NRC's primary responsibilities are to develop and enforce guidelines on building and operating nuclear facilities. It is also heavily involved in fire protection relating to the nuclear industry. Address: 1717 H Street N.W., Washington, DC 20555.

Congressional Fire Services Caucus

Although it is not a federal agency, the Congressional Fire Services Caucus is a function of the federal government. The Congressional Fire Services Caucus was founded in November 1987. Pennsylvania Congressman Curt Weldon founded the Caucus to direct Congress's attention to the broad concerns of the fire safety constituency. This constituency includes everyone from volunteers in small fire departments to major international industries. Advancing the concerns of the entire fire safety constituency, the Caucus marks the first attempt within Congress to comprehensively address America's fire problem.

Members of the Congress are made aware of major fire safety issues and legislation through educational seminars, legislative updates, and policy analyses. The Fire Service Caucus has become the largest caucus on Capitol Hill. Address: 1233 Longworth, House Office Building, Washington, DC 20515.

Congressional Fire Services Institute

In 1989, the Congressional Fire Services Institute was formed. This Institute enables the Caucus to expand its membership within Congress and reach out into the fire service community. The Institute will track legislation, monitor hearings, develop policy, identify consensus priorities of the fire service, and report these findings to the Caucus and the public. The Institute will educate members of the Congress about the fire problem and at the same time instruct the fire service on how to make government more responsive. Address: Railway Express Building, 900 Second Street N.E., Suite 207, Washington, DC 20002.

United States Department Of Interior (DOI)

DOI has several internal agencies that provide important fire protection services. The Bureau of Land Management (BLM) provides protection against wildland fires on 545 million acres of public land. The BLM also supports the Interagency Fire Center in Boise, Idaho. The National Park Service (NPS) also has major operations in the area of fire prevention, management, and suppression in the national park system. Addresses: BLM, U.S. Dept. of Interior/BLM, Suite 5660, 1849 C Street, Washington, DC 20240; NPS, U.S. Dept. of Interior/NPS, P.O. Box 37127, Washington, DC 20013-7127.

Bureau Of Alcohol, Tobacco, And Firearms (BATF or ATF)

ATF assists local agencies in major arson investigations and regulates the storage and transportation of explosives. ATF is a division of the Department of Treasury. Address: 650 Massachusetts Avenue N.W., Washington, DC 20226.

Consumer Product Safety Commission (CPSC)

CPSC conducts research on the safety of consumer goods and also on injury and loss patterns. Address: Westwood Towers, 5401 Westwood Avenue, Bethesda, MD 20816.

STATE/PROVINCIAL ORGANIZATIONS

The concern about the fire problem at the state/provincial level has helped to establish state fire protection agencies. The majority of fire protection agencies are operated and maintained by state government, although some are independent. Brief descriptions of the most common agencies are presented in this section to make firefighters aware of the organizations that may exist in their states. A state agency may have the same name as an agency in another state; however, the agency may have different responsibilities. Also, some of these agencies may not exist in all states. These descriptions are only general in nature.

State Fire Marshal

The state fire marshal's office is the principal authority on fire protection in forty-seven states. The powers are usually delegated by the state legislative body and carry the effect of law. The responsibilities of the fire marshal vary from state to state because of different opinions on what the office should do. In some states, the fire marshal's office is an independent government office. In other states, the fire marshal's office is a function of the state police. Following is a list of the typical responsibilities of the state fire marshal's office:

- To review and approve construction plans for fire safety
- To conduct fire prevention activities
- To investigate and determine fire causes (Figure 3.5)
- To actively fight arson
- To regulate the storage and use of combustibles, hazardous materials, and explosives
- To provide specifications for required exits, detection systems, alarm systems, and extinguishing systems

State/Provincial Fire Training

Most states and provinces have a training organization for firefighters and officers. These programs have full-time staff as administrators and instructors. They also have a part-time staff of instructors spread across the state or province to conduct classes at local fire departments. These state-level organizations are associated with state universities, fire marshal offices, and vocational-technical programs (Figure 3.6). In some cases, they provide technical assistance to fire departments as well as training programs.

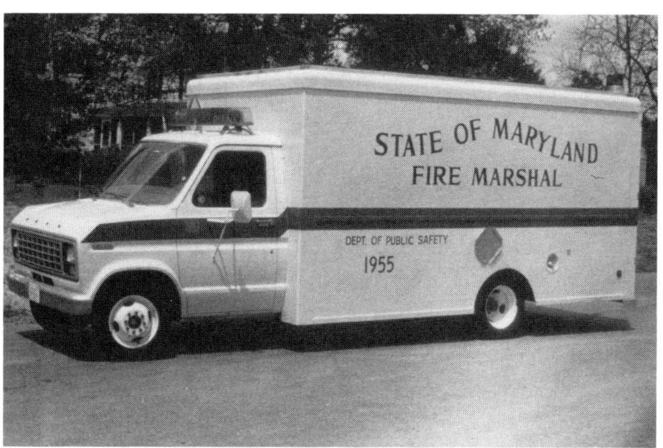

Figure 3.5 State fire marshals can be called in to assist local investigators. *Courtesy of Joel Woods, University of Maryland Fire and Rescue Institute.*

Fire Commission

Several states have appointed fire commissions to establish standards for fire fighting and fire officers. These commissions are funded by state legislatures and use the money to assist in training, testing, and administering the state certification program for the fire service. Most fire commissions have a director who works directly with the training delivery mechanisms of the area whether they are state, county, or local agencies.

Figure 3.6 Fire academies have a variety of training structures.

State Fire Chiefs Association

In some states, fire chiefs have organized a state association. At meetings, they can discuss common problems and suggest solutions. They can also present an organized force to lobby for legislation to benefit the state's fire protection efforts. Many state associations hold an annual conference with educational activities for professional development.

State Firefighter Association

These organizations are formed by the members of departments across the state to bring firefighters together to work toward common goals. The association may lobby, develop insurance plans, work on pension legislation or administration, promote fire prevention activities, or assist in training. Many firefighter associations hold an annual conference with contests, guest speakers, and social activities.

State Police

Many state police forces provide an arson investigation unit that contains highly technical equipment used to uncover hard-to-find evidence. State police often work with fire department arson squads to solve difficult cases. State police may also help firefighters with hazardous materials, traffic control, and personal protection during riots. In some states, the state fire marshal's office is a division of the state police.

State Highway Department Or Turnpike Commission

The primary relationship that highway departments and turnpike commissions may have with fire departments involves road, bridge, and route design. Fire departments must have unobstructed access to all areas under their jurisdiction. The fire department should also be notified anytime a highway or bridge is closed for repairs to eliminate surprises during emergencies. In some cases where specialized or heavy equipment is required, pre-incident planning may include the cooperation of the highway department or turnpike commission (Figure 3.7). The department or commission may also provide materials, such as sand, for hazardous materials incidents.

State Environmental Protection Agency

State environmental agencies usually become involved with local fire departments when a fire or disaster might contaminate the environment with hazardous materials. The agency usually sends a representative to monitor and report on the situation.

State Occupational Safety And Health Administration

States become involved in firefighter safety through their occupational safety and health agencies. When required by the legislature, the agencies write specifications for equipment to be used by firefighters. States that manage their own occupational safety and health programs are required to have requirements that are equal to or greater than the requirements of the federal OSHA regulations.

State Health Department

After a fire, the health department may inspect a facility to see whether any potential detriment to the public exists because of the fire and extinguishing operations. This is especially true for establishments that provide food or lodging. The fire department may interact with the health department and assist in the investigation.

State Forestry Department

In wildland fires, fire departments often have to work with the state forestry department to contain and control the blaze. The forestry department has heavy equipment, such as bulldozers, and also has the equipment and expertise to conduct operations such as backfiring.

Office Of Emergency Preparedness Or Civil Defense

Civil Defense interacts with the fire department during natural disasters, large wildland fires,

Figure 3.7 Highway department crews may provide equipment and materials on special incidents.

civil unrest, and other larger emergency situations. The office can provide personnel, vehicles, and communication equipment and is always available to help.

Special Task Forces

Special groups are often called together to attack specific problems that arise within a state. An example could be an arson task force that would bring law enforcement, fire service, insurance, and state agencies to a joint effort against arson. Another example would be a haz mat group formed to address the hazardous materials problem.

Other State Organizations

Each state has its own departments that interface with the fire service. Firefighters should become familiar with the agencies in their state such as water resources, natural resources, transportation, and parks and recreation.

LOCAL ORGANIZATIONS

Most of a firefighter's interaction with outside agencies will be at the local level. Local people and groups will be familiar because firefighters will have day-to-day interactions with them, and these local groups will often be topics of discussion. In this section, some of these groups will be reviewed to provide firefighters an overview of their functions.

Local Government

Local government at the town, village, borough, township, city, parish, or county level consists of elected officials responsible for enacting legislation to govern the people under their jurisdiction (Figures 3.8 a and b). These officials may also establish the fire department if it is within their power. Depending on the local structure, the governing body may have control over hiring practices and other matters involving the fire department.

Local government may also finance the fire department. Funds come from taxes and are budgeted to various departments, including the fire department. The chief, who is ultimately responsible for fire department finances, must have a good working relationship with local government so that the fire department can get its fair share of financing.

Figure 3.8 City (a) and county (b) governments enact legislation to govern their people.

Local Law Enforcement

Because fire and law enforcement personnel have the same goal, which is to protect the public, the two must work together successfully. The fire department depends on local police for such things as traffic control, crowd control, and personal protection during civil unrest (Figure 3.9). Cooperation between the two agencies will undoubtedly make their job easier to accomplish.

Figure 3.9 Police can assist with traffic control.

Building Department

The local building department is responsible for enforcing various codes and regulations adopted by local government. The department may review and approve plans for new buildings and remodeling before construction begins. The department may check its own standards as well as fire prevention codes. An effective building department program is an asset to the local fire department. It provides a medium through which the fire department can get fire prevention code requirements integrated into local construction. This provides safer structures and reduces the amount of injuries and damage from fire. It is extremely important for the fire department fire prevention staff and building officials to have an excellent working relationship.

Water Department

The fire department's water supply system often means the difference between a successful stop and a total loss. Therefore, the water department must provide enough water at proper pressure to satisfy the fire protection needs of a community (Figure 3.10). The fire department must work with the water department to determine such things as water main size and location, fire flow determination, hydrant locations, and pumping and storage capacity. The fire department must also be notified when parts of the system are closed so that firefighters can arrange for alternate water supplies.

Zoning Commission

The zoning commission is responsible for planning community growth. The commission determines the divisions between residential and commercial districts; this is important because the fire protection needs of the two may be different. The difference dictates where the fire department locates fire stations and places apparatus.

Street Department

The street department is responsible for building and maintaining public thruways. The fire department must know when roads will be closed so that it can establish alternate routes. The fire department may want to help design roadways and bridges to make sure that they are accessible for large apparatus. In some cities, the street department also provides equipment, such as automatic traffic signal changers, that allow firefighters on the apparatus to change signal lights from red to green (Figures 3.11 a and b). As with state highway departments, the local street department may also be able to provide equipment and services to abate hazardous materials or other emergencies.

Figure 3.11a The Opticom® sensor is mounted on the traffic standard.

Figure 3.11b The emitter is located on the vehicle.

Figure 3.10 Cooperation with the water authority is essential for good fire protection.

Local Judicial System

The fire department's primary contact with the judicial system often concerns two situations: fire department personnel testifying in court and court orders. Fire department personnel are called to testify in arson and insurance claim cases, and firefighters are often called as witnesses to incidents that occurred on the fireground. In order to force the correction of code violations, the fire department often needs a judge to issue a court order. When fire marshals carry the power of the law, they deal directly with the court system to perform their duties.

Office Of Emergency Preparedness Or Civil Defense

Local emergency preparedness groups assist the fire department during large-scale disasters and provide personnel and equipment. They are also instrumental in the pre-incident planning and stockpiling of supplies for large-scale disasters.

Civic Groups

Community civic groups are an excellent resource for departments to use when trying to publicize their fire prevention message. The groups can provide a core of interested citizens who are willing and able to assist the department in becoming an integral part of the community. Scouting organizations, such as the Boy Scouts of America, may assist fire departments with community service and public education activities. Major corporations may be able to provide fire departments with facts and information on projected community growth. This may be possible because corporations prepare these studies when planning locations for their restaurants or retail stores. Through cooperative and effective working relationships with organizations, such as the local Chamber of Commerce, fire departments may also gain political support for their needs. Some of the more common local civic groups include the Lions, Rotary, Kiwanis, and Jaycee clubs as well as American Legion and Veterans of Foreign Wars (VFW) organizations.

Chapter 3
Application And Review Activities

DIRECTIONS

The following activities are designed to help you comprehend and apply the information in Chapter 3 of **Orientation and Terminology**. To receive the maximum learning experience from these activities, it is recommended that you use the following procedure:

1. Read the chapter, underlining or highlighting important terms, topics, and subject matter. Study the photographs and illustrations, and read the captions under each.
2. Review the list of vocabulary words to ensure that you know the chapter-related meaning of each. If you are unsure of the meaning of a vocabulary word, look the word up in a dictionary, and then study its context in the chapter.

   NOTE: Some words have different meanings as different parts of speech. Abbreviations after certain words stand for the part of speech (v., verb; n., noun; adj., adjective; adv., adverb) of the word as it is used in the chapter.
3. On a separate sheet of paper, complete all assigned or selected application and review activities before checking your answers.
4. After you have finished, check your answers against those on the pages referenced in parentheses.
5. Correct any incorrect answers, and review material that was answered incorrectly.

VOCABULARY

Be sure that you know the chapter-related meanings of the following terms.

- Abate *(60)*
- Accredited *(53)*
- Caucus *(56)*
- Certification *(51)*
- Chartered (adv.) *(49)*
- Civil *(52)*
- Consensus *(50)*
- Consolidation *(52)*
- Constituency *(56)*
- Correlating *(50)*
- Detriment *(58)*
- Disseminate *(51)*
- Federal *(49)*
- Forum *(52)*
- Incorporated *(52)*
- Integral *(61)*
- Interface (v.) *(59)*
- Interstate *(53)*
- Jurisdiction*(54)*
- Liaison *(50)*
- Lobby (v.) *(57)*
- Mitigating *(52)*
- Municipal *(50)*
- Supplement *(53)*
- Suppression *(52)*

APPLICATION OF KNOWLEDGE

1. With which of the following fire service related trade organizations were you familiar before reading this chapter? How did you learn of these organizations, and what was (is) the extent of your involvement? *(Local protocol)*

- JCNFCO
- IAFF
- IAFC
- Metro Chiefs
- IAAI
- ISFSI
- IABPFF
- NFPA
- FMANA
- NVFC
- IFSTA
- IMSA
- BOCA
- ICBO
- SBCCI
- ICMA
- ANSI
- UL
- FM
- ISO
- CRS
- WFS
- NASDFTE

2. With which of the following fire service related federal organizations were you familiar before reading this chapter? How did you learn of these organizations, and what was (is) the extent of your involvement? *(Local protocol)*

- FEMA
- USFA
- NFA
- EMI
- USFS
- DOT
- FAA
- OSHA
- NIOSH
- EPA
- NRC
- DOI
- ATF
- CPSC
- Congressional Fire Services Caucus
- Congressional Fire Services Institute

3. With what state/provincial and local organizations have you had experience? Briefly describe. *(Local protocol)*

REVIEW ACTIVITIES

1. Write the full names of ten of the following trade organizations.

- JCNFCO *(49)*
- IAFF *(49)*
- IAFC *(49)*
- Metro Chiefs *(50)*
- IAAI *(50)*
- ISFSI *(50)*
- IABPFF *(50)*
- NFPA *(50)*
- FMANA *(50)*
- NVFC *(50)*
- IFSTA *(50)*
- IMSA *(50)*
- BOCA *(51)*
- ICBO *(51)*
- SBCCI *(51)*
- ICMA *(51)*
- ANSI *(51)*
- UL *(51)*
- FM *(52)*
- ISO *(52)*
- CRS *(52)*
- WFS *(52)*
- NASDFTE *(52)*

2. Write the full names of ten of the following federal organizations.
   - FEMA *(52)*
   - USFA *(53)*
   - NFA *(53)*
   - EMI *(53)*
   - USFS *(53)*
   - NIST (53)
   - DOT *(53)*
   - FAA *(54)*
   - OSHA *(54)*
   - DOL *(55)*
   - NIOSH *(55)*
   - EPA *(56)*
   - NRC *(56)*
   - DOI *(56)*
   - ATF *(56)*
   - CPSC *(56)*
3. Explain the differences between trade organizations and state and federal organizations. *(49 ff)*
4. Discuss the Joint Council of National Fire Service Organizations' original purpose, major accomplishments, and reasons for disbandment. *(49, 52)*
5. Describe two trade organizations that were formed to provide support networks for minorities and women. *(50, 52)*
6. List three trade organizations that identify and develop building codes and standards. Explain how these organizations differ from each other. *(51)*
7. Describe two trade organizations whose primary purpose is to develop national fire service standards. *(50 & 51)*
8. Explain the goal of Underwriters Laboratories Incorporated. *(51)*
9. List three trade organizations concerned with fire service training and instruction. Explain how these organizations differ from each other. *(50, 52)*
10. Describe the organization and purposes of the Federal Emergency Management Agency (FEMA), listing the programs that this agency encompasses. *(52)*
11. List the purposes of the United States Fire Administration (USFA). *(53)*
12. Describe the purpose and programs of the National Fire Academy. *(53)*
13. Compare and contrast the purposes of NFA and EMI. *(53)*
14. Explain how the U.S. Department of Transportation affects the fire service. *(53)*
15. State the purpose of OSHA, and name its enforcement and research support organizations. *(54)*
16. Explain how the Congressional Fire Services Caucus, while not a federal agency, is a function of the federal government. *(56)*
17. Describe how the Congressional Fire Services Institute differs from the Congressional Fire Services Caucus. *(56)*
18. List the typical responsibilities of the state fire marshal's office. *(56)*
19. Describe the purposes and funding of state fire commissions. *(57)*
20. Explain how state OSHA differs from the federal OSHA. *(54, 58)*
21. Explain how the state Office of Emergency Preparedness or Civil Defense differs from FEMA. *(52, 58)*
22. Describe the fire service related functions of at least three local organizations in your area or jurisdiction. *(59-61)*

4
Fire Department Facilities And Apparatus

Chapter 4
Fire Department Facilities And Apparatus

The operating functions of a fire department are centered around its personnel, facilities, apparatus, and equipment. As a firefighter begins his or her career on the fire department, there are various types of fire department facilities and apparatus with which he or she must become familiar. Depending on the size and resources of any particular department, it may not have all of the types of facilities or equipment covered in this chapter. Therefore, firefighters should concentrate on their individual department's resources.

FIRE DEPARTMENT FACILITIES

Various types of facilities are required for the operation of a fire department. Depending on the size of the department, some or all of these facilities may be found at one location, or the facilities may be separate structures located throughout the jurisdiction. Fire department facilities include:

- Fire stations
- Administrative offices and buildings
- Dispatch centers
- Training centers
- Maintenance shops

Fire Stations

Fire stations, known in some jurisdictions as firehouses or fire halls, are used to shelter fire apparatus and equipment. The required number and size of fire stations vary with the size of the department. A small community may have a fire department with only a small building to house its apparatus (Figure 4.1). Larger cities may have many fire stations to house multiple pieces of apparatus (Figure 4.2).

The layout and contents of fire stations vary widely. Each fire department has requirements for its stations; however, some components are present in all stations. The most obvious component, of course, is the apparatus bay or garage area. This is the portion of the station where the apparatus is

Figure 4.1 Small communities have small fire stations.

Figure 4.2 Departments that have a large number of apparatus need large stations in which to store them.

parked (Figure 4.3). The apparatus bay may contain the following equipment and utilities for servicing the apparatus:

- Water for refilling the apparatus water tank
- A battery charging system for keeping the apparatus electrical system at peak capacity
- Compressed air for filling tires or keeping air brake systems ready during periods of inactivity
- Apparatus exhaust removal systems to help maintain air quality throughout the entire station

All fire stations must have an area in which to keep tools and equipment for station and apparatus maintenance (Figure 4.4). The size of this area and the tools provided depend on how much maintenance work the firefighters actually perform. For example, volunteer fire stations have large work areas because they do much of the maintenance work themselves.

Figure 4.3 The apparatus bay is the portion of the station where the vehicles are parked.

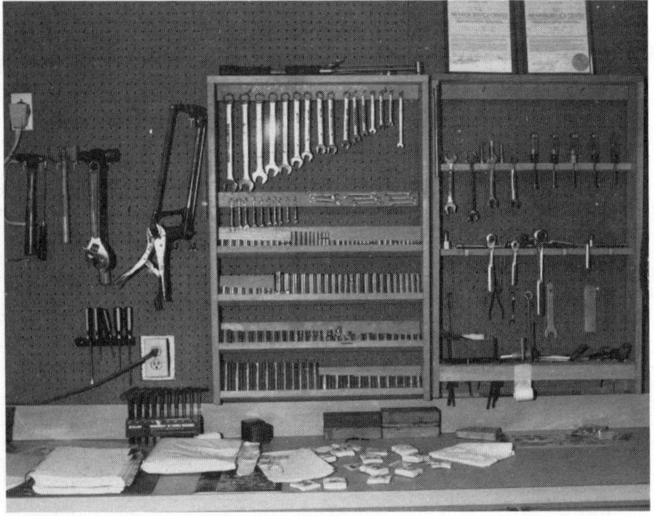

Figure 4.4 Some fire stations have maintenance and repair areas.

Each station should be equipped with an appropriate area for the storage of personal protective equipment. This area may be in the form of racks, lockers, or cubicles (Figures 4.5 a and b). The storage arrangement must provide for adequate ventilation, which allows for proper drying of the equipment. The fire station may be equipped with an air cascade system or breathing-air compressor from which self-contained breathing apparatus cylinders can be filled.

Figure 4.5 Turnout clothing may be stored on (a) racks or in (b) lockers.

Beyond these basics, the features of the fire station vary widely. Stations that are used to house paid firefighters need living accommodations, which includes eating, sleeping, bathing, and recreational spaces. Volunteer and paid departments often have training or meeting rooms built into the station. These rooms allow large groups to hold meetings or classroom instructional sessions. Smaller paid and volunteer departments may have office facilities in the station for their officers. Volunteer stations may also be equipped with facilities that are used for fund-raising purposes. These include banquet facilities, club rooms, bowling alleys, and bingo halls (Figure 4.6).

Administrative Offices And Buildings

Larger fire departments require office space for administrative purposes. This office space may be attached to a fire station — typically a headquarters fire station — or it may be in a separate

Figure 4.6 Some volunteer fire departments have social halls that are used to raise money.

building (Figure 4.7). These offices house the administrative chief officers of the department; the staff for research and planning, safety, and personnel; and other related entities. Depending on the size and organization of the department, the dispatch, investigation, inspection, and training staffs may also be located in the main administrative building.

Administrative buildings must have appropriate office space for all professional and clerical staff. These buildings may also contain records storage sections, meeting rooms, press rooms, and other special-function rooms as required by the department.

Figure 4.7 Some administration buildings are attached to fire stations.

Dispatch Centers

The dispatch center is the focal point for all fire department communications. It is considered the "brain" of the fire department's central nervous system. Depending on local requirements, the dispatch center may be located at fire department headquarters, in a fire station, or at a separate facility. In some cases, the dispatch center is a joint facility that dispatches various services, such as police, fire, and emergency medical services, for the same municipality (Figure 4.8). In other cases, it may be a facility that dispatches many different fire departments or agencies within the same county or region.

Figure 4.8 Some dispatch centers house police, fire, and EMS communications.

The primary function of the dispatcher is to take calls for help and to assign companies to respond to those calls. The dispatch center keeps track of the companies that are in the field and serves as an information center during emergency operations (Figure 4.9). The dispatch center is equipped with a multitude of phone and radio equipment. Tape recording machines are used to record telephone calls and radio transmissions. Modern dispatch centers are equipped with computer-aided-dispatch (CAD) systems that stream-

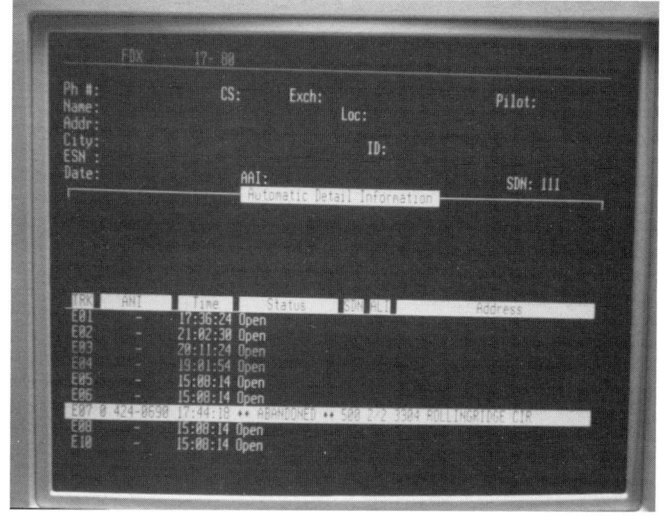

Figure 4.9 Computers are used to keep track of calls and unit assignments.

line the dispatch operation by providing exact information on locations and assigned responses (Figure 4.10).

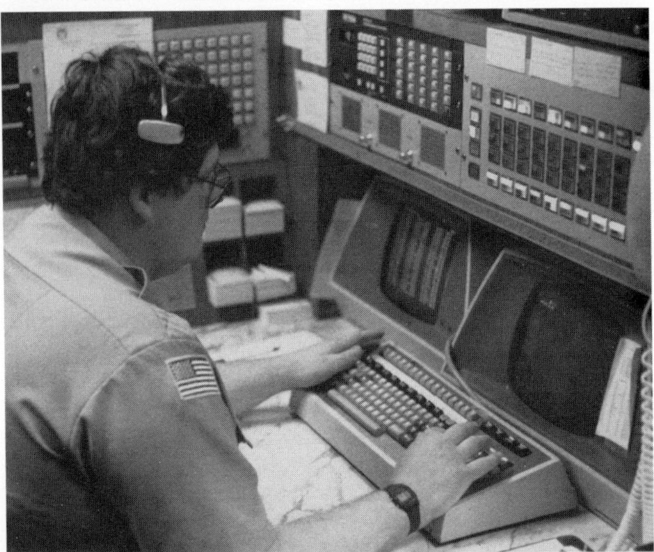

Figure 4.10 A dispatcher who uses computer-aided systems must be highly trained in their use. *Courtesy of Montgomery County (PA) Emergency Communications Center.*

Training Centers

The training center is where all formal educational activities take place. The training administration building may contain the following (Figure 4.11):

- Administrative offices
- Classroom and laboratory
- Auditorium
- Cafeteria
- Dressing and locker areas
- Storage for equipment, supplies, and apparatus

The training center also has buildings designed for specific educational purposes. These buildings are discussed in the following sections.

Figure 4.11 Most training centers have a main administration building and a classroom building.

BURN BUILDING

A burn building is designed to be set on fire repeatedly for the purpose of allowing firefighters to practice interior structural fire attacks (Figure 4.12). Typically, a burn building is of masonry construction, utilizing special fire bricks and mortar. The fire in many of these buildings is provided by burning straw or wood. More modern buildings use piped-in natural gas to provide the fire. This allows for more control over the conditions in the building. The fire can be shut off immediately if a problem arises.

Figure 4.12 A burn building is designed for repetitive live-fire evolutions.

DRILL TOWER

A drill tower is used for ladder, rope, and other types of training that require a tall structure — usually three to seven stories (Figure 4.13). It is equipped with interior stairways that allow access to the upper floors of the structure. These stairways can also be used for high-rise training. If the tower is used frequently for rope rescue and rappelling, it may also be equipped with safety nets around the outside. These nets are designed to catch a firefighter in the event he or she falls from the rope or structure.

Figure 4.13 A drill tower has a variety of uses, including ladder and rope training.

SMOKEHOUSE

This structure is designed to provide simulated smoke conditions for firefighters. Simulated smoke conditions help the firefighters develop their confidence and skills when performing interior searches under poor visibility conditions (Figure 4.14). Some smokehouses may be designed to have an interior similar to that of a house. Others are designed with obstacle-type courses that can be changed by moving partitions or dividers. The smoke for these structures is nontoxic and is produced by a special machine that uses a vegetable oil type fluid. The smokehouse should have adequate access points so that panicky students may be removed. The smokehouse should also have a venting system that can quickly clear the structure if needed.

Figure 4.14 A smokehouse is not designed to contain live fires.

TRAINING PADS

Training centers may be equipped with a variety of training pads, or areas, that are designed for a specific purpose. These include:

- Flammable and combustible liquids and gas fire fighting
- Driver/operator training
- Vehicle extrication
- Hazardous materials abatement props
- Trench and confined space rescue props
- Other specialized props (Figure 4.15)

Figure 4.15 A special pad, or area, may be constructed for specialized training evolutions such as hazardous materials exercises.

Maintenance Facilities

The job of a fire department is highly dependent on the apparatus and equipment firefighters use. The maintenance of this equipment requires special facilities and personnel. Small fire departments have maintenance areas built into the fire station where apparatus and equipment can be worked on. Larger fire departments have separate facilities for these activities. Apparatus maintenance shops look like and are equipped much like any commercial truck repair facility (Figure 4.16).

Maintenance facilities are also needed for the upkeep of fire department equipment, which includes the repair of self-contained breathing apparatus, fire hose, electrical equipment, ladders, and hand tools. Each type of equipment requires special tools and machines in order to be repaired or maintained. Most fire departments prefer to keep all tools and machines in a central location.

Figure 4.16 Larger fire departments have their own apparatus maintenance facilities.

FIRE DEPARTMENT APPARATUS

Fire departments have an array of apparatus for firefighters to choose from to help them perform their duties. Each type of apparatus is designed for a specific function. All departments do not have all the types of apparatus listed in the following sections; however, these types of apparatus are commonly used throughout North America.

The Pumper

The name "pumper" or "engine" is derived from the function of the apparatus and from the pump, which is the apparatus's main feature. The primary purpose of the pumper or engine company is to confine and extinguish fires with water delivered through hoselines under pump pressure

(Figures 4.17 a through c). The pumper is the most basic of all fire department apparatus. The personnel of pumper companies usually consists of a company officer, a driver/operator or engineer, and two or more firefighters.

Figure 4.17a A fire department pumper is the most basic of all fire department apparatus.

Figure 4.17b Pumpers are designed to meet requirements set forth in the NFPA 1901 standard. *Courtesy of Joel Woods, University of Maryland Fire and Rescue Institute.*

Figure 4.17c A fire department pumper is designed to deliver water through hoselines under pump pressure.

Pumpers are designed to meet the requirements set forth in NFPA 1901, *Standard for Pumper Fire Apparatus*. Standard pumpers are equipped with fire pumps with the following rated capacities:

- 750 gpm (3 000 L/min)
- 1,000 gpm (4 000 L/min)
- 1,250 gpm (5 000 L/min)
- 1,500 gpm (6 000 L/min)
- 1,750 gpm (7 000 L/min)
- 2,000 gpm (8 000 L/min)

Gauges and other instruments are provided for the pump operator. Controls regulate the speed of the pump, and the speed affects the pressure and volume of the water (Figure 4.18). A pumper usually has a water tank, sometimes referred to as a booster tank, with capacities ranging from 500 to 1,500 gallons (2 000 L to 6 000 L). This water is used to start a fire attack before the pumper can be connected to an external water supply. There may also be a smaller tank for special extinguishing agents such as foam concentrate. A proportioning device on the main fire pump mixes the foam concentrate with water to produce a foam fire stream for use on structural or flammable and combustible liquids fires.

Most pumpers have bins or compartments, called hose beds, located around the apparatus for carry-

Figure 4.18 The pump panel contains the controls from which the driver/operator operates the fire pump.

ing the various sizes of fire hose. Most of the hose used for water supply to the apparatus is kept on the main hose bed at the rear of the apparatus (Figure 4.19). Some attack lines may also be carried on the rear hose bed. Other attack lines may be carried in hose beds on different portions of the apparatus such as the front bumper or above the pump panel area (Figures 4.20 a and b). In many cases, these attack lines are preconnected to a discharge for rapid deployment. NFPA 1901 requires each pumper to carry a minimum of 400 feet (120 m) of small attack hose (1½-inch [38 mm], 1¾-inch [45 mm], or 2-inch [50 mm]) and 1,200 feet (360 m) of supply hose larger than 2½ inches (65 mm) in diameter. Apparatus may also be equipped with a booster reel (Figure 4.21). This is a reel of small (1-inch [25 mm] diameter or less), noncollapsible hose used for extinguishing small exterior fires or for overhaul operations.

Figure 4.19 Most of the fire hose is carried on the rear hose bed.

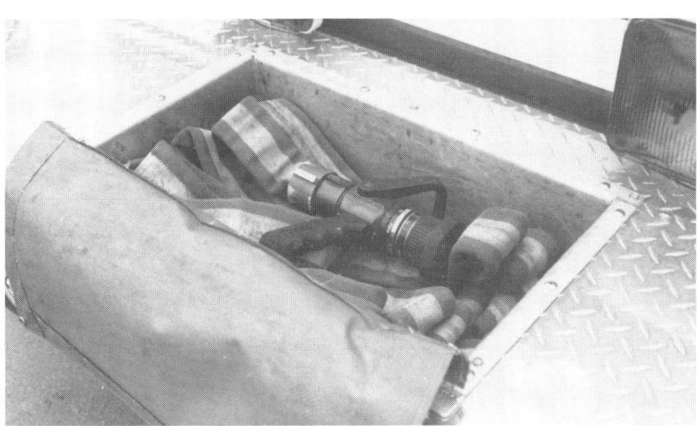

Figure 4.20a Some preconnected attack lines are found on the front bumper.

Figure 4.20b Mattydale preconnected lines are found above the pump panel.

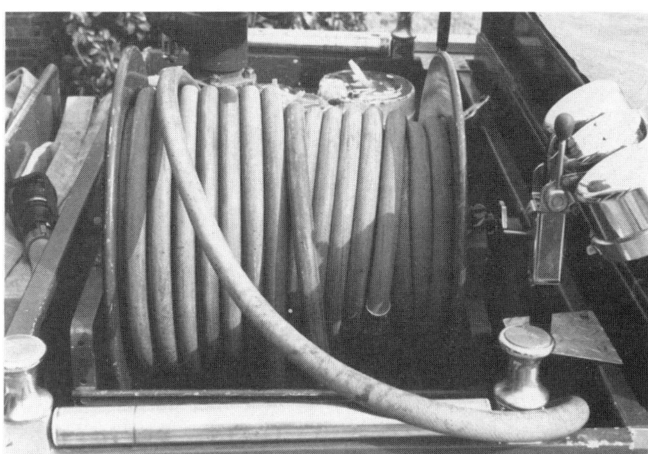

Figure 4.21 Booster lines may be used for small exterior fires.

In addition to hose, pumpers carry a variety of equipment for fire and rescue operations. Most pumpers carry the following:

- Ladders
- Forcible entry tools
- Nozzles
- Hose adapters and appliances
- Hose tools
- Protective breathing equipment
- Portable fire extinguishers
- Pike poles
- Salvage covers
- Other tools the company uses

Depending on the functions of the engine company in a particular municipality, the pumper may carry specialized equipment such as the following:

- Rescue and extrication tools
- Emergency medical equipment
- Ventilation equipment
- Portable water tanks for shuttle operations

Pumpers that carry this special equipment may have special body configurations (Figure 4.22).

Figure 4.22 Rescue pumpers carry standard pumper equipment plus extrication and rescue equipment. *Courtesy of Ron Bogardus.*

Pumpers Equipped With Elevating Water Towers

Some pumpers are equipped with an elevating water tower that allows fire streams to be deployed above the apparatus. This elevating water tower has a height that ranges from 50 to 75 feet (15 m to 23 m). The water tower is hydraulically operated and is equipped with a waterway to the tip of the device. At the end of the waterway is a nozzle capable of flowing at least 1,000 gpm (4 000 L/min). The tower may be either articulating or telescoping (Figures 4.23 a and b). Pumpers equipped with elevating water towers carry other equipment as described for pumpers in the previous section.

Figure 4.23a An articulating elevated master stream device. *Courtesy of Joel Woods, University of Maryland Fire and Rescue Institute.*

Figure 4.23b A telescoping elevated master stream device. *Courtesy of Joel Woods, University of Maryland Fire and Rescue Institute.*

Initial Attack Fire Apparatus

The initial attack fire apparatus is known by many different names throughout the fire service. Different names used include the following:

- Mini-pumper
- Midi-pumper
- Quick attack apparatus
- Booster apparatus
- Rapid intervention vehicle
- Attack pumper
- Quick response vehicle (Figures 4.24 a and b)

Figure 4.24a An initial attack apparatus is designed to handle small fires.

Figure 4.24b NFPA 1902 contains the design requirements for an initial attack apparatus.

An initial attack fire apparatus is designed to handle small fires that do not require the capacity and personnel of a larger pumper. This unit also enables a fire department to save on fuel and apparatus replacement costs while still having larger pumpers ready for action. NFPA 1902, *Standard for Initial Attack Fire Apparatus*, contains requirements for the design of these vehicles.

An initial attack fire apparatus is most often mounted on a pickup chassis with a custom-made body. Its fire pump must have a capacity of at least 250 gpm (1 000 L/min). Typically, it carries 100 to

300 gallons (400 L to 1 200 L) of water. Much of the equipment carried on a larger pumper is also carried on an initial attack fire apparatus, although in smaller numbers. Some of the apparatus also carries medical equipment, which enables it to serve as a rescue unit as well as a fire fighting unit. Some initial attack fire apparatus are also equipped with a turret gun that can be supplied directly from another pumper. The small size and maneuverability of this pumper allows it to get into small spaces and set up a master stream where a larger pumper would not be able to fit.

An initial attack apparatus operates with a crew of two to five people. A crew of more than three people requires a four-door cab vehicle to carry all the crew members. Some fire departments use the initial attack apparatus as part of a "mini-maxi" concept. They use the initial attack apparatus as a "first-in" quick attack unit (Figures 4.25 a and b). The full-sized pumper, often a quint, can then lay in supply hoselines and provide additional support.

Mobile Water Supply Apparatus

The mobile water supply apparatus, known as a tanker or tender, is widely used to transport water to areas beyond a water system or to areas where water supply is inadequate. Most attack pumpers carry water, but not in large enough quantities to sustain an extended attack. A mobile water supply apparatus has water tanks that are larger than those generally found on a standard pumper.

The size of a mobile water supply apparatus's water tank depends upon a number of variables:

- Terrain — The mobile water supply apparatus may be required to climb steep hills or to operate on winding roads.
- Bridge weight limits — Bridges in the protected area may be too old or may not be designed to bear the weight of heavy mobile water supply apparatus. This presents a danger to firefighters as they drive over these bridges when alternate routes are not available.
- Monetary constraints — The fire department may not have enough money to purchase a large mobile water supply apparatus.
- Size of other mobile water supply apparatus in the area — Mobile water supply apparatus shuttle operations flow more easily when mobile water supply apparatus of the same or similar size are used.

Figure 4.25a This initial attack apparatus is paired with a quint.

Figure 4.25b The quint forms the major part of the attack-quint task force.

If an approved mobile water supply apparatus is desired, the requirements of NFPA 1903, *Standard for Mobile Water Supply Fire Apparatus*, should be met. The road tests and weight distribution requirements generally limit tank capacity to 1,500 gallons (6 000 L) or less for single rear-axle vehicles (Figure 4.26). When tanks of capacities greater than 1,500 gallons (6 000 L) are desired, either tandem rear axles or a tractor-trailer design should be considered (Figure 4.27). Straight-chassis apparatus have tanks up to 4,000 gallons (12 000 L). Anything larger than that requires a tractor-trailer arrangement (Figure 4.28). Some mobile water supply apparatus are equipped with full-size fire pumps and equipment similar to that described for pumpers (Figure 4.29). This apparatus is called a pumper-tanker or a tanker-pumper, and it can operate as either a pumper or a mobile water supply apparatus depending on the requirements of the call.

Figure 4.26 Smaller tankers require only a single rear axle.

Figure 4.27 Large tankers require tandem rear axles.

Figure 4.28 Some departments use tractor-trailer apparatus for large tankers. *Courtesy of Bob Esposito.*

Figure 4.29 Pumper-tankers carry large water tanks and fire pumps.

Wildland Fire Apparatus

Because it can go places that are inaccessible to larger apparatus, a lightweight, highly maneuverable vehicle is needed to control wildland fires. The fire apparatus specifically adapted for fighting wildland fires is designed to fulfill these requirements and should meet the requirements of NFPA 1902, *Standard for Initial Attack Fire Apparatus*. This unit is usually built on a utility-type vehicle chassis, and most have all-wheel drive (Figures 4.30 a through c). Booster tanks for wildland apparatus vary from approximately 50 gallons (200 L) on jeeps to around 1,000 gallons (4 000 L) on larger apparatus.

Figure 4.30a Brush apparatus can go places inaccessible to larger apparatus.

Figure 4.30b A typical brush apparatus.

Figure 4.30c Typical brush apparatus is lightweight and highly maneuverable. *Courtesy of Joel Woods, University of Maryland Fire and Rescue Institute.*

Figure 4.31 Though common, this method of attacking brush fires is not advisable.

Wildland apparatus is usually equipped with either a portable pump, auxiliary-engine-driven pump, or a PTO-powered pump. Although NFPA 1902 requires a pump capacity of at least 250 gpm (1 000 L/min) for initial attack apparatus, many wildland rigs have smaller pumps. Fire pumps range from 50 to 500 gpm (200 L/min to 2 000 L/min). A PTO-powered pump on wildland apparatus normally has a larger gpm (L/min) capacity than a portable pump, but it has a smaller capacity than an auxiliary pump. The PTO-powered pump is easily put into operation and requires little maintenance of the power source other than normal apparatus engine service. An auxiliary-powered pump delivers a constant flow regardless of the apparatus engine speed. A portable pump may serve as the main pump for wildland apparatus or may be carried as a backup unit for PTO-driven or auxiliary-driven pumps.

Although there is no standard that approves this method, many fire departments control natural cover fires on flat terrain by having their firefighters attack the fire while riding on the apparatus. Extended front bumpers or platforms are added to the apparatus for firefighters to ride upon while the truck is moving (Figure 4.31). Some use areas behind the cab (Figure 4.32). All firefighters should be secured to the apparatus by a strap if they are standing or by a seat belt if they are sitting. Appropriate speed limits and some form of communication should be established between the driver and riders of the apparatus. This technique must not be used in areas where the potential for an apparatus rollover exists.

Figure 4.32 Riding positions behind the cab offer more protection to the firefighters than do bumper positions.

WARNING:

Although riding on the exterior of wildland fire apparatus is a prevalent practice in many areas of the country, it is specifically prohibited by most applicable codes or standards. This practice is not recommended by IFSTA, and suitable alternatives should be found.

Most brush fire vehicles use booster hose as attack lines. However, using short sections of 1½-inch (38 mm) hose and adjustable flow nozzles reduces friction loss and gives the nozzleman a choice of flows to combat the volume and intensity of fire. A ground sweep nozzle may be useful if the number of personnel is limited and the fuel is short and slow burning. A brush fire apparatus may also carry small diameter, single-jacket forestry hose that allows for handlines to be stretched far from the apparatus. In addition to hose, brush fire apparatus carries a variety of related equipment such as rakes, axes, backpack water tanks, backfire torches, and shovels.

Aerial Apparatus

An aerial apparatus is a large vehicle with a powered aerial device that provides firefighters access to the upper levels of a structure. At fireground operations, the company of firefighters assigned to the aerial apparatus is most commonly charged with search and rescue operations, forcible entry, and ventilation. The members assigned to the aerial apparatus are called the "truck" or "ladder" company. The truck or ladder companies usually consist of a company officer, a driver/operator or engineer, and two or more firefighters. All aerial apparatus fall under the requirements set forth by NFPA 1904, *Standard for Aerial Ladder and Elevating Platform Fire Apparatus.*

IFSTA divides aerial apparatus into four distinct categories:

- Aerial ladder apparatus
- Aerial ladder platform apparatus
- Telescoping aerial platform apparatus
- Articulating aerial platform apparatus

AERIAL LADDER APPARATUS

An aerial ladder is a power-operated ladder mounted on a special truck chassis. The full extended length (also referred to as the working height) of North American-made aerial ladders is 50 to 135 feet (15 m to 41 m). The working height for aerial ladders is measured from the ground to the highest ladder rung with the ladder at maximum elevation and extension. Models manufactured in other countries may exceed these heights. The main uses of aerial ladders are:

- Rescue
- Ventilation
- Elevated master stream application
- Gaining access to upper levels

To accomplish these objectives, the aerial ladder apparatus carries a complement of ground ladders, tools, and other equipment. Most aerial ladders are power operated with hydraulic pumps, cylinders, and motors. An electric or mechanical backup system must be provided for the truck to meet the specifications of NFPA 1904.

The aerial ladder may be mounted on either a two- or three-axle, single-chassis vehicle or on a three-axle tractor-trailer vehicle (Figures 4.33 a through c). The single-chassis vehicle is usually equipped with dual rear wheels and is shorter than the tractor-trailer vehicle.

Figure 4.33a A single-axle aerial ladder apparatus. *Courtesy of Joel Woods, University of Maryland Fire and Rescue Institute.*

Figure 4.33b Larger aerial apparatus require tandem axles.

Figure 4.33c Tractor-tiller aerial apparatus are highly maneuverable.

A tractor-trailer apparatus, also known as a tiller truck, is equipped with steerable rear wheels on the trailer. The tiller operator is required to steer the rear wheels of this type of vehicle (Figure 4.34). A tractor-trailer truck is more maneuverable than a single-chassis vehicle. This maneuverability is an asset when the apparatus must negotiate narrow streets or heavy traffic.

Figure 4.34 The tiller station is located at the rear of the trailer.

AERIAL LADDER PLATFORM APPARATUS

An aerial ladder platform apparatus is similar to an aerial ladder apparatus except that a work platform is attached to the end of the aerial ladder. This vehicle is always single chassis and is usually of three-axle design (Figures 4.35 a and b). Most aerial ladder platform apparatus have a rear-mounted aerial device. The aerial ladder platform combines the safe work area of a platform with a safe, climbable aerial ladder. NFPA 1904 requires that platforms be constructed of metal; they are usually made of steel or aluminum alloy. The platform is usually encased by a heat protective shield that offers protection to occupants of the platform. The working height of all types of elevating platforms is measured from the ground to the top surface of the highest platform handrail with the aerial device at maximum extension and elevation. Aerial ladder platforms range in size from 85 to 110 feet (26 m to 34 m).

Figure 4.35a Aerial ladder platforms offer the advantages of both aerial ladder and platform apparatus. *Courtesy of Joel Woods, University of Maryland Fire and Rescue Institute.*

Figure 4.35b An aerial ladder platform. *Courtesy of Joel Woods, University of Maryland Fire and Rescue Institute.*

Fire fighting equipment on the platform typically includes a permanently mounted turret nozzle supplied by a water system incorporated with the booms or the ladder (Figure 4.36). A shower spray nozzle is also located beneath the platform to provide extra protection to the platform and its occupants during high heat situations (Figure 4.37).

Figure 4.36 The platforms are equipped with a master stream device.

Figure 4.37 A shower-curtain nozzle protects the underside of the platform.

The shower nozzle is operated by a foot pedal in the platform. Electrical, air, and hydraulic outlets are usually provided in the platform. Floodlighting and forcible entry equipment may also be in or attached to the platform. A backup hydraulic system is required. Two operating control stations are required—one at street level and one in the platform. A communication system between the two control stations is also necessary. Many platforms are provided with outlets to provide handlines and a mobile standpipe to upper floors (Figure 4.38).

Figure 4.38 Many platforms are equipped with standpipe lines or connections from which interior attacks may be made.

TELESCOPING AERIAL PLATFORM APPARATUS

NFPA places the aerial ladder platform and the telescoping aerial platform under the same definition. However, each type of apparatus has different capabilities on the fireground. The primary difference between the two is that an aerial ladder platform is designed with a large ladder that allows firefighters to climb back and forth from the platform. A telescoping aerial platform is equipped with a small ladder attached to the boom, which is designed primarily as an escape ladder for firefighters in the platform to use during an emergency (Figures 4.39 a and b). The escape ladder is shown in Figure 4.40. The equipment carried on this type of apparatus is typical of all aerial apparatus.

A telescoping aerial platform device has two or more sections and is made of either box-beam construction or tubular truss-beam construction. Box-beam construction consists of four sides welded together to form a box shape with a hollow center (Figure 4.41). Hydraulic lines, air lines, electrical cords, and waterways may be encased within the center or on the outside of the box beam. Tubular truss-beam construction is similar in design to the truss construction of aerial ladders. Tubular steel is welded to form a box shape using cantilever or triangular truss design (Figure 4.42).

Figure 4.39a Telescoping aerial platforms are not designed to be climbed. *Courtesy of Joel Woods, University of Maryland Fire and Rescue Institute.*

Figure 4.39b A telescoping aerial platform.

Figure 4.40 Telescoping aerial platforms are equipped with escape ladders that are to be used only as a last resort.

Figure 4.41 Some telescoping aerial platforms are of solid-side, box-beam construction. *Courtesy of Joel Woods, University of Maryland Fire and Rescue Institute.*

Figure 4.42 This telescoping aerial platform is of truss construction.

ARTICULATING AERIAL PLATFORM APPARATUS

The articulating aerial platform apparatus is similar to the telescoping aerial platform apparatus (Figure 4.43). The primary difference is in the operation of the aerial device. Instead of telescoping into each other, the boom sections are connected by a hinge and fold like an elbow. The boom is constructed in basically the same manner as the telescoping platform. This unit is often used along with or in place of aerial ladder apparatus. It performs many of the same functions such as rescue, ventilation, master stream application, and accessing upper floors.

Figure 4.43 An articulating aerial platform. *Courtesy of Joel Woods, University of Maryland Fire and Rescue Institute.*

NFPA 1904 requires that articulating aerial platform apparatus and all other platform apparatus have a permanent turret nozzle and supply system. Air, water, and electric power are piped or wired to the platform to facilitate fire fighting and rescue operations. These may be either inside the booms or attached to the outside.

Quintuple Aerial Apparatus (Quint)

A properly equipped aerial apparatus can also be operated as a quint. In addition to the aerial device, a quint is equipped with pumps, water tanks, ground ladders, and hose beds (Figures 4.44 a and b). Many fire departments are experimenting with the quint as a replacement for traditional pumper and ladder companies.

Figure 4.44a A quintuple aerial apparatus (quint). *Courtesy of Joel Woods, University of Maryland Fire and Rescue Institute.*

Figure 4.44b A full-sized quint.

Many departments are also starting to use a standard fire pumper that is equipped with a 65- to 75-foot (20 m to 23 m) aerial ladder or platform (Figures 4.45 a and b). This pumper lacks the space to carry a full complement of ground ladders or other truck company equipment; however, it can perform many of the same functions as an aerial apparatus.

Figure 4.45a Some pumpers are equipped with aerial ladders. *Courtesy of Joel Woods, University of Maryland Fire and Rescue Institute.*

Figure 4.45b A pumper equipped with an aerial ladder.

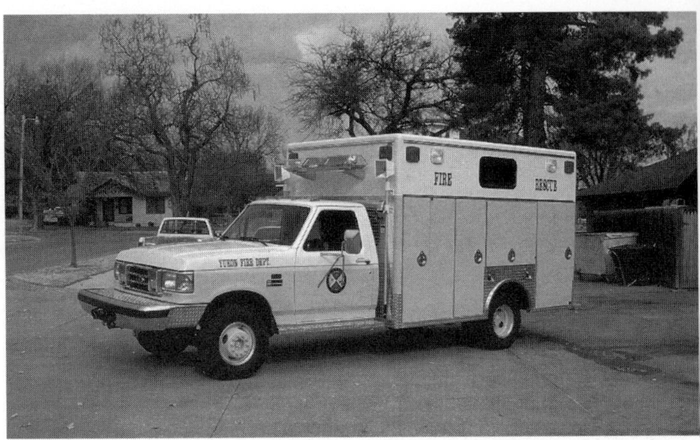

Figure 4.46a Light rescue trucks are generally built on a 1 or 1½-ton chassis.

Figure 4.46b Light rescue trucks carry basic equipment.

Rescue Apparatus

A rescue apparatus is used to transport specially trained firefighters and their equipment. As the name implies, its primary function is to rescue people from positions of danger such as fires, automobile accidents, trench cave-ins, structural collapses, and many other emergencies. The number of personnel assigned to a rescue company depends on the type of service provided, the type of apparatus, and local needs. There are three types of rescue apparatus: light, medium, and heavy rescue vehicles.

LIGHT RESCUE VEHICLE

A light rescue vehicle is designed to handle only basic extrication and life-support functions; therefore, it carries only basic hand tools and small equipment. Often, a light rescue unit functions as a first responder; that is, the crew attempts to stabilize the situation until heavier equipment arrives. The standard equipment carried on ladder and engine companies also gives them light rescue capabilities.

A light rescue vehicle is generally built on a 1-ton or a 1½-ton chassis (Figures 4.46 a and b). The rescue unit's body resembles a multiple-compartment utility truck. The size of this vehicle limits the amount of equipment it can carry. A light rescue vehicle can carry a variety of small hand tools, such as saws, jacks, and pry bars, as well as smaller hydraulic rescue equipment and small quantities of emergency medical supplies. This vehicle is generally capable of transporting two to seven rescue team members. A vehicle carrying more than three people requires either a four-door cab or an enclosed crew compartment in the body of the vehicle.

MEDIUM RESCUE VEHICLE

The medium rescue vehicle has more capabilities than the light rescue vehicle (Figures 4.47 a and b). In addition to basic hand tools, this vehicle may carry:

- Powered hydraulic spreading tools and cutters
- Air bag lifting systems
- Power saws
- Acetylene cutting equipment
- Ropes and rigging equipment

Figure 4.47a A medium rescue apparatus has more capabilities than the light rescue vehicle. *Courtesy of Saulsbury Fire Apparatus.*

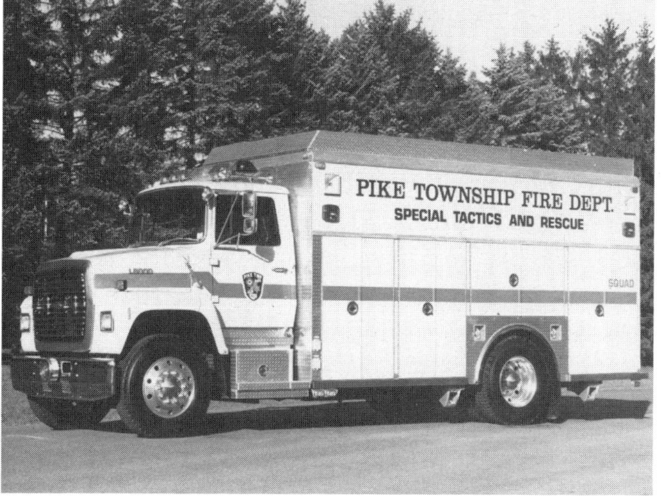

Figure 4.47b A medium rescue apparatus. *Courtesy of Saulsbury Fire Apparatus.*

A medium rescue unit is capable of handling the majority of rescue incidents. It may carry a variety of fire fighting equipment, which makes it a dual-purpose unit. This vehicle can carry as many as eight to ten rescue team members.

HEAVY RESCUE VEHICLE

A heavy rescue unit must be capable of providing the support necessary to extricate victims from almost any entrapment. As its name implies, the heavy rescue unit has heavier and more specialized equipment than smaller units (Figures 4.48 a and b). Additional types of equipment carried by the heavy rescue unit are:

- A-frames or gin poles
- Cascade systems
- Larger power plants
- Trenching and shoring equipment
- Small pumps and foam equipment
- Large winches

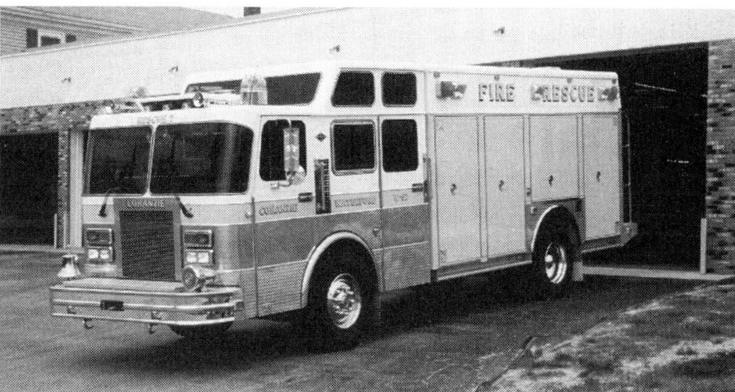

Figure 4.48a Heavy rescue vehicles carry extensive amounts of rescue and extrication equipment.

Figure 4.48b A heavy rescue vehicle.

- Hydraulic booms
- Large quantities of rope and rigging equipment
- Air compressors
- Ladders

Other specialized equipment may be carried according to the responsibilities of the rescue unit and the special needs of the department. The heavy rescue unit is frequently oriented more toward fire fighting than the smaller unit because it has more space available for fire fighting equipment. It can also carry a greater number of rescue personnel. Many units have seating for 12 or more people.

Aircraft Rescue And Fire Fighting Apparatus

Aircraft rescue and fire fighting (ARFF) apparatus is specifically designed and built to combat aircraft fires. There are several types of ARFF apparatus. The primary type is a very large vehicle that carries water and sufficient quantities of foam concentrate in a separate tank, which is mixed with the water. The foam is used to combat flammable liquid fires by smothering or by causing a blanketing effect on these fires. This apparatus has water tanks that range in capacity from 1,500 to 6,000 gallons (6 000 L to 24 000 L) (Figure 4.49). Foam concentrate tanks vary in size up to about 1,000 gallons (4 000 L). Fire pumps have a capacity of up to 2,000 gpm (8 000 L/min).

Figure 4.49 Large ARFF vehicles can carry up to 6,000 gallons (24 000 L) of water.

ARFF apparatus has the ability to discharge its fire streams while the vehicle is moving (often called pump and roll capability). This is crucial when combating aircraft fires. The large master stream nozzles on the roof of the apparatus are operated from within the cab. Many of the ARFF apparatus also carry foam-compatible fire extinguishing agents, such as carbon dioxide, dry chemical, and Halon, and the equipment needed to deliver them simultaneously with or separately from the foam. The ARFF apparatus also carries ladders, extrication equipment, and an assortment of hand tools.

Because not all work is performed on paved or hard surfaces, the ARFF apparatus is built on a special chassis with power to all the wheels. ARFF apparatus is usually supported by a tanker or fed by supply lines from a pumper for a continuous fire fighting operation.

A rapid intervention vehicle (RIV) is also used to provide protection at airports (Figure 4.50). It is designed to be the first unit to arrive at the scene of an aircraft emergency. Designed to be operated by one firefighter, this vehicle is capable of extinguishing incipient fires. An RIV must carry at least 600 gallons (2 400 L) of water, an appropriate amount of foam concentrate, and 500 pounds (227 kg) of dry chemical or Halon. Some airports may also have structural fire fighting apparatus that have been modified to assist on aircraft emergencies. These units serve the dual role of providing protection to the terminal area and responding to aircraft emergencies.

Figure 4.50 ARFF rapid intervention vehicles are designed to make quick attacks.

Hazardous Materials Response Unit

Many fire departments now assume the responsibility for stabilizing hazardous materials incidents. This requires additional training and specialized tools and equipment. Specially designed apparatus is required to carry the hazardous materials crew members and their equipment (Figures 4.51 a and b). The most important feature of the hazardous materials response unit is that it must be staffed by personnel who are thoroughly trained to identify hazardous materials and to deal with the hazards they present. This unit carries the

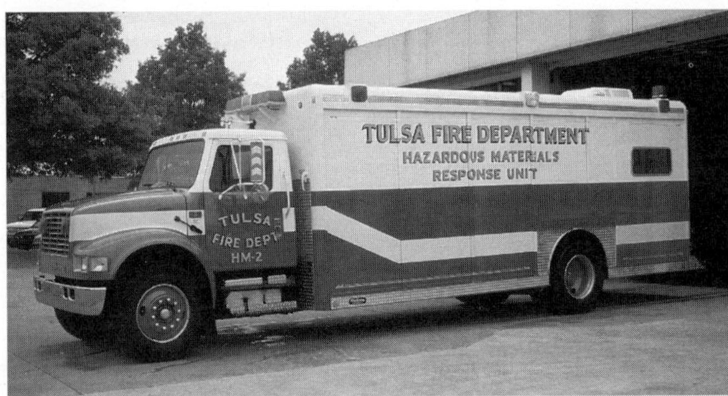

Figure 4.51a Hazardous materials apparatus carry highly specialized equipment.

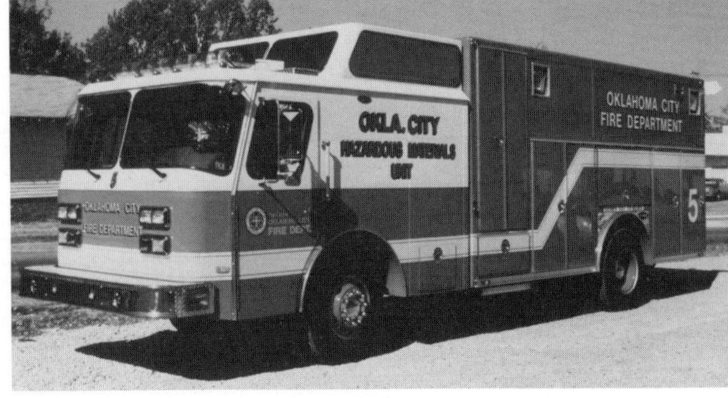

Figure 4.51b A hazardous materials apparatus.

usual array of standard hand tools, such as screwdrivers, wrenches, hammers, and saws, although many departments use nonsparking copper-beryllium alloy tools. This unit can also carry the following:

- All types of common patches from sheet metal screws to wooden plugs and duct tape
- Special kits designed for specific cylinders and containers
- A variety of special protective clothing
- SCBA
- Litmus paper for testing acidity and alkalinity
- Radiological detectors and various gas "sniffers"
- A variety of reference materials in the form of books and documents
- Onboard computers and modems that allow response personnel to tap into data bases and other sources of information for more information on the hazardous material (Figure 4.52)
- Cellular telephones and facsimile (fax) machines that allow for direct communications with other individuals or companies
- A variety of radio equipment that allows the members to communicate with anyone on the emergency scene
- Weather monitoring equipment so that conditions that may affect the incident can be anticipated and dealt with (Figure 4.53)

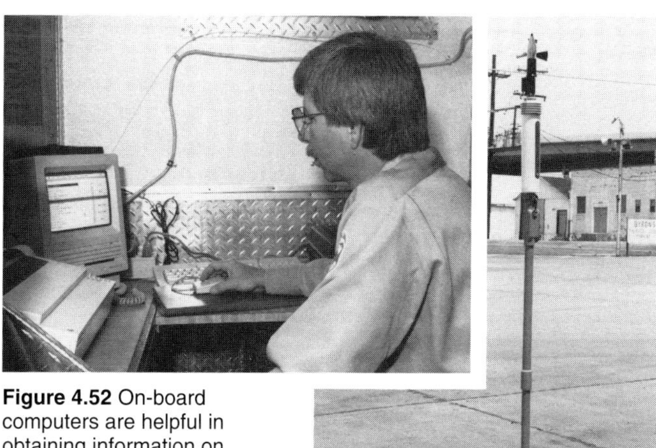

Figure 4.52 On-board computers are helpful in obtaining information on chemicals.

Figure 4.53 Weather-monitoring equipment, such as this wind gauge, helps provide information for incident management.

Mobile Air Supply Unit

Many fire departments and county organizations are placing the mobile air supply unit in service. Its primary purpose is to refill exhausted self-contained breathing apparatus cylinders at the scene of an emergency (Figures 4.54 a and b). This unit may simply carry a large number of air cylinders for replacement, may be a single or multiple cascade of three to five or more large cylinders, or may include an air compressor to refill a series of storage cylinders (Figure 4.55). The compressor is fitted with a purification system and various controls to ensure safe operation (Figure 4.56). Tools and parts are carried on the unit to make field repairs, adjustments, and replacements to damaged SCBA.

The types of vehicles used range from pickup trucks with trailers to larger vans or custom-designed apparatus. These units may be combined with other operations such as light apparatus and rescue.

Figure 4.54a Air units are useful for extended incidents.

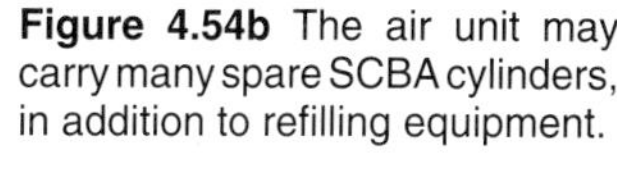

Figure 4.54b The air unit may carry many spare SCBA cylinders, in addition to refilling equipment.

Figure 4.55 Cascade systems have limited refill capabilities.

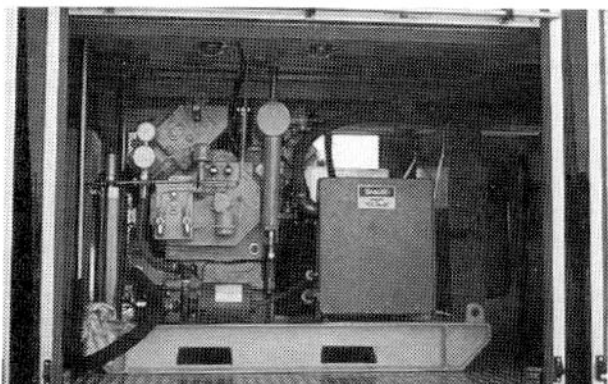

Figure 4.56 Air compressors fill cylinders as long as there is power to run the unit.

For safety, the mobile unit should have an adequate refilling station. With sufficient storage cylinders (more than six) and proper planning, several SCBA cylinders can be filled simultaneously. Each mobile air unit should meet the following safety standards:

- Those units with a compressor must position the air intake at a high level.
- All vehicle exhaust piping should discharge at a maximum practical distance from the air compressor intake.
- Each unit must have carbon monoxide monitoring equipment with an automatic shutoff switch that is activated when carbon monoxide exceeds acceptable limits.
- An air purification system must be installed and properly maintained on the discharge side of the compressor.
- Proper training must be given to all personnel operating these units.

Mobile Command Post

A mobile command post brings needed communication and reference materials directly to the emergency scene (Figure 4.57). For most incidents, a staff vehicle, station wagon, or pickup truck has sufficient space to carry radio equipment, area and water system maps, pre-incident plans, hazardous material references, and unit status boards. But at major emergencies with many pieces of equipment or when the incident lasts a long time, the unit must be a combination field dispatch center and temporary headquarters (Figure 4.58).

Figure 4.57 Mobile command post units bring needed resources to the scene.

Figure 4.58 The inside of the command post is furnished with radios, computers, and other equipment.

The larger mobile command post may be a step-van, converted bus, trailer, motor home, or a custom-designed unit (Figure 4.59). This unit is equipped with a wide variety of radio and telephone communications equipment, computers, television and video equipment, and other resources needed in that locale. It generally has an electrical generator that allows it to operate independent of outside utilities.

Figure 4.59 Many types of vehicles can be converted into mobile command post units.

Fireboat

Cities on a waterfront usually have fireboats to protect docks, wharves, piers, and boats. A fireboat may be a small, high-speed, shallow-draft vessel, or it may be the size of a river, harbor, or ocean-going tug depending on its duties and the area to be covered (Figures 4.60 a and b). The number of personnel varies with the size of the apparatus.

Using self-contained underwater breathing apparatus (SCUBA) equipment is an effective way to attack pier and waterfront fires. Specially trained and outfitted firefighters, usually working from

Figure 4.60a Small fire boats may be carried on trailers.

Figure 4.60b Large fire boats have pumping capacities of up to 20,000 gpm (80 000 L/min). *Courtesy of Joel Woods, University of Maryland Fire and Rescue Institute.*

fireboats, can approach a burning pier and deploy a floating nozzle to attack a fire burning underneath or deploy a water curtain to protect exposures. The SCUBA fire fighting company can be used for water search and rescue.

The fireboat can also be used to relay water to land-based companies. The two phases of fire fighting to which fireboats are particularly adapted are pumping through large master stream devices and providing additional water for onshore fire fighting operations. Fireboats have been built to deliver as much as 26,000 gpm (104 000 L/min). Individual master stream turrets that discharge 2,000 to 3,000 gpm (8 000 L/min to 12 000 L/min) are common.

Some of the smaller fireboats are propelled by water jets, but the larger types use conventional propellers. Most of the heavy-duty fireboats are powered by marine-type diesel engines. Dual-purpose engines for propulsion and pumping have also been used. All large fireboats need at least one auxiliary power generator and provisions for receiving shore power, fire alarms, and fresh water.

Power And Light Unit

Some fire departments have special apparatus to furnish lights and power at the scene of an incident (Figure 4.61). Large-capacity generators are used to power electric tools, provide standby power to buildings, and light the emergency scene. An auxiliary motor powers the trailer- or truck-mounted generator. Banks of floodlights and telescoping towers are provided, as well as an ample supply of extension cords, adapters, and portable lights. Personnel may be specially assigned to this company and used only on special calls. In many cases, power and light units are combined with air supply units onto one vehicle. These are called air/power/light units (Figure 4.62).

Figure 4.61 Power and light units are helpful on night calls. *Courtesy of Ron Jeffers.*

Figure 4.62 Some departments combine air, power, and light units into one vehicle.

Mobile Fire Investigation Unit

The mobile fire investigation unit carries materials and equipment necessary to detect arson (Figure 4.63). This includes supplies for the collection, preservation, and preliminary evaluation of physical evidence. Equipment carried on this unit includes:

- Flammable liquids detectors
- Gas chromatographs
- Magnifying lenses
- Common hand tools
- Lighting equipment
- Cameras
- Tape recorders
- Fingerprint kits
- Sifting screens
- Materials for making plaster casts and crime sketches
- Containers, such as plastic bags, steel cans with lids, and boxes, for storing evidence

Figure 4.63 Mobile investigation units are like on-scene labs. *Courtesy of Ron Jeffers.*

Fire Fighting Aircraft

Fixed-wing aircraft (planes) and helicopters are used to supplement ground-based fire fighting units in many areas (Figure 4.64). The use of airplanes is usually limited to dropping fire-retardant materials and parachute deployment of hand-tool crews (smoke jumpers) on natural cover fires. Aircraft commonly used include converted antisubmarine warfare planes (the S-2 and the amphibious PB-Y), other military aircraft (B-17 and C-119), and commercial aircraft (DC-3, DC-6 and DC-7). These planes can carry from 700 to 3,000 gallons (2 800 L to 12 000 L) of retardant material or water. The aircraft pilot can choose the amount of product released by using multiple bay doors, giving the drop different characteristics of penetrating power, length, and width. While extremely useful at fires, aircraft do not replace wildland fire fighting forces.

Figure 4.64 Fire fighting aircraft are useful on large wildland fires. *Courtesy of Canadair.*

Like fixed-wing aircraft, the helicopter can be used to drop retardant or water on natural cover fires from a suspended bucket or a tank attached underneath. A helicopter is limited in the amount of retardant material it can carry, but its ability to hover adds the advantage of pinpoint accuracy. The helicopter is also used for airborne command posts, aerial photography, and fire area mapping. A helicopter is useful for water or rough terrain rescues; an outside winch can be used to lower rescuers and retrieve victims. Specially equipped helicopters are also used to transport critically injured persons from an accident to a medical facility (Figure 4.65).

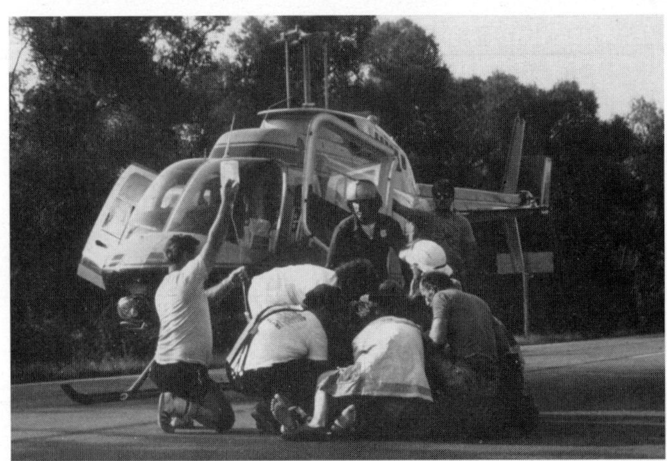

Figure 4.65 Medevac helicopters speed the removal of victims to a hospital. *Courtesy of Joel Woods, University of Maryland Fire and Rescue Institute.*

Other Special Units

Other special companies can be designed to fulfill local needs. Some special fire fighting companies include high-expansion foam, dry chemical units, hose monitor or deluge, and smoke ejector companies (Figure 4.66 a through d). Some special units do not have fire fighting functions, but are necessary for efficient operations such as:

- Gasoline or diesel service trucks
- Mechanical service trucks
- Wreckers
- Thawing apparatus
- Fire alarm service trucks
- Fire hydrant maintenance vehicles (Figures 4.67 a through c)

Variations and combinations of all the previously discussed companies may be necessary, particularly in smaller departments where one piece of apparatus may be required to perform several functions.

Figure 4.66a A high-expansion foam unit. *Courtesy of Ron Bogardus.*

Figure 4.66c A twin-agent unit.

Figure 4.66b A large master stream/foam unit. *Courtesy of Harvey Eisner.*

Figure 4.66d A large-volume smoke blower apparatus. *Courtesy of Joel Woods, University of Maryland Fire and Rescue Institute.*

Figure 4.67a A fire department wrecker.

Figure 4.67b A fire department fueler.

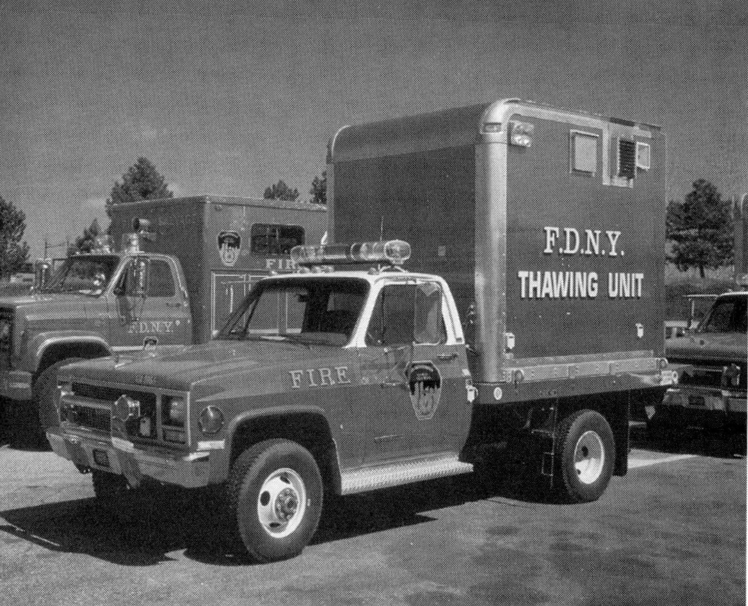

Figure 4.67c A thawing unit. *Courtesy of Ron Jeffers.*

Chapter 4
Application And Review Activities

DIRECTIONS

The following activities are designed to help you comprehend and apply the information in Chapter 4 of **Orientation and Terminology**. To receive the maximum learning experience from these activities, it is recommended that you use the following procedure:

1. Read the chapter, underlining or highlighting important terms, topics, and subject matter. Study the photographs and illustrations, and read the captions under each.
2. Review the list of vocabulary words to ensure that you know the chapter-related meaning of each. If you are unsure of the meaning of a vocabulary word, look the word up in a dictionary, and then study its context in the chapter.

   NOTE: Some words have different meanings as different parts of speech. Abbreviations after certain words stand for the part of speech (v., verb; n., noun; adj., adjective; adv., adverb) of the word as it is used in the chapter.
3. On a separate sheet of paper, complete all assigned or selected application and review activities before checking your answers.
4. After you have finished, check your answers against those on the pages referenced in parentheses.
5. Correct any incorrect answers, and review material that was answered incorrectly.

VOCABULARY

Be sure that you know the chapter-related meanings of the following terms.

- Apparatus *(67)*
- Appliance vs. tool *(73)*
- Arson *(88)*
- Articulating (adj.) *(74)*
- Auxiliary *(77)*
- Cantilever *(80)*
- Chassis *(74)*
- Concentrate (n.) *(83)*
- Dispatch *(69)*
- Extrication *(71)*
- Facsimile *(85)*
- Fireground *(78)*
- Hydraulic *(78)*
- Incipient *(84)*
- Rigging *(82)*
- Shoring *(83)*
- Telescoping (adj.) *(74)*
- Terrain *(77)*
- Trenching *(83)*
- Turret *(79)*
- Ventilation *(78)*
- Wildland *(76)*

APPLICATION OF KNOWLEDGE

1. Which of the fire apparatus described in this chapter does your local fire department have? Does the department have any specially designed apparatus that does not clearly fit into one of the categories this chapter covers? If so, describe the apparatus. *(Local protocol)*

2. Describe your local fire department's facilities. How many fire stations does it have? Are the administrative offices housed in or separate from the fire stations? Where is the dispatch center? What is the training center like? Where do firefighters perform maintenance on apparatus and equipment? *(Local protocol)*

3. What might happen if a firefighter fought a wildland fire while riding on the wildland apparatus? Find and identify three standards that prohibit the practice of riding on the apparatus while fighting a fire. *(Local protocol)*

REVIEW ACTIVITIES

1. List and describe the five areas or components of fire departments. *(67)*

2. Describe the typical contents of an apparatus bay. *(68)*

3. List three uses of drill towers. *(70)*

4. Explain the purpose of smokehouse training.*(71)*

5. Explain why pumpers carry water to a fire location equipped with hydrants. *(72)*

6. List at least eight pieces of equipment that most pumpers carry for fire and rescue. *(73)*

7. Explain the advantage of the small initial attack fire apparatus over a larger pumper. *(74)*

8. Describe how a fire department might determine the size and type of mobile water supply apparatus to buy. *(75)*

9. Distinguish among the four types of aerial apparatus. *(78-81)*

10. Explain why driver/operators working narrow, crowded city streets might prefer a tiller truck over a single-chassis apparatus. *(79)*

11. Name at least four required components of any aerial ladder platform. *(79 & 80)*

12. Distinguish between a telescoping aerial platform and an articulating aerial platform. *(80 & 81)*

13. Name the five major components of a quint. *(81)*

14. Compare and contrast the three types of rescue vehicles. *(82 & 83)*

15. List at least six pieces of rescue equipment that a heavy rescue vehicle might carry. *(83)*

16. Name two types of fire apparatus designed with all-wheel drive. *(76, 84)*

17. List three extinguishing agents that a rapid intervention vehicle (RIV) must carry. *(84)*

18. List at least four types of equipment or materials that a hazardous materials unit would carry. *(85)*

19. Describe the three types of mobile air supply units.*(85)*

20. List the materials that a mobile command post brings to the emergency scene. *(86)*

21. Describe at least two tasks that firefighters can perform from a fireboat. *(86 & 87)*

22. Discuss the advantages and disadvantages of helicopters versus airplanes in fighting wildland fires. *(88)*

23. List at least three services for which a fire department may need special, nonfire units. *(89)*

24. Identify eight of the following in one or two phrases.
    - ARFF *(83)*
    - Boom *(79)*
    - Booster tank *(72)*
    - Box beam *(80)*
    - CAD *(69)*
    - Cascade system *(68)*
    - Gas chromatograph *(88)*
    - Gin pole *(83)*
    - Hose bed *(72)*
    - psi *(258)*
    - RIV *(84)*
    - SCBA *(85)*
    - SCUBA *(86*
    - Smoke jumper *(88)*
    - Training pad *(71)*
    - Truss beam *(289)*
    - Working height *(78)*

5
Fire Department Organization

Chapter 5
Fire Department Organization

Before entering into any discussion on fire department organization, it is necessary to preface this section with one qualifying statement: Virtually no two fire departments in North America are organized the same. Therefore, any discussion on fire department organization must be made in a very general way. The purpose of this chapter is to introduce the reader to the following:

- Principles of organization
- Local government structures
- Types of fire departments
- Fire department funding
- Work schedules
- Polices and procedures
- Incident management systems
- Fire department planning
- Industrial fire brigades

PRINCIPLES OF ORGANIZATION

A fire department is composed of individuals with different backgrounds and different ideas about life. The success of a fire department depends on the willingness of its members to put aside their differences and work for the benefit of the department. To ensure that department members cooperate effectively, the methods of cooperation are outlined in policies, job descriptions, and organizational charts.

An organizational chart shows the structure of the fire department and its chain of command. The complexity of a department is represented on its organizational chart. Small fire departments have a relatively simple chain of command, while large departments have a considerably more complex chart. Figures 5.1 through 5.3 show sample organizational charts for small, medium, and large fire departments. These are meant only to serve as a reference. Charts for local municipalities vary.

In order for the firefighter to operate effectively as a team member, there are four basic organizational principles of which the firefighter should be aware:

- Unity of command
- Span of control
- Division of labor
- Discipline

Unity of Command

Unity of command is an important concept to the fire department. The principle behind unity of command is that a person can only report to one supervisor. Directly, each subordinate reports to one boss; however, indirectly everyone reports to the fire chief through the chain of command (Figure 5.4). The chain of command is the pathway of responsibility from the highest level of the department to the lowest level. The fire chief issues general orders that filter through the chain of command and turn into specific work assignments for the firefighter. The unity of command ensures that all fire department personnel are aware of and understand the chief's orders. In this way, work can be broken down into specific job assignments without loss of control.

If a firefighter is put into a position that requires reporting to more than one supervisor, a number of difficult situations can result. For example, a firefighter at a fire scene is given an order

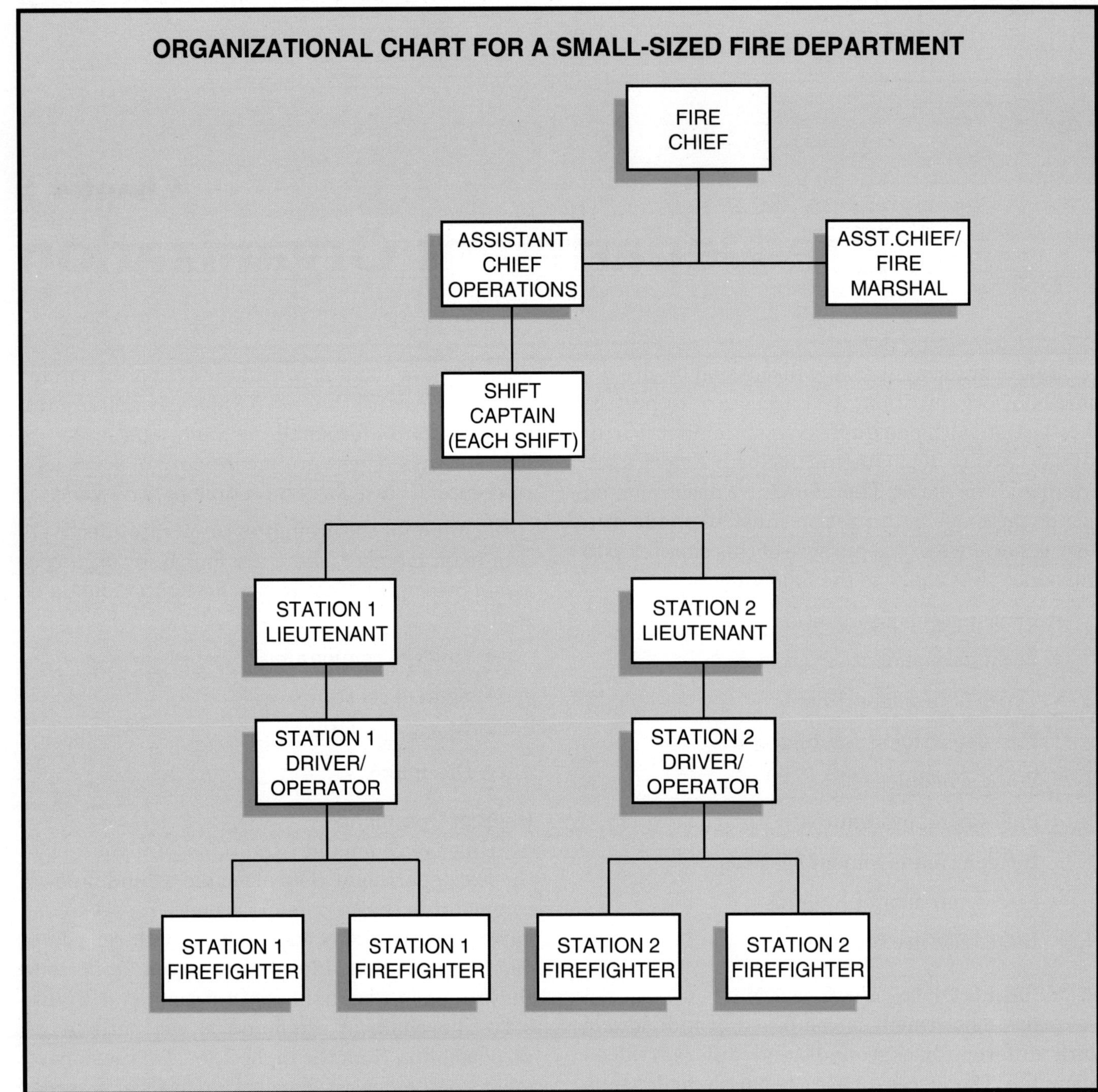

Figure 5.1 Small departments have relatively simple organizational charts.

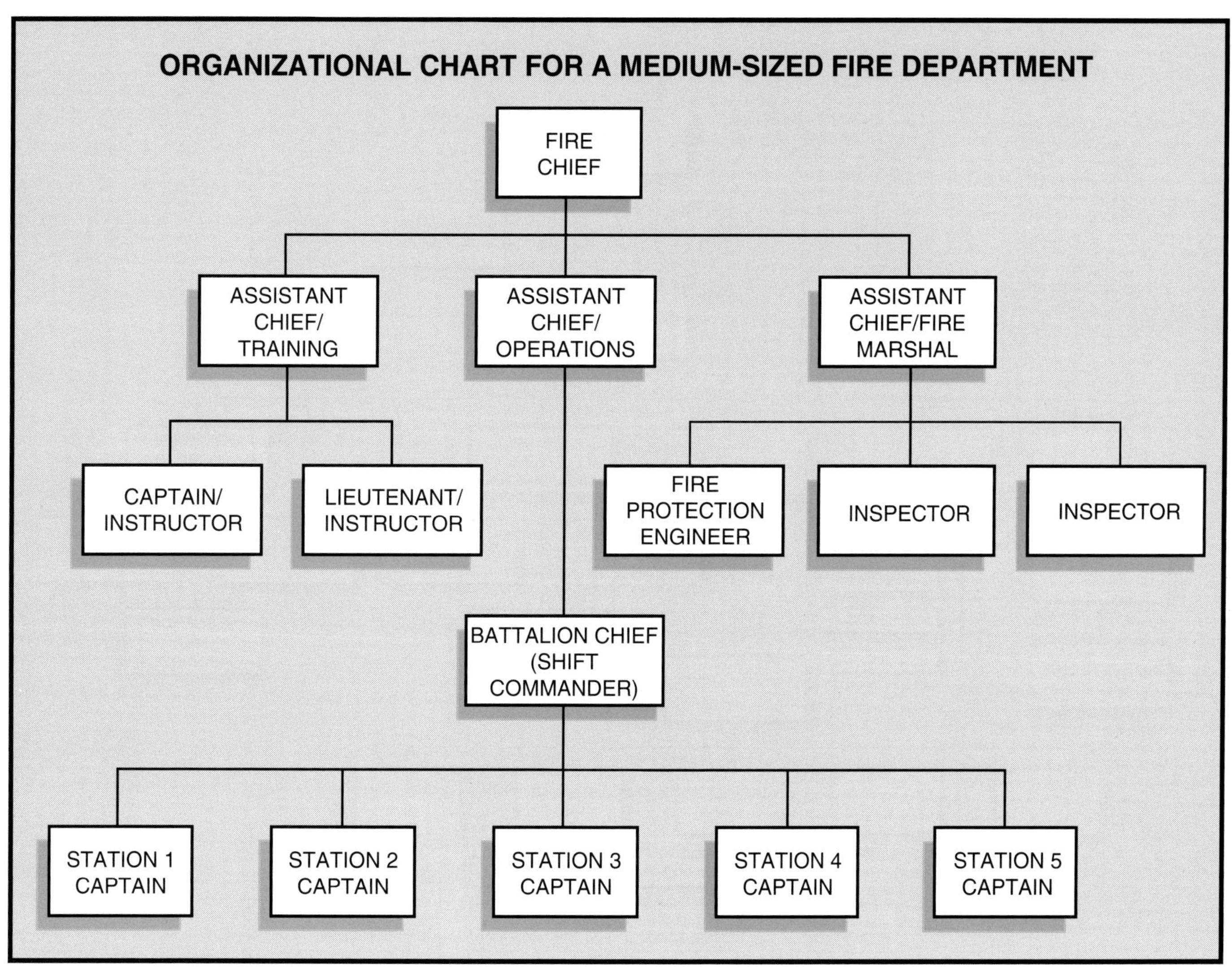

Figure 5.2 Medium-sized departments have more resources to manage than do the small departments.

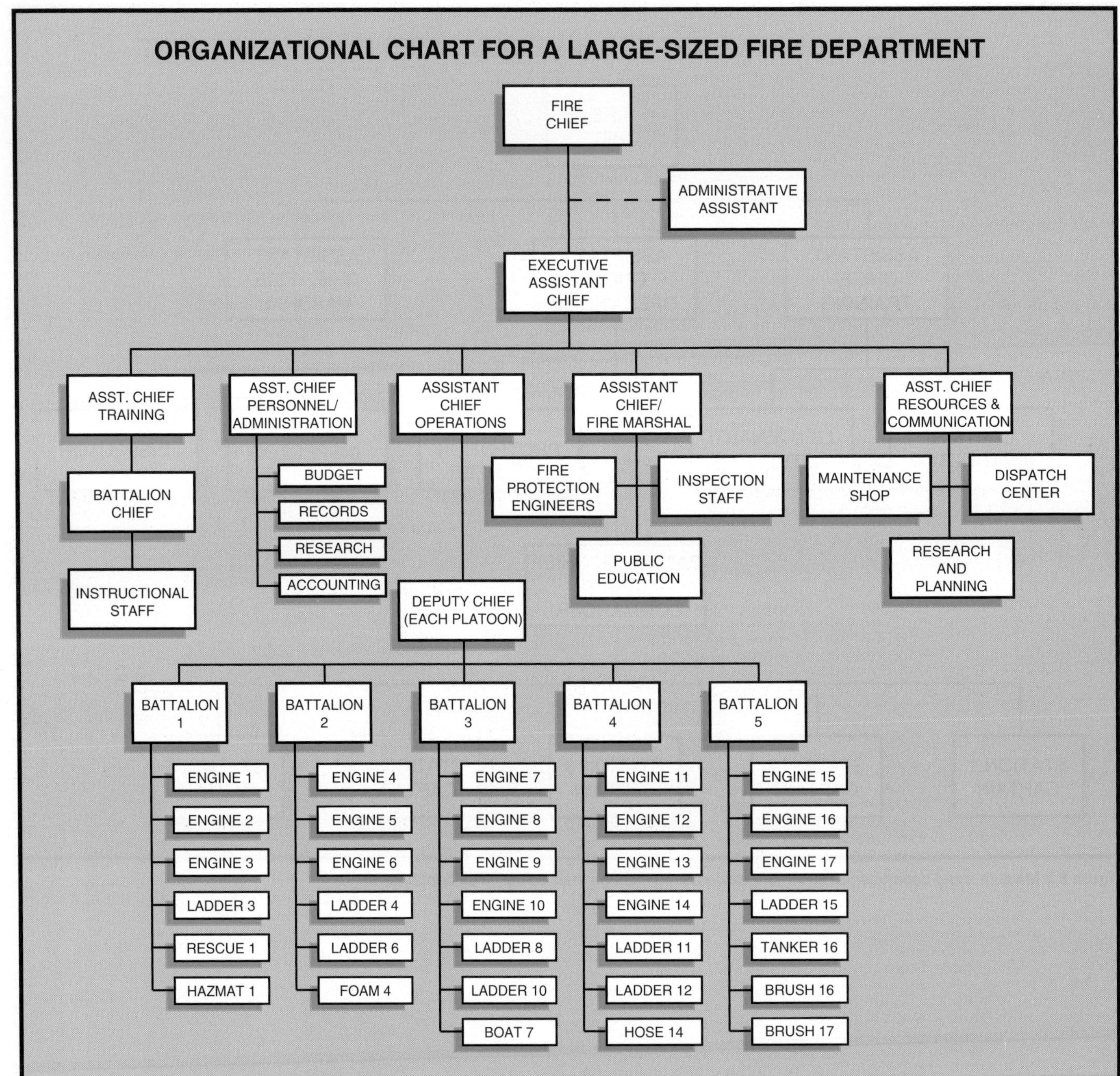

Figure 5.3 Large fire departments have complex organizational structures.

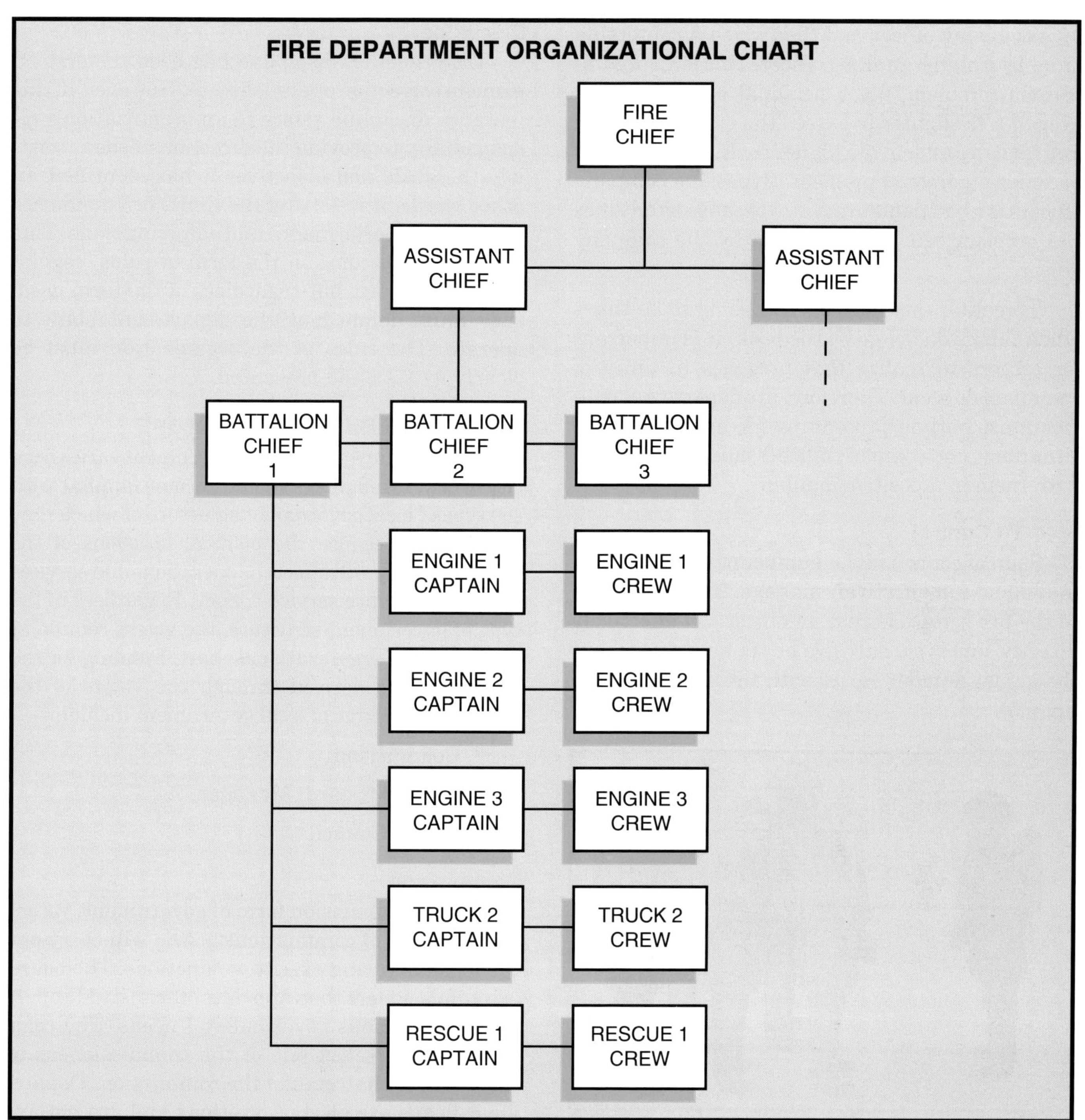

Figure 5.4 This simple organizational chart shows the department's chain of command..

by a company officer and then given a conflicting order by a higher ranking officer. This is an organizational problem, not a personal problem. However, if a firefighter bypasses the company officer and takes a problem to a higher ranking officer, this becomes a personal problem. Bypassing company officers is a bad habit to get into because oftentimes the problem can be best solved by the company officer.

In reality, there are always going to be times when things do not go by the book. It is important for officers to realize that breaches in unity of command do occur. Therefore, fire department policies must outline procedures for handling these situations, and company officers must learn to deal with them in a positive manner.

Span Of Control

Span of control is the number of personnel one individual can effectively manage. A rule of thumb in the fire service is that an officer can effectively directly supervise only five or six firefighters, but the actual number varies with the situation (Figure 5.5).

Figure 5.5 A five-to-one span of control is desirable.

Division Of Labor

Division of labor is breaking large jobs into small jobs. These small jobs are then assigned to specific individuals. The division of labor concept is necessary in the fire service for the following reasons:

- To assign responsibility
- To prevent duplication of effort
- To make specific and clear-cut assignments

Discipline

Traditionally, discipline has been understood to mean correction or punishment. However, in this instance discipline refers to an organization's responsibility to provide the direction needed to satisfy the goals and objectives it has identified. In other words, it is setting the limits or boundaries for expected performance and enforcing them. This direction may come in the form of rules, regulations, or policies, but regardless of the term used, they must define how the department plans to operate. The rules of the organization must be clearly written and presented.

LOCAL GOVERNMENT STRUCTURE

The structure of the local government varies from city to city. Firefighters should become familiar with the type of local government structure of which they are a part, because the political decisions of the governing body will affect the operations and services offered by the fire service agency. Regardless of the type of government structure, the voters remain at the top of the organizational chart. Funding for the department is derived through the voters of the community. Forms of local government include:

- Commission
- Council (Board) Manager
- Mayor/Council

Commission

In the Commission form of government, voters elect a board of commissioners who will carry out the legislative and executive functions. The board of commissioners then appoints officials and supervisors for various governmental needs. The commission may select one of the commissioners to serve as the chairman of the commission. Department heads are elected positions and are not appointed by the commissioners.

Council (Board) Manager

In the Council (Board) Manager form of government, voters elect a council or board of officials who carry out the legislative responsibilities. These elected officials appoint a professional manager to handle the administrative (executive) matters. This manager appoints the department heads to execute the needs of the council within their specific areas of responsibility.

Mayor/Council

In the Mayor/Council form of government, voters elect a mayor and a council to govern the community. The mayor plays the role of an elected independent executive who is both policy advocate and chief executive officer. The mayor, acting as a manager, appoints the department heads.

TYPES OF FIRE DEPARTMENTS

What is an *adequate* level of fire protection? What is a *reasonable* community cost? These are basic questions that every community must face. The acceptable level of risk assumed by the local government is a political and community decision. Every community must define what level of fire protection is acceptable once the extent of the problem has been determined. The community must also determine what it is willing to pay for in emergency and nonemergency services. The values, trends, and community forces all play a part in determining the types and levels of services that the fire department provides.

Fire departments generally function under the local government, although some departments are independent. Some states furnish fire fighting and rescue services on state turnpikes or other large state roads, for forests and parks, and for state institutions. The federal government has little or no control over local fire protection, although there are some foreign countries in which fire protection is controlled and operated solely by the national government. The military branches of the United States maintain their own fire protection forces, and the personnel are military specialists or civil service employees. The federal government does, however, furnish fire protection for its national parks and forests. The National Park Service and the U.S. Forestry Service have extensive fire prevention and suppression activities and contract for mutual aid with other local fire departments.

Paid Departments

Paid fire departments are manned by career firefighters who work regular shifts at the fire station in return for financial compensation. Paid departments are mostly found in medium and large cities or other heavily populated areas. Some private industrial or government complexes may also have full-time fire protection staff.

Volunteer Departments

Volunteer departments are manned by personnel who donate their time for the cause of fire protection in their community. Their only reward, in many cases, is the feeling of self-satisfaction they get from helping others. Most volunteer firefighters receive no financial compensation for their services. However, some may receive pension benefits after they serve a specified period of time.

Paid-Call Departments

Paid-call firefighters are often technically considered volunteers, although they are not volunteers in the true sense. Paid-call firefighters are members of a department who receive a monthly or per-call stipend for responding to emergencies, attending training, and participating in associated activities. This stipend is not enough to live on, and in most cases, belonging to the department is not the individual's primary job.

Combination Departments

Combination departments have full-time personnel on duty at the fire station, and their full-time firefighters are backed up with a cadre of volunteer or paid-call firefighters. The volunteers or paid-call personnel provide assistance when incidents are larger than the capabilities of the duty staff.

Factors That Affect Fire Department Type

The type of fire department used to protect any given municipality or area is dependent on many factors such as the following:

- The inherent hazards of the area — These must be considered to identify the extent of the problem.
- The type of community and its needs — For example, emergency medical calls may exceed fire and hazardous materials responses.
- The availability of personnel — Urban and suburban areas that have a high volume of emergency calls may require career departments with full-time staffing in the fire stations. This is particularly true if a shortage of potential volunteers exists. Rural areas and small communities may be staffed by volunteers or a combination of paid and volunteer personnel if the call volume is not sufficient for total career staffing.

- The financial resources of the community — These resources influence the decision as to the type of department to serve the community. Larger metropolitan and suburban areas have more money available for fire protection than do smaller rural areas (Figures 5.6 a and b). This allows for career fire departments to be established and adequately funded.

Figure 5.6a The resources of a large city differ from those of a small town.

Figure 5.6b Small towns require less resources than large cities.

FIRE DEPARTMENT FUNDING

In many respects, a fire department is like a private business — money is required for capital and personnel expenses. In order to remain operational, this flow of revenue must be continuous and well maintained. A fire department can be funded through its municipality, independently through alternative revenue sources, or through its fire district. Private sector departments may fall under any one of these funding strategies and are discussed later in this section.

A department funded by its municipality relies on monies that are allocated in the local government's operating budget. The fire department receives a portion of the money that is collected through the local government's established tax system. This tax could be of the earned income, property, or sales variety. In most cases, the local governing body, either a council or commission, has the ultimate approval control over the fire department's spending.

Most independently funded fire departments are volunteer organizations. These departments rely on alternative revenue sources, as opposed to taxes, for their income. Revenues are raised by fund drives, raffles, car washes, carnivals, dinners and dances, bingo, coin tosses, and businesses run by the department. In these fund-raising events, the fire department has autonomous control over expenditures.

Fire protection districts usually have separate governing bodies and are financed by taxes or membership fees, similar to a school or a water district. Fire protection districts may be either paid or volunteer fire departments. The members of the fire district's board of directors have final approval over expenditures.

A private sector fire department is an organization that provides fire service to the public for profit. The department receives its funding from either subscription fees paid by individual property owners or from municipal funding through taxes. The department itself may be a corporation, a partnership, or a sole proprietorship. The private sector department either purchases or leases fire equipment (including trucks) and a building for housing the equipment.

WORK SCHEDULES

Paid firefighters work a variety of schedules. While a very few work eight-hour shifts as in other professions, most work a different, longer scheduled shift. The first thing upon which the work schedule depends is the number of platoons, or shift crews, the department uses. Fire departments may have a two-, three-, or four-platoon system. Two-platoon systems are fairly rare, although much of the American military fire service still operates with two platoons. The most common work schedule for each platoon under the two-platoon system is a straight 24 hours on duty and 24 hours off duty.

The majority of the North American paid fire service operates under the three-platoon system. A variety of work schedules are used under the three-platoon system; however, all revolve around 24-hour work shifts. Although many variations exist, the most common shift is the straight 24 hours on duty and 48 hours off duty (Figure 5.7). Another shift may involve extra days off, which are called Kelly days. One such schedule is the 24 on, 24 off, 24 on, 24 off, 24 on, and 96 (four days) off (Figure 5.8). Other variations exist.

Some cities, particularly large cities with heavy run loads, use a four-platoon system. Most commonly, the four- platoon system revolves around shortened work periods such as 10-hour day shifts and 14-hour night shifts (or 9s and 15s). Other variations exist, but one common schedule is for a crew to work two day shifts and then two night shifts, followed by four days off (Figure 5.9). Again, other variations exist.

Volunteer departments may or may not have work schedules. Most smaller departments depend on all volunteers to respond anytime they are available. Larger volunteer organizations and those with paid-call firefighters may have personnel assigned to duty crews that respond only during specific times.

POLICIES AND PROCEDURES

When a firefighter joins a fire department, he or she is familiarized with the department's regulations and procedures. If a firefighter has questions about these activities, he or she should contact a supervisor to clear up any misunderstanding that could cause trouble later on. The intent of this section is to provide new firefighters with an idea of some of the rules and regulations that most departments generally follow.

Before entering this discussion, it is important to understand the difference between policy and procedure. *Policy* is a guide to decision making within an organization. Policy originates mostly with top management in the fire department and

24 ON, 48 OFF SHIFT SCHEDULE

SUNDAY	MONDAY	TUESDAY	WEDNESDAY	THURSDAY	FRIDAY	SATURDAY
6	7 ON DUTY 8:00 a.m.	8 OFF DUTY 8:00 a.m.	9	10 ON DUTY 8:00 a.m.	11 OFF DUTY 8:00 a.m.	12
13 ON DUTY 8:00 a.m.	14 OFF DUTY 8:00 a.m.	15	16 ON DUTY 8:00 a.m.	17 OFF DUTY 8:00 a.m.	18	19 ON DUTY 8:00 a.m.

Figure 5.7 A sample 24 on, 48 off work schedule.

KELLY SCHEDULE

SUNDAY	MONDAY	TUESDAY	WEDNESDAY	THURSDAY	FRIDAY	SATURDAY
6	7 OFF DUTY 8:00 a.m.	8	9 OFF DUTY 8:00 a.m.	10	11 OFF DUTY 8:00 a.m.	12
ON DUTY 8:00 a.m.		ON DUTY 8:00 a.m.		ON DUTY 8:00 a.m.		
13	14	15	16 OFF DUTY 8:00 a.m.	17	18 OFF DUTY 8:00 a.m.	19
		ON DUTY 8:00 a.m.		ON DUTY 8:00 a.m.		ON DUTY 8:00 a.m.

Figure 5.8 A different work schedule using 24-hour shifts.

10s and 14s SCHEDULE

SUNDAY	MONDAY	TUESDAY	WEDNESDAY	THURSDAY	FRIDAY	SATURDAY
6	7	8	9	10 OFF DUTY 8:00 a.m	11 OFF DUTY 8:00 a.m	12
	ON DUTY 8:00 a.m. OFF DUTY 6:00 p.m.	ON DUTY 8:00 a.m. OFF DUTY 6:00 p.m.	ON DUTY 6:00 p.m.	ON DUTY 6:00 p.m.		
13	14	15	16	17	18 OFF DUTY 8:00 a.m	19 OFF DUTY 8:00 a.m
		ON DUTY 8:00 a.m. OFF DUTY 6:00 p.m.	ON DUTY 8:00 a.m. OFF DUTY 6:00 p.m.	ON DUTY 6:00 p.m.	ON DUTY 6:00 p.m.	

Figure 5.9 A four-platoon, 10s and 14s work schedule.

points to the kinds of decisions that must be made by fire officers or other management personnel in specified situations.

A *procedure* is a kind of formal communication closely related to policy. Whereas policy is a guide to thinking or decision making, a procedure is a detailed guide to action. A procedure details in writing the steps to be followed in carrying out organizational policy for some specific, recurring problem or situation.

Orders and directives may be either written or verbal. An order is based upon the administrative policy or procedure, and directives are not based on policy or procedure. Yet, both are essential for implementing the formal guidelines of the department. On the fireground, fire officers issue many instructions, directives, and requests (Figure 5.10). However, because of the seriousness of the situation, all of these utterances are generally considered orders.

Figure 5.10 Officers must not hesitate to give orders on the emergency scene. *Courtesy of Joe Marino.*

Uniforms And Dress

Proper dress is usually defined in the department regulations, which may include requirements for dress uniform, work clothing, and protective clothing. The dress uniform, sometimes referred to as the Class A uniform, is used for public appearances, special events, parades, inspections, and some social functions (Figure 5.11). A dress uniform generally consists of a uniform pant and jacket, white shirt for officers, colored shirt for firefighters, tie, black shoes, appropriate color brass, badge, name tag, and uniform hat.

Station work clothing comes in several forms. Work clothes are usually worn while on duty or on special work details. Some departments prefer the uniform-type work clothing (Figure 5.12). Others wear golf or tee shirts and flame-resistant trousers. Coveralls may be worn for especially dirty work (Figure 5.13). Regardless of the style chosen by the fire department, all work uniforms must comply with the requirements set forth in NFPA 1975, *Standard on Station / Work Uniforms for Fire Fighters.*

Figure 5.11 Class A uniforms are often worn during official ceremonies or presentations.

Volunteer firefighters do not usually have the opportunity to wear an approved work uniform when responding to an emergency (Figure 5.14). However, volunteer departments are encouraged to establish guidelines for proper dress when responding to an alarm. All volunteers should wear shirts, socks, and, preferably, long trousers, in addition to full personal protective clothing. When possible, natural fibers such as cotton or wool are preferred.

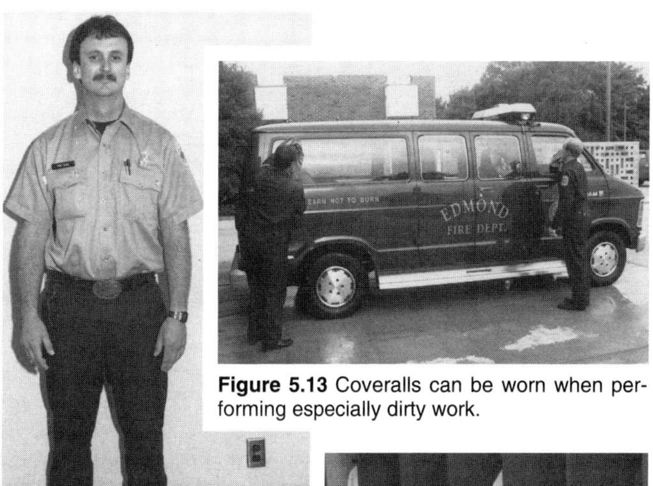

Figure 5.13 Coveralls can be worn when performing especially dirty work.

Figure 5.12 Station uniforms are worn during normal duties.

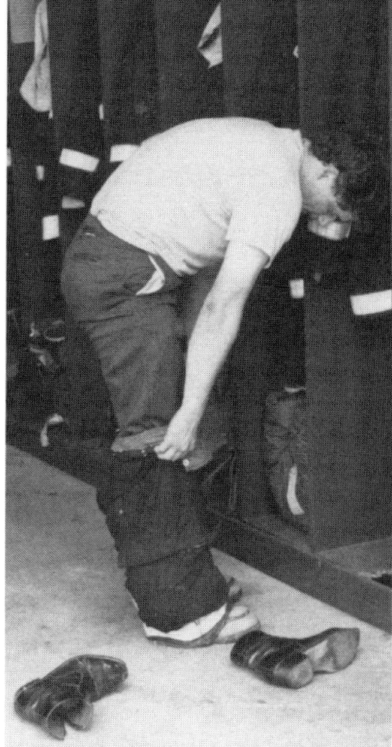

Figure 5.14 Volunteers don protective clothing over whatever they happen to be wearing at the time of the call.

All firefighters must be wearing personal protective clothing when responding to and working at emergencies. Full personal protective clothing consists of a turnout coat and pants, helmet, eye protection, boots, and gloves for fire fighting (Figure 5.15). When working in atmospheres that are hazardous or have the potential to become so, firefighters must wear self-contained breathing apparatus (SCBA) and personal alert safety systems (PASS devices) (Figure 5.16).

Figure 5.15 A firefighter in full personal protective clothing.

Figure 5.16 A firefighter in full personal protective equipment, including a self-contained breathing apparatus and a personal alert safety system.

Conduct

Members of the fire service must behave properly for the department to be successful. No activity should be undertaken that would lower the public's or the local government's respect for the department. Fire department members should not be permitted to report for duty under the influence of any intoxicating liquor or drug. Off-duty members should not appear at any station in an intoxicated condition. Scuffling, horseplay, or any other form of physical encounter incompatible with accepted standards of conduct should be prohibited in or around any fire department facility. Fire department members should avoid swearing and rudeness while on duty. The general rule for new firefighters is to use common sense when it comes to their behavior.

Standard Operating Procedures

Some fire departments have a predetermined plan or written policy for nearly every type of emergency that they can conceive of occurring. This plan or written policy is known as the department's standard operating procedure (SOP). The SOP is usually initiated by the first fire companies that reach the scene. The SOP may vary considerably in different localities, but the principle is usually the same. The procedure is primarily a means to get the fire attack started. Its use does not replace size-up, decisions based on professional judgment, evaluation, or command. In addition, there may be several SOPs from which to choose depending on fire severity, location, and the ability of first-in units to achieve control.

The SOP should be established to follow the most commonly accepted order of fireground priorities:

- Rescue
- Fire control
- Property conservation

The need to save lives in danger is always the first consideration. Once all possible victims have been rescued, attention is turned to controlling the fire, which includes protecting the exposures as well. Last, firefighters should make all possible efforts to minimize damage to the structure. This can be accomplished through proper fire fighting tactics and good salvage and overhaul techniques.

SOPs are used to standardize general activities at any emergency scene (Figure 5.17). Special SOPs can be implemented to make operations at target hazards more efficient. The use of SOPs reduces confusion and increases efficiency on the fireground.

Standard operating procedures do not have to be limited to the emergency scene. Many departments prefer to carry out the administrative and personnel functions of the department through SOPs. SOPs may include regulations on dress, conduct, vacation and sick leave, station life and duties, and other departmental policies.

Figure 5.17 SOPs should be used on all incidents, even routine ones. *Courtesy of Joe Marino.*

Discipline Procedures

Fire departments have discipline procedures for members who stray from the established rules or standard operating procedures. Disciplinary measures taken against an individual may vary depending on several of the following factors:

- The severity of the offense
- The number of occurrences for a specific offense
- The previous record of the individual
- Precedence on similar previous occurrences

The type of disciplinary actions taken also depends on the type of department. Paid departments have levels of action that start at a verbal warning and proceed through time off without pay or even termination. Volunteer departments may warn individuals, suspend them for a period of time, or terminate their membership.

Formal Communications

Communication is the exchange of ideas and information that conveys an intended meaning in a form that is understood. It involves messages being sent and understood. Yet, there are many barriers to effective communication.

The term used to describe the common organizational structure in the fire service is "scalar." Scalar is defined as "having an uninterrupted series of steps" or a "chain of authority." The scalar organization is a paramilitary, pyramid-type of organization with authority centralized at the top. Decisions are directed down from the top of the structure through intermediate levels to the base. Information in turn is transmitted up from the bottom through the structure to the positions at the top.

Due to the scalar organizational structure, each level of the organization acts as a filter that reduces the quality and quantity of information passed down. Many human factors affect the interpretation of the message, and oftentimes subordinates are reluctant to communicate upward with their superiors, especially if there is bad news to pass on. Verbal communication is not the most effective method for dissemination of information to the department on a large scale; therefore, there is a need for formal written communication. Policies and procedures are examples of "standing" or "repeat-use" plans designed to deal with the recurring problems of an organization. Formal communication of these policies and procedures in writing helps to ensure that the organizational objectives are met throughout all divisions of the department.

INCIDENT MANAGEMENT SYSTEMS

Confusion can cause personnel to work against each other instead of working against the fire. If a firefighter is confused about orders, he or she could hesitate in performing a specific duty at a vital time. For example, conflicting orders could cause personnel to open up the roof before interior crews are ready. Or, a lack of command could result in crews pushing the fire into unburned portions of the structure or, worse yet, into other crews. Coordination of all personnel at the scene is absolutely necessary for operations to be conducted safely. To avoid chaos and confusion at the emergency scene, a unifying system must be employed to establish roles and responsibilities.

Many systems exist throughout the nation for the command and control of resources at emergency incidents. The National Fire Academy (NFA) has adopted the Incident Command System (ICS) as its base for teaching the concepts of incident command. ICS is a system that is well documented and has been successfully used in managing available resources at a variety of emergency operations (Figure 5.18). The procedures will not fit all departments perfectly. The system does not need to be fully implemented for all situations the fire department encounters, especially for routine responses.

The system consists of procedures for controlling personnel, facilities, equipment, and communications. It is designed to expand as needed from the time an incident occurs until the requirements for management and operations no longer exist. The ICS should be staffed and operated by qualified personnel from any emergency services agency and may involve personnel from a variety of agencies.

The system can be used for any type or size of emergency, ranging from a minor incident involving a single unit to a major emergency involving several agencies. The Incident Command System allows agencies to communicate using common

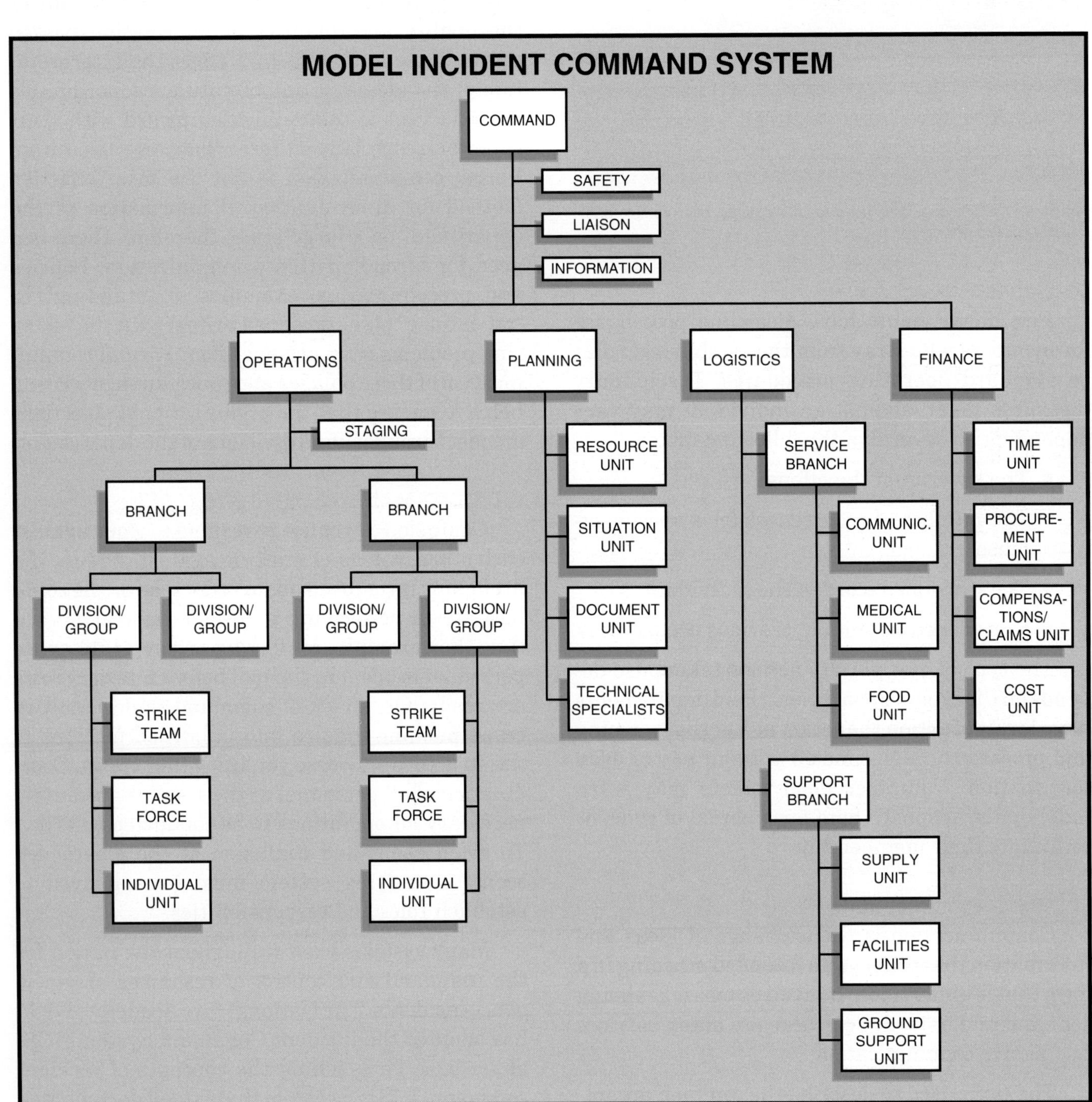

Figure 5.18 The basic incident command system chart.

terminology and operating procedures and allows for the timely combining of resources during an emergency.

Components Of The ICS

The Incident Command System has a number of components. The following interactive components provide the basis for an effective ICS operation:

- Common terminology
- Modular organization
- Integrated communications
- Unified command structure
- Consolidated action plans
- Manageable span of control
- Predesignated incident facilities
- Comprehensible resource management

Organization And Operations

All members of the department should be trained in the Incident Command System, and standard operating procedures should be designed in accordance with this system. This procedure enables personnel to know what is expected of them and what role and responsibilities they have at any given incident. The integration of SOPs with the five major functional areas of the ICS eliminates confusion at the emergency scene and helps operations run smoothly and safely. The five major functional areas of the Incident Command System are as follows (Figure 5.19):

- Command
- Operations
- Planning
- Logistics
- Finance

COMMAND

An operation cannot be implemented unless someone is in charge. The incident commander is in charge of the operation. Command is responsible for all incident activities, including the development and implementation of strategic decisions. The responsibility of incident activities also includes dealing with the results of these strategic decisions. Command is the authority over the ordering and releasing of resources. There may be a

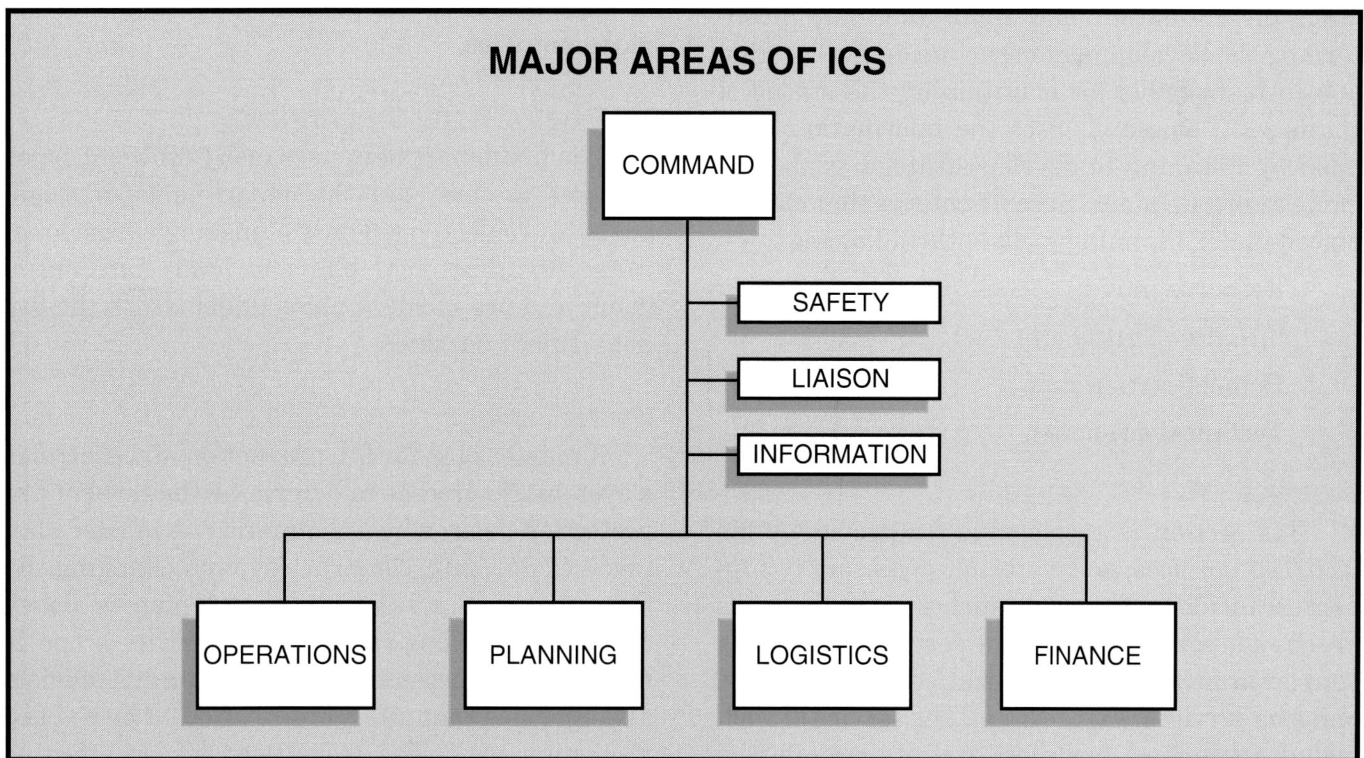

Figure 5.19 There are five major units within ICS.

limited number of staff positions within the command area such as the safety officer, liaison, and the public information officer.

OPERATIONS

This area is responsible for the management of all operations directly applicable to the primary mission. Its function is to direct the organization's tactical operations to meet the strategic goals developed by Command (Figure 5.20). Operations is divided into branches that may be further divided into groups or divisions. Groups are teams that are assigned to perform a particular task such as ventilation or rescue.

Figure 5.20 Command posts are used to control incidents.

PLANNING

This area is responsible for the collection, evaluation, dissemination, and use of information concerning the development of the incident. Planning is also responsible for maintaining the status of resources. Command uses the information compiled by Planning to develop strategic goals and make alternate plans. Specific entities that may be placed under Planning include the following:

- Resource unit
- Situation status unit
- Demobilization unit
- Technical specialist

LOGISTICS

This section is responsible for providing the facilities, services, and materials necessary to support the incident. The two branches within logistics are the support branch and the service branch. The support branch includes medical, communications, and food services (Figure 5.21). The service branch includes supplies, facilities, and ground support (vehicle services).

Figure 5.21 Canteen units provide food and drinks at extended incidents.

FINANCE

This area has the responsibility for all costs and financial aspects of the incident. Finances are generally of concern only at large-scale, long-term incidents.

Other Incident Management Systems

Other incident management systems exist and are in use throughout the fire service such as the Fireground Command System. Many individual departments have local systems that are unique. At the time this manual was written, a multiagency consortium was working toward a single system that could be adopted nationally. Firefighters must be well versed in the particular system their department uses.

FIRE DEPARTMENT PLANNING

The fire department uses many different types of plans to carry out the department's mission, goals, and objectives. These plans range from long-range organizational plans to immediate emergency and pre-incident plans under which the fire department operates.

Master Planning

A master plan for fire prevention and control is a systematic process to determine the level of fire protection desired by a community. A master plan involves devising, constructing, and changing the fire protection system. A master plan is policy oriented with long-range goals, and its scope is broad. The process involves community officials and agencies that affect or are affected by the fire protection plan. The steps used for an effective master plan are as follows:

Step 1: Analyze data.

Step 2: Identify options.

Step 3: Evaluate options.

Step 4: Propose program.

After completion, the plan becomes the management document that guides the implementation and evaluation of fire and emergency response programs.

Disaster Planning (Community Fire Defense Planning)

A disaster plan outlines the duties and areas of responsibilities for agencies that handle large-scale incidents (Figure 5.22). A disaster plan also defines roles and responsibilities and provides a predetermined course of action in the first operational period of a major disaster. Organizations accounted for in the disaster plan include, but are not limited to, police, fire, emergency medical services, emergency management agencies, Red Cross, National Guard, and other local service organizations.

Figure 5.22 Mock disaster incidents help prepare personnel for the real thing. *Courtesy of Ron Jeffers.*

Mutual Aid Planning

A mutual aid plan includes an agreed-upon method for requesting response and the level of response that will be supplied to neighboring agencies. Mutual aid is needed from neighboring agencies when a single agency does not have the equipment and personnel to control an emergency (Figure 5.23).

Figure 5.23 Some incidents involve massive mutual aid responses. Coordination of resources is essential on these incidents. *Courtesy of Bob Esposito.*

Automatic Aid Planning

An automatic aid plan is an agreement between neighboring agencies to have equipment and personnel that are closest to an emergency respond without regard to normal jurisdictional boundary lines. Typically, this results in a larger response than the original jurisdiction would be capable of providing.

Pre-Incident Planning

A pre-incident plan is the gathering of information on an occupancy, including the anticipated fire loading, fuels stored at the location, special hazards, life safety considerations, and other needed information (Figure 5.24). This information makes the size-up of an emergency go smoother and warns responders of potential hazards or special concerns. This plan lays out the course of actions for initial responders so that they may take positive steps to abate the emergency immediately.

Figure 5.24 Pre-incident planning is essential to fire operations.

INDUSTRIAL FIRE BRIGADES

In addition to the municipal fire department structure and organization, it is important for firefighters to realize the important role that industrial fire brigades play in the overall fire protection picture. The fire brigade is responsible for the primary response to emergencies at its facility. Depending on the organization of the brigade, fire brigade members may respond to fire, hazardous materials, and medical emergencies.

Each industrial location determines the level of fire protection it desires and the capabilities of its brigade. Small facilities with few hazards may have a small group of people who are trained only in incipient fire fighting procedures such as the use of portable fire extinguishers. Large industrial facilities, such as petrochemical plants or multibuilding manufacturing facilities, may have fully trained fire brigades with their own apparatus (Figures 5.25 a and b). Though most brigades are composed of employees from various disciplines within the facility, some large facilities have full-time fire fighting personnel.

Effective fire brigades help minimize emergency situations and reduce losses considerably. In many cases, they control the situation before the arrival of the municipal fire department. Larger brigades may respond to emergencies on their own and only call for the local fire department when additional aid is required.

Figure 5.25a Many industrial sites have their own emergency apparatus. *Courtesy of Ron Jeffers.*

Figure 5.25b An industrial fire apparatus. *Courtesy of Joel Woods.*

An effective brigade has to be well planned, well organized, and well trained. Top management must give extensive financial and administrative support. The chief and officers should be well qualified and knowledgeable of all operations within the plant. Fire brigade members should be trained to the level to which they are expected to perform, and they must be willing to take on extra work. It takes all of these things to have a successful fire brigade; any deficiency may result in failure.

Fire Brigade Responsibilities

The following list contains examples of activities for which fire brigades are normally responsible.

- Preventing fires and eliminating hazards
- Seeing that all fire fighting and safety equipment is properly maintained and available for immediate use (Figure 5.26)

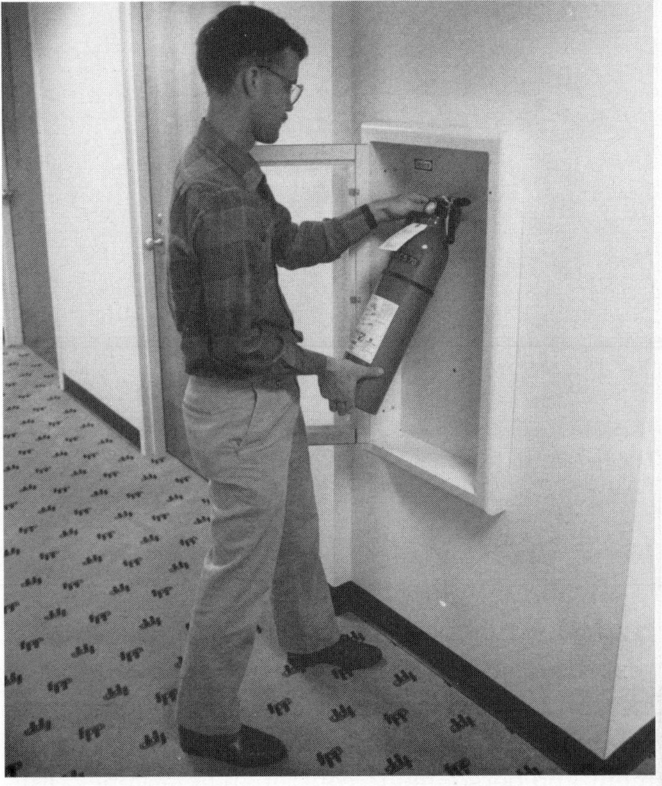

Figure 5.26 Fire brigade members may be responsible for the upkeep of on-site fire equipment.

- Assisting department managers in training employees in fire prevention, safety, and proper use of first aid fire equipment
- Responding to and handling all fire alarms and reports of fires
- Handling other emergency situations such as bomb threats, hazardous materials incidents, and medical emergencies
- Coordinating plant emergency operations with the local fire department

Organizational Structure

Developing a suitable fire brigade organizational structure is important. There is no one organizational structure suitable for all industrial plants. The number of brigade members, the assigned brigade responsibilities, and the plant's physical characteristics make each organizational plan unique (Figures 5.27 and 5.28). Each plant must choose an organizational structure that will work best for its operation and accomplish its objectives and responsibilities. The organization

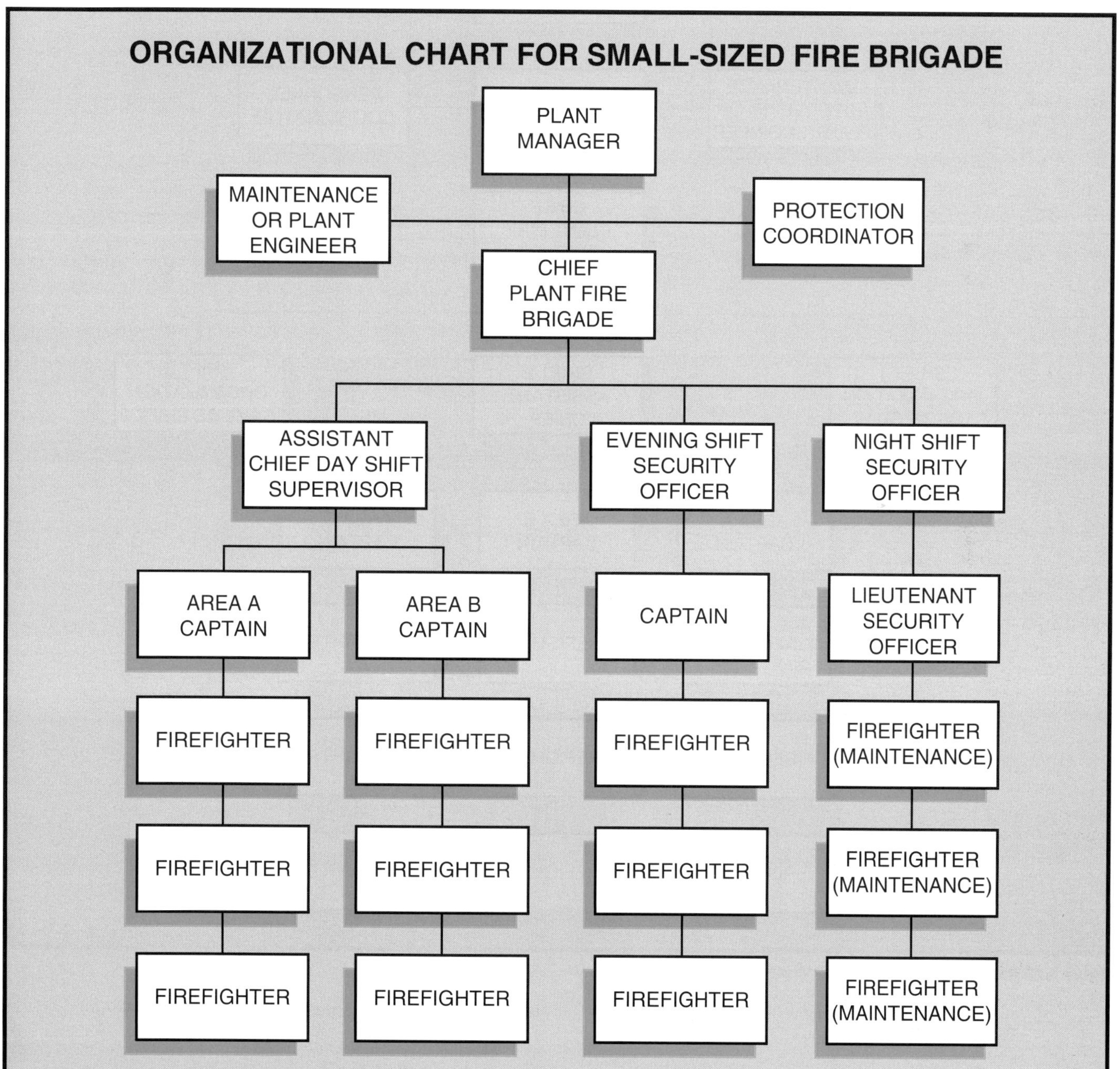

Figure 5.27 A small fire brigade organizational chart.

must also provide protection during all shifts, weekends, and holidays. Coordination with the local fire department is essential.

Because the interface between the fire brigade and the local fire department is very important, each should be familiar with the other's capabilities and standard operating procedures. Joint training sessions may be held to acquaint line personnel with each other. These exercises are beneficial during emergency situations when both agencies will be working together. For more information on fire brigades, see IFSTA's **Industrial Fire Protection** manual.

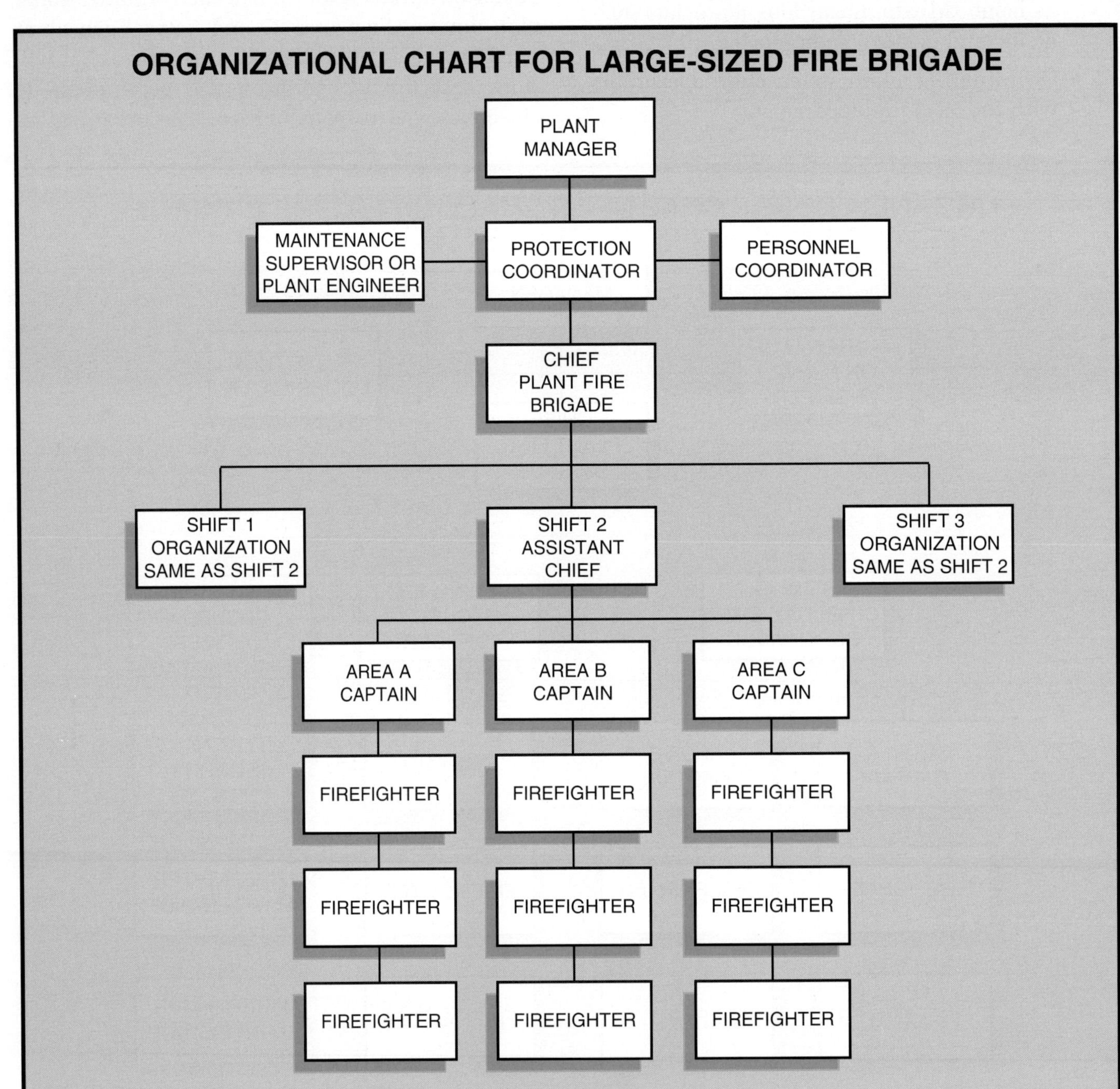

Figure 5.28 A large fire brigade organizational chart.

Chapter 5
Application And Review Activities

DIRECTIONS

The following activities are designed to help you comprehend and apply the information in Chapter 5 of **Orientation and Terminology**. To receive the maximum learning experience from these activities, it is recommended that you use the following procedure:

1. Read the chapter, underlining or highlighting important terms, topics, and subject matter. Study the photographs and illustrations, and read the captions under each.
2. Review the list of vocabulary words to ensure that you know the chapter-related meaning of each. If you are unsure of the meaning of a vocabulary word, look the word up in a dictionary, and then study its context in the chapter.

   NOTE: Some words have different meanings as different parts of speech. Abbreviations after certain words stand for the part of speech (v., verb; n., noun; adj., adjective; adv., adverb) of the word as it is used in the chapter.
3. On a separate sheet of paper, complete all assigned or selected application and review activities before checking your answers.
4. After you have finished, check your answers against those on the pages referenced in parentheses.
5. Correct any incorrect answers, and review material that was answered incorrectly.

VOCABULARY

Be sure that you know the chapter-related meanings of the following terms.

- Allocate *(102)*
- Autonomous *(102)*
- Breach *(100)*
- Cadre *(101)*
- Consortium *(110)*
- Discipline *(95)*
- Entity *(110)*
- Exposure (n.) *(106)*
- Implement (v.) *(104)*
- Incipient *(112)*
- Inherent *(101)*
- Jurisdiction *(111)*
- Overhaul *(106)*
- Platoon *(103)*
- Revenue *(102)*
- Salvage *(106)*
- Sector *(102)*
- Strategic *(109)*

APPLICATION OF KNOWLEDGE

1. Draw an organizational chart representative of your fire department. *(Local protocol)*
2. Examine the workings of your fire department. Does it adhere to the principles of unity of command, span of control, and division of labor? Explain. *(Local protocol)*

3. Describe the local government structure in your municipality. Use actual names as well as descriptive titles. Describe also the type of funding your department receives. *(Local protocol)*

4. List at least four of your department rules and regulations in regard to each of the following: *(Local protocol)*
   - Dress
   - Conduct
   - Shifts
   - Discipline
   - Standard operating procedures

REVIEW ACTIVITIES

1. Describe an organizational chart. *(95)*

2. Define *unity of command*, and provide an example to support your definition. *(95)*

3. Explain what is meant by a breach in unity of command. *(100)*

4. Define *span of control,* and provide an example to support your definition. *(100)*

5. Define *division of labor*, and provide an example to support your definition. *(100)*

6. List three reasons for the necessity of division of labor in the fire service. *(100)*

7. Explain why firefighters should be familiar with the structure of their local governments. *(100)*

8. Describe the Commission form of local government. *(100)*

9. Explain the differences between legislative versus executive functions in a city commission. *(100)*

10. Describe the Council (Board) Manager form of local government. *(100)*

11. Describe the Mayor/Council form of local government. *(101)*

12. Explain how communities determine what is an adequate level of fire protection at a reasonable community cost. *(101)*

13. Explain how fire service is furnished to the branches of the U.S. military and to U.S. national parks and forests. *(101)*

14. Briefly compare and contrast each of the following types of fire departments:
    - Paid department *(101)*
    - Volunteer department *(101)*
    - Paid-call department *(101)*
    - Combination department *(101)*

15. List and explain factors that affect the type of fire department used by any given municipality. *(101)*

16. Explain how a municipality-funded fire department obtains money for its operating budget. *(102)*

17. Explain how an independently funded department obtains money for its operating budget. *(102)*

18. Define *private sector fire department*, and describe how it obtains money for its operating budget. *(102)*

19. Outline the most common work schedules for the following systems:
    - Two-platoon system *(103)*
    - Three-platoon system *(103)*
    - Four-platoon system *(103)*

20. Define *policy*. *(103)*

21. Define *procedure*. *(104)*

22. Distinguish among orders, directives, and requests. *(104)*

23. Describe common fire service uniform and dress regulations in the following areas:
    - Dress uniforms *(105)*
    - Station work clothing *(105)*
    - Emergency response dress *(106)*

24. List several rules of conduct common to most fire departments. *(106)*

25. Define and explain *standard operating procedure (SOP)*. *(106)*

26. List the commonly accepted order of fireground priorities. *(106)*

27. List the primary factors on which fire service disciplinary action is based. *(107)*

28. Compare and contrast the disciplinary action taken by paid departments and that taken by volunteer departments. *(107)*

29. Define *communication*. *(107)*

30. Define *scalar,* and explain fire department scalar organizational structure. *(107)*

31. Explain the need for a unifying system at the emergency scene. *(107)*

32. List the components of a typical incident management system. *(108)*

33. Identify the responsibilities of each of the following incident command areas:
    - Command *(109)*
    - Operations *(110)*
    - Planning *(110)*
    - Logistics *(110)*
    - Finance *(110)*

34. Define each of the following plans:
    - Master plan *(110)*
    - Disaster plan *(111)*
    - Mutual aid plan *(111)*
    - Automatic aid plan *(111)*
    - Pre-incident plan *(111)*

35. Describe the organization and responsibilities of a typical industrial fire brigade. *(112-114)*

6
Roles Of Fire Department Personnel

Chapter 6
Roles of Fire Department Personnel

From a distance, the responsibility of a fire department — to put out fires — seems simple. At closer inspection, however, things become more complicated. Many questions, such as the following, are raised:

- Who is in command?
- Who drives the truck?
- Who buys equipment?

These questions are only a minute sampling of the details that must be handled in operating a fire department. New firefighters will see sides of the fire service the public never sees. They will realize there is more to a fire department than "putting out fires." They will also realize that roles exist for fire department personnel other than riding the apparatus, pulling hoselines, or raising ladders. This chapter will cover many of the common roles found within the fire service. Depending on local requirements and customs, additional specialized personnel may be used. The duties and requirements of these positions will vary depending on local needs and procedures.

FIRE SUPPRESSION (OPERATIONS) PERSONNEL

The primary mission of the fire service is fire prevention. When all else fails and a fire starts, it is the job of the fire department to extinguish it (Figure 6.1). As fire departments have improved over time, they have learned that certain objectives must be accomplished in a coordinated manner for successful fire fighting. These objectives are:

- Rescue
- Exposure protection
- Fire confinement

Figure 6.1 Suppression forces handle fire incidents. *Courtesy of Harvey Eisner.*

- Fire extinguishment
- Salvage and overhaul
- Fire cause determination

Conducting these operations are the primary objectives of suppression personnel. By accomplishing these objectives, firefighters can control fire.

The intent of this section is to present a detailed description of the following positions among fire suppression personnel:

- Firefighter
- Fire apparatus driver/operator
- Company officer
- Battalion or district chief
- Safety officer
- Public information officer
- Assistant or deputy chief
- Fire chief

Before discussing the personnel positions, the fire company will be addressed. This section outlines its organization and the roles of different types of companies.

Fire Companies

The standard operating unit of a fire department is the "company." A company consists of a group of firefighters assigned to a particular piece of fire apparatus. The number of personnel varies depending upon:

- The type of company
- The size of apparatus
- The number of personnel available

A company consists of a company officer, a driver/operator, and one or more firefighters (Figure 6.2).

A fire company is organized, equipped, and trained for a definite function. The functions and duties of a fire company of the same type may vary in different localities because of the inherent hazards of the area, the size of the department, and the scope of the department's activities. A small fire department may have only one fire company to carry out the functions that would normally be performed by several companies in a larger city. A group of fire companies assigned to work together constitutes a task force (assorted types of units) or strike team (a group of similar units). Apparatus and assigned groups have considerable influence on how, when, and where each company operates. The type of apparatus and equipment corresponds to the purpose and duty of the fire company. The following general descriptions of fire companies illustrate how they are organized and how they operate.

THE ENGINE COMPANY

The basic role of the engine company in structural fire fighting is to deploy hoselines for fire attack and exposure protection. This may be accomplished by stretching and operating hoselines into structures, operating portable master stream devices from outside the structure, or supplying water to aerial apparatus operating elevated master stream devices (Figure 6.3). While engine company members may also perform rescue, forcible entry, or other functions while preparing to make a fire attack, these are not typically their responsibilities.

The engine company is responsible for the pri-

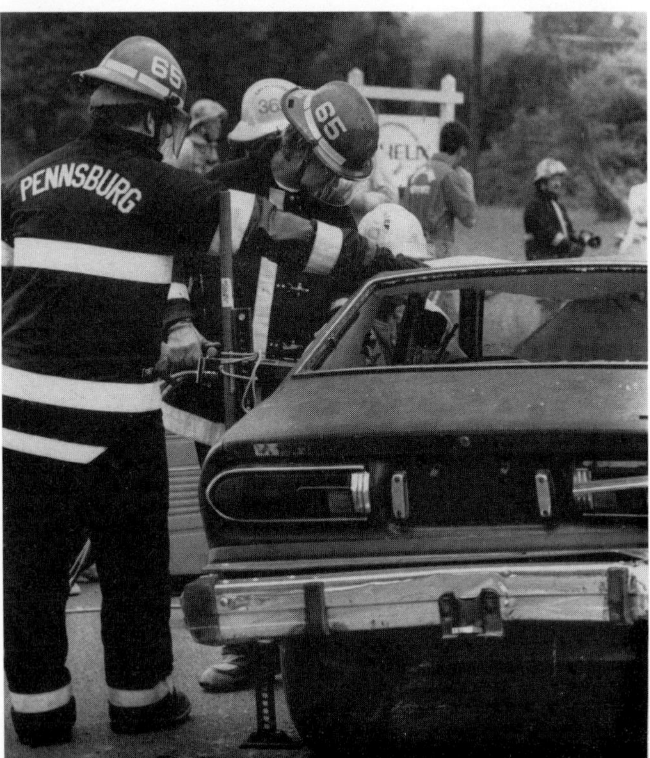

Figure 6.2 The members of a company work together at all times. *Courtesy of Bob Esposito.*

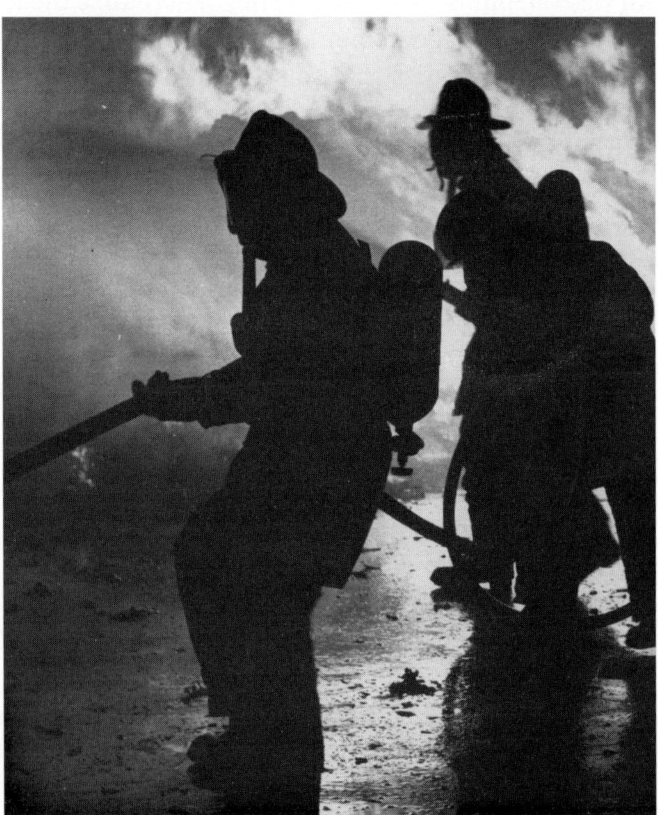

Figure 6.3 Engine companies put water on the fire. *Courtesy of Joe Marino.*

mary fire attack on nonstructural fires such as automobiles, trash dumpsters, and natural cover fires. Depending on local policies, the engine company may also respond to medical emergencies, accidents, and citizen assist calls.

THE TRUCK COMPANY

The role of the truck (ladder) company in structural fire fighting is to perform forcible entry, search and rescue, ventilation, salvage and overhaul, and provide access to upper levels (Figure 6.4). In many cases, it is necessary for the truck company to perform two of these functions simultaneously. This necessitates splitting the crew to handle the various jobs. Truck companies place ground ladders in addition to the apparatus's main aerial device. The truck company may also be required to operate an elevated master stream for fire attack or exposure protection (Figure 6.5).

In some municipalities, the truck company responds to medical emergencies and citizen assist calls. Because the aerial apparatus has a large amount of compartmentation, many departments have the truck company carry rescue equipment and perform rescue operations such as vehicle extrications and cave-in rescues or recoveries.

THE RESCUE/SQUAD COMPANY

The role of the rescue or squad company varies from department to department. Typically, its primary responsibility is the removal of victims from areas of danger or entrapment (Figure 6.6). This includes vehicle extrications, industrial and agricultural extrications, trench and structural collapse rescues, and high-angle (rope) rescues. Frequently, the rescue company is assigned to respond on structural fires as well. The duties of the rescue company on the fireground vary depending on departmental procedures and what is needed at the scene. Many times the rescue company assists engine or truck companies, performs first aid on victims, refills air cylinders, provides floodlighting, or performs other duties.

Figure 6.4 One of the duties of a truck company is to perform forcible entry. *Courtesy of Bob Esposito.*

Figure 6.5 Elevated master streams are used to control large fires. *Courtesy of Ron Jeffers.*

Figure 6.6 Rescue companies perform a myriad of rescues.

The Firefighter

Fire fighting requires skill in combating, extinguishing, and preventing fires; answering emergency calls; and operating and maintaining fire department equipment, apparatus, and quarters. The work involves extensive training in performing fire fighting and rescue activities. Firefighters are required to learn and participate in operating apparatus and performing hazardous tasks under emergency conditions, all of which require strenuous exertion with handicaps such as smoke and cramped surroundings (Figure 6.7). Although fire fighting and rescue work are the most difficult and

Figure 6.7 Firefighters work under strenuous conditions. *Courtesy of Bob Esposito.*

responsible areas of work, a significant portion of time is spent doing inspections, training, and performing station duties. The following are some of the typical duties of a firefighter:

- Attend training courses; read and study assigned materials related to fire fighting and fire prevention.
- Respond to fire alarms with the company, operate fire fighting equipment, lay and connect hose, maneuver nozzles and direct fire streams, raise and climb ladders, and use extinguishers and all fire fighting hand tools.
- Ventilate burning buildings by opening windows and skylights or by cutting holes in roofs or floors.
- Remove people from danger and administer first aid.
- Perform salvage operations, which include placing salvage covers, sweeping water, and removing debris.
- Complete overhaul operations with the goal of ensuring total fire extinguishment (Figure 6.8).
- Relay instructions, orders, and information and give locations of alarms received from the dispatcher.
- Exercise precautions to avoid injury while performing duties.

Figure 6.8 Overhaul is one task that firefighters must complete on the fire scene. *Courtesy of Joe Marino.*

- Exercise precautions to avoid unnecessary damage to or loss of property.
- Ensure safekeeping and proper care of all fire department property.
- Perform assigned fire inspections and checks of buildings and structures for compliance with fire prevention ordinances.

In addition to specific duties, firefighters are expected to adhere to the following rules of conduct:

- Be ready to perform duties and not be absent from duty without specific permission from the company officer.
- Be obedient, respectful, and courteous to superiors and to those performing duties of higher rank.
- Be respectful and courteous to the general public.

Being a firefighter demands an individual who

can perform many functions. A firefighter needs to have certain knowledge and skills that allow him or her to function effectively in the position. For the firefighter to function effectively, he or she is required to meet the following requirements:

- Meet the requirements set forth in NFPA 1001, *Standard for Fire Fighter Professional Qualifications.*
- Know department organization, operation, and procedures.
- Know the district or city street system and physical layout.
- Meet minimum health and physical fitness standards.
- Climb ladders and work at considerable heights.
- Learn a wide variety of fire fighting and rescue duties within a reasonable working test period.
- Establish and maintain effective working relationships with other employees and the general public.
- Understand and follow oral and written instructions.

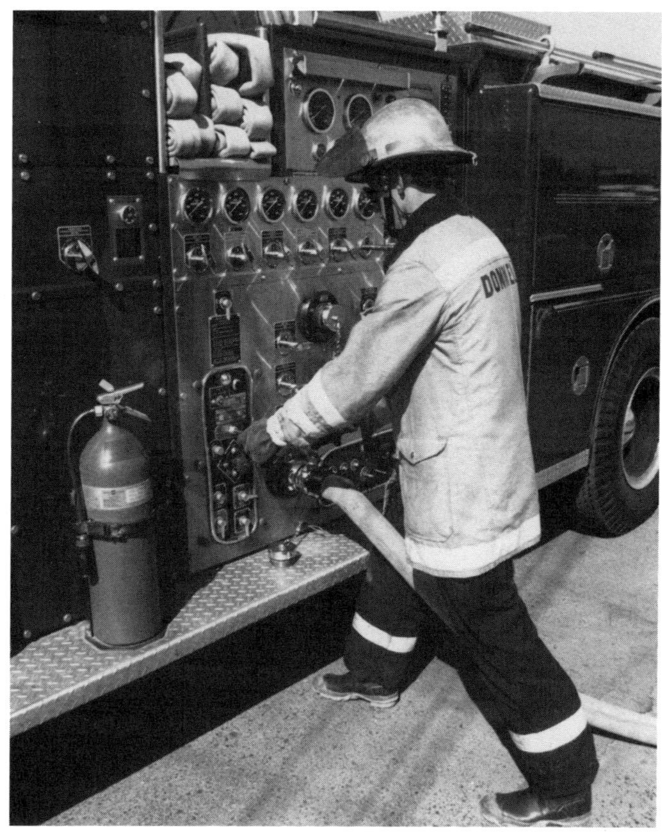

Figure 6.9 Driver/operators must be proficient in pump operations.

The Fire Apparatus Driver/Operator

Operating mechanical apparatus and equipment is skilled fire fighting work. A driver/operator has the responsibilities of a firefighter and the additional general duties related to the care and use of departmental equipment and property. A driver/operator is responsible for safely driving assigned fire apparatus to and from fire and emergency scenes and for operating pumps, aerial devices, or other mechanical equipment as required (Figure 6.9). Work usually is performed under the direction of a company officer and is reviewed by observation. The driver/operator position is typically the first level of promotion in the fire department's organizational chain. A driver/operator is expected to perform the following duties:

- Drive assigned fire fighting apparatus to and from emergencies or other assigned activities; operate its pumps, aerial device, and other mechanical equipment as required (Figure 6.10); and keep inventory of tools and equipment on the apparatus.
- Clean and service the assigned apparatus,

Figure 6.10 The driver/operator must understand the limitations of the aerial device.

keep the apparatus ready, report mechanical failures or difficulties to the proper person, and help the department's mechanic make minor apparatus repairs.

- Perform general fire fighting duties as assigned and participate in company inspections.
- Perform assigned housekeeping duties at the fire station.
- Attend appropriate training sessions and instruct relief driver in equipment operation.
- Act in a supervisory capacity over the company in the absence of the company officer.

A fire apparatus driver/operator is one of the most important members of the company. Because of his or her position, an operator must be trained to a higher level than a firefighter. To be eligible for the apparatus driver/operator position, a firefighter must meet the following requirements:

- Meet the requirements for Fire Fighter I in NFPA 1001 and the appropriate requirements contained in NFPA 1002, *Standard for Fire Apparatus Driver/Operator Professional Qualifications.*
- Be legally licensed within the state or province to operate heavy vehicles.
- Know the location of streets, fire alarm boxes, and fire hydrants and know the types of building construction in the district.
- Know the mechanical principles involved in operating fire apparatus and allied equipment.
- Know the rules and regulations of the fire department.
- Know modern fire fighting, fire prevention practices, and first aid.
- Understand and follow oral and written instructions, react quickly in emergencies, and display proper judgment in making work decisions.
- Make quick, mental mathematical calculations.
- Establish and maintain effective working relationships with other employees and the general public.
- Operate mechanical and automotive fire equipment.

For more information on fire apparatus driver/operators, see the IFSTA **Fire Department Pumping Apparatus** and **Fire Department Aerial Apparatus** manuals.

The Company Officer

The company officer supervises a fire company in the station and at the fire scene (Figure 6.11). The authority for this position is delegated from the chief officer. The work involves responsibility for proper maintenance and operation of the fire station and fire fighting equipment.

The company officer performs a wide variety of fire fighting and related duties, including inspections of equipment, personnel, and public buildings. Routine duties are performed with independence within established regulations but under the general direction of a chief officer. The company officer is evaluated by observation of work in progress, by results obtained, and by inspections of

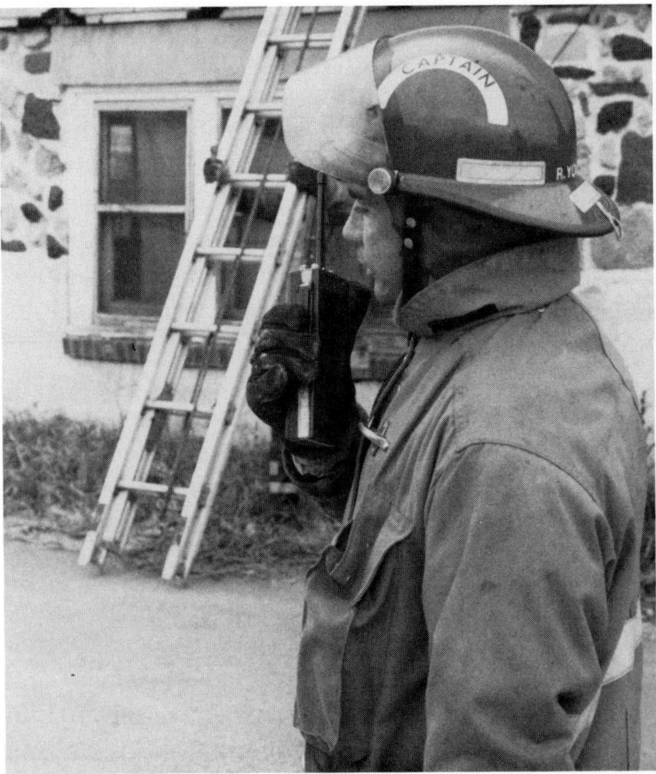

Figure 6.11 Company officers have supervisory responsibilities on the fireground.

quarters and equipment. Depending on the structure of the fire department, the company officer holds the rank of lieutenant, captain, major, or a similar title. A company officer is expected to perform the following duties:

- Respond to all fire and emergency alarms assigned to the company, advise the driver/operator on the route to follow, evaluate the scene conditions, and direct the company's initial actions.
- Direct and assist subordinates at the emergency scene and at the station unless command is assumed by a chief officer.
- Inspect conditions at the fire scene to prevent reignition.
- Inspect apparatus, equipment, grounds, and station to ensure proper order and condition.
- Inspect public buildings, businesses, hospitals, schools, and places of public assembly for fire hazards or conditions dangerous to life and property; give fire prevention talks; and assist in fire cause determination.
- Prepare and conduct employee training courses using lectures, practice sessions, and demonstrations; test methods of teaching; and perform special duties in the training school.
- Perform clerical work (Figure 6.12); report on fires, personnel absences, and company activities; and prepare requisitions for supplies.

The job requirements for company officers are extensive because of their tremendous responsibilities. Because the company officer is the leader, expectations of the person in this position are extremely high. Many fire service leaders view the company officer as the most important cog in the fire department's wheel of success. A company officer must have the following qualifications:

- Ability to meet the appropriate requirements in NFPA 1021, *Standard for Fire Officer Professional Qualifications*
- Considerable knowledge of streets, principal buildings, fire hydrants, and fire alarm boxes in the city
- Considerable knowledge of the principles and practices of fire fighting, fire prevention, and first aid and the ability to apply them

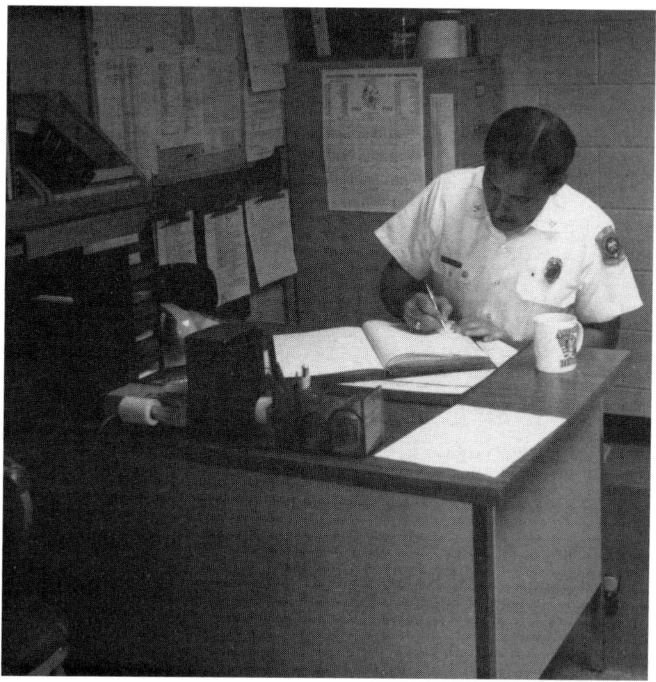

Figure 6.12 Company officers must fill out reports on incidents.

- Ability to evaluate emergency situations, recognize danger, and take immediate action to protect life and property
- Ability to inspect buildings, recognize and determine fire or other hazardous conditions, and make written and oral reports of such conditions with recommendations for their correction
- Ability to establish and maintain effective working relationships with other employees and the general public

For more information on the role of a company officer, refer to the IFSTA **Fire Department Company Officer** manual.

The Battalion/District Chief

The role of the battalion or district chief (referred to herein as the battalion chief) varies depending on the size of the fire department. In small departments, the battalion chief may actually be the shift commander in charge of all duty crews. For the purpose of this section, a battalion chief is the first level of chief officer in a large department. The battalion chief is assigned the responsibility of supervising a group of fire companies in a specified geographical region of the city (Figure 6.13). Typically, each battalion chief supervises 5 to 10 companies. In many departments, the battalion chief responds to incidents that require the response of three or more companies. A battalion chief is required to perform the following duties:

- Supervise all fire fighting and rescue activities within the battalion during an assigned tour of duty, review records and reports of operations, and take appropriate corrective action when required (Figure 6.14).
- Inspect fire stations, equipment, and apparatus and make recommendations or issue orders to comply with established standards of appearance and condition.
- Provide direction to the company officers of that battalion and handle administrative or personnel matters when required.
- Provide assistance to other battalion chiefs in the event of a multiple-alarm emergency in their district.
- Assist higher chief officers with special projects and requests for help or information when required.

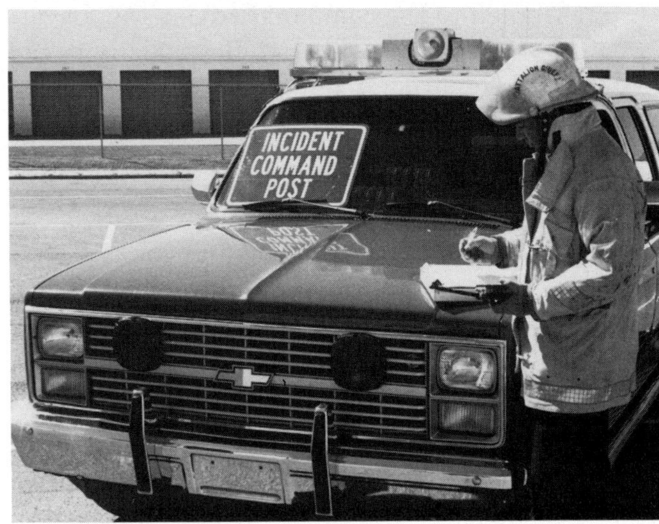

Figure 6.14 The battalion chief may take over command of an incident from company officers.

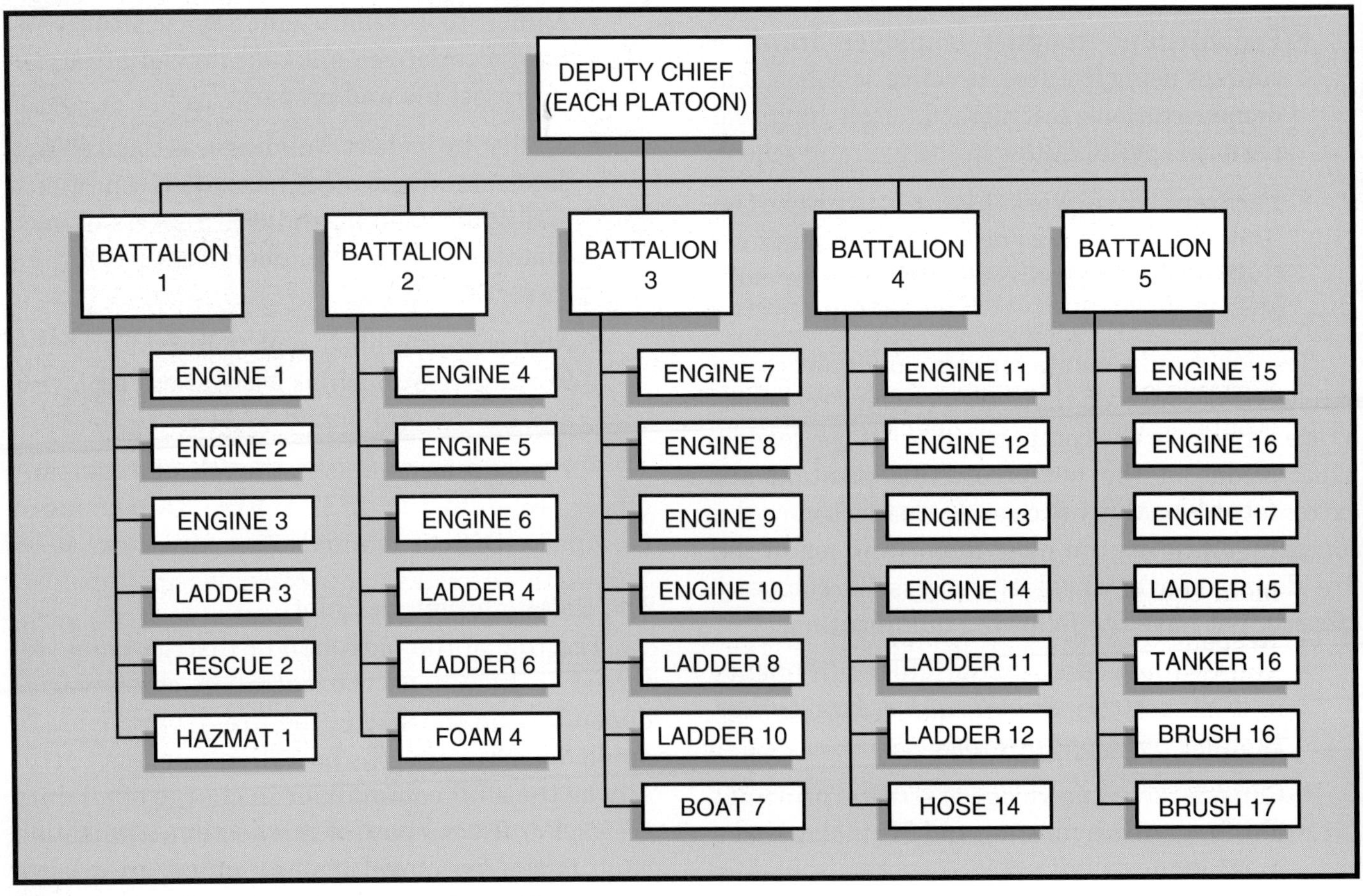

DEPUTY CHIEF (EACH PLATOON)

BATTALION 1	BATTALION 2	BATTALION 3	BATTALION 4	BATTALION 5
ENGINE 1	ENGINE 4	ENGINE 7	ENGINE 11	ENGINE 15
ENGINE 2	ENGINE 5	ENGINE 8	ENGINE 12	ENGINE 16
ENGINE 3	ENGINE 6	ENGINE 9	ENGINE 13	ENGINE 17
LADDER 3	LADDER 4	ENGINE 10	ENGINE 14	LADDER 15
RESCUE 2	LADDER 6	LADDER 8	LADDER 11	TANKER 16
HAZMAT 1	FOAM 4	LADDER 10	LADDER 12	BRUSH 16
		BOAT 7	HOSE 14	BRUSH 17

Figure 6.13 Battalion chiefs supervise a group of companies.

Because the battalion chief is the first level of chief officer, the person holding this position must have exemplary technical and administrative skills. A battalion chief must have the following qualifications:

- Ability to meet the appropriate requirements in NFPA 1021, *Standard for Fire Officer Professional Qualifications*
- Ability to evaluate fires, recognize danger, use sound judgment, and react calmly in emergencies
- Thorough knowledge of fire fighting and rescue tactics and strategy; ability to organize the emergency scene through the use of the department's incident management system
- Extensive knowledge of the rules and regulations of the fire department; geography of the city; location of streets; and the nature and location of hazardous premises, principal buildings, fire hydrants, and fire alarm boxes in the city

The Safety Officer

The safety officer is the individual charged with overseeing a fire department's occupational safety and health program. Depending on the department, this individual may hold the rank of company officer or battalion chief, or this individual could be a civilian employee. The safety officer must be well respected, compassionate, and able to work effectively with all members of the department from the fire chief on down the line. The safety officer is required to perform the following duties:

- Formulate and administer the department's occupational safety and health program.
- Maintain an accident investigation and record-keeping system (Figure 6.15).
- Coordinate safety inspections of all department equipment, apparatus, and facilities.
- Respond to emergency incidents to view operations with the goal of maintaining crew safety; coordinate with the incident commander, and stop or modify operations when serious safety concerns arise (Figure 6.16).
- Perform research and provide recommendations on new equipment, apparatus, and facilities in relation to safety issues.

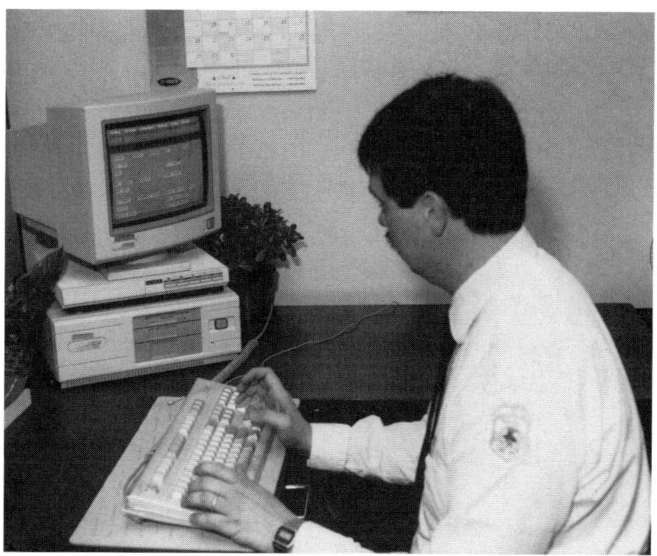

Figure 6.15 The safety officer may use a computer to keep records and statistics.

Figure 6.16 On the emergency scene, the safety officer serves as an advisor to the incident commander.

Because the safety officer has a variety of duties, there are a variety of skills required of him or her. The safety officer must have the following qualifications:

- Ability to meet the requirements established by NFPA 1521, *Standard for Fire Department Safety Officer*
- Extensive knowledge of emergency operations, building construction, hazardous materials, and incident management

- Ability to effectively communicate with members at all levels of the department
- Ability to carry out research projects, document results, and maintain an effective record-keeping system

For more information on the role of a safety officer, see the IFSTA **Fire Department Occupational Safety** manual.

The Public Information Officer

The public information officer (PIO) is responsible for maintaining a positive relationship between the fire department and the media. The PIO is also responsible for maintaining a positive relationship between the fire department and the general public. Depending on the department, this individual may hold the rank of company officer or battalion chief, or the individual could be a civilian employee. The PIO is required to perform the following duties:

- Coordinate all departmental news releases and public service announcements, acting as a contact source for media representatives.
- Respond to major emergency incidents to act as a liaison between the incident commander and the news media (Figure 6.17).

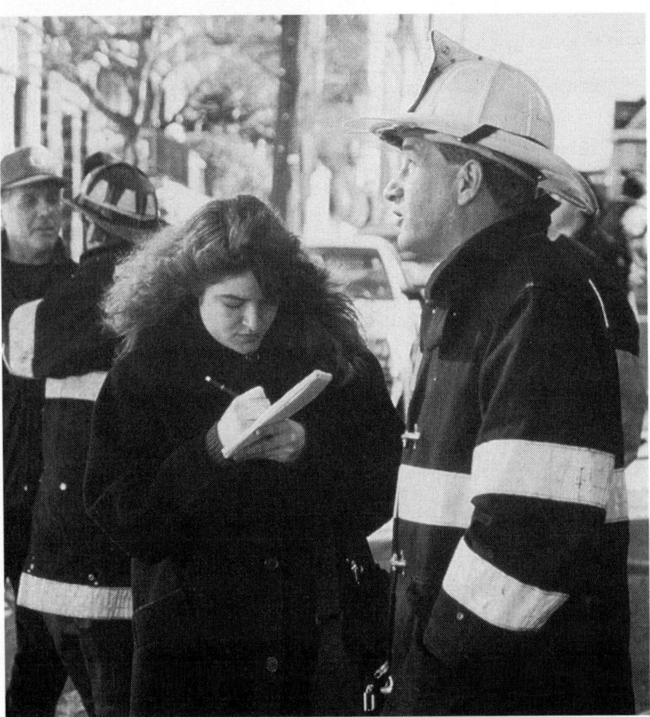

Figure 6.17 The public information officer acts as a liaison between the incident commander and the media. *Courtesy of Ron Jeffers.*

- Serve as a departmental spokesperson before neighborhood, civic, and other groups.

Because the PIO is often the only direct view that the public has of the fire department, it is important that he or she have the following qualifications:

- Ability to effectively convey information to the media and the general public, often without a script or adequate preparation
- Ability to discriminate between information that can be released and information that should not be released
- Ability to maintain excellent rapport with all members of the fire department, news media, and general public
- Ability to communicate well in a written format

The Assistant/Deputy Chief

Fire departments usually have one or more assistant/ deputy chiefs, referred to herein as assistant chiefs. These titles are used interchangeably from department to department. An assistant chief is part of the fire department senior management staff. Typically, a fire department has several assistant chiefs, each one assigned a specific function or portion of the department to manage. Some of the roles assigned to an assistant chief include operations, personnel/administration, fire prevention, resources, and planning (Figure 6.18). The assistant chief is expected to perform the following duties:

- Supervise the operation of the division of the department to which he or she is assigned.
- Respond to major emergency incidents, when required, and assist in the command structure as needed.
- Provide input to or carry out the major administrative duties of the fire department. This includes activities such as budgeting, policy development, research and planning, personnel matters, and public relations.
- Assume the duties of the fire chief when required.

To successfully complete the duties of an assistant chief, the individual needs to have a wide

- FIRE CHIEF
  - ADMINISTRATIVE ASSISTANT
  - EXECUTIVE ASSISTANT CHIEF
    - ASST. CHIEF TRAINING
      - BATTALION CHIEF
        - INSTRUCTIONAL STAFF
    - ASST. CHIEF PERSONNEL/ ADMINISTRATION
      - BUDGET
      - RECORDS
      - RESEARCH
      - ACCOUNTING
    - ASSISTANT CHIEF OPERATIONS
      - DEPUTY CHIEF (EACH PLATOON)
    - ASSISTANT CHIEF/ FIRE MARSHAL
      - FIRE PROTECTION ENGINEERS
      - INSPECTION STAFF
      - PUBLIC EDUCATION
    - ASST. CHIEF RESOURCES & COMMUNICATION
      - MAINTENANCE SHOP
      - DISPATCH CENTER
      - RESEARCH AND PLANNING

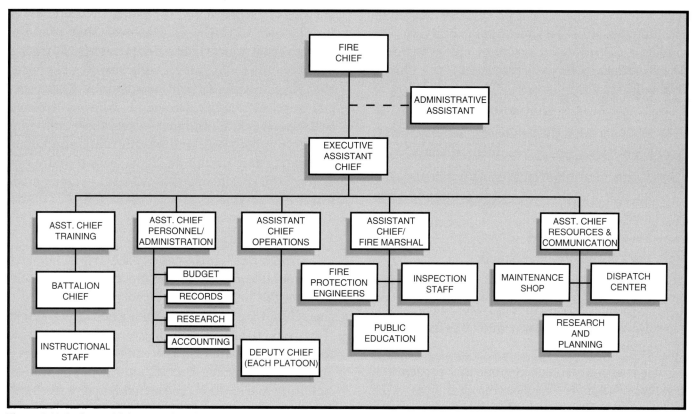

Figure 6.18 Assistant chiefs are assigned to various functions within the fire department.

variety of personal and professional abilities. The assistant chief must have the following qualifications:

- Ability to meet the appropriate requirements in NFPA 1021, *Standard for Fire Officer Professional Qualifications*
- A college degree or some education above the high school level
- Extensive knowledge of the fire department's administrative structure and process
- Excellent written and oral communication skills
- Thorough knowledge of fire fighting and rescue tactics and strategy; ability to organize the emergency scene through the use of the department's incident management system

The IFSTA **Chief Officer** manual provides more information on the job and requirements for chief officers.

The Fire Chief

The fire chief is the chief executive officer of the fire department (Figure 6.19). The fire chief is ultimately responsible for all operations within the fire department. In turn, the fire chief is responsible to the city manager, mayor, council, district board members, and the members of the fire department. Although the responsibilities remain the same, the activities of the fire chief vary depending on the size of the fire department. In small

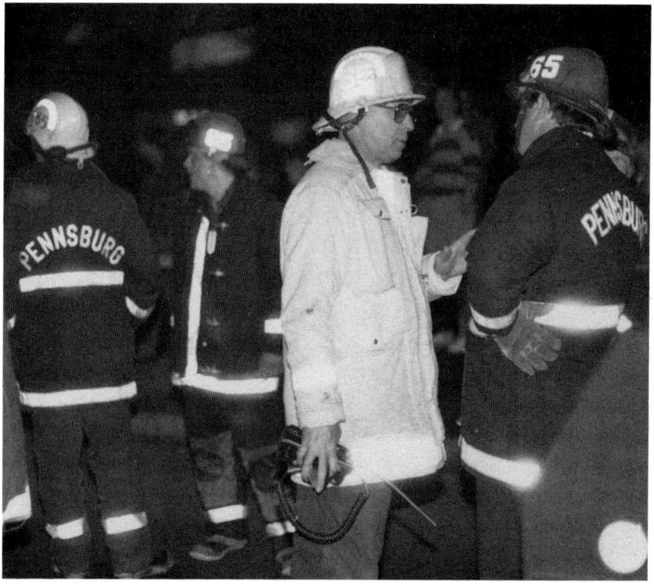

Figure 6.19 The fire chief may respond to and take command of large incidents. *Courtesy of Pennsburg (PA) Fire-Rescue.*

departments, the fire chief has a close interaction with line personnel and may handle functions that would be delegated to assistant chiefs in larger departments. In large departments, the chief is primarily an administrator. The fire chief is expected to perform the following duties:

- Interact with the heads of other city departments and local government officials.
- Respond to major emergency incidents, when required, and assist in the command structure as needed.
- Provide leadership and direction to all members of the fire department.
- Participate directly in the city or county budgeting process.
- Develop policy, plans, and objectives for the department.

The position of fire chief is one that presents the greatest challenge. To meet this challenge, a person must be fully prepared for the job. Some of the requirements for the fire chief are listed below.

- Ability to meet the appropriate requirements in NFPA 1021, *Standard for Fire Officer Professional Qualifications*
- A college degree or some education above the high school level
- Extensive knowledge of the fire department's administrative structure and process
- Excellent written and oral communication skills
- Thorough knowledge of fire fighting and rescue tactics and strategy; ability to organize the emergency scene through the use of the department's incident management system
- Ability to deal with local government officials and processes
- Labor negotiations skills

The IFSTA **Chief Officer** manual provides more information on the job and requirements for chief officers.

SPECIAL OPERATIONS PERSONNEL

If fire departments only provided standard structural fire protection to their communities, the line positions discussed to this point in the chapter would cover all the bases. However, this is not the case in most modern fire departments. Most fire departments today have a wide variety of services that they provide to their jurisdictions. These special services require personnel who are trained with special skills. In many cases, these individuals serve as both regular firefighters and specialists in a particular discipline. This section addresses some of the special operations found in many modern fire departments.

The Airport Firefighter

Airport fire fighting and rescue work involves responsibility for protecting life and property, controlling fire hazards, and performing general duties related to airport operations and aircraft safety (Figure 6.20). Airport firefighters are responsible for driving fire apparatus to and from fire scenes, standing by during aircraft emergency landings, handling fuel spills on the airfield, and performing fire fighting and rescue procedures on downed aircraft. In some cases, airport firefighters also provide conventional fire protection and emergency medical services to the airport facility. The following are duties of the airport firefighter:

- Respond to all fires and standby alarms at an airport; position equipment according to prearranged runway positions; and take into consideration the type of aircraft, number of passengers, windage, and other factors.
- Perform rescue, fire fighting, and first aid duties in connection with aircraft emergencies.
- Operate aircraft rescue and fire fighting vehicles; fire pumps; turret nozzles; and foam, dry chemical, and water extinguishers (Figure 6.21).
- Use specialized tools specific to aircraft emergencies.
- Perform structural fire fighting, emergency medical services, fire prevention duties, and other functions as required on the airport property.
- Attend training courses and drills as required.

Figure 6.20 Airport firefighters wear special equipment and are trained to handle incidents involving all kinds of aircraft.

Figure 6.21 Crash vehicles can apply large volumes of foam and water through their turrets.

Airport firefighters must have all the skills of a structural firefighter and those specific to the aircraft industry. Because airport firefighters must work at traumatic incidents, he or she must have the following special qualifications:

- Ability to meet the requirements in NFPA 1003, *Standard for Professional Qualifications for Airport Fire Fighters*
- Knowledge of the proper use and care of aircraft rescue and fire fighting equipment
- Knowledge of modern fire fighting methods used in aircraft rescue and fire fighting and structural fire fighting and the fundamentals of first aid
- Ability to cope firmly with emergencies with maximum effectiveness
- Ability to analyze situations quickly and objectively and to determine the proper course of action
- Ability to learn and apply correct techniques to combat airfield and aircraft fires
- Skill in driving and operating aircraft rescue and fire fighting vehicles, fire trucks, and related equipment
- Sufficient physical strength and agility to perform prolonged and arduous work under adverse conditions
- Knowledge of aircraft types and characteristics
- Knowledge of the airport facility and its rules and regulations

The IFSTA **Aircraft Rescue and Fire Fighting** manual provides additional information on the role of an airport firefighter.

The Hazardous Materials Technician

With the increasing number of hazardous materials incidents, every department will be called upon to handle or become involved with such an incident. Hazardous materials can be found in every community. All fire departments must be prepared to handle hazardous materials emergencies. Some departments will do this by using regular engine, truck, and rescue company personnel to handle the incidents. Others will have dedicated hazardous materials response units and teams to control such emergencies. In most cases, the hazardous materials technician is a firefighter who has received additional, specialized training on the topic (Figure 6.22). The hazardous materials technician is expected to perform the following duties:

- Conduct fire safety/hazardous materials inspections for compliance with applicable codes and standards.

Figure 6.22 Hazardous material personnel wear special protective equipment. *Courtesy of Bob Esposito.*

- Respond to and assist with the mitigation of hazardous materials incidents.
- Assist with the development of departmental programs related to hazardous materials.
- Participate in extensive specialized hazardous materials training.

The seriousness of the health threat posed by many hazardous materials emergencies requires that personnel assigned to mitigate these emergencies be extremely competent. The hazardous materials technician must meet the following major requirements:

- NFPA 472, *Standard for Professional Competence of Responders to Hazardous Materials Incidents*
- Excellent physical condition
- Extensive knowledge in chemistry and other physical sciences
- Knowledge of specific departmental operating procedures for hazardous materials incidents

The IFSTA **Hazardous Materials for First Responders** manual and Fire Protection Publications' **Hazardous Materials: Managing the Incident** manual provide additional information in this area.

The SCUBA Diver

Many fire departments are responsible for the response to and handling of water rescues and recoveries. Water emergencies occur in rivers, ponds, lakes, swimming pools, treatment plants, and industrial plants. The handling of these incidents requires specially trained crews for both topside and underwater functions. The underwater operations are performed by divers who wear self-contained underwater breathing apparatus (SCUBA) (Figure 6.23). SCUBA apparatus is similar to, but somewhat different than, the SCBA used for fire fighting operations. SCUBA divers wear or carry a variety of equipment such as wet or dry suits, weight belts, flashlights, small hand tools, and a diver's knife. The SCUBA diver is expected to perform the following duties:

- Maintain all SCUBA and diving equipment in a constant state of readiness.
- Respond to incidents involving submerged victims with the goal of quickly locating them and moving them to a place of safety.
- Assist law enforcement personnel with searches for evidence thrown into the water.

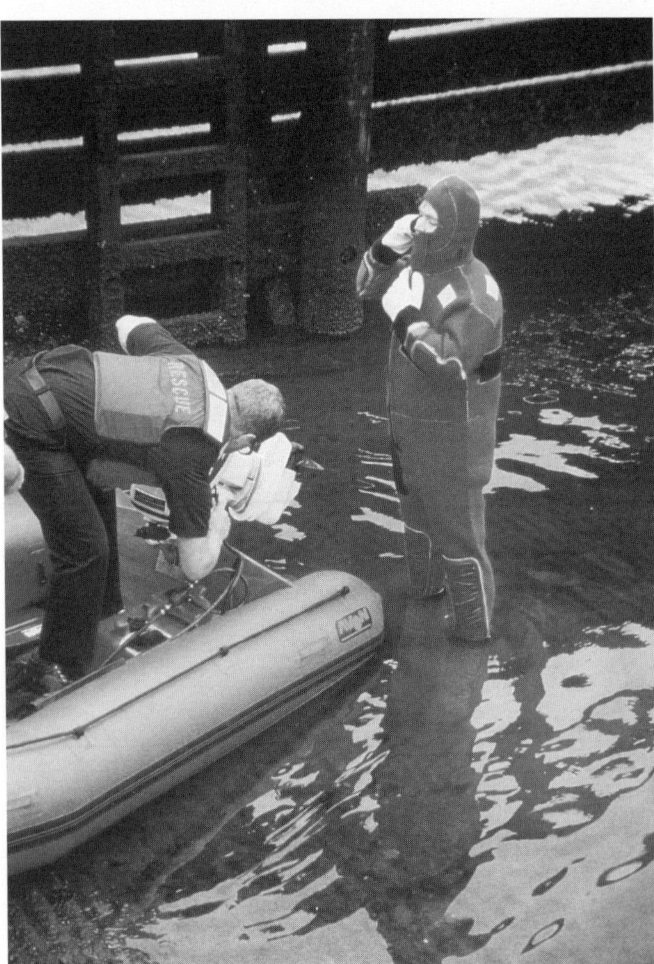

Figure 6.23 A fire department diver in action. *Courtesy of Ron Jeffers.*

Because SCUBA operations are significantly different than fire fighting operations, special needs and skills are required of the SCUBA diver.

- The diver should successfully complete an approved diver certification course.
- The diver should complete a boat and water safety operations course (Figure 6.24).
- The diver must have extensive training in the department's system for handling water emergencies.

Figure 6.24 Dive team personnel must be trained in safe boating operations.

The Special Rescue Technician

The myriad of special rescue situations that could face a fire department requires some of the personnel to be trained to handle them. Some of the special rescue situations include:

- High-angle (rope) rescue
- Trench and structural collapse
- Confined space entry
- Industrial extrication
- Agricultural extrication
- Transportation extrication
- Cave or mine rescue (Figure 6.25)

Some departments choose to have different teams for each type of potential emergency. Other departments have one team of specialized personnel, known as the rescue company or heavy rescue squad, who handle all rescue situations. The special rescue technician is expected to perform the following duties:

- Respond to special rescue situations, fires, and other emergencies as dictated by fire department standard operating procedures.

Figure 6.25 Rescue technicians perform high-angle and other types of rescues.

- Maintain rescue equipment in a state of readiness.
- Participate in special training sessions.
- Provide input to department administrators on equipment needs and specifications.

Most special rescue technicians are firefighters who have been trained to a higher level for these particular rescue situations. The special rescue technician must have the following qualifications:

- Ability to meet the requirements in NFPA 1001, *Standard for Fire Fighter Professional Qualifications*
- Specialized training on the equipment and methods used for special rescue situations to which the individual will be assigned
- Mechanical aptitude to adapt to the conditions presented by particular situations

The IFSTA **Principles of Extrication** and **Fire Service Rescue Practices** manuals contain more information for special rescue personnel.

FIRE PREVENTION PERSONNEL

As part of the overall role of public protection, the fire prevention division of a fire department is extremely important. An effective fire prevention program decreases the need for suppression activities and thereby reduces the cost and risk of extinguishing fire. But having an effective fire prevention program requires more than a lackadaisical effort. It requires aggressiveness and enterprising action to make it successful. For a fire department to be complete, it must have a competent fire prevention program. The fire prevention division of a fire department is typically headed by an assistant chief of the department. Depending on local customs, this person may be called the assistant chief in charge of fire prevention or the fire marshal. This individual has subordinate officers to fill the various roles within the division. Depending on local customs, fire prevention personnel may be sworn members of the fire department or they may be civilian employees.

The fire prevention division generally includes three major positions:

- Fire and arson investigator
- Public fire education specialist
- Fire protection engineer/specialist

The purpose of this section is to present the functions of each of these positions and to describe the type of personnel required to fill them.

The Fire Prevention Officer/Inspector

The fire prevention officer conducts technical and supervisory work in the fire prevention program. The work involves supervising and participating in field enforcement of local and state or provincial laws and ordinances relative to fire prevention. Considerable effort is required to correct fire hazards, and emphasis is placed on public assembly inspections and those areas where special hazards are present. The work allows considerable latitude for independent judgment and is reviewed through observing the results. A fire prevention officer/inspector is expected to perform the following duties:

- Assist the fire chief or fire marshal in planning and implementing the local fire prevention program.
- Inspect places of public assembly, such as halls, auditoriums, theaters, businesses, and industrial establishments, for existing or potential fire hazards and order correction of dangerous conditions (Figure 6.26).
- Receive complaints on fire hazards, investigate them, and recommend or order methods of correction.

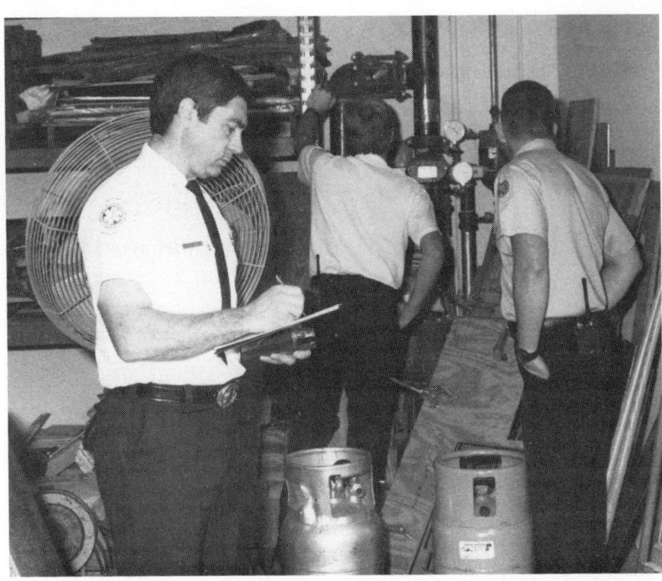

Figure 6.26 Inspectors may work with companies or work on their own.

- Inspect schools for fire hazards, conduct fire drills, and give talks to students on fire hazards and drill procedures.
- Cooperate with inspectors or field service workers of other municipal departments when making inspections to correct or remove hazards involving structural, electrical, and utility service safety.
- Cooperate with and assist fire companies in district fire prevention and inspection activities.
- Prepare reports of inspections and maintain files on all records.

The fire prevention officer/inspector is obviously responsible for a wide range of duties. To effectively perform these functions, the officer must have the following qualifications:

- Ability to meet the requirements in NFPA 1031, *Standard for Professional Qualifications for Fire Inspector*
- Thorough knowledge of fire safety laws, fire hazards, and methods of fire prevention
- Knowledge of the principles and practices of building construction and maintenance
- Ability to recognize existing and potential fire and casualty hazards in a wide variety of structures and installations
- Ability to establish and maintain effective working relationships with property owners, other employees, and the general public

- Ability to express factual information clearly and concisely — orally and in writing
- Ability to enforce rules and regulations firmly, tactfully, and impartially

The IFSTA **Fire Inspection and Code Enforcement** manual provides additional information on this subject.

Fire And Arson Investigator

The purpose of a fire investigation is to determine the cause of the fire. The results are then used to settle insurance claims, prosecute criminals, and protect the innocent. The responsibility of fire investigations may fall on several different sources. A fire department may handle the fire investigations in its area with specially trained personnel. The state or provincial fire marshal's office usually provides fire investigators for areas that do not have their own personnel. Large cities may use police and fire personnel to form a strike force. Many state police forces organize fire and arson investigation teams. Federal agencies, such as the Bureau of Alcohol, Tobacco, and Firearms or the FBI, may provide assistance on large incidents.

The field of fire investigation has become highly technical. It is now possible to discover things that a few years ago would have been impossible to discover. The use of space-age technology has improved the efficiency of many investigative methods. The methods used vary depending on whether the investigator is undertaking a fire or an arson investigation. A fire investigator is responsible for determining the cause of all fires, regardless of size. An arson investigator is needed to answer specific questions once the fire cause is determined to be arson. The job functions and requirements are similar because each investigator must make analytic judgments based on the remains at the fire scene. A fire and arson investigator is expected to perform the following duties:

- Respond to the fire scene as part of routine duties or respond when summoned.
- Make preliminary observations of the location, including the exterior of the fire area, the condition of the involved location, and the position of surrounding objects.
- Conduct the investigation of the fire area, and use all available means to determine the origin of the fire, the fire cause, and the results (Figure 6.27).
- Attempt to determine the sequence of events by using evidence, technical data, outside agencies, and witnesses.
- Appear in court to express an expert opinion about the fire cause and the results of investigations.
- Participate in arson awareness and prevention programs.

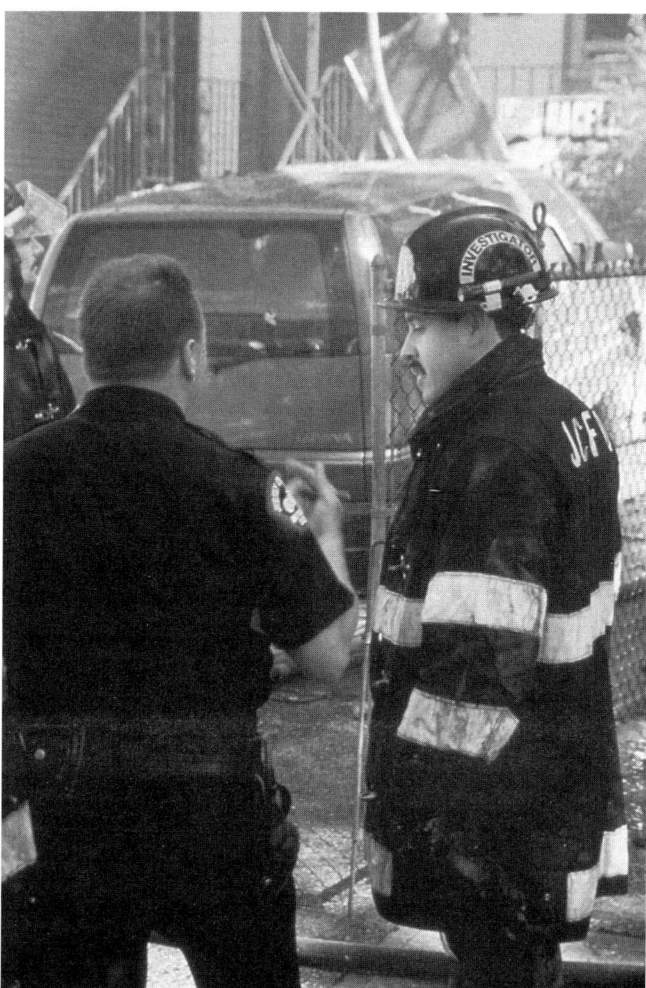

Figure 6.27 Fire investigators determine fire cause. *Courtesy of Ron Jeffers.*

A fire and arson investigator must have the following qualifications:

- Ability to meet the requirements in NFPA 1033, *Standard for Professional Qualifications for Fire Investigator*

- Thorough knowledge of all applicable areas of fire science, including fire chemistry, fuel types, burn patterns, and ignition sources
- Thorough knowledge of fire environment, including building construction, utility services, motor vehicles, and weather
- Ability to do strenuous activity, see well, and perceive colors accurately
- Ability to make pertinent observations and to take complete and coherent notes
- Ability to use tools, cameras, gas detection devices, microscopes, and other technical equipment efficiently and correctly
- Ability to converse and work with property owners, other agencies, witnesses, and the general public
- Ability to express factual information clearly and concisely — orally and in writing

Public Fire Education Specialist

Public fire education consists of informing the public about fire hazards, fire causes, precautions, and actions to take during a fire. To reduce fires in the community, the public fire specialist should focus on fire prevention in the home. The public is encouraged to use smoke detectors, fire extinguishers, and exit drills. Through these efforts, the loss of life and property is reduced.

The public fire education specialist is the hub of the public fire education program (Figure 6.28). To be effective, the specialist must be energetic and believe firmly in the program. The public fire education specialist is required to perform the following duties:

- Assist the fire chief and fire marshal in planning and implementing the local public fire education program.
- Design and develop training aids to use in public demonstrations and learning sessions.
- Work with newspapers, radio, and television to disseminate information to the public.
- Develop flyers and pamphlets that contain pertinent information.
- Conduct education activities for the public.

Figure 6.28 Public fire education is geared toward fire prevention. *Courtesy of Joe Marino.*

- Provide information to fellow firefighters about public fire education so that they can effectively represent the department's program.

A public fire education specialist must have the following qualifications:

- Ability to meet the requirements in NFPA 1035, *Standard for Professional Qualifications for Public Fire Educator*
- Thorough knowledge of current fire education principles and techniques
- Knowledge of human motivation and how to make the information desirable to learn
- Ability to work with news media professionals
- Ability to effectively communicate and to present oneself effectively
- Ability to portray confidence and to present an image acceptable to the public

For more information on public fire education and the responsibility of the educator, see the IFSTA **Public Fire Education** manual.

Fire Protection Engineer/Specialist

The use of fire protection engineers or specialists (referred to herein as FPEs) by municipal fire departments has increased significantly in recent years. FPEs are civilian employees who have an educational background in one of the following: fire protection engineering, safety engineering, civil engineering, mechanical engineering, or engineering technology. Primarily, the FPE acts as a consultant to the upper administration of the department. FPEs are used in both the operations and prevention sections of a department, although it is more common for the FPE to work in the prevention section. In operations, the FPE provides assistance in research and planning, purchasing equipment and apparatus, facilities specifications, hazardous materials problems and responses, water supply issues, and emergency scene safety. Fire prevention FPEs handle building plans reviews, fire protection systems plans reviews, systems tests, apparatus access issues, and other fire prevention and code enforcement concerns (Figure 6.29). The typical duties of a fire protection engineer/specialist include the following:

- Review site and building plans, note code violations, and make recommendations for changes.
- Review fire protection systems plans, note deficiencies, and make recommendations for improving systems.
- Inspect, review, and test fire protection systems.
- Consult with those involved in preliminary planning for building construction or change and give advice on current legal requirements.
- Interact with officials of all departments involved in regulating construction and use.
- Provide assistance in issues related to the municipal water supply system.
- Perform research, assist in planning functions, prepare specifications, and perform other services as required by operations personnel.

A fire protection engineer/specialist must have the following qualifications:

- College degree in one of the following: fire protection engineering, safety engineering, civil engineering, mechanical engineering, or engineering technology

Figure 6.29 Fire protection engineers perform many roles within the fire department.

- Appropriate professional registry such as a Professional Engineer (PE) or a Certified Safety Professional (CSP)
- Thorough knowledge of all applicable state or provincial and local laws and codes concerning fire protection
- Ability to review and evaluate plans and proposals for fire hazards
- Ability to provide appropriate recommendations relating to the review and evaluation process
- Ability to communicate appropriate recommendations relating to the review and evaluation process
- Ability to effectively communicate orally and in writing
- Ability to establish working relationships with members of other regulatory agencies
- Ability to provide information on a burning building's structural condition, on water hydraulics problems, and on the nature of hazardous materials involved in an incident

EMERGENCY MEDICAL SERVICES

The fire department's role in the emergency medical service has increased since the late 1920s when firefighters from a few fire departments were giving aid to citizens who were experiencing breathing problems and heart attack symptoms. By the early 1960s, the techniques of emergency life support were being perfected, and public demand for these services rose. As the decade of the '60s passed into the '70s, a few departments started to use specialized paramedic technicians to provide advanced life support for victims of accidents and illness. These services were provided to complement the ambulance and first aid service that many departments already provided.

Today, the fire service's involvement in the provision of emergency medical services (EMS) is dependent on local needs and customs.

- Some fire departments still do not have any responsibility for EMS.
- Some departments provide first response to priority calls.
- Some departments provide first response to all calls.
- Many departments handle all the EMS responsibilities for their districts, including the transport of patients to the hospital (Figures 6.30 a and b).

Figure 6.30a Some fire departments provide ambulance service for their jurisdictions. *Courtesy of Ron Jeffers.*

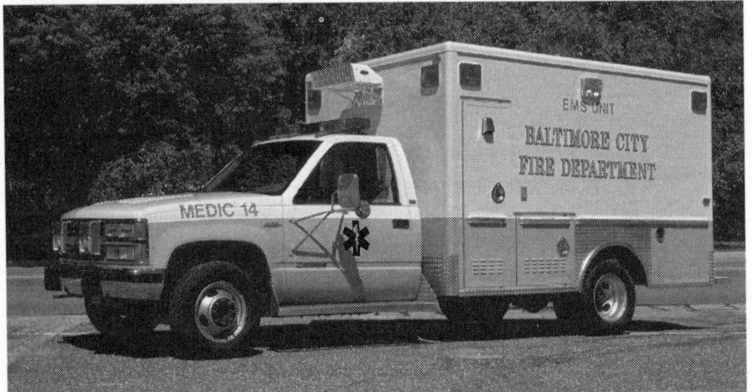

Figure 6.30b A fire department ambulance. *Courtesy of Joel Woods, University of Maryland Fire and Rescue Institute.*

Departments may use civilian EMS personnel or cross-trained firefighters.

Departments that provide first response to EMS incidents have trained first aid responders on regular fire companies such as engines, trucks, or squads (Figure 6.31). These personnel may be trained to the first responder, emergency medical technician, or paramedic levels. The ambulance that responds to transport the victim also has trained crew members on board.

The following sections highlight the capabilities of personnel who are trained to the first responder, emergency medical technician, or paramedic levels. Remember that in most cases these duties are in addition to those of a firefighter.

Figure 6.31 Fire companies are commonly assigned to medical calls.

First Responder

The first responder is likely to be the first person who responds to an emergency scene. The primary function of the first responder is to sustain life until more competent medical personnel arrive (Figure 6.32). A first responder has minimal emergency care equipment and a limited amount of tools to gain access to the victim. The first responder is not usually responsible for transporting the victim to the hospital.

The first responder is only responsible for the medical conditions of the victim that present an immediate hazard to life. The job consists of stabilizing the victim. As a result, the medical conditions that the first responder treats are limited. Some of these conditions treated by the first responder are as follows:

Figure 6.32 First responders are trained in basic first aid techniques.

- Respiratory distress or arrest
- Heart attack or cardiac arrest
- Extensive bleeding
- Poisoning
- Shock
- Emergency childbirth
- Substance abuse
- Stroke
- Diabetic coma and insulin shock
- Fractures
- Sprains
- Seizures
- Animal bites
- Severe exposure and burns

The first responder is trained to apply emergency first aid to those having any of these listed conditions, and he or she is effectively equipped to do so. For more details, see the IFSTA **Fire Service First Responder** manual.

Emergency Medical Technician

The emergency medical technician (EMT) provides basic life support for those whose lives are in danger. The EMT has been trained in a program of at least 120 hours and certified proficient by a regulatory agency. As compared to the first responder, the EMT is responsible for more care to the victim and will have more equipment to do so. The EMT may be responsible for transporting the victim. The EMT is expected to perform the following duties:

- Conduct examinations to determine the extent of illness or injury.
- Stabilize the victim before taking him or her to a hospital (Figure 6.33):
  - — Maintain victim's respiration.
  - — Use mechanical aids like suction and oxygen equipment to aid breathing.
  - — Take blood pressure and other vital signs.
  - — Dress and bandage wounds.
  - — Immobilize fractures in all areas of the body.
- Use proper methods for moving victims to the ambulance.
- Transport victims safely to the hospital while taking proper care of them.
- Extricate victims from automobiles and other sources of entrapment.
- Maintain proper control over the accident scene until police arrive.
- Be familiar with and use proper communication procedures.
- Maintain proper records of activities.

These listed duties are those expected of a basic level EMT. Many jurisdictions have certification levels for EMTs that exceed these minimums. EMTs who are certified to these ad-

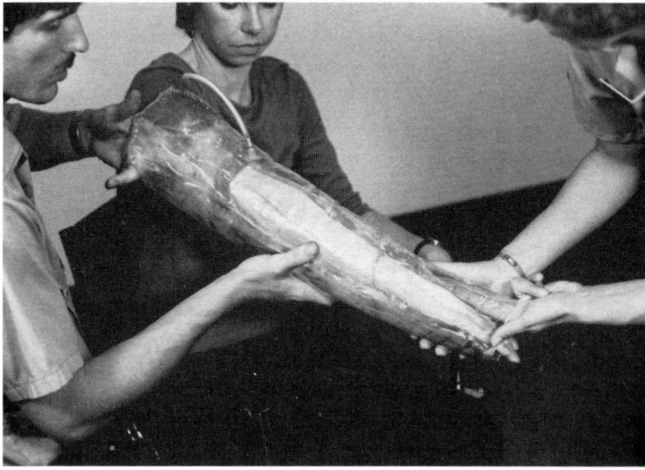

Figure 6.33 EMTs can apply splints to injured limbs.

vanced levels may provide more advanced care than the basic level EMTs. Emergency Medical Technician Defibrillators (EMT-Ds) are trained in the use of defibrillation equipment for cardiac emergencies. EMT Intermediates (EMT-I) are trained in the establishment of intubation tubes and intravenous fluids (IVs).

Paramedic

A paramedic is the highest position within the emergency medical service. This is the only position qualified to provide advanced life support. As a minimum, paramedics must complete a training program and be certified by a regulatory agency in the state. This training will consist of 800 or more hours, depending on the jurisdiction. The program includes course work, practical instruction, and a field internship. Paramedics work under the supervision of a physician.

As compared to the first responder and EMT, the paramedic maintains the most responsibility. Paramedics handle incidents similar to those handled by EMTs, but they are able to provide advanced life support where EMTs are limited to basic life support (Figure 6.34). Thus, the paramedic's knowledge must be more in-depth. To be competent, paramedics must be able to perform the following duties:

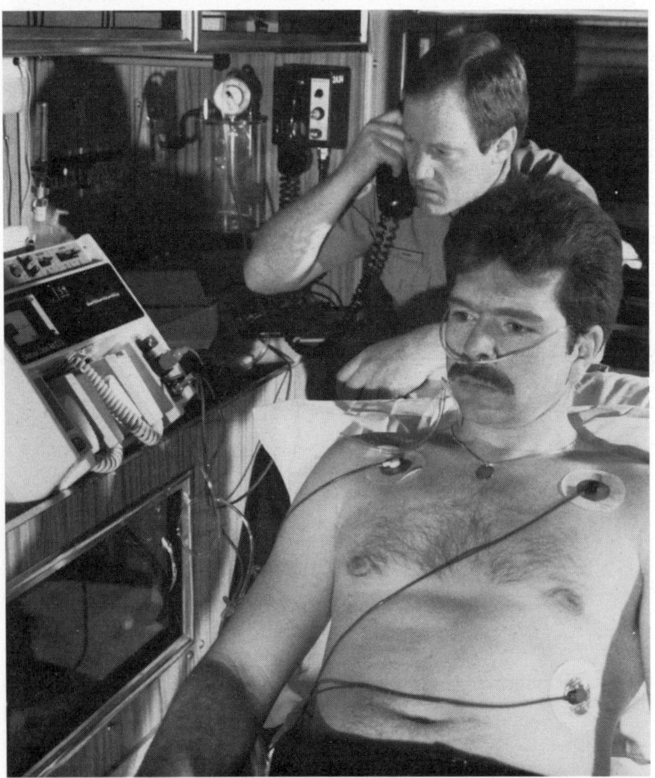

Figure 6.34 Paramedics are the most highly trained emergency medical personnel.

- Recognize and assess medical emergencies.
- Decide priorities of medical treatment and communicate necessary data to the responsible physician.
- Follow the directions of the physician concerning treatment and report the progress of treatment.
- Function and exercise judgment in stabilizing the victim when out of contact with the physician; formal protocols (standing orders) may be established by medical command and must be followed by the paramedic in these situations.
- Administer intravenous fluids and drugs, including narcotics.
- Perform airway management, including intubation.
- Direct the proper transport of the victim.
- Maintain proper records.
- Maintain emergency equipment and supplies.

Paramedics also accompany victims to the hospital. During the trip, paramedics stay in contact with the hospital to handle situations as they arise.

TRAINING PERSONNEL

The training that new firefighters receive is one of the most important aspects of job indoctrination. Training under realistic conditions does more toward preparing firefighters for the job than movies or stories. Firefighters responding to an emergency must be properly prepared to perform effectively. Much depends on firefighters accomplishing their tasks expediently and efficiently: the lives of the victims and fellow firefighters, the saving of property, fire extinguishment, and exposure protection.

A firefighter's training never ends. Even the firefighter who has been with the department for 20 years has something to learn. The fire service is ever changing. New ideas and tactics present new methods that have to be learned. New materials and technology present challenges that never before existed. It is imperative that the fire service remain abreast of these changes. This is accomplished only by frequent and intense training that is constantly improved and updated to make it effective.

The manning of the training staff is dependent on the size of the department. Small departments have a single training officer who acts as both the administrator and trainer. Larger departments have a chief of training and instructors to carry out the delivery. This section details the roles of the administrator of training programs (the training officer) and the instructor.

The Training Officer/Chief Of Training/ Drillmaster

Of primary importance to most departments is the intradepartmental training they establish and conduct. The training officer (sometimes called the chief of training or drillmaster) actually runs the program. The training officer's responsibilities involve the administration of all fire department training activities. Typically, the training officer reports directly to the chief. The training officer is expected to perform the following duties:

- Plan, organize, and supervise the work of subordinate instructors.
- Determine the need for new training material and evaluate new techniques, methods, and procedures.
- Appropriate the necessary resources to conduct training exercises and classes.
- Oversee the maintenance of department personnel training records.
- Oversee the maintenance of training facilities and equipment.

The training officer must have the following qualifications:

- Ability to meet the appropriate requirements contained in NFPA 1041, *Standard for Fire Service Instructor Professional Qualifications*
- Extensive background in educational theory and methodology
- Knowledge of the fire department's record-keeping system
- Ability to interact with the other administrators of the department and convert their concerns into appropriate training courses

The Instructor

The instructor is responsible for the actual delivery of the training courses to the other members of the department (Figure 6.35). These courses could be entry (recruit) level or advanced training and may be delivered at the training center or out in the field. The instructor takes direction from the chief of training. The instructor is expected to perform the following duties:

- Deliver prepared training courses using a variety of classroom delivery methods and practical exercises.
- Prepare curriculum for new courses at the request of the chief of training.
- Monitor practical exercises for safety hazards, and correct them immediately when noted.
- File appropriate paperwork to record the progress and completion of course work for all students.

Figure 6.35 Instructors prepare firefighters to respond to real emergencies.

The instructor must have the following qualifications:

- Ability to meet the appropriate requirements contained in NFPA 1041, *Standard for Fire Service Instructor Professional Qualifications*
- Knowledge of the fire department's operating procedures and the ability to convey them with the training material

- Good verbal communications skills
- Thorough knowledge of all the skills and theories conveyed to the class

For more information on the role of a fire service instructor, see the IFSTA **Fire Service Instructor** manual.

OTHER FIRE DEPARTMENT PERSONNEL

In order to carry out the mission of the fire department, personnel other than the previously described line personnel are required. This section describes some of these personnel.

Communications/Dispatch Personnel

The radio communications system of the fire department is the operation's central nervous system. The backbone of this system is the dispatcher who runs the system (Figure 6.36). If the dispatcher does his or her job professionally and efficiently, all operations will run more smoothly. Typically, dispatchers work 8- to 12-hour shifts. Some departments have their dispatchers work the same shifts as the line companies. The dispatcher may be a civilian or sworn member of the department. The duties of the dispatcher include the following:

- Take emergency and nonemergency phone calls and process the information appropriately.
- Dispatch the appropriate units to handle reported emergencies.

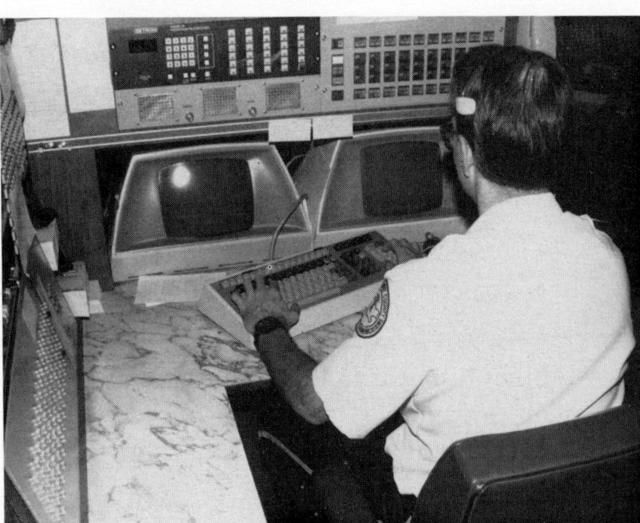

Figure 6.36 Dispatchers are the vital link in any fire department communications system.

- Maintain contact with companies that are in service and provide communications assistance when required.
- Follow departmental guidelines to relocate nonassigned companies to fill empty stations during an extended incident.
- Follow departmental policy in relaying information to the media.
- Record all information according to departmental policy.

The dispatcher must have the following qualifications:

- Ability to communicate clearly and concisely
- Ability to remain calm during stressful situations
- Ability to assign and relocate companies according to fire department standard operating procedures
- Ability to operate communications equipment, including radios, telephones, computers, fire alarm equipment, and recording equipment

Fire Alarm Maintenance Personnel

Some fire departments still maintain municipal fire alarm systems. These systems consist of some type of alarm box positioned at various locations around the city and signaling equipment located at the dispatch center. Most of these systems are of the hard-wire variety and require maintenance similar to that for a telephone system. The system is maintained by fire alarm maintenance personnel who are typically civilian employees of the department. The duties of the maintenance personnel include the following:

- Maintain all equipment within the municipal fire alarm system in a state of readiness.
- Add additional boxes as required and directed by fire department administration.

The fire alarm maintenance personnel should have the following qualifications:

- Knowledge of the operation of the municipal fire alarm system
- Knowledge of the basic principles of wiring for communications systems
- Ability to operate heavy equipment, including aerial lift devices

Apparatus And Equipment Maintenance Personnel

To keep the fire department running properly, maintenance personnel are required for the fire apparatus and equipment. Apparatus maintenance personnel need to have all the same skills as any automotive or truck mechanic, with the added skills of maintaining fire equipment such as pumps, aerial devices, and generators. Fire equipment maintenance personnel are responsible for maintaining all portable equipment on the apparatus. The following are typical duties for apparatus maintenance personnel:

- Perform routine maintenance on all mechanical components of the vehicle (Figure 6.37).
- Perform repairs on all mechanical components of the vehicle.
- Repair damage to the body of the vehicle as required.
- Maintain and repair all fire related portions of the apparatus, including fire pumps and aerial devices.
- Perform service tests on aerial devices and fire pumps.
- Inspect the vehicle according to state or provincial requirements.
- Maintain records of all work performed on each apparatus.

Figure 6.37 Apparatus mechanics must be capable of fixing all apparatus systems.

The typical duties for equipment maintenance personnel include the following:

- Maintain portable equipment such as hose, ladders, SCBAs, hand and power tools, and lighting or electrical equipment (Figure 6.38).
- Service test equipment after repairs or on an annual basis as required by applicable standards.
- Stock extra parts for potential repairs.
- Maintain a record system for recording repairs and testing.

Apparatus maintenance personnel should have the following qualifications:

- Appropriate automotive mechanic certification for the types of vehicles to be worked on
- Training in the maintenance of equipment specific to fire apparatus
- Certification to perform state or provincial inspections
- Ability to operate towing vehicles if required

Equipment maintenance personnel should have the following qualifications:

- Knowledge of the proper repair and testing procedures for all equipment
- Manufacturer's certification for servicing specialized equipment such as SCBA
- Ability to analyze equipment for hidden problems

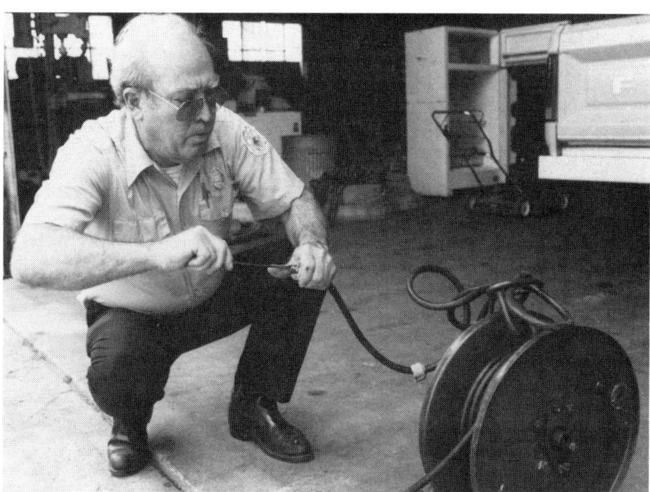

Figure 6.38 Fire departments have a multitude of equipment that requires regular repair.

Fire Police

Many communities, particularly smaller communities with volunteer fire departments, use fire police to assist in emergency operations. In many cases, small communities have only one or two police officers on duty, and they are involved at the scene doing an investigation. The fire police then handle the duties that would otherwise be police functions. Fire police assist with traffic control, crowd control, and securing the scene (Figure 6.39). Fire police are typically actual members of the fire department who operate in this auxiliary role. The following are typical duties of fire police:

- Route traffic around the emergency scene.
- Maintain crowd control at the emergency scene.
- Secure the emergency scene until investigators or law enforcement officials arrive to take over.
- Assist police with similar duties at public gatherings and other nonemergency functions.

Fire police should have the following qualifications:

- Training in traffic safety routing
- Understanding of the emergency scene and potential danger zones

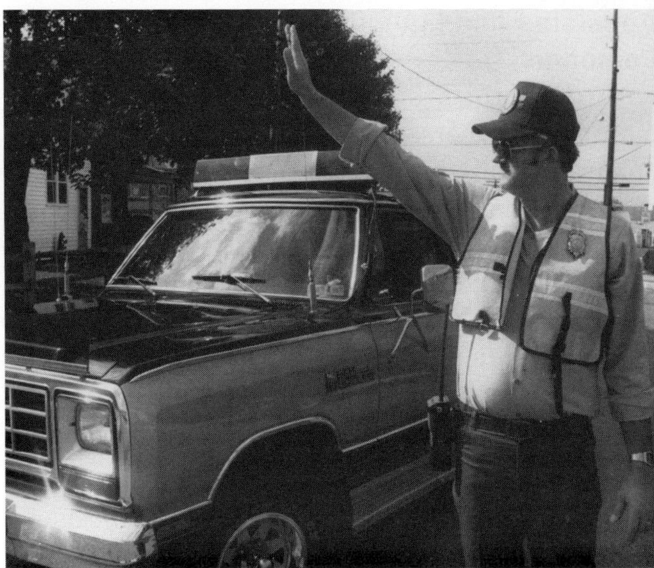

Figure 6.39 Fire police assist with traffic and crowd control. *Courtesy of Bob Esposito.*

- Understanding of the operation of traffic control equipment such as flares, signs, and flashers
- Any certification or legal swearing in as required

This chapter has covered many of the common roles found within the fire service. Depending on local requirements and customs, other specialized personnel may be used. Their duties and requirements vary depending on local needs and procedures.

Chapter 6
Application And Review Activities

DIRECTIONS

The following activities are designed to help you comprehend and apply the information in Chapter 6 of **Orientation and Terminology**. To receive the maximum learning experience from these activities, it is recommended that you use the following procedure:

1. Read the chapter, underlining or highlighting important terms, topics, and subject matter. Study the photographs and illustrations, and read the captions under each.
2. Review the list of vocabulary words to ensure that you know the chapter-related meaning of each. If you are unsure of the meaning of a vocabulary word, look the word up in a dictionary, and then study its context in the chapter.

   NOTE: Some words have different meanings as different parts of speech. Abbreviations after certain words stand for the part of speech (v., verb; n., noun; adj., adjective; adv., adverb) of the word as it is used in the chapter.
3. On a separate sheet of paper, complete all assigned or selected application and review activities before checking your answers.
4. After you have finished, check your answers against those on the pages referenced in parentheses.

VOCABULARY

Be sure that you know the chapter-related meanings of the following terms.

- Arson *(136)*
- Civic *(130)*
- Coherent *(138)*
- Compliance *(124)*
- Defibrillation *(142)*
- Delegate (v.) *(126)*
- Dispatch (v.) *(124)*
- Disseminate *(138)*
- Expedient *(142)*
- Impartial *(137)*
- Implement (v.) *(136)*
- Indoctrination *(142)*
- Internship *(142)*
- Intravenous *(142)*
- Inventory *(125)*
- Law vs. ordinance *(136)*
- Mitigation *(134)*
- Myriad *(135)*
- Protocol *(142)*
- Requisition *(127)*
- Traumatic *(133)*

APPLICATION OF KNOWLEDGE

1. What is your fire service career goal? Why? What types of training or qualifications must you obtain to meet your career goal? Outline your plan to meet your career goal. *(Local protocol)*

2. Write a job description describing the position you presently hold. Describe your major responsibilities, the approximate amount of time you spend in each area, and the specific duties you perform to meet these responsibilities. *(Local protocol)*

REVIEW ACTIVITIES

1. Explain the difference between fire apparatus and fire equipment. *(201, 206)*

2. Define each of the following:
   - Fire department company *(122)*
   - Task force *(122)*
   - Strike team *(122)*
   - High-angle rescue *(123)*

3. Explain the differences between being licensed and being certified. *(126, 141-142)*

4. Distinguish among administrative, supervisory, and line personnel. *(122, 126-128)*

5. Explain the difference between a rescue and a recovery. *(123)*

6. List the primary and six basic objectives of all fire departments. *(121)*

7. Compare and contrast the composition and duties of each of the following fire companies:
   - Engine company *(122)*
   - Truck company *(123)*
   - Rescue squad/company *(123)*

8. Identify and list at least three primary duties for each of the following fire suppression (operations) personnel:
   - Firefighter *(123)*
   - Fire apparatus driver/operator *(125)*
   - Company officer *(126)*
   - Battalion chief *(127)*
   - Safety officer *(129)*
   - Public information officer *(130)*
   - Assistant or deputy chief *(130)*
   - Fire chief *(131)*

9. List four qualifications required for each of the fire suppression (operations) personnel listed in Activity 8. *(123-131)*

10. Explain the differences between operations personnel and special operations personnel. *(121, 132)*

11. Identify and list at least three primary duties for each of the following fire special operations personnel:
    - Airport firefighter *(132)*
    - Hazardous materials technician *(133)*
    - SCUBA diver *(134)*
    - Special rescue technician *(135)*

12. List four qualifications that are required for each of the fire special operations personnel listed in Activity 11. *(132-135)*

13. Explain the general role of fire prevention personnel. *(135)*

14. Identify and list at least three primary duties for each of the following fire prevention personnel:
    - Fire prevention officer/inspector *(136)*
    - Fire and arson investigator *(137)*
    - Public fire education specialist *(138)*
    - Fire protection engineer/specialist *(139)*

15. List four qualifications that are required for each of the fire prevention personnel listed in Activity 14. *(136-139)*

16. Outline a brief chronological history of the fire service's involvement in the provision of emergency medical services. *(139 & 140)*

17. Identify and list at least three primary duties for each of the following medical service personnel:
    - First responder *(140)*
    - Emergency medical technician *(141)*
    - Paramedic *(142)*

18. Identify and list at least three primary duties and three qualifications for fire service training officers and instructors. *(140-142)*

19. Identify and list three primary duties for each of the following fire department personnel:
    - Communications/dispatch personnel *(144)*
    - Fire alarm maintenance personnel *(144)*
    - Apparatus maintenance personnel *(145)*
    - Equipment maintenance personnel *(145)*
    - Fire police *(146)*

20. List four qualifications required for each of the fire department personnel listed in Activity 19. *(144-146)*

APPENDIX A

NATIONAL FIRE PROTECTION ASSOCIATION (NFPA) STANDARDS THAT COMMONLY APPLY TO THE FIRE SERVICE

The following list contains those NFPA standards that are most commonly used within the fire service. Other standards may be applicable; however, their usage by everyday fire personnel would be rare.

NFPA 1, *Fire Prevention Code*

NFPA 10, *Standard for Portable Fire Extinguishers*

NFPA 11, *Standard for Low Expansion Foam and Combined Agent Systems*

NFPA 11A, *Standard for Medium- and High-Expansion Foam Systems*

NFPA 11C, *Standard for Mobile Foam Apparatus*

NFPA 13, *Standard for the Installation of Sprinkler Systems*

NFPA 13D, *Standard for the Installation of Sprinkler Systems in One- and Two-Family Dwellings and Mobile Homes*

NFPA 13R, *Standard for the Installation of Sprinkler Systems in Residential Occupancies up to Four Stories in Height*

NFPA 14, *Standard for the Installation of Standpipe and Hose Systems*

NFPA 30, *Flammable and Combustible Liquids Code*

NFPA 70, *National Electrical Code®*

NFPA 101®, *Code for Safety to Life from Fire in Buildings and Structures* (The Life Safety Code)

NFPA 291, *Standard for Fire Flow Testing and Marking of Hydrants*

NFPA 295, *Standard for Wildfire Control*

NFPA 297, *Standard for Telecommunications Systems — Principles and Practices for Rural and Forestry Services*

NFPA 298, *Standard on Foam Chemicals for Wildland Fire Control*

NFPA 299, *Standard for Protection of Life and Property from Wildfire*

NFPA 402M, *Manual for Aircraft Rescue and Fire Fighting Operations*

NFPA 403, *Standard for Aircraft Rescue and Fire Fighting Services at Airports*

NFPA 412, *Standard for Evaluating Aircraft Rescue and Fire Fighting Foam Equipment*

NFPA 414, *Standard for Aircraft Rescue and Fire Fighting Vehicles*

NFPA 471, *Standard for Responding to Hazardous Materials Incidents*

NFPA 472, *Standard for Professional Competence of Responders to Hazardous Materials Incidents*

NFPA 473, *Standard for Competencies for EMS Personnel Responding to Hazardous Materials Incidents*

NFPA 600, *Standard on Industrial Fire Brigades*

NFPA 1001, *Standard for Fire Fighter Professional Qualifications*

FPA 1002, *Standard for Fire Apparatus Driver / Operator Professional Qualifications*

NFPA 1003, *Standard for Professional Qualifications for Airport Fire Fighters*

NFPA 1021, *Standard for Fire Officer Professional Qualifications*

NFPA 1031, *Standard for Professional Qualifications for Fire Inspector*

NFPA 1033, *Standard for Professional Qualifications for Fire Investigator*

NFPA 1035, *Standard for Professional Qualifications for Public Fire Educator*

NFPA 1041, *Standard for Fire Service Instructor Professional Qualifications*

NFPA 1051, *Standard for Wildland Fire Fighter Professional Qualifications* (Proposed)

NFPA 1061, *Standard for Fire Service Telecommunicator Professional Qualifications* (Proposed)

NFPA 1201, *Standard for Developing Fire Protection Services for the Public*

NFPA 1221, *Standard for the Installation, Maintenance, and Use of Public Fire Service Communications Systems*

NFPA 1231, *Standard on Water Supplies for Suburban and Rural Fire Fighting*

NFPA 1401, *Recommended Practice for Fire Service Training Reports and Records*

NFPA 1402, *Guide to Building Fire Service Training Centers*

NFPA 1403, *Standard on Live Fire Training Evolutions in Structures*

NFPA 1404, *Standard for a Fire Department Self-Contained Breathing Apparatus Program*

NFPA 1405, *Guide for Land-Based Fire Fighters Who Respond to Marine Vessel Fires*

NFPA 1410, *A Training Standard on Initial Fire Attack*

NFPA 1452, *Guide for Training Fire Service Personnel to Make Dwelling Fire Safety Surveys*

NFPA 1500, *Standard on Fire Department Occupational Safety and Health Program*

NFPA 1521, *Standard for Fire Department Safety Officer*

NFPA 1561, *Standard on Fire Department Incident Management System*

NFPA 1581, *Standard on Fire Department Infection Control Program*

NFPA 1582, *Standard on Medical Requirements for Fire Fighters*

NFPA 1901, *Standard for Pumper Fire Apparatus*

NFPA 1902, *Standard for Initial Attack Fire Apparatus*

NFPA 1903, *Standard for Mobile Water Supply Fire Apparatus*

NFPA 1904, *Standard for Aerial Ladder and Elevating Platform Fire Apparatus*

NFPA 1911, *Standard for Service Tests of Pumps on Fire Department Apparatus*

NFPA 1914, *Standard for Testing Fire Department Aerial Devices*

NFPA 1921, *Standard for Fire Department Portable Pumping Units*

NFPA 1931, *Standard on Design of and Design Verification Tests for Fire Department Ground Ladders*

NFPA 1932, *Standard on Use, Maintenance, and Service Testing of Fire Department Ground Ladders*

NFPA 1961, *Standard on Fire Hose*

NFPA 1962, *Standard for the Care, Use, and Service Testing of Fire Hose Including Couplings and Nozzles*

NFPA 1963, *Standard for Screw Threads and Gaskets for Fire Hose Connections*

NFPA 1964, *Standard for Spray Nozzles (Shutoff and Tip)*

NFPA 1971, *Standard on Protective Clothing for Structural Fire Fighting*

NFPA 1972, *Standard on Helmets for Structural Fire Fighting*

NFPA 1973, *Standard on Gloves for Structural Fire Fighting*

NFPA 1974, *Standard on Protective Footwear for Structural Fire Fighting*

NFPA 1975, *Standard on Station / Work Uniforms for Fire Fighters*

NFPA 1981, *Standard on Open-Circuit Self-Contained Breathing Apparatus For Fire Fighters*

NFPA 1982, *Standard on Personal Alert Safety Systems (PASS) for Fire Fighters*

NFPA 1983, *Standard on Fire Service Life Safety Rope, Harness, and Hardware*

NFPA 1991, *Standard on Vapor-Protective Suits for Hazardous Chemical Emergencies*

NFPA 1992, *Standard on Liquid Splash-Protective Suits for Hazardous Chemical Emergencies*

NFPA 1993, *Standard on Support Function Protective Garments for Hazardous Chemical Operations*

NFPA 1999, *Standard on Protective Clothing for Emergency Medical Operations*

Glossary

Glossary

This glossary contains an extensive list of fire service terms and their definitions. Only the fire service definitions are given for the provided terms. In many cases, certain terms may have nonfire service applications that are not covered here. Also, the spellings and definitions are consistent with IFSTA and Fire Protection Publications policy and may differ slightly from those used by other fire service organizations. Example: IFSTA uses one word for "firefighter," while the NFPA uses two words for "fire fighter."

A

Abandonment
Termination of a first responder/patient relationship by the first responder without consent of the patient and without care to the patient by qualified medical volunteers.

ABC Extinguisher
See Multipurpose Fire Extinguisher.

ABC's
Airway, Breathing, Circulation, and Severe Bleeding; the first three steps in the basic life support examination of any patient.

Abdominal Cavity
Large body cavity below the diaphragm and above the pelvis containing the following organs: stomach with lower portion of esophagus, small and large intestines (except sigmoid colon and rectum), liver, gallbladder, spleen, pancreas, kidney, and ureter.

Abort
(1) Act of terminating a planned aircraft maneuver such as the takeoff or landing. (2) To terminate prematurely. (3) To stop in the early stages.

Abortion
Premature expulsion of the products of conception from the uterus. Abortion can occur naturally or can be artificially induced.

Abrasion
Injury consisting of the loss of a partial thickness of skin from rubbing or scraping on a hard, rough surface. Also called Brush Burn or Friction Burn.

Absence Seizure
Type of seizure characterized by a momentary loss of awareness, staring, or blinking of the eyes. It is especially prevalent in children aged 4 to 14. Also known as a Petit Mal Seizure.

Absorbent
Substance that allows another substance to penetrate into the interior of its structure. Absorbent material is commonly used in the abatement of hazardous materials spills.

Absorption
(1) To take in and make part of an existent whole. (2) Passage of toxic materials through some body surface into body fluids and tissue.

Academy
Training school; a place to train, learn, study, and achieve.

Accelerant
Flammable or combustible liquid that is used to initiate or increase the speed of a fire.

Accelerator
(1) Device attached to a dry-pipe sprinkler system for rapid removal of air in the system when a sprinkler is fused. (2) Device, usually in the form of a foot pedal, used to control the speed of a vehicle by regulating the fuel supply.

Acceptance Testing (Proof Test)
Preservice tests on fire apparatus or equipment performed at the factory or after delivery to assure the purchaser that the apparatus or equipment meets bid specifications.

Access Hole
(1) Starter hole into which a cutting tool may be inserted to continue cutting a piece of sheet metal.

(2) Space made in a door crack with a manual prying tool to facilitate the placement of a spreading tool.

Accessibility
Ability of fire apparatus to get close enough to a building to conduct emergency operations.

Accident
Unplanned, uncontrolled event that results from unsafe acts of people and/or unsafe occupational conditions, either of which can result in injury.

Accordion Fold
Method of folding a salvage cover; when completed resembles the bellows of an accordion.

Accordion Load
Arrangement of fire hose in a hose bed or compartment in which the hose lies on edge with the folds adjacent to each other.

Acetylene [C_2H_2]
Colorless gas that has an explosive range from 2.5 percent to 100 percent; used as a fuel gas for cutting and welding operations.

Acquired Immune Deficiency Syndrome (AIDS)
Fatal viral disease that is spread through direct contact with bodily fluids from a previously infected individual.

Acquired Structure
Structure that is acquired for the purpose of conducting live fire fighting or rescue training evolutions.

Acrolein (CH_2=CHCHO)
Toxic gas produced when wood, paper, cotton, plastic materials, and oils and fats burn. Inhaled, acrolein can cause nose and throat irritation, nausea, shortness of breath, pulmonary edema, lung damage, and can eventually lead to death.

Action Plan
Written plan of how objectives are to be achieved.

Actuate
To set into operation, especially an installed fire protection system.

Actuator Valve
Valve that controls the flow of hydraulic oil from an aerial apparatus hydraulic system to the hydraulic cylinders.

Acute
Characterized by sharpness or severity; having rapid onset and a relatively short duration.

Acute Abdomen
Severe pain, tenderness, and muscular rigidity caused by inflammation, infection, or obstruction of an organ within the abdominal cavity.

Acute Myocardial Infarction (AMI)
Acute phase of a heart attack where blockage of a coronary artery produces a number of signs and symptoms, particularly chest pain, nausea, heavy sweating, anxiety, and pallor. Also called Heart Attack.

Adam's Apple
Projection on the front of the neck formed by the thyroid cartilage of the larynx.

Adapter
Fitting for connecting hose couplings with dissimilar threads but with the same inside diameter.

Addiction
State of being strongly dependent upon some agent such as drugs, tobacco, or alcohol.

Adjunct
Accessory or auxiliary agent. An oral airway is an airway adjunct.

Adjustable Flow Nozzle
Nozzle designed so that the amount of water flowing through the nozzle can be increased or decreased at the nozzle.

Adjutant
Firefighter assigned to drive and assist a chief officer. Also called Chief's Aide.

Admission
Statement; tending to implicate the speaker in the commission of a crime.

Admission Valve
Pressure regulator valve that lets the air flow to the user.

Adrenaline
Chemical released by the body that causes the breathing rate to increase and the body to prepare for "fight or flight."

Adsorbent
Material, such as activated carbon, that has the ability to condense or hold molecules of other substances on its surface.

Advanced Life Support
Basic life support and the additional use of invasive procedures or drugs.

Advancing Line
A line of fire hose that is moved forward.

Adverse Weather Condition
Any atmospheric condition, such as rain, snow, and cold, that creates additional problems or considerations for emergency personnel.

Adz or Adze
Chopping tool characterized by a thin, arched blade set at a right angle to the handle.

Aerate
Act of mixing with air.

Aerial Apparatus
Fire fighting vehicle equipped with a hydraulically operated ladder or elevating platform for the purpose of placing personnel and/or water streams in elevated positions.

Aerial Device
General term used to describe the hydraulically operated ladder or elevating platform attached to a specially designed fire apparatus.

Aerial Device Certification Testing
Preservice testing, usually performed by a third-party testing agency, designed to give an unbiased opinion to determine if a piece of apparatus meets its designed requirements and if it is worthy of being placed in service.

Aerial Ladder
Power-operated (usually hydraulically) ladder mounted on a special truck chassis.

Aerial Ladder Platform
Power-operated (usually hydraulically) ladder with a passenger-carrying device attached to the end of the ladder.

Aerial Ladder Truss
Assembly of bracing bars or rods in triangular shapes to form a rigid framework for the aerial device.

Aerobic Capacity
Measure of cardiovascular fitness that takes into account oxygen capacity and efficiency of the lungs and blood in the cardiovascular and respiratory systems.

Aerodrome
See Airport.

Affective Learning
Learning that relates to interests, attitudes, and values.

AFFF
Abbreviation for Aqueous Film Forming Foam.

Affidavit
Sworn written statement.

Affirmative
Clear text radio term for "yes."

Affirmative Action
Employment programs designed to make a special effort to identify, hire, and promote special populations where the current labor force in a jurisdiction or labor market is not representative of the overall population.

A-Frame
(1) Vertical lifting device that can be attached to the front or rear of the apparatus. It consists of two poles attached several feet (meters) apart on the apparatus and whose working ends are connected to form the letter A. A pulley or block and tackle through which a rope or cable is passed is attached to the end of the frame. (2) A type of building construction in which a steep, gabled roof forms the major structural supports for the entire building.

A-Frame Ladder
Type of ladder that is hinged in the middle and can be used as a stepladder or a short extension ladder.

A-Frame Stabilizer
Stabilizing device that extends at an angle down and away from the chassis of an aerial fire apparatus.

Aft/After
Near, toward, or in the stern of a ship or the tail of an aircraft.

Aftercooler
Air compressor component that cools the air that has been heated during compression.

Agency Representative
Individual from an assisting or cooperating agency who has been assigned to an incident and has full authority to make decisions on all matters affecting that agency's participation at the incident. Agency Representatives report to the Incident Liaison Officer.

Agent
Generic term used for materials that are used to extinguish fires.

Aggravate
To worsen; to make worse.

Aggregate
(1) Gravel, stone, sand, or other inert materials used in concrete. (2) Used in fire prevention and building codes to describe the sum total of individual parts or components of an assembly or feature such as in units of exit.

AIDS
Acronym for Acquired Immune Deficiency Syndrome.

Aileron
Movable hinged rear portion of an airplane wing. Its primary function is to roll or bank the aircraft in flight.

Air
Gaseous mixture that composes the earth's atmosphere; composed of approximately 21 percent oxygen, 79 percent nitrogen, plus trace gases

Air-Aspirating Foam Nozzle
Foam nozzle especially designed to provide the aeration required to make the highest quality foam possible; most effective appliance for the generation of low-expansion foam.

Air Attack
(1) Using airplanes or helicopters to apply fire retardants or extinguishing agents on a wildland fire. (2) ICS term for the air attack coordinator.

Air Bag
(1) Inflatable bag designed into the steering wheel or dashboard of an automobile that inflates immediately when the front of the vehicle is impacted. (2) Large inflatable bag into which persons can leap to escape danger. *Also see* Air Lifting Bag.

Air Bank
See Air Cascade System.

Air Bill
Shipping document prepared from a bill of lading that accompanies each piece or each lot of air cargo.

Air Bottle
See Air Cylinder.

Air Cascade System
Three or more large air cylinders, each usually with a capacity of 300 cubic feet (8 490 L), from which SCBA cylinders are recharged.

Air Chamber
Chamber filled with air that eliminates pulsations caused by the operation of piston or rotary-gear pumps.

Air Chisel
See Pneumatic Chisel/Hammer.

Airco
One of several names for the plane carrying the air attack coordinator.

Aircraft Accident
Occurrence during the operation of an aircraft in which any person suffers death or serious injury or in which the aircraft receives damage.

Aircraft Classes
Classification of aircraft by weight for various purposes. (Canadian terms are in parentheses.) *Heavy (Heavy)* aircraft capable of takeoff weight of 300,000 pounds (136 078 kg) or more, whether or not the aircraft is operating at this weight during a particular phase of flight. *Large (Medium)* aircraft capable of takeoff weight of more than 12,500 pounds (5 670 kg), maximum certified takeoff weight up to 300,000 pounds (136 078 kg). *Small (Light)* aircraft capable of takeoff weight of 12,500 pounds (5 670 kg) or less.

Aircraft Familiarization
Process of teaching personnel to become familiar with the various aircraft operated in an airport. This familiarization includes fuel capacity, fuel tank locations, emergency exit locations, operation of emergency exits, passenger seating capacity, etc.

Aircraft Fire Apparatus
Fire apparatus specifically designed for aircraft crash fire fighting/rescue operations.

Aircraft Incident
Occurrence, other than an accident, associated with the operation of an aircraft that affects or could affect continued safe operation if not corrected.

Aircraft Rescue And Fire Fighting (ARFF)
Term used to describe actions required by rescue and fire fighting personnel to handle aircraft incidents and accidents.

Air Cylinder
Metal or composite cylinder that contains compressed air for the breathing apparatus. Also called Air Tank.

Air Drop
The process of dropping water or fire retardant from an aircraft onto a wildland fire.

Air-Entrained Concrete
Concrete with air entrapped in its structure to improve its resistance to freezing.

Airfield
See Airport.

Air Foam
Term used to describe mechanical foam, as differentiated from chemical foam; the type of foam concentrate added to water and agitated or aerated to produce the agent.

Airfoil
Any surface, such as an airplane wing, aileron, elevator, rudder, or helicopter rotor, designed to obtain reaction from the air through which it travels. This reaction keeps the aircraft aloft and controls its flight attitude and direction.

Airframe
(1) Major components, such as the fuselage, wings, stabilizers, and flight control surfaces, of an aircraft that are necessary for flight. (2) Basic model of an aircraft; for example, the Boeing 707 airframe has both civilian and military applications in a variety of configurations.

Air-Handling System
See HVAC System.

Air Inversion
Meteorological condition in which the temperature of the air some distance above the earth's surface is higher than the temperature of the air at the surface. Normally, air temperatures decrease as altitude increases. An air inversion traps air, releases gases and vapors near the surface, and impedes their dispersion.

Air Lift Axle
Single air-operated axle that, when lowered, will convert a vehicle into a multiaxle unit, providing the vehicle with a greater load carrying capacity.

Air Lifting Bag
Inflatable envelope-type device that may be inserted between the ground and an object and then inflated to lift the object. It can also be used to separate objects. Depending on the size of the bag, it may have lifting capabilities in excess of 75 tons (68 040 kg).

Air Line Connection
See Chuck.

Airline System
System in which breathing air is continuously supplied to the SCBA wearer from a remote source of air.

Air Lock
(1) Intermediate chamber between places of unequal atmospheric pressure or temperature. (2) Situation that can develop in a centrifugal pump that has not been properly primed. The rapid revolution of the impeller may create an air lock, which prevents priming the pump.

Air Mask
See Self-Contained Breathing Apparatus.

Air Pack
See Self-Contained Breathing Apparatus.

Air Pocket
(1) Condition that occurs during drafting when a portion of hard suction hose is elevated higher than the intake of the pump. (2) Void created by a cave-in. (3) Confined space where air is trapped in the top of a vehicle that has sunk beneath the water. (4) Condition of the atmosphere (as a local down current) that causes an airplane to drop suddenly.

Airport
Land used for aircraft takeoffs and landings.

Airport Control Tower
Unit established to provide traffic control service for the movement of aircraft and other vehicles in the airport operations area.

Airport Emergency Plan
Plan formulated by airport authorities to ensure prompt response to all emergencies and other unusual conditions in order to minimize the extent of personal and property damage.

Airport Familiarization
Knowledge of airport buildings, runways and taxiways, access roads, and surface features that may enhance or obstruct the prompt and safe response to accidents/incidents on the airport.

Airport Fire Protection
Specialized branch of the fire service dealing with airports or aircraft.

Airport Flight Information Service
Air traffic service units that provide services for airport flight information, search and rescue, alerting aircraft at noncontrolled airports, and aircraft emergency situations.

Airport Ground Control
Control of aircraft and other vehicular traffic operating in the airport movement area by the airport control tower.

Air Operations Area (AOA)
Area of an airport such as taxiways, runways, and ramps, where aircraft are expected to operate .

Air-Pressure Sprinkler System
Sprinkler system in which air pressure is used to force water from a storage tank into the system.

Air Purifier
Air-filtration system for compressed breathing air.

Air-Reactive Materials
Substances that ignite when exposed to air at normal temperatures. Also called Pyrophoric.

Air Scoop
Hood or open end of an air duct that introduces air into an automobile or aircraft engine for combustion, cooling, ventilating, etc.

Air Spring
Flexible, air-inflated chamber on a truck or trailer in which the air pressure is controlled and varied to support the load and absorb road shocks.

Air-Supply Unit
Apparatus designed to refill exhausted SCBA air cylinders at the scene of an ongoing emergency.

Air Surface Detection Equipment (ASDE)
Short-range radar, displaying the airport surface, used to track and guide surface traffic in low-visibility weather conditions. ASDE may be used to direct radio-equipped emergency vehicles to known accident sites.

Air Tank
See Air Cylinder.

Air Tanker
Aircraft used to drop retardant or water during an air attack.

Air Traffic Control (ATC)
Federal Aviation Administration (FAA) division that operates control towers at major airports.

Airway
(1) Metal or plastic framework designed to fit the curvature of the mouth and throat to prevent air passageways from closing. (2) Channel of a designated radio frequency for broadcasting or other radio communications. (3) Designated route along which airplanes fly from airport to airport.

Alarm
(1) Any signal indicating the need for emergency fire service response. (2) Predetermined number of fire units assigned to respond to an emergency. (3) Radio designation for the dispatch center; for example, "Engine 65 to Alarm, we are returning and available."

Alarm Check Valve
The valve in an automatic sprinkler system that activates the alarm signal when water is flowing in the system.

Alarm Circuit
Electrical circuit connecting two points in an alarm system; for example, from the signal device to the fire station, from the central alarm center to all fire stations, or from the sending device to the audible alarm services.

Alarm-Initiating Device
Mechanical or electrical device that activates an alarm system. There are three basic types of alarm-initiating devices: manual, products-of-combustion detectors, and extinguishing system activation devices.

All Clear
(1) Signal given when all victims have been extricated from an entrapment. (2) Signal that a danger has passed. (3) Signal given to incident commander that a specific area has been checked for victims and none have been found or all found victims have been removed.

Allergic Reaction
Local or general (systemic) reaction to an allergen; usually characterized by hives, tissue swelling, or difficulty breathing.

All Hands
Fire service jargon for an emergency incident engaging all companies on the first-alarm assignment; may be followed by multiple alarms.

Allocated Resources
Resources dispatched to an incident that have not been checked in with the incident commander.

Alloy
Substance composed of two or more metals fused together and dissolved in each other when molten.

Alternate Airport
Airport to which an aircraft may proceed if a landing at the intended airport becomes inadvisable.

Altitude
Geographical position of a location or object in relation to sea level. The location may be either above, below, or at sea level.

Aluminize
To coat with aluminum.

Aluminum Alloy Ladder
Ladder made of aluminum and other materials, such as magnesium, to make the ladder lightweight but strong.

Alveoli
Air sacs of the lungs; place where oxygen is passed to the blood and carbon dioxide is passed from the blood.

Ambu-bag
Trade name for a device that is used to provide the manual ventilation of a victim during cardiopulmonary resuscitation.

Ambulance
Special vehicle equipped to transport sick or injured people to medical facilities.

American National Standards Institute (ANSI)
Voluntary standards-setting organization that examines and certifies existing standards and creates new standards.

American Society for Testing and Materials
Voluntary standards-setting organization that sets standards for systems, materials, and services.

Ammeter
(1) Instrument for measuring electric current in amperes. (2) Gauge that indicates both the amount of electrical current being drawn from and provided to the vehicle's battery.

Ampere
(1) Amount of current sent by one volt through one ohm of resistance. (2) Unit of measurement of electrical current.

Amputation
Complete removal of an appendage.

Anaphylaxis (Anaphylactic Shock)
Severe systemic allergic reaction characterized by hives, itching, difficulty breathing, and possible circulatory collapse.

Anatomy
Structure of the body or the study of body structure.

Anchor
(1) Metal device used to hold down the ends of trusses or heavy timber members at the walls. (2) Reliable or principal support. (3) Something that serves to hold an object firmly.

Anchor Point
(1) Solid base or point from which pulling or pushing operations can be initiated. (2) Point from which a fire line is begun; usually, a natural or man-made barrier that prevents fire spread and the possibility of the crew being "flanked" while constructing the fire line. Examples are lakes and ponds, streams, roads, earlier burns, rock slides, and cliffs.

Ancillary Ladder
Small ladder attached to an elevating platform to be used as an escape route for platform passengers in the event of a mechanical failure of the aerial device.

Angina Pectoris
Spasmodic pain in the chest caused by insufficient blood supply to the heart; aggravated by exercise or tension and relieved by rest or medication.

Angle Of Approach
Angle formed by level ground and a line from the point where the front tires of a vehicle touch the ground to the lowest projection at the front of the apparatus. The angle of approach should be at least 16 degrees.

Angle Of Departure
Angle formed by level ground and a line from the point where the rear tires of a vehicle touch the ground to the lowest projection at the rear of the apparatus. The angle of departure should be at least 8 degrees.

Annual Leave
Vacation time allowed firefighters per year.

ANSI
Acronym for American National Standards Institute.

Anterior
(1) Situated in front of, or in the forward part of. (2) In anatomy, used in reference to the belly surface of the body.

Anti-Electrocution Platform
Slide-out platform mounted beneath the side running board or rear step of an apparatus equipped with an aerial device. This platform is designed to minimize the chance of the driver/operator being electrocuted should the aerial device come in contact with energized electrical wires or equipment.

Antifogging Chemical
Chemical used to prohibit fogging inside the facepiece.

Anti-Shim Device
See Dead Latch.

Anus
Outlet of the rectum lying in the cleft between the buttocks.

Anxiety
Feeling of apprehension, uncertainty, and fear.

Aorta
Largest artery in the body; originates at the left ventricle.

Apgar Score
Method developed by Dr. Virginia Apgar for assessing the newborn infant at 1 minute of age by designating a score of 0, 1, or 2 for the following: A = Appearance, P = Pulse Rate, G = Grimace, A = Activity, and R = Respiration.

Apnea
Cessation of breathing; the absence of respiration.

A-Post
Front post area of a vehicle where the door is connected to the body.

Apparatus
Vehicle or group of vehicles of any variety used in the fire service.

Apparatus Bay (Apparatus Room)
Area of the fire station where apparatus are parked.

Apparatus Engine
Diesel or gasoline engine that powers the apparatus drive chain and associated fire equipment. Also called Power Plant.

Appendicitis
Condition in which the appendix becomes swollen and infected; characterized by sharp pain in the lower right abdomen.

Appliance
Generic term applied to any nozzle, wye, siamese, deluge monitor, or other piece of hardware used in conjunction with fire hose for the purpose of delivering water.

Application Step
Third step, in the four-step teaching method of conducting a lesson, in which the learner is given the opportunity to apply what has been learned and to perform under supervision and assistance as necessary.

Applicator Pipe
Curved pipe attached to a nozzle for precisely applying water over a burning object.

Apprenticeship
Labor organization professional development program requiring at least three years of fire service experience supplemented with related technical instruction. Apprentices are subject to probationary periods, the length of which is stipulated in local programs. The fire service apprenticeship training program was developed by the International Association of Fire Chiefs and the International Association of Fire Fighters and accepted by the U.S. Department of Labor's Bureau of Apprenticeship and Training on July 11, 1975.

Approach-Avoidance
Decision-making problem; refers to an inner conflict within the person in charge that results in an inability to make a decision.

Approach Clothing
Special personal protective clothing designed to protect the firefighter from radiant heat while approaching the fire. It typically consists of standard turnout gear with an aluminized outer coating.

Approach Lights
System of lights arranged to assist an airplane pilot in aligning his or her aircraft with the runway for landing.

Approach Sequence
Order in which aircraft are positioned while on approach or while awaiting approach clearance.

Apron
Area on airports intended to accommodate aircraft for purposes of loading or unloading passengers or cargo, refueling, parking, or maintenance.

Aqueous Film Forming Foam (AFFF)
Synthetic foam concentrate that, when combined with water, is a highly effective extinguishing and blanketing agent on hydrocarbon fuels.

Arched Roof
Any of several different types of roofs of which all are curved or arch shaped, resembling the top half of a horizontal cylinder. Typical applications are on supermarkets, auditoriums, bowling centers, sports arenas, and aircraft hangars.

Area Ignition
Simultaneous or nearly simultaneous ignition of several natural cover fires in an area that are spaced in such a way as to add to and influence the main body of the fire. Area ignition is a cause of blowup and great fire spread.

Area Of Origin
Localized area where a fire originated.

Area Of Refuge
Two-hour-rated building compartment containing one elevator to the ground floor and at least one enclosed exit stairway.

ARFF
Acronym for Aircraft Rescue and Fire Fighting.

Arrest
(1) Sudden cessation or stoppage. (2) Restricting a person's movement or freedom, usually in a legal or law enforcement action.

Arresting System
Device used to engage an aircraft and absorb forward momentum in case of an aborted takeoff and/or landing.

Arrhythmia
Any disturbance in the rhythm of the heart.

Arson
Willful and malicious burning of the property of oneself or another.

Arson Hotline
Telephone line and operation set up for the purpose of receiving information, often anonymously given, on arson crimes.

Arsonist
Person who commits an act of arson.

Arson Kit
Kit containing equipment used to detect, collect, protect, and preserve evidence of arson and to aid in determining the cause of a fire.

Arson Task Force
Group of individuals who convene to analyze, investigate, and reduce the arson problem in a particular region.

Arteriosclerosis
Generic name for several conditions that cause the walls of the arteries to become thickened, hard, and inelastic.

Artery
Blood vessel that carries blood away from the heart.

Articulating Aerial Platform
Aerial device that consists of two or more booms that are attached with hinges and operate in a folding manner. A passenger-carrying platform is attached to the working end of the device.

Articulating Boom
Arm portion of the articulating aerial platform.

Articulation
(1) The action or manner of jointing or interrelating. (2) A joint or juncture between bones or cartilages.

Artificial Respiration
Movement of air into and out of the lungs by artificial means. Also known as Rescue Breathing, Artificial Resuscitation, and Pulmonary Resuscitation.

Artificial Resuscitation
See Artificial Respiration.

Asbestos
Carcinogenic fibrous substance used for insulation and ceiling materials in older buildings. Inhaled asbestos fibers travel to the lungs, causing scarring, reduced lung capacity, and cancer.

Asbestosis
Emphysemalike condition caused by respiratory exposure to asbestos.

Ascender
Mechanical contrivance, used when climbing rope, that allows upward movement but not downward movement.

Aspect
(1) Position facing a particular direction; exposure. (2) Compass direction toward which a slope faces.

Asphyxia
Suffocation.

Asphyxiant
Any substance that prevents oxygen from combining in sufficient quantities with the blood or being used by body tissues.

Asphyxiating Materials
Substances that can cause death by displacing the oxygen in the air.

Asphyxiation
Condition that causes death because of a deficient amount of oxygen and an excessive amount of carbon monoxide and/or other gases in the blood.

Aspirate
To inhale foreign material into the lungs.

Aspirator
Suction device for removing undesirable material from the throat of a victim.

Assembly
Manufactured parts fitted together to make a complete machine, structure, or unit.

Assigned Resources
Resources checked in and assigned an objective on an incident.

Assisting Agency
Agency directly contributing suppression, rescue, support, or service resources to another agency.

Asthma
Respiratory condition marked by attacks of labored breathing, wheezing, a sense of constriction in the chest, and coughing or gasping.

ASTM
Abbreviation for American Society for Testing and Materials.

Astragal
Molding that covers the narrow opening between adjacent double doors in the closed position.

Atherosclerosis
Common form of arteriosclerosis characterized by fat deposits in the walls of the arteries.

Atmospheric Ceiling
Level in the atmosphere at which a heated column ceases to rise.

Atmospheric Displacement
System or method of applying water fog in a superheated area causing the water to be converted into steam that expands and displaces the atmosphere in a burning room or building.

Atmospheric Pressure
Pressure exerted by the atmosphere at the surface of the earth due to the weight of air. Atmospheric pressure at sea level is about 14.7 psi (101 kPa). Atmospheric pressure increases as elevation is decreased below sea level and decreases as elevation increases above sea level.

Atomic Number
Number of protons in an atom.

Atomic Weights
Relate to the weights of molecules and atoms. A standard for atomic weights has been adopted to a relative scale in which that for carbon has been set at 12, although its true atomic weight is 12.01115.

Atrium
(1) Upper chamber of the left or right side of the heart. (2) Open area in the center of a building, similar to a courtyard but usually covered by a skylight, to allow natural light and ventilation to interior rooms.

Attack
(1) To set upon forcefully. (2) Any action to control fire.

Attack Hose
Hose between the attack pumper and the nozzle(s); also, any hose used in a handline to control and extinguish fire. Minimum size is 1½ inch (38 mm).

Attack Lines
Hoselines or fire streams used to attack, contain, or prevent the spread of a fire.

Attack Pumper
(1) Pumper that is positioned at the fire scene and is directly supplying attack lines. (2) Light truck equipped with a small pump and water tank. Also called a Minipumper or Midipumper.

Attic
Concealed and often unfinished space between the ceiling of the top floor and the roof of a building.

Attic Fold
Method of folding a salvage cover that aids in spreading within the tight confines of an attic where lateral movement is difficult.

Attic Ladder
Collapsible ladder especially useful for inside work; comes in 6- to 14-foot (2 m to 4 m) lengths.

Attitude
Position of an aircraft determined by the relationship between its axes and a reference datum (as the horizon or a particular star).

Audible Alarm
(1) Bell, whistle, or other sound-producing alerting device attached to a self-contained breathing apparatus or personal alert safety system. (2) Sound-producing alerting device attached to a fixed fire protection system.

Audiometric Test
Examinations used to determine the extent of temporary or permanent shifts in thresholds of hearing acuity. These tests make it possible to grade occupational noise exposures and, when necessary, recommend appropriate hearing conservation procedures.

Auditorium Raise
Method of extending a ladder perpendicular and holding it in place from four opposite points of the compass by four guy ropes attached to the top of the ladder. Also called Church Raise or Steeple Raise.

Auger
(1) Screwlike shaft that is turned to move grain or other commodities through a farm implement. (2) Tool for boring holes in floors.

Auger Wagon
Large wagon containing a PTO-driven auger for unloading purposes. Widely used in agriculture to transport and unload grain, silage, loose forage, stover, and other loose materials.

Authority
Relates to the empowered duties of an official to perform certain tasks.

Authority Having Jurisdiction
Term used in codes and standards to identify the legal entity that has the ability to approve or require equipment, procedures, and building-codes concerns in a municipality.

Autoexposure
See Lapping.

Autoignition
Ignition that occurs when a substance in air, whether solid, liquid, or gaseous, is heated sufficiently to initiate or cause self-sustained combustion independently of the heat source.

Autoignition Temperature
See Ignition Temperatures.

Automatic Alarm
(1) Alarm actuated by heat, smoke, flame-sensing devices, or the waterflow in a sprinkler system conveyed to local alarm bells and/or the fire station. (2) Alarm boxes that automatically transmit a coded signal to the fire station to give the location of the alarm box.

Automatic Hydrant Valve
Valve that when connected to a hydrant opens automatically to permit water to flow into the supply line.

Automatic Nozzle
Fog stream nozzle that automatically corrects itself to provide a good stream at the proper nozzle pressure.

Automatic Sprinkler Kit
Kit containing the tools and equipment required to close an open sprinkler head.

Automatic Sprinkler System
System of water pipes, discharge nozzles, and control valves designed to activate during fires by automatically discharging enough water to control or extinguish a fire. Also called Sprinkler System.

Autonomic Nervous System
Part of the nervous system concerned with the regulation of body functions not controlled by conscious thought.

Autorotation
Flight condition in which the lifting rotor of a rotary wing aircraft is driven entirely by action of the air when in flight or, as in the case of a helicopter, after an engine failure.

Auxiliary
(1) Additional fire fighting equipment or staffing that are not part of the regular complement assigned to the fire service. (2) Ladies' group organized to assist the fire department.

Auxiliary Deadbolt
Deadbolt bored lock. Also called Tubular Deadbolt.

Auxiliary Hydraulic Pump
Electrically operated, positive displacement pump used to supply hydraulic oil through the hydraulic system of an aerial device in the event that the main hydraulic pump fails.

Auxiliary Lock
Lock added to a door to increase security.

Auxiliary Power Unit (APU)
(1) Power unit installed in most large aircraft to provide electrical power and pneumatics for ground power, air conditioning, engine start, and backup power in flight. (2) Mobile units that are moved from one aircraft to another to provide a power boost during engine startup.

Available Fire Flow
Actual amount of water available from a given hydrant; determined by testing.

Available Resources
Resources not assigned to an incident and available for an assignment.

Average Daily Consumption
Average of the total amount of water used each day during a one-year period.

Avoidance
Effect of a decision-making problem. The person in charge might try to avoid being in charge, especially when faced with an approach-avoidance dilemma.

Awning Window
Type of swinging window that is hinged at the top and swings outward, often having two or more sections.

Axe
Forcible entry tool that has a pick or flat head and a blade attached to a wood or fiberglass handle. Also called Firefighter's Axe.

B

B.A.
Abbreviation for Breathing Apparatus. *See* Self-Contained Breathing Apparatus.

Back Burn
The process of burning plots of land to establish a fire break that is intended to stop the spread of a wildland fire.

Backdraft
Instantaneous explosion or rapid burning of superheated gases that occurs when oxygen is introduced into an oxygen-depleted confined space. It may occur because of inadequate or improper ventilation procedures.

Backfill
Coarse dirt or other material used to build up the ground level around the foundation walls to provide a slope for drainage away from the foundation.

Backfiring
(1) Technique used in the indirect attack method for natural cover fires; intentionally setting a fire between the control line and the advancing fire. The intent is for the backfire to meet the advancing fire some distance from the control line. Backfiring can be dangerous and is illegal in some places. (2) Improperly timed explosion of fuel mixture in the cylinder of an internal-combustion engine.

Back Flushing
The cleaning of a fire pump or piping by flowing water through it in the opposite direction of normal flow.

Backlash
(1) Sudden violent backward movement or reaction. (2) Reverse bouncing motion that occurs when the motion of an aerial device is abruptly halted.

Backpack
(1) Tank-type extinguisher carried on the firefighter's back by straps. The unit has a pump built into the nozzle; used extensively to fight natural cover fires. (2) Pack used to carry hose on firefighters' backs. (3) Assembly that holds the air cylinder and regulator of the self-contained breathing apparatus to the wearer.

Back Plate
See Backpack (3).

Back Pressure
Pressure loss or gain created by changes in elevation between the nozzle and pump.

Backsplash
Vertical surface at the back of a countertop.

Backwards
Slang for making a reverse hose lay; as in "Lay a backwards."

Badge
Indicator of rank worn on a firefighter's or an officer's uniform.

Baffle
(1) Intermediate partial bulkhead that reduces the surge effect in a partially loaded liquid tank. (2) Divider used to separate beds of hose into two or more compartments.

Bagging
For salvage and overhaul purposes it is the spreading of a salvage cover to catch water from above, particularly in an attic.

Bag-Valve Mask
Portable artificial ventilation unit consisting of a face mask, a one-way valve, and an inflatable bag; can be used on a nonbreathing or breathing patient.

Balanced Pressure Proportioner
A foam concentrate proportioner that operates in tandem with a fire water pump to ensure a proper foam concentrate-to-water mixture.

Bale Hook/Baling Hook
Tool used for moving bales or boxed goods and for moving and overhauling stuffed furniture or mattresses. Also called Hay Hook.

Balloon-Frame Construction
Type of structural framing used in some single-story and multistory buildings wherein the studs are continuous from the foundation to the roof. There may be no fire stops between the studs.

Balloon Throw
Method of spreading a salvage cover that utilizes air trapped under the cover to float it into place over materials to be protected.

Ball Valve
Valve having a ball-shaped internal component with a hole through its center that permits water to flow through when aligned with the waterway.

Baluster
Vertical member supporting a handrail.

Balustrade
Entire assembly of a handrail including its supporting members (newel posts and balusters).

Bandage
Material used to hold a dressing in place.

Banding Method
Means of attaching a coupling to a fire hose with tightly wound strands of narrow-gauge wire or steel bands.

Bangor Ladder
See Pole Ladder.

Bang Out
Slang for "to dispatch" or "to be dispatched."

Barometer
Instrument used for the measurement of atmospheric pressure.

Barrel Strainer
Cylindrical strainer that is attached to a hard suction hose to prevent the induction of foreign debris into the pump during drafting operations.

Bar-Screw Jack
Jack used to hold loads under compression. It is commonly used in shoring work or other similar evolutions.

Basal Skull Fracture
Fracture involving the base of the cranium.

Base
(1) Bottom of something; considered as its support; foundation. (2) Location at which the primary incident command logistics functions are coordinated and administered. The incident command post may be co-located with the base. There is only one base per incident.

Base Leg
Flight path at right angles to the landing runway off the approach end.

Basement Plans
Drawings showing the below ground view of a building. The thickness and external dimensions of the basement walls are given, as are floor joist locations, strip footings, and other attached foundations.

Base Section
See Bed Section.

Basic Life Support
Maintenance of airway, breathing, and circulation, as well as basic bandaging and splinting, without the use of adjunctive equipment.

Basket Stabilizer
Device used to support the platform (basket) portion of an elevating platform device in the stowed position during road travel.

Battalion
Fire department subdivision consisting of all fire service equipment and personnel in a designated geographic area.

Battalion Chief
Chief officer assigned to command a fire department battalion.

Batten Door
See Ledge Door.

Battering
Act of creating an opening in a building component by striking and breaking it with a tool such as a sledge or ram.

Battering Ram
Large metal pipe with handles used to break down doors or create holes in walls.

Battery
(1) Intentional and unauthorized touching of a person without his or her consent. (2) Grouping of artillery pieces for tactical purposes. (3) Number of similar articles, items, or devices arranged, connected, or used together.

Battery Bank
Group of vehicle batteries clustered in one location.

Batt Insulation
Blanket insulation cut in widths to fit between studs and in short lengths to facilitate handling.

Battle's Sign
Purplish discoloration above the bone behind the ear indicating a skull fracture.

Bay
Compartment or section in a fire station where the fire apparatus is parked.

Beam
(1) Structural member subjected to loads perpendicular to its length. (2) Main structural member of a ladder supporting the rungs or rung blocks.

Beam Block
See Truss Block.

Beam Bolts
Bolts that pass through both rails at the truss block of a wooden ladder to tie the two truss rails together.

Beam Raise
Raising a ladder to the vertical position with only one beam in contact with the ground instead of both beams being on the ground as with a flat raise.

Bearing Wall
Wall that supports itself and the weight of the roof and/or other structural components above it.

Becket Bend
Knot used for joining two ropes. It is particularly well suited for joining ropes of unequal diameters or joining a rope and a chain. Also called Sheet Bend.

Bed Ladder
Lowest section of a multisection ladder.

Bed Ladder Pipe
Nontelescoping section of pipe, usually 3 or 3½ inches (77 mm or 90 mm) in diameter, attached to the underside of the bed section of the aerial ladder for the purpose of deploying an elevated master stream.

Bed Section
Bottom section of an extension ladder. Also called Base Section.

Behavioral Objective
Measurable statement of behavior required to demonstrate that learning has occurred.

Below Minimum
Weather conditions below the minimum prescribed by regulation for a particular operation such as the takeoff or landing of aircraft.

Belt System
See Loop System.

Bench Mark
(1) Mark on some object firmly fixed in the ground from which distances and elevations are measured. (2) Anything that serves as a standard against which others may be measured; usually Benchmark.

Bent
Supporting legs of a bridge in a plane perpendicular to its length.

Benzene (C_6H_6)
Highly toxic carcinogen produced when PVC plastics and gasoline burn. Inhalation of high levels can cause unconsciousness and death from respiratory paralysis.

Bernoulli's Equation
Mathematical expression of the principle of conservation of energy.

Bid Bond
Deposit provided to the apparatus purchaser from the manufacturer in order to ensure that the manufacturer will take the bid made if offered. This prevents damages to the purchaser should the bidder default on any part of the deal. The bond is returned to the manufacturer when the contract is executed.

Bifold Doors
Doors designed to fold in half vertically.

Bight
Element of a knot formed by simply bending the rope back on itself while keeping the sides parallel.

Big Line
Slang for a hoseline of at least 2½-inch (65 mm) diameter, especially when used as a handline.

Big Stick
Slang for a mechanically raised main ladder or an aerial ladder truck. Originally, aerial ladders were made of wood, hence the term "big stick."

Bile
Fluid secreted by the liver that is concentrated and stored in the gall bladder.

Bill Of Lading
Shipping paper used by the trucking industry indicating origin, destination, route, and product. There is a bill of lading in the cab of every truck tractor.

Billy Pugh Net
Rope net or basket designed to be suspended beneath a helicopter for transporting personnel and/or equipment.

Bimetallic
Strip or disk composed of two different metals that are bonded together; used in heat detection equipment.

Biological Death
Condition present when irreversible brain damage has occurred, usually 4 to 10 minutes after cardiac arrest.

Bird Box
See Connection Box.

Bird Cage Construction
See Integral Construction.

Birth Canal
Canal through which the fetus passes during childbirth; composed of the cervix, vagina, and vulva.

Bitter End
See Working End.

Blacken
To "knock down" a fire; to reduce a fire by extinguishing all visible flame. As the flame is extinguished, the fire is said to be blackened.

Bladder
Membranous sac that stores urine.

Blanch
To become white or pale.

Blanket
(1) Thick layer of insulating material between two layers of heavy waterproof paper. (2) Layer of foam over a fuel.

Blast Area
Area affected by the blast wave from an explosion.

Bleed
(1) Process of releasing a liquid or gas under pressure. (2) Release of air from the regulator or cylinder of a self-contained breathing apparatus.

Bleeder Valve
Valve on a gate intake that allows air from an incoming supply line to be bled off before allowing the water into the pump.

BLEVE
Acronym for Boiling Liquid Expanding Vapor Explosion.

Blitz Attack
To aggressively attack a fire from the exterior with a large caliber (2½-inch [65 mm] or larger) fire stream.

Block
Division of an occupational analysis consisting of a group of related tasks with one factor in common.

Block And Tackle
Series of pulleys (sheaves) contained within a wood or metal frame. They are used with rope to provide a mechanical advantage for pulling operations.

Blood
Fluid that circulates through the heart, arteries, veins, and capillaries, carrying nutrients and oxygen to the body cells and removing waste products, such as carbon dioxide, for excretion.

Blood Pressure (BP)
Pressure exerted by the flow of blood against the arterial walls.

Blood Volume
Total amount of blood in the heart and the blood vessels.

Blow-Down Valve
Manually operated valve whose function is to quickly reduce tank pressure to atmospheric.

Blower
Large-volume fan used to blow fresh air into a building or other confined space. Often used in positive-pressure ventilation (PPV), blowers are most often powered by gasoline engines, but some have electric motors.

Blowup
Dangerously rapid increase in natural cover fire spread caused by any one or more of several factors: strong or erratic wind, uphill slopes, large open areas, and easily ignited fuels.

Blunt Start
See Higbee Cut.

Board Of Appeals
Group of five to seven people with experience in fire prevention and code enforcement who arbitrate differences in opinion between fire inspectors and property owners or occupants.

Body Bag
Device used to remove the bodies of deceased victims. The bags are made of rubber or plastic and are widely used at disasters.

Body-On-Chassis Construction
Method of school bus or recreational vehicle construction where the school bus body manufacturer installs the body unit onto a commercially available chassis constructed by another manufacturer.

Bogie
Tandem arrangement of aircraft landing gear wheels with a central strut. The bogie swivels up and down so all wheels stay on the ground as the attitude of the aircraft changes or as the slope of the ground surface changes.

Boiling Liquid Expanding Vapor Explosion (BLEVE)
Major failure of a closed liquid container into two or more pieces when the temperature of the liquid is well above its boiling point at normal atmospheric pressure.

Boiling Point
Temperature of a substance when the vapor pressure exceeds atmospheric pressure. At this temperature, the rate of evaporation exceeds the rate of condensation. At this point, more liquid is turning into gas than gas is turning back into a liquid.

Boilover
Overflow of crude oil from its container when the heat wave reaches the water level in the tank. The water flashes to steam causing a violent expulsion of the material as a froth.

Bolster
See Chair.

Bolt Cutters
Cutting tool designed to make a precise, controlled cut; used for cutting wire, fencing, bolts, and small steel bars.

Bomb Line
Slang for a portable master stream device that is preconnected to a short length (less than 200 feet [60 m]) of hose for rapid deployment.

Bomb Squad
Crew of emergency responders specially trained and equipped to deal with explosive devices.

Bonding
(1) Connection of two objects with a metal chain or strap in order to neutralize the static electrical charge between the two. (2) Gluing two objects together.

Booms
Telescoping or articulating arm portions of an elevating platform aerial device.

Booster Apparatus
See Brush Apparatus.

Booster Hose
Fabric reinforced, rubber-covered, rubber-lined hose. Booster hose is generally carried on apparatus on a reel and is used for the initial attack and extinguishment of incipient and smoldering fires. Also called Hard Line and Red Line.

Booster Pump
Fire pump used to boost the pressure of the existing water supply within a fixed fire protection system.

Booster Reel
Mounted reel on which booster hose is carried.

Booster Tank
See Water Tank.

Bored Lock
Lock installed within right angle holes bored in a door. Also called Cylindrical Lock.

Bourdon Gauge
Most common device used to measure water system pressures.

Bourdon Tube
Part of a pressure gauge that has a curved, flat tube that changes its curvature as pressure changes. This movement is then transferred mechanically to a pointer on the dial.

Bowline Knot
Knot used to form a loop in natural fiber rope.

Box
Short term for public or private fire alarm box.

Box Alarm
(1) Signal transmitted from a fire alarm box. (2) Predetermined response assignment to an emergency call.

Box-Beam Construction
Method of construction for aerial device booms consisting of four sides welded together to form a box shape with a hollow center. Hydraulic lines, air lines, electrical cords, and waterways may be encased within the center or on the outside of the box beam.

Box Crib
Stabilization platform constructed by creating opposing layers of pieces of cribbing.

Box Lock
Lock mortised into a door. Also called Mortise Lock.

Box Stabilizer
Two-piece aerial apparatus stabilization device consisting of an extension arm that extends directly out from the vehicle and a lifting jack that extends from the end of the extension arm to the ground. Also called H-Jack.

Boyle's Law
Law that states that the volume of a gas varies inversely with the applied pressure. The formula is: $P_1V_1=P_2V_2$ where P_1 = original pressure, V_1 = original volume, P_2 = final pressure, and V_2 = final volume.

BP
Abbreviation for Blood Pressure.

B-Post
Post between the front and rear doors on a four-door vehicle, or the door-handle-end post on a two-door car.

Brace Lock
Rim lock equipped with a metal rod that serves as a brace against the door.

Brachial Artery
Main artery of the upper arm.

Bradycardia
Abnormally slow heart rate, usually any rate less than 60 beats per minute.

Braided Hose
Nonwoven rubber hose manufactured by braiding one or more layers of yarn, each separated by a rubber layer, over a rubber tube and encased in a rubber cover.

Braided Rope
Rope constructed by uniformly intertwining strands of rope together (similar to braiding a person's hair).

Braid-On-Braid Rope
Rope constructed with both a braided core and a braided sheath. The appearance of the sheath is that of a herringbone pattern.

Brain
Large, soft mass of nerve tissue that is contained within the cranium.

Brain Stem
Stemlike portion of the brain that connects the brain with the spinal cord.

Brake Limiting Valve
Valve that allows the vehicle's brakes to be adjusted for the current road conditions.

Braking Distance
Distance the vehicle travels from the time the brakes are applied until it comes to a complete stop.

Branch
Organizational level of an incident management system having functional/geographic responsibility for major segments of incident operations. The branch level is organizationally between section and division/sector/group.

Branch Line
Those pipes in an automatic sprinkler system to which the sprinklers are directly attached.

Brands
(1) Large, burning embers that are lifted by a fire's thermal column and carried away with the wind. (2) Small burning pieces of wood or charcoal used to test the fire resistance of roof coverings and roof deck assemblies.

Brass
(1) Brasswork or brass appliances carried on fire apparatus; may now be chrome-plated or made of lightweight alloys. (2) Slang for upper management personnel or chief officers.

Breach
To make an opening in a wall for rescue, hoseline operation, ventilation, or other reasons.

Break A Line
To disconnect hoselines for any purpose, especially to break and roll up hose after a fire operation; to disconnect a hose coupling.

Breakaway/Frangible Fences And Gates
Fences and gates designed and constructed to collapse when impacted by large vehicles to allow rapid access to accident sites.

Breakover Angle
Angle formed by level ground and a line from the point where the rear tires of a vehicle touch the ground to the bottom of the frame at the wheelbase midpoint. This angle should be at least 10 degrees.

Breast Timber
Strut that holds a horizontal compression load, keeping sheeting in place for shoring.

Breathing Air
Compressed air that is filtered and contains no more contaminants than are allowed by standards.

Breathing-Air Compressor
Compressor specifically designed to compress air for breathing-air cylinders.

Breathing Tube
Low-pressure hose that extends from the regulator to the facepiece on SCBA.

Breech Delivery
Delivery of a fetus with some part of the body other than the head appearing first. Usually the buttocks appear first in a breech birth.

Bresnan Distributor Nozzle
Cellar nozzle in which the head rotates when water flows through it.

Brick-Joisted
Brick or masonry wall structure with wooden floors and roof. Commonly known as ordinary construction.

Brick Veneer
Single layer of bricks applied to the inside or outside surface of a wall for esthetic and/or insulation purposes.

Bridge
To place a ladder to span a gap, usually between two structures.

Bridge Truss
Heavy-duty truss, usually made of heavy wooden members with steel tie rods, that has horizontal top and bottom chords and steeply sloped ends.

Bridging
Diagonal bracing between joists.

British Thermal Unit (Btu)
Amount of heat energy required to raise the temperature of one pound of water one degree Fahrenheit. One Btu = 1.055 kJ.

Broadside Collision
Collision in which one vehicle sustains direct side impact. Also called T-Bone Collision.

Broken Stream
Stream of water that has been broken into coarsely divided drops.

Bronchial Asthma
Constriction of the bronchial tubes in response to irritation, allergies, or other stimulus.

Bronchus
One of the two main branches of the trachea that lead to the right and left lungs.

Bruise
Injury that does not break the skin but causes rupture of small underlying blood vessels with resulting tissue discoloration. Also known as a Contusion.

Brush
Bushes and small trees of little or no commercial value.

Brush Apparatus
Fire department apparatus designed specifically for fighting ground cover fires. Also called Booster Apparatus, Brush Patrol, Brush Pumper, and Field Unit.

Brush Burn
Scrape or adhesion created when the skin is rubbed across a rough surface; not actually a thermal or chemical burn. Also called Abrasion.

Brush Patrol
See Brush Apparatus.

Brush Pumper
See Brush Apparatus.

Buddy Breathing
Method of sharing another person's SCBA.

Buddy System
See Emergency Escape Breathing Support System.

Buff
Person, other than a firefighter, who is interested in fires, fire departments, and firefighters. Also called Spark.

Buggie
Slang for a chief's vehicle.

Bugles
Insignia depicting early speaking trumpets used to designate the rank of fire department personnel.

Building
Relatively permanent walled and roofed structure that stands alone and separate from other structures.

Building Code
List of rules, usually adopted by city ordinance, to regulate the safe construction of buildings. There are several building codes that are widely adopted in the United States including the Southern Standard Building Code, the Uniform Building Code, the Basic Building Code, and the National Building Code.

Building Engineer
Person who is familiar with and responsible for the operation of a building's heating, ventilating, and air-conditioning (HVAC) system and other essential equipment.

Building Survey
Portion of the pre-incident planning process during which the company travels to a building and gathers the necessary information to develop a pre-incident plan for the building.

Built-Up Roof
Roof covering made of several alternate layers of roofing paper and tar, with the final layer of tar being covered with pea gravel or crushed slag. Also called Tar and Gravel Roof.

Bulk Container
Cargo tank container attached to a flatbed truck or rail flat car used to transport materials in bulk. This may carry liquids or gases.

Bulkhead
(1) Upright partition that separates one aircraft compartment from another. Bulkheads may strengthen or help give shape to the structure and may be used for the mounting of equipment and accessories. (2) Structure on the roof of a building through which the interior stairway opens onto the roof.

Bumper
Structure designed to provide front or rear end protection of a vehicle.

Bumper Line
Preconnected hoseline located on the apparatus bumper.

Bunk
Firefighter's bed.

Bunker Clothes
See Personal Protective Equipment.

Bunk Room
Dormitory area where firefighters sleep.

Bureau Of Alcohol, Tobacco, And Firearms (BATF)
Division of the U.S. Department of Treasury that regulates the storage, handling, and transportation of explosives.

Burn
(1) To be on fire; to consume fuel during rapid combustion. (2) Geographical area over which a fire has passed. (3) Tissue injury caused by heat, electrical current, or chemicals.

Burn Building
Training structure specially designed to contain live fires for the purpose of fire suppression training.

Burn Center
Medical facility especially designed, equipped, and staffed to treat severely burned patients.

Burning Out
Intentionally setting a fire to natural cover fuels inside the control line to widen the line; used as a direct attack technique, usually within 10 feet (3 m) of the line.

Burning Point
See Fire Point.

Burnout
(1) Building that has been denuded of almost all combustible material. Also refers to a burned wildland area. (2) A work-related psychological disorder resulting from stress.

Burn Pattern
Obvious design of burned material and the burning path of travel from a point of fire origin.

Burns, Degree Of
First degree: reddened skin; second degree: blisters; third degree: deep skin destruction. Major types of burns: heat, chemical, electrical, and radiation.

Burst Test
Destructive test on a 3-foot (1 m) length of hose to determine its maximum strength.

Butt
(1) One coupling of a fire hose. (2) Hydrant outlet. (3) Heel (lower end) of a ladder. (4) Act of steadying a ladder that is being climbed.

Butterfly Roof
V-shaped roof style resembling two opposing shed roofs joined along their lower edges.

Butterfly Valve
Type of control valve that uses a flat baffle operated by a quarter-turn handle.

Buttress
Structure projecting from a wall designed to receive lateral pressure action at a particular point.

Butt Spurs
Metal safety plates or spikes attached to the butt end of ground ladder beams.

Bypass Breathing
Emergency procedure in which the SCBA wearer closes the mainline valve and opens the bypass valve for air when a regulator malfunctions.

Bypass Valve
Valve on a self-contained breathing apparatus that when opened lets air bypass its normal route through the regulator; used when a regulator malfunctions

C

Cabin
Aircraft passenger compartment that may be separated and may contain a cargo area.

Cable Hanger
Device used to test the structural strength of aerial ladders.

Caisson
(1) Watertight structure within which construction work is carried out underwater. (2) Large box used to hold ammunition.

Calendering
Fire hose inner tube manufacturing process in which rubber is pressed between opposing rollers to produce a flat sheet. A tube is then formed by lapping and bonding together the edges of the sized sheet.

Calibrate
To standardize or adjust the increments on a measuring instrument.

Call Back
Process of notifying off-duty firefighters to return to their stations for service.

Call Box
See Telephone Alarm Box.

Call Firefighter
See Paid-On-Call Firefighter.

Calorie
Amount of heat needed to raise the temperature of one gram of water one degree Centigrade.

Cam
Part of a mortise lock cylinder that moves the bolt or latch as the key is turned.

Camber
Low vertical arch placed in a beam or girder to counteract deflection caused by loading.

Camlock Fastener
Trade name given to a quick-disconnect screw-type fastener, designed to open with a quarter or half turn.

Canister Apparatus
Type of breathing apparatus that uses filtration, adsorption, or absorption to remove toxic substances from the air. Generally referred to as a Gas Mask; canister apparatus are not acceptable for use in fire fighting operations or IDLH atmospheres.

Canister, Oxygen-Generating
Container of chemicals that generate oxygen when the moisture of an individual's breath is mixed with them.

Can Man
Slang for a firefighter, usually from a truck or ladder company, whose role is to carry a pump can and some other tool, often a pike pole.

Cannula
Tube used to enter a duct or cavity. A nasal cannula is often used to administer supplemental oxygen.

Canopy
(1) Transparent enclosure over the cockpit of some aircraft. (2) Leaves of trees and brush.

Canteen Unit
Emergency vehicle that provides food, drinks, and other rehabilitative services to emergency workers at extended incidents.

Cantilever
Projecting beam or slab supported at one end.

Cantilever Operation
See Unsupported Tip.

Cant Strip
Angular board installed at the intersection of a roof deck and a wall to avoid a sharp right angle when the roofing is installed.

CANUTEC
Canadian hazardous material hotline, similar to CHEMTREC in the U.S.

Capacity
Maximum ability of a pump or water distribution system to deliver water.

Capacity Indicators
Device installed on a tank to indicate capacity at a specific level.

Capillaries
Tiny blood vessels in the body's tissues in which the exchange of oxygen and carbon dioxide take place.

Captain
Rank used in some departments for a company officer.

Carabiner
D-shaped metal device used in connection with ascending or descending a rope.

Carbonaceous
Made of or containing carbon.

Carbonaceous Material
Material that contains carbon.

Carbon Dioxide (CO_2)
(1) Colorless, odorless gas that neither supports combustion nor burns; a waste product of aerobic metabolism. (2) Common extinguishing agent used in portable fire extinguishers.

Carbon Monoxide (CO)
Colorless, odorless, dangerous gas formed by the incomplete combustion of carbon. It combines more than 200 times as quickly with hemoglobin as oxygen.

Carboxyhemoglobin
Hemoglobin saturated with carbon monoxide and therefore unable to absorb needed oxygen.

Carcinogen
Cancer-producing substance.

Cardiac Arrest
Sudden cessation of heartbeat.

Cardiac Neurosis
Stress-caused reaction resembling heart attack in a healthy heart.

Cardiopulmonary Resuscitation (CPR)
Application of rescue breathing and external cardiac compression in patients with cardiac arrest to provide an adequate circulation to support life. Also called Rescue Breathing.

Cardiopulmonary System
Heart and lungs.

Cardiovascular System
Body's system of blood vessels and associated organs that support the flow of blood through the body.

Career Fire
Jargon used to describe a large fire.

Cargo Container
See Container.

Cargo Manifest
Shipping paper listing all contents carried by a vehicle or vessel.

Carline Supports
Structural members used in the construction of buses. They are designed to strengthen the sidewall of the bus where it might come into contact with a car during a collision.

Carotid Artery
Principal artery of the neck, easily felt on either side of the trachea.

Carriage
Main support for the stair treads and risers. Also called a Stringer (1).

Carryall
Waterproof carrier or bag used to carry and catch debris or used as a water sump basin for immersing small burning objects.

Cartilage
Tough, elastic tissue that lines the joints of large bones and separates the vertebrae, providing structure and cushioning.

Cascade Air Cylinders
Large air cylinders that are used to refill smaller SCBA cylinders.

Cascade System
Three or more large air cylinders, each usually with a capacity of 300 cubic feet (8 490 L), that are interconnected and from which smaller SCBA cylinders are recharged.

Case
Housing for any locking mechanism.

Casement Window
Window hinged along one side, usually designed to swing outward, with the screen on the inside.

Cast Coupling
Coupling manufactured by a process in which molten metal is poured into a mold and allowed to cool, and then the mold is removed from the hardened coupling.

Caster/Castor
Roller on the bottom of a chair or piece of furniture.

Catalyst
Substance that modifies (usually increases) the rate of a chemical reaction without being consumed in the process.

Catch A Hydrant
Process in which a firefighter dismounts the fire apparatus at the hydrant, connects the fire hose to the hydrant, and turns on the water.

Catchall
Retaining basin, usually made from salvage covers, to impound water dripping from above.

Catch Basin
See Portable Tank.

Catenary System
System of overhead wiring that provides a power source for electric trains.

Caulk (Calk)
Nonhardening paste used to fill cracks and crevices.

Caustic
Corrosive material that burns or destroys tissue by chemical action, as opposed to heat.

Cavitation
Condition in which vacuum pockets form in a pump and cause vibrations, loss of efficiency, and possibly damage.

Cavity
Hollow or space, especially within the body or one of its organs. For example, the abdominal cavity is bounded by the abdominal walls, the diaphragm, and the pelvis.

Ceiling
(1) Height above the ground of the base of the lowest layer of clouds when over half of the sky is obscured. (2) Nonbearing structural component separating a living/working space from the underside of the floor or roof immediately above.

Cell
(1) Small cavity or compartment. (2) Least structural unit of living matter capable of functioning independently.

Cellar Pipe
Special nozzle for attacking fires in basements, cellars, and other spaces below the attack level.

Cell Electrolyte Level
In apparatus terms, the level of water that is within the vehicle's batteries.

Celsius Scale
Temperature scale in which the freezing point of water is 0 degrees and the boiling point at sea level is 100 degrees. Also known as Centigrade Scale.

Cement
(1) Any adhesive material. (2) Clay mixture called portland cement is combined with sand and/or other aggregates and water to produce mortar or concrete.

Center Rafter Cut
See Louver Cut.

Centigrade Scale
See Celsius Scale.

Central Fire Station
Headquarters station that contains administrative offices, special equipment, fire apparatus, and personnel.

Central Nervous System
Portion of the nervous system consisting of the brain and spinal cord.

Central Neurogenic Hyperventilation
Abnormal pattern of breathing seen in severe illness or injury involving the brain and characterized by very heavy, rapid breathing.

Central Processing Unit (CPU)
Part of a computer that actually possesses information.

Centrifugal Pump
Pump with one or more impellers that utilizes centrifugal force to move the water. Most modern fire pumps are of this type.

Cerebellum
Large posterior portion of the brain just below the cerebrum.

Cerebrospinal Fluid
Clear, watery fluid surrounding the meninges that protects the brain and spinal cord.

Cerebrovascular Accident (CVA)
Hemorrhage or blood clot within a blood vessel in the brain. Also called a Stroke.

Cerebrum
Largest portion of the brain. It controls major body functions, including movement, sensation, thinking, and emotions.

Certification Tests
Preservice tests for aerial device, ladder, pump, and other equipment conducted by an independent testing laboratory prior to delivery of an apparatus. These tests assure that the apparatus or equipment will perform as expected after being placed into service.

Certified Shop Test Curves
Results, which are plotted on a graph, of the test performed by the manufacturer on its pump before shipping the pump.

Cervical Collar
Device used to immobilize and support the neck.

Cervical Spine
First seven bones of the vertebral column, located in the neck.

Cervix
Lower portion, or neck, of the uterus.

C-Factor
Factor that indicates the roughness of the inner surface of piping. The C-factor decreases as the sediment, incrustation, and tuberculation within the pipe increases.

CFM
Abbreviation for Cubic Feet Per Minute.

CFR
(1) Abbreviation for Code of Federal Regulations. (2) Abbreviation for Crash Fire Rescue.

Chafing Block
Blocks placed under hoselines to protect the hose covering from damage due to rubbing against the ground or concrete.

Chain Hose Tool
Tool used to carry, secure, and otherwise aid in handling hose.

Chain Of Command
Order of rank and authority in the fire service.

Chain Of Custody
Continuous possession of physical "evidence" that must be established in court to admit such material into evidence.

Chain Reaction
Series of self-sustaining changes each of which causes or influences a similar reaction.

Chain Saw
Gas- or electric-powered saw that operates by rotating a chain of small cutting blades around an oblong bar.

Chair
Device of bent wire used to hold reinforcing bars in position. Also called Bolster.

Chamois
Soft pliant leather used for drying furniture and contents or for removing small amounts of water.

Char
Carbonaceous material formed by incomplete combustion of an organic material, commonly wood; the remains of burned materials.

Charge
To pressurize a fire hose or fire extinguisher.

Charged Building
Building heavily laden with heat, smoke, and gases and possibly in danger of having a backdraft.

Charged Line
Hose loaded with water under pressure and prepared for use.

Charging Station
Group of equipment assembled in a location to refill self-contained breathing apparatus cylinders.

Charles's Law
Law of physics that states that a gas will expand or contract in direct proportion to an increase or decrease in temperature. If a gas is confined so it cannot expand, its pressure will increase or decrease in direct proportion to temperature.

Charter Bus
See Commercial Motor Coach.

Chase
See Pipe Chase.

Chassis
Frame upon which the body of the fire apparatus rests.

Chauffeur
See Fire Apparatus Driver/Operator.

Cheater Bar
Piece of pipe added to a prying tool to lengthen the handle and provide additional leverage.

Checklists
Detailed lists generally prepared for the maintenance of equipment or apparatus or for installed fire protection equipment to ensure that the inspector does not overlook an item that needs to be checked regularly. They may also be used during pre-incident planning and fire prevention inspections.

Checkrail Window
Type of window usually consisting of two sashes, known as the upper and lower sashes, that meet in the center of the window. Checkrail or double-hung windows may be made of either wood or metal, but the construction design is quite similar.

Checks
Cracks or breaks in wood.

Check Valve
Automatic valve that permits liquid flow in only one direction.

Chemical Chain Reaction
One of the four sides of the fire tetrahedron representing a process occurring during a fire: Vapor or gases are distilled from flammable materials during initial burning. Atoms and molecules are released from these vapors and combine with other radicals to form new compounds. These compounds are again disturbed by the heat releasing more atoms and radicals that again form new compounds and so on.

Chemical Compound
New homogeneous substance consisting of two or more elements and having properties different from the constituent elements.

Chemical Entry Suit
Protective apparel designed to protect the firefighter's body from certain liquid or gaseous chemicals. May be used to describe both Level A and Level B protection.

Chemical Flame Inhibition
The extinguishment of a fire by interruption of the chemical chain reaction.

Chemical Foam
Foam formed when an alkaline solution and an acid solution unite to form a gas (carbon dioxide) in the presence of a foaming agent that traps the gas in fire-resistive bubbles. Chemical foam is not commonly used today.

Chemical Heat Energy
Heat of combustion, spontaneous heating, heat of decomposition, heat of solution. This occurs as a result of materials being improperly used or stored. The materials may come in contact with each other and react, or they may decompose and generate heat.

Chemical Properties
Relating to the way a substance is able to change into other substances. These properties reflect the ability to burn, react, explode, or produce toxic substances hazardous to people or the environment.

CHEMTREC
Manufacturing Chemists Association's name for its Chemical Transportation Emergency Center. The center provides immediate information about handling hazardous materials incidents. The toll-free number is 1-800-424-9300 (1-202-483-7616 in Washington, D.C., Alaska, and Hawaii).

Cheyne-Stokes Respiration
Abnormal breathing pattern characterized by rhythmic increase and decrease in depth of ventilations, with regularly recurring periods during which breathing stops.

Chief
(1) Incident management system title for individuals responsible for command of the functional sections: operations, planning, logistics, and finance/administrative. (2) Short for "chief of department" or "fire chief." (3) Term used to verbally address any chief officer.

Chief Complaint
Problem for which a patient seeks help; usually stated in a word or short phrase.

Chief Of Department
Highest ranking member of the fire department; in some instances, designated as the director or administrator.

Chief Officer
Any of the higher officer grades, from district or battalion chief to the chief of the fire department.

Chief's Aide
See Adjutant.

Chills
Sensation of cold with convulsive shaking of the body.

Chimney Brush
Wire brush connected to the end of a series of poles; used to clean soot from the inside of a chimney.

Chimney Effect
Created when a ventilation opening is made in the upper portion of a building and air currents throughout the building are drawn in the direction of the opening; also occurs in wildland fires when the fire advances up a V-shaped drainage swale.

Chimney Rods
Poles connected to a chimney brush.

Chocks
Wooden, plastic, or metal blocks constructed to fit the curvature of a tire; placed against the tire to prevent apparatus rolling. Also called Wheel Blocks.

Cholesterol
Steroid alcohol that is present in body fluids and has been linked to arteriosclerosis.

Chord
Top or bottom longitudinal member of a truss.

Chronic
Of long duration or recurring over a period of time.

Chronic Obstructive Pulmonary Disease (COPD)
Term for several diseases that result in obstructive problems in the airways.

Chuck
Portable fire hydrant carried on the apparatus with one or more gated connections for the hose. The device screws into a special flush hydrant connection on the water main or a special main. Also called Air Line Connection.

Chuck Key
Key used to tighten or loosen the bit in a power drill.

Church Raise
See Auditorium Raise.

Churning
When smoke is being blown out of a ventilation opening only to be drawn back inside by the negative pressure created by the ejector because the open area around the ejector has not been sealed.

Chute
Salvage cover arrangement that channels excess water from a building. A modified version can be made with larger sizes of fire hose.

Cilia
Tiny hairlike projections that help move mucus from the lungs.

Circle System
See Loop System.

Circuit
Complete path of an electrical current.

Circuit Breaker
Device that interrupts the flow of electricity in a circuit when it becomes overloaded.

Circular Saw
Gas- or electric-powered saw whose circular blade rotates at a high speed to produce a cutting action. A variety of blades may be used, depending on the material being cut. Also called Rotary Rescue Saw.

Circulating Feed
Fire hydrant that receives water from two or more directions.

Circulating System
See Loop System.

Circulation Relief Valve
Small relief valve that opens and provides enough water flow into and out of the pump to prevent the pump from overheating when it is operating at churn against a closed system.

Circulator Valve
Device in a pump that routes water from the pump to the supply to keep the pump cool when hoselines are shut down.

Circulatory System
Body system consisting of the heart and blood vessels.

Circumstantial Evidence
Facts from which presumptions or inferences are made; indirect evidence. For example, seeing a person flee from the scene of an arson is circumstantial or indirect evidence that the person committed the crime. Seeing the person set the fire is direct evidence.

Cistern
Water storage receptacle that is usually underground and may be supplied by a well or rainwater runoff.

Citation
Legal reprimand for failure to comply with existing laws or regulations.

Cladding
Exterior finish or skin.

Clappered Siamese
Hose appliance that has one discharge and two or more intakes equipped with hinged gates that prevent water from being discharged through an open intake.

Clapper Valve
Hinged valve that permits the flow of water in one direction only.

Class A Fire
Fires involving ordinary combustibles such as wood, paper, cloth, and so on.

Class A Foam
Foam specially designed for use on Class A combustibles. These foams are becoming increasingly popular for use in wildland and structural fire fighting. Class A foams are essentially wetting agents that reduce the surface tension of water and allow it to soak into combustible materials easier than plain water.

Class A Poison
Poisonous gases or liquids of such nature that a very small amount of the gas or vapor of the liquid is dangerous to life.

Class B Fire
Fires of flammable and combustible liquids and gases such as gasoline, kerosene, and propane.

Class B Poison
Substance known to be so toxic to humans as to effect a severe health hazard if released during transportation.

Class C Fire
Fires involving energized electrical equipment.

Class D Fire
Fires of combustible metals such as magnesium, sodium, and titanium.

Class E Fire
Fires involving nuclear materials; nuclear fusion.

Class I Harness
Ladder-belt-type harness that is worn around the wearer's waist and used only to secure firefighters to a ladder or other object. Also called Pompier Belt. *Also see* Life Safety Harness.

Class II Harness
Sit-type harness designed to support the weight of two people (victim and rescuer). *Also see* Life Safety Harness.

Class III Harness
Sit-type harness designed to support two people. However, this type has additional support over the shoulders that is designed to prevent the wearer from becoming inverted on the rope. *Also see* Life Safety Harness.

Class I (1) Patient
Type of classification used within the method for communicating a patient's condition to the dispatcher or the hospital. A Class I patient is in immediate danger of dying if action is not taken.

Class II (2) Patient
Type of classification used within the method for communicating a patient's condition to the dispatcher or the hospital. A Class II patient is moderately injured and could worsen without prompt treatment.

Class III (3) Patient
Type of classification used within the method for communicating a patient's condition to the dispatcher or the hospital. A Class III patient has minor injuries and is in no immediate danger.

Class IV (4) Patient
Type of classification used within the method for communicating a patient's condition to the dispatcher or the hospital. A Class IV patient is one suffering from a psychiatric problem or emergency.

Class V (5) Patient
Type of classification used within the method for communicating a patient's condition to the dispatcher or the hospital. A Class V patient is one who is deceased.

Claustrophobia
Pathological fear of confined spaces.

Clavicle
Collarbone; attaches to the uppermost part of the sternum and joins the scapula to form the point of the shoulder.

Claw Tool
Forcible entry tool having a hook and a fulcrum at one end and a prying blade at the other.

Cleanout Fitting
Fitting installed in the top of a tank to facilitate washing the tank's interior.

Clear Text
Use of plain English in radio communications transmissions. No ten codes or agency specific codes are used when using clear text.

Clearway/Overrun
Area beyond the end of the runway that has been cleared of nonfrangible obstacles and strengthened to allow overruns without serious damage to the aircraft.

Clerestory
Windowed space that rises above lower stories to admit air, light, or both.

Clevis
U-shaped shackle attached with a pin or bolt to the end of a chain.

Clinical Death
Term that refers to the lack of signs of life, where there is no pulse and no blood pressure; occurs immediately after the onset of cardiac arrest.

Closed-Circuit Apparatus
Breathing apparatus in which the wearer's exhalations are recycled after carbon dioxide and moisture are removed and some oxygen is added; usually a long-duration device.

Closed Fracture
Fracture in which there is no break in the overlying skin.

Clot
Semisolid mass of fibrin and cells.

Clove Hitch
Knot that consists essentially of two half hitches. Its principal use is to attach a rope to an object such as a pole, post, or hose.

CNG
Abbreviation for Compressed Natural Gas.

CO_2
Carbon Dioxide.

Coach Space
Standard seating areas within a train car or airliner.

Coccyx
Lowest part of the spine; composed of four small, fused vertebrae. Also called Tailbone.

Cockloft
Concealed space between the top floor and the roof of a structure.

Cockpit
Fuselage compartment occupied by pilots while flying the aircraft.

Cockpit Voice Recorder
Recording device installed in most large civilian aircraft to record crew conversation and communications. It is intended to assist in an accident investigation to determine probable cause of the accident.

Code 1
(1) Operation of an emergency vehicle under nonemergency response conditions. No warning devices are being used, and all traffic laws are followed. (2) Driver proceeds at his or her convenience, obeys all traffic laws, and does not use warning devices.

Code 2
(1) Operation of an emergency vehicle using visual warning devices but no audible warning devices. This is prohibited in most jurisdictions. (2) The driver proceeds immediately, obeys all traffic laws, and does not use warning devices.

Code 3
Operation of an emergency vehicle under emergency response conditions using visual and audible warning devices.

Code For Safety To Life From Fire In Buildings And Structures
NFPA 101; a building standard designed to protect lives in the event of a fire. Also called Life Safety Code®.

Code Of Federal Regulations (CFR)
Formal name given to the books or documents containing the specific regulations provided for by law.

Codes
Rules or laws used to enforce requirements for fire protection, life safety, or building construction.

Coefficient Of Discharge
Correction factor relating to the shape of the hydrant discharge outlet; used when computing the flow from a hydrant.

Coercion
To compel to an act or choice by force, threat, or other pressure.

COFC
Abbreviation for Container-on-Flatcar.

Coffee Grounds Vomitus
Vomitus having the appearance and consistency of coffee grounds; indicates slow bleeding in the stomach.

Coffer Dam
Watertight enclosure, usually made of sheet piling, that can be pumped dry to permit construction inside.

Cognitive Learning
Learning that relates to knowledge and intellectual skills.

Cold Smoke
Smoke from a fire that lacks any substantial heat.

Cold Trailing
Constructing a minimum fire line along the perimeter of a natural cover fire after the perimeter is relatively cold; done to ensure no further advance of the fire.

Collar Method
Means of attaching a coupling to a hose with a two- or three-piece collar, which is bolted into place.

Collision Beam
Heavy-gauge steel member strategically located in the sidewall of a bus. Its purpose is to limit penetration of an object into the passenger compartment.

Colon
See Large Intestine.

Column
Vertical supporting member.

Combination Apparatus
Piece of fire apparatus designed to perform more than one function; usually called triple combinations, quads, or quints.

Combination Attack
Battling a fire by using both a direct and an indirect attack. This method combines the steam-generating technique of a ceiling level attack with an attack on the burning materials near floor level.

Combination Ladder
Ladder that can be used as either a single, extension, or A-frame ladder.

Combination Lay
Hose lay in which two or more hoselines are laid in either direction — water source to fire or fire to water source.

Combination Nozzle
Nozzle designed to provide a straight stream and a fog stream.

Combination Spreader/Shears
Powered hydraulic tool consisting of two arms equipped with spreader tips that can be used for pulling or pushing. The insides of the arms contain cutting shears.

Combination System
Water supply system that is a combination of both gravity and direct pumping systems. It is the most common type of municipal water supply system.

Combine
Large, self-propelled machine that cuts, threshes, and cleans crops as it drives across a field.

Combplate
Grooved plate at the top of an escalator. The grooves in the plate mesh with matching ridges in the stair treads to prevent shoes from being caught in the crevice as the stair treads move under the plate.

Combustible Liquid
Liquid having a flash point at or above 100°F (37.8°C) and below 200°F (93.3°C).

Combustion
Self-sustaining process of rapid oxidation of a fuel, which produces heat and light.

Come-Along
Manually operated pulling tool that uses a ratchet/pulley arrangement to provide a mechanical advantage.

Command
Act of directing, ordering, and/or controlling resources by virtue of explicit legal, agency, or delegated authority.

Command Post
Command and control point where the incident commander and command staff function and where those in charge of emergency units report to be briefed on their respective assignments.

Command Staff
Information officer, safety officer, and liaison officer, who report directly to the incident commander.

Comm Center
See Communications Center.

Commercial Chassis
Truck chassis produced by a commercial truck manufacturer. The chassis is in turn outfitted with a rescue or fire fighting body.

Commercial Motor Coach
Custom-built buses designed to carry groups of people to a specific destination, usually a long distance away. These buses may run regularly scheduled routes, or they may be specially chartered. Also called Charter Bus and Touring Bus.

Commissioner
Member of city or county government. The fire commissioner represents the fire department on the government ruling body. In some departments, there is no commissioner and the fire chief is the ranking official directly responsible to the government.

Common Brick
Fired clay brick with a plain, unfinished surface.

Common Freight
Goods, other than passenger baggage, transported to a specific destination by a regularly scheduled hauler such as a bus or train.

Common Hazard
Condition likely to be found in almost all occupancies and generally not associated with a specific occupancy or activity.

Communicable Disease
Disease that is transmissible from one person to another.

Communication
The exchange of ideas and information that conveys an intended meaning in a form that is understood.

Communications Center
Point through which nearly all information flows, is processed, and then acted upon. Also called Comm Center.

Communications Unit
(1) Functional unit within the service branch of the logistics section of the incident management system. This unit is responsible for the incident communications plan, installation and repair of communications equipment, and operation of the incident communications center. (2) Vehicle used to provide the major part of an incident communications center.

Community Master Plan
Medium- to long-range plan for the growth and development of a community in a planned, orderly manner. The master plan is generally written through the interaction of all city agencies that may be affected by future developments.

Company
Basic fire fighting organizational unit consisting of firefighters and apparatus; headed by a company officer.

Company Log
Record of the activities of a fire company; usually kept by a company officer.

Company Officer
Individual responsible for command of a company. This designation is not specific to any particular fire department rank (may be a firefighter, lieutenant, captain, or chief officer if responsible for command of a single company).

Compensation/Claims Unit
Functional unit within the finance/administrative section of an incident management system. Responsible for financial concerns resulting from injuries or fatalities at an incident.

Competency-Based Learning (CBL)
Training based upon the competencies of a profession or job. Competencies are the absolute standards or criteria of performance. Emphasis is on what the learner will learn. Same as Criterion-Referenced and Performance-Based Learning.

Complaint
Objection to existing conditions that is brought to the attention of the fire inspection bureau.

Complement
(1) All firefighters assigned to a working unit, or the number of units assigned to a given alarm. (2) Equipment assigned to a piece of apparatus.

Complex Loop
Piping system that is characterized by one or more of the following: more than one inflow point, more than one outflow point, and/or more than two paths between inflow and outflow points. Also called Grid and Gridded Piping System.

Compliance
Meeting the minimum standards set forth by applicable codes or regulations.

Composite Cylinder
Lightweight air cylinder made of more than one material; often aluminum wrapped with fiberglass.

Composite Materials
Plastics, metals, ceramics, or carbon-fiber materials with built-in strengthening agents. These materials are much lighter and stronger than the metals formerly used for such aircraft components as panels, skin, and flight controls.

Compound Fracture
Open fracture; a fracture in which there is an open wound of the skin and soft tissues.

Compound Gauge
(1) Pressure gauge capable of measuring positive or negative pressures. (2) Term used to describe the gauge that measures the intake pressure on a fire pump.

Compound Tackle
Two or more blocks reeved with more than one rope.

Compress
Folded cloth or pad used for applying pressure to stop hemorrhage or as a wet dressing.

Compressed Air
Air under greater than atmospheric pressure; used as a portable supply of breathing air for SCBA.

Compressed Gas
Gas that, at normal temperature, exists solely as a gas when pressurized in a container.

Compressed Gas Association (CGA)
Association that writes standards relating to compressed gases.

Compressed Natural Gas
Natural gas that is stored in a vessel at pressures of 2,400 to 3,600 psi (16 800 kPa to 25 200 kPa).

Compression
Those vertical or horizontal forces that tend to press things together. For example, the force exerted on the top chord of a truss.

Compressor
Machine designed to compress air or gas.

Computer-Aided Instruction (CAI)
Instructional approach that uses the computer to present instruction to the student on an individualized, self-paced basis.

Concealed Space
Area between walls or partitions, ceilings and roofs, and floors and basement ceilings through which fire may spread undetected; also soffits and other enclosed vertical or horizontal shafts through which fire may spread.

Concrete
Mixture of portland cement and an aggregate filler/binder to which water is added to form a rigid building material. In structural concrete, the filler/binder is usually sand and/or gravel. Lightweight concrete, used as sound-proofing material, may use sand and/or vermiculite.

Conduction
Transfer of heat energy from one body to another by direct contact or through a solid medium.

Conductivity Readings
Form of nondestructive testing used on aluminum aerial devices. Changes in the integrity of material in a certain area will be reflected by a divergence of conductivity readings.

Conductor
Substance that transmits electrical or thermal energy.

Confession
Acknowledgment of guilt by a party accused of an offense.

Confined Space
Any space not intended for continuous occupation, having limited openings for entry or exit, and providing unfavorable natural ventilation.

Confinement
Fire fighting operations required to prevent fire from extending to uninvolved areas or structures.

Conflagration
Large, uncontrollable fire covering a considerable area and crossing natural fire barriers such as streets; usually involves buildings in more than one block and causes a large fire loss. Forest fires can also be considered conflagrations.

Congestive Heart Failure (CHF)
Excessive fluid in the lungs or tissues caused by the failure of the heart to effectively pump blood.

Conjunctiva
Delicate membrane that lines the eyelids and covers the exposed surface of the eyeball.

Connection Box
Contains fittings for trailer emergency and service brake connections and electrical connector to which the lines from the towing vehicle may be connected. Formerly called junction box, light box, or bird box.

Consignee
Person who is to receive a shipment.

Consist
Rail shipping paper containing a list of cars in the train by order. Those containing hazardous materials are indicated. Some railroads include information on emergency operations for the hazardous materials on board with the consist. Also called Train Consist.

Constant Pressure Relay
Method of establishing a relay water supply utilizing two or more pumpers to supply the attack pumper. This method reduces the need for time-consuming and often confusing fireground calculations of friction loss.

Constrict
To be made smaller by drawing together or squeezing.

Construction Classification
Rating given to a particular building based on construction materials and methods and its ability to resist the effects of a fire situation.

Contact Paper
Vinyl or paperlike material that has a strong adhesive preapplied to one side.

Contained Fire
Fire whose progress has been stopped but for which the control line is not yet finished.

Container
Article of transport equipment that is: (a) of a permanent character and strong enough for repeated use; (b) specifically designed to facilitate the carriage of goods by one or more modes of transport without intermediate reloading; and (c) fitted with devices permitting its ready handling, particularly its transfer from one mode to another. The term “container” does not include vehicles. Also referred to as Freight Container, Cargo Container, and Intermodal Container.

Container Chassis
Trailer chassis consisting of a frame with locking devices for securing and transporting a container as a wheeled vehicle.

Container-on-Flatcar (COFC)
Rail flatcar used to transport highway transport containers.

Container Ship
Ship specially equipped to transport large freight containers in horizontal or more commonly, vertical container cells. The containers are usually loaded and unloaded by special cranes.

Container Specification Number
Shipping container number preceded by "DOT" that indicates the container has been built to federal specifications.

Contaminants
Any foreign substance that compromises the purity of a given substance.

Contents
Furnishings, merchandise, and any machinery or equipment not part of the building structure.

Contractual Sleeve Binding
Method of attaching couplings to fire hose with a tension ring that compresses a nylon sleeve to lock the hose onto the coupling shank.

Control
Progress of a fire that has been halted. When the fire is under control, the release of fire fighting resources can begin.

Control Agents
Materials used to contain, confine, neutralize, or extinguish a hazardous material or its vapor.

Control Center
Communications or dispatch center used by the fire service for emergency communications. There are also mobile command posts that can be taken directly to the fire scene and function as the incident operational control center.

Controlled Airport
Airport having a control tower in operation. The tower is usually, but not always, staffed by FAA personnel.

Controlled Breathing
Technique for consciously reducing air consumption by forcing exhalation from the mouth and allowing natural inhalation through the nose.

Controlled Burning
Process of burning grass and brush to prevent the occurrence of uncontrolled wildland fires.

Controller
Electric control panel used to switch a pump on and off and to control its operation.

Control Line
Combination of natural or constructed barriers that ultimately contain the fire; not to be confused with fire line.

Control Pedestal
Central location for most or all of the aerial device controls. Depending on the type and manufacturer of the apparatus, the control pedestal may be located on the turntable, on the rear or side of the apparatus, or in the elevating platform. Also called Pedestal.

Contusion
See Bruise.

Convection
Transfer of heat by the movement of fluids or gases; usually in an upward direction.

Convection Column
Rising column of heated air or gases above a continuing heat or fire source. Also known as Thermal Column.

Convenience Outlet
Electrical outlet that can be used for lamps and other appliances.

Conversion Hysteria
Unfounded belief that part of the body has ceased normal function.

Convulsion
(1) Violent involuntary contraction or series of contractions of the voluntary muscles. (2) Seizure.

Cooling
Reduction of heat by the quenching action or heat absorption of the extinguishing agent.

Coon's Eyes
Bruising around both eyes, which may indicate skull fracture.

Cooperating Agency
Agency supplying assistance other than direct suppression, rescue, support, or service functions to the incident control effort (Red Cross, law enforcement agency, telephone company, etc.).

Cope Steel
To cut a flange section in order to avoid interference with other structural members.

Copyright Law
Law designed to protect the competitive advantage developed by an individual or organization as a result of their creativity.

Core Temperature
Body temperature measured in deep structures such as the lungs or liver.

Cornea
Transparent structure covering the pupil of the eye.

Corner Fittings
Strong metal devices located at the corners of a container having several apertures that normally provide the means for handling, stacking, and securing the freight container.

Corner Structures
Vertical frame components located at the corners of a container; integral with the corner fittings.

Cornice
Concealed space near the eave of a building; usually overhanging the area adjacent to exterior walls.

Coronary Arteries
Blood vessels that supply blood to the walls of the heart.

Corpus Delicti
Evidence of substantial and fundamental facts necessary to prove the commission of a crime.

Corrosive Materials
Liquids or solids that can destroy human skin tissue or liquids that can severely corrode steel.

Corrosives
Those materials that cause harm to living organisms by destroying body tissue.

Corrugated
Formed into ridges or grooves.

Corrugated Hose
Hose shaped into folds or parallel and alternating ridges and grooves to improve flexibility.

Cost Unit
Functional unit within the finance/administrative section of an incident management system; responsible for tracking costs, analyzing cost data, making cost estimates, and recommending cost-saving measures.

Counterbalance Valve
Valves designed to prevent unintentional or undesirable motion of an aerial device from position.

Coupling
Fitting permanently attached to the end of a hose; used to connect two hoselines together or a hoseline to such devices as nozzles, appliances, discharge valves, or hydrants.

Course Description
Relates the basic goals and objectives of the course in a broad, general manner. It is designed to provide a framework and guide for further development of the course and also communicate the course content.

Course Objectives
Specific identification of the planned results of a course of instruction.

Course Outline
List of jobs and information to be taught to fulfill previously identified needs and objectives.

Cover
(1) Practice of moving unassigned fire companies into stations that have been emptied by another emergency. (2) To cover exposures by placing primary fire streams in advantageous positions to protect buildings or rooms exposed to heat and fire. (3) To protect with a salvage cover. (4) General term used to described brush, grasses, and other natural ground covers.

Cowl Flaps
Adjustable sections or hinged panels on the engine cowling of reciprocating engines. They are used to control the engine temperature.

Cowling
Removable covering around aircraft engines.

C-Post
Post nearest the rear door handle on a four-door vehicle. On a two-door vehicle, the rear roof post is considered to be the C-post.

CPR
Abbreviation for Cardiopulmonary Resuscitation.

CPU
Abbreviation for Central Processing Unit.

Cradle
Rest designed to support the free end of the aerial device during road travel.

Cramp
Painful spasm, usually of a muscle; a gripping pain in the abdominal area.

Cranium
Skull; the portion of the skull enclosing the brain.

Crash Fire Rescue (CFR)
Old term used to describe the fire and rescue services provided at airport facilities. Also see Aircraft Rescue and Fire Fighting for a more modern description.

Crawl Space
Area between ground and floor, ceiling and floor, or ceiling and roof, the dimensions of which are such that a person cannot stand up; often used for duct work, water pipes, and similar structural adjuncts.

Crazing
Cracking of glass, such as windows and mirrors, from the heat of fire.

Crepitus
Grating sound heard when the fractured ends of a bone rub together.

Crew
Specific number of personnel assembled for an assignment such as search, ventilation, or hoseline deployment and operations. The number of personnel in a crew should not exceed recommended span-of-control limits of three to seven people. A crew operates under the direct supervision of a crew leader.

Cribbing
(1) Varying lengths of hardwood, usually 4 x 4 inches (100 mm by 100 mm) or larger, used to stabilize objects. (2) Process of arranging planks into a cratelike construction. Also called Shoring.

Crib Death
See Sudden Infant Death Syndrome.

Criteria
One of the three requirements of evaluation; the standard against which learning is compared after instruction; the expected learning outcome. Examples are behavioral objectives or NFPA standards.

Criterion-Referenced Learning
See Competency-Based Learning.

Criterion-Referenced Testing
Measurement of individual performance against a set standard or criteria, not against other students. Mastery learning is the key element to criterion-referenced testing.

Critical Incident Stress Debriefing
See Post-Traumatic Incident Debriefing

Critical Rescue And Fire Fighting Access Area (CRFFAA)
Rectangular area surrounding any given runway. Its width extends 500 feet (150 m) outward from each side of the runway centerline, and its length is 3,300 feet (1 000 m) beyond each runway end.

Crossover Line
Installed in tank piping systems to allow unloading from either side of the tank.

Croup
Common viral infection seen in small children; characterized by spasm of the larynx and resulting upper airway obstruction.

Crowbar
Prying tool with a blade at either end. One end is significantly curved to provide additional mechanical advantage.

Crown Fire
Fire that sweeps through the canopy of closely spaced trees or bushes without involving ground fuels at the same time.

Crowning
Condition where the presenting part of a baby, usually the head, first bulges out of the vaginal opening.

Cruising
Driving a vehicle in such a manner that an even speed and engine rpm is maintained. It is best to operate at 200 to 300 rpm below the maximum rpm recommended by the manufacturer.

Crush Points
Places within the frame of a vehicle that are designed to collapse, crush, deform, and otherwise absorb (not transmit) forces so as to minimize the impact on the passengers.

Cryogenics
Gases that are converted into liquids by being cooled below -150°F (-101°C).

Cryogens
Gases that are cooled to a very low temperature, usually below -150°F (-101°C), to change to a liquid. Also called Refrigerated Liquids.

Cubic Feet Per Minute
Measure of a volume of material flowing past or through a specified measuring point.

Curbside
Side of a trailer nearest the curb when trailer is traveling in a normal forward direction (right-hand side); opposite to roadside.

Curing
(1) Maintaining conditions to achieve proper strength during the hardening of concrete. (2) Manufacturing step in making fire hose; the process of applying heat and pressure to "set" the shape of the tube and to increase its smoothness.

Curtain Boards
See Draft Curtains.

Curtain Door
Door used as a barrier to fire, consisting of interlocking steel plates or of a continuous formed spring steel "curtain." Curtain doors are often mounted in pairs, one door on the inside and the other on the outside of an opening.

Curtain Wall
Nonload-bearing wall.

Custom Chassis
Truck chassis designed solely for use as a fire or rescue apparatus.

Cutters
See Powered Hydraulic Shears.

Cutting Tool
Any one of a number of hand or power tools used to cut a specific kind of material.

CVA
Abbreviation for Cerebrovascular Accident.

Cyanosis
Blueness of the skin due to insufficient oxygen in the blood.

Cylinder
(1) Component of a locking mechanism that contains coded information for operating that lock, usually with a key. (2) Air tank portion of a self-contained breathing apparatus.

Cylinder Guard
Metal plate that covers a lock cylinder to prevent forceful removal.

Cylinder Plug
Part of a lock cylinder that receives the key. Also called Key Plug.

Cylinder Pressure Gauge
Gauge attached to the cylinder outlet that indicates the pressure in the cylinder.

Cylinder Shell
External case of a lock cylinder.

Cylindrical Lock
Lock having the lock cylinder contained in the knob. Also called Bored Lock .

D

Dangerous Cargo Manifest
Invoice of cargo used on ships containing a list of all hazardous materials on board and their location on the ship.

Dangerous Goods
(1) Any product, substance, or organism included by its nature or by the regulation in any of the nine United Nations classifications of hazardous materials. (2) Term used to describe hazardous materials in Canada. (3) Term used in the U.S. and Canada for hazardous materials aboard aircraft.

Darcy-Weisbach Method
Technique used to establish the pressure lost to friction in a piping system.

Day Book
See Journal.

Deadbolt
Movable part of a deadbolt lock that extends from the lock mechanism into the door frame to secure the door in a locked position.

Dead-End Hydrant
Fire hydrant that receives water from only one direction.

Dead-End Main
Water main that is not looped and in which water can flow in only one direction.

Dead Latch
Sliding pin or plunger that operates as part of a dead-locking latch bolt. Also called Anti-Shim Device.

Dead Load
Weight of the structure, structural members, building components, and any other feature that is constant and immobile.

Dead Locking
See Latch Bolt.

Deadman Switch
Foot pedal located below the aerial device control pedestal. This pedal must be depressed in order for the aerial device controls to be operable.

Dead Shore
Shore that is applied vertically to support a horizontal load; for example, an unstable floor. Also called Vertical Shore.

Decerebrate Posture
Posture assumed by a patient with severe brain injury characterized by extension and internal rotation of the arms and extension of the legs.

Decibel
Unit used to express relative difference in power between acoustic and electrical signals; equal to 10 times the logarithm of the ratio of the two levels.

Deck Gun
See Turret Pipe.

Decking
See Sheathing (2).

Deck Pipe
See Turret Pipe.

Decomposition
Chemical change of a substance that results in the creation of two or more different substances.

Decontaminate
To remove a foreign substance that could cause harm; frequently used to describe removal of a hazardous material from the person, clothing, or area.

Decorticate Posture
Posture assumed by patients with a severe brain injury characterized by tightly flexed arms, clenched fists, and slightly extended legs.

Deep-Seated Fire
Fire that has moved deep into piled or bulk materials such as hay, baled cotton, or paper.

Defense Mechanism
Systems, such as nasal hair, mucus, or cilia, that protect the body from invasion by foreign particles and injury.

Defensive Attack
Exterior fire attack with emphasis on exposure protection.

Defensive Mode
Commitment of a fire department's resources to protect exposures when the fire has progressed to a point where an offensive attack is not effective.

Defibrillation
Process of stopping very rapid contractions of the heart (fibrillation) by delivering a direct electric shock to the patient's heart with a device called a defibrillator. This is a common emergency procedure that is administered by paramedics and other specially trained emergency medical technicians.

Deflagration
Chemical reaction producing vigorous heat and sparks or flame and moving through the material (as black or smokeless powder) at less than the speed of sound. A major difference among explosives is the speed of the reaction; can also refer to intense burning; a characteristic of Class B explosives.

Deformation
(1) Alteration of form or shape. (2) Projections on the surface of reinforcing bars to prevent the bars from slipping through the concrete. Also called Set.

Delirium Tremens (D.T.'s)
Serious and sometimes fatal reaction to sudden withdrawal of alcohol in the alcoholic. Symptoms include loss of appetite, difficulty in sleeping, excitement, mental confusion, and hallucinations.

Deluge Sprinkler System
Fire protection sprinkler system in which the sprinkler heads are always open. The system is controlled by a valve that operates automatically by a thermostatically actuated device. Also called Open-Head System.

Demand Apparatus
Breathing apparatus with a regulator that supplies air to the facepiece only when the wearer inhales or when the bypass valve has been opened; not to be used for fire fighting or IDLH atmospheres.

Demand Valve
Valve within the self-contained breathing apparatus regulator that lets breathing air pass to the wearer when the wearer inhales.

Demand Valve Unit
Intermittent, positive-pressure breathing unit used to assist or control ventilation.

Demobilization Unit
Functional unit within the planning section of an incident management system; responsible for assuring orderly, safe, and efficient demobilization of resources committed to the incident.

Demonstration
Teaching method that includes the act of showing a person how to do something.

Density
Weight per unit of volume of a substance. The density of any substance is obtained by dividing the weight by the volume.

Deodorization
Action taken following a fire to remove smoke odors from an atmosphere.

Department Of Transportation (DOT)
Administrative body of the executive branch of the federal government responsible for transportation policy, regulation, and enforcement.

Deposition
Sworn testimony taken out of court.

Depression
Emotional state in which there are extreme feelings of sadness, dejection, lack of worth, and emptiness. The obvious signs range from a slight lack of motivation and failure to concentrate to severe changes of body functions.

Dermatitis
Inflammation of the skin that is noticeable by redness, pain, or itching.

Dermis
True skin; a dense, elastic layer of fibrous tissue that lies beneath the epidermis (the outer skin). It is laced with blood vessels, nerve fibers, and receptor organs for sensations of touch, pain, heat, and cold. It contains muscular elements, hair follicles, and oil and sweat glands.

Desiccant
Substance that has a high affinity for water and is used as a drying agent.

Desktop Publishing
Using a computer to develop manuals, handouts, and so on.

Detailed View
Additional, close-up information shown on a particular section of a larger drawing.

Det Cord
See Detonator Cord (1) and (2).

Detention Window
Window designed to prevent exit through the opening.

Detonation
Supersonic thermal decomposition, which is accompanied by a shock wave in the decomposing material.

Detonator Cord
(1) Flexible explosive tape put around the outer edge of the inside of the canopy of some military aircraft to separate the Plexiglas® from the metal frame to facilitate rescue or egress. (2) Fuse used to trigger an explosion in more powerful explosives. (3) Also called Det Cord.

Dew Point
Temperature at which the water vapor in air precipitates as droplets of liquid.

Diabetes Mellitus
Complex disorder that is mainly caused by the failure of the pancreas to release enough insulin into the body; high levels of sugar in the blood and urine. Symptoms include the need to urinate often, increased thirst, weight loss, and increased appetite.

Diabetic Ketoacidosis
Condition that results when there is too much sugar in the blood and not enough insulin to metabolize it. The body then metabolizes fats, which causes acid waste products to build up in the blood.

Diaphoresis
Profuse sweating that occurs with a fever, physical exertion, exposure to heat, or stress.

Diaphragm
Dome-shaped muscle that separates the chest cavity from the abdominal cavity. This muscle has holes through which pass the large artery (aorta), esophagus, and large vein (vena cava).

Diastole
Period of time between contractions of the heart. During this state, blood enters the relaxed chambers of the heart to be pumped throughout the body.

Dielectric
Nonconductor of direct electric current.

Dielectric Heating
Heating that occurs as a result of the action of pulsating either direct current (DC) or alternating current (AC) at high frequency on a nonconductive material.

Differential Dry-Pipe Valve
Valve in a dry-pipe sprinkler system in which air pressure is used to hold the valve closed and thus hold the water back.

Differential Manometer
Device whose primary application is to reflect the difference in pressures between two points in a system.

Diffusion
(1) Process by which oxygen moves from alveoli to the blood cells in the thin-walled capillaries. (2) Process by which hazardous materials pass through protective clothing.

Digester
Large, circular container used at sewage treatment plants to cleanse raw sewage.

Digestion
Process that takes place in the stomach and intestines where food is converted into substances that can be absorbed by the body.

Dike
(1) Temporary dam constructed of readily available objects to obstruct the flow of a shallow stream of water to a depth that will facilitate drafting operations. (2) Temporary or permanent barriers that prevent liquids from flowing into certain areas or that direct the flow as desired.

Dilated Pupil
Pupil enlarged beyond its normal size.

Dimensioning
Drawing that places a building on a site plan to clearly show its size and arrangement relative to existing conditions.

Dimpled
Depressed or indented (as on a metal surface) to aid in gripping.

Dip Tube
Installed for pressure unloading of product out of the top of the tank.

Direct Attack
(1) To attack a natural cover fire directly at or close to the burning edge. (2) Application of a fire stream directly onto a burning fuel.

Directive
Authoritative instrument or order issued by a superior officer.

Director
Title for individuals responsible for command of a branch in an incident management system.

Direct Pumping System
Water supply system supplied directly by a system of pumps rather than elevated storage tanks.

Disc (Disk)
Cartilaginous pad between the vertebrae that separates and cushions them.

Discharge Velocity
Rate at which water travels from an orifice.

Discussion
Teaching method where students contribute to the class session by using their knowledge and experience to provide input.

Disinfect
Destroy, neutralize, or inhibit the growth of harmful microorganisms.

Disk
See Disc.

Dislocation
State of being misaligned; the condition that results when the surfaces of two bones are no longer in proper contact.

Dispatch
(1) To direct fire companies to respond to an alarm. (2) Radio designation for the dispatch center; for example, "Engine 65 to Dispatch, send me a second alarm."

Dispatcher
Person who works in the communications center and processes information from the public and emergency responders.

Displaced Runway Threshold
Temporary relocation of a runway threshold (beginning or end) because of maintenance or other activity on the runway.

Displacement
(1) Volume or weight of a fluid displaced by a floating body of equal weight. (2) Amount of water forced into the pump thus displacing air.

Distal
Located away from the trunk of the body.

Distention
State of being expanded or swollen, particularly of the abdomen.

Distortion
State of being twisted out of normal or natural shape or position.

Distress
More stress than a person can reasonably be expected to handle; in other words, when stress controls the person.

Distribution System
That part of an overall water supply system which receives the water from the pumping station and delivers it throughout the area to be served.

Distributor Nozzle
Nozzle used to create a broken stream that is usually used on basement fires.

District
See Response District.

Diverter Valve
See Selector Valve.

Diving Accident Network
Hotline that can advise physicians and rescue personnel about diving mishaps.

Division
Subunit of the incident command system. It is composed of a number of individual units that are assigned to operate within a defined geographical area.

Documentation Unit
Functional unit within the planning section of an incident management system; responsible for recording/protecting all documents relevant to the incident.

Dogs
See Pawls.

Domains Of Learning
Areas of learning and classification of learning objectives, which are often referred to as cognitive (knowledge), affective (attitude), and psychomotor (skill) learning.

Dome Roof
Hemispherical roof assembly, usually supported only at the outer walls of a circular structure.

Domestic Consumption
Water consumed from the water supply system by residential and commercial occupancies.

Domineering Attitude
Effect of a decision-making problem in which the leader tries to control every facet of the operation.

Donning Mode
State of positive-pressure SCBA when the donning switch is activated.

Donning Switch
Device on a positive-pressure regulator that when activated stops airflow while the unit is being donned. Airflow is resumed with the user's first inhalation.

Donut Roll
Length of hose rolled up for storage and transport.

Doorjamb
Sides of the doorway opening.

Dosimeter
Small, nuclear-radiation detection device that registers the total amount of radiation to which it has been exposed.

DOT
Abbreviation for Department of Transportation (U.S.).

DOT 3AA
DOT specification for type and material of steel self-contained breathing apparatus or cascade cylinder construction.

Double-Acting Hydraulic Cylinder
Hydraulic cylinder capable of transmitting power in either direction.

Double-Edge Snap Throw
Method of spreading a salvage cover similar to the single-edge snap throw; intended to cover two groupings located on either side of a narrow aisle.

Double Figure Of Eight Knot
Knot used to tie ropes of equal diameters together.

Double-Hung Window
Window having two vertically moving sashes.

Doubles
Truck combination consisting of a truck tractor and two semitrailers coupled together. Formerly called double-trailer or double-bottom.

Downstream
(1) Direction of airflow from a high-pressure source to a low-pressure source; for example, the facepiece is downstream from the air cylinder. (2) Direction in which the current of a moving body of water is flowing.

Downwind Leg
Flight path parallel to the landing runway in the direction opposite to landing.

Draft
Process of obtaining water from a static source into a pump that is above the source's level. Atmospheric pressure on the water surface forces the water into the pump where a partial vacuum has been created.

Draft Curtains
Dividers hung from the ceiling in large open areas that are designed to minimize the mushrooming effect of heat and smoke. Also called Curtain Boards and Draft Stop.

Drafting Operation
See Draft.

Drafting Pit
Underground reservoir of water from which to draft for pumper testing; usually located at a training center.

Draft Stop
See Draft Curtains.

Drag
(1) Procedure of dragging hooks through water to find drowning victims. (2) Rescue procedure for removing victims from a fire area.

Drag Chute
Parachute device installed on some aircraft that is deployed on landing to aid in slowing the aircraft to taxi speed.

Drain Valve
(1) Valve on a pump discharge that facilitates the removal of pressure from a hoseline after the discharge has been closed. (2) Valve on an elevated waterway system to facilitate the drainage of water from the system before stowing.

Dressing
Clean or sterile covering applied directly to wound; used to stop bleeding and to prevent contamination of the wound.

Drift Smoke
Smoke that has drifted from its area of origin and is not columnar.

Drill Schedule
Calendar for training sessions in manipulative skills for firefighters or fire companies.

Drill Tower
Training structure, normally more than three stories, used by training personnel to develop realistic fire service situations. Particularly used for ladder and rope evolutions. Also called Tower.

Driver/Operator
See Fire Apparatus Driver/Operator.

Driver Reaction Distance
Distance a vehicle travels while a driver is transferring the foot from the accelerator to the brake pedal after perceiving the need for stopping.

Drivers
(1) Engine or motor used to turn a pump. (2) *See also* Fire Apparatus Driver/Operator.

Drivewheel Horsepower
Power available at the wheels to move the vehicle.

Drop
To drop water or retardant from an aircraft.

Drop Bar
Metal or wooden bar that serves as a locking device when placed or dropped into brackets across a swinging door.

Drop-Forged Coupling
Coupling made by raising and dropping a drop hammer onto a block of metal as it rests on a forging die, thus forming the metal into the desired shape.

Drop Frame
Two-level frame section of a trailer that provides proper coupler height at the forward end and a lower height for the remainder of the length.

Droplet Contact
Means of transmitting a communicable disease indirectly by spray droplets from an infected person's coughing or sneezing.

Drop Panel
Type of concrete floor construction in which an area above each column is dropped below the bottom level of the rest of the slab.

Drowning Machine
Colloquial term for the convection currents resulting when water floods over a low-head dam.

Dry-Barrel Hydrant
Fire hydrant that has its opening valve at the water main rather than in the barrel of the hydrant. When operating properly, there is no water in the

barrel of the hydrant when it is not in use. These hydrants are used in areas where freezing could occur.

Dry Chemical
Any one of a number of powdery extinguishing agents used to extinguish fires. The most common include sodium or potassium bicarbonate, monoammonium phosphate, or potassium chloride.

Dry Hoseline
Hoseline without water in it; an uncharged hoseline.

Dry Hydrant
Permanently installed pipe that has pumper suction connections installed at static water sources to speed drafting operations.

Dry Lightning Storm
Lightning storm during which little or no rain reaches the ground.

Dry-Pipe Sprinkler Systems
Fire protection sprinkler system that has air instead of water under pressure in its piping. Dry systems are often installed in areas subject to freezing.

Dry Powder
Extinguishing agent suitable for use on combustible metal fires.

Dry Standpipe System
Standpipe system that has closed water supply valves or that lacks a fixed water supply.

Drywall
See Wallboard.

D.T.'s
Abbreviation for Delirium Tremens.

Dual Pumping
Operation where a strong hydrant is used to supply two pumpers by connecting the pumpers intake-to-intake. The second pumper receives the excess water not being pumped by the first pumper, which is directly connected to the water supply source. Sometimes incorrectly referred to as tandem pumping.

Duct
(1) Tube or passage that confines and conducts airflow throughout the aircraft for pressurization, air conditioning, etc. (2) Channel or enclosure, usually of sheet metal, used to move heating and cooling air through a building.

Duff
Matted, partly decomposed leaves, twigs, and bark beneath trees and brush.

Dummy Coupler
Fitting used to seal the opening in an air brake hose connection (gladhands) when the connection is not in use; a dust cap.

Dust Explosion
Rapid burning (deflagration), with explosive force, of any combustible dust. Dust explosions generally are two explosions: a small explosion or shock wave creates additional dust in an atmosphere causing the second and larger explosion.

Dutchman
Extra fold placed along the length of a section of hose as it is loaded so that its coupling rests in proper position.

Dye-Penetrant Testing
Form of nondestructive testing in which the surface of the test material is saturated with a dye or fluorescent penetrant, and a developer is applied. Dyes bleed visibly to the surface indicating defects; fluorescents show the defect areas under ultraviolet light.

Dynamic Load
Addition of a moving load force to an aerial device or structure. Also called Shock Loading.

Dynamic Rope
Rope that stretches farther than a static rope stretches.

Dynamic Stress
Stress imposed on an aerial device while it is in motion.

Dysconjugate Gaze
Condition in which the two eyes are not aligned but stare in different directions.

Dyspnea
Painful or difficult breathing; rapid, shallow respirations.

Dzus Fastener
Trade name given to a half-turn fastener with a slotted head. This type of fastener is used on engine cowlings, cover plates, and access panels throughout the aircraft.

E

EAP
Abbreviation for Employee Assistance Program.

Eave
Lower border of a roof that overhangs the wall.

Ecchymosis
Escape of blood into the tissues from ruptured blood vessels. Also known as a bruise.

Eclampsia
Toxic condition of pregnancy, associated with high blood pressure, edema, convulsions, and possible coma. Also called Toxemia of Pregnancy.

E.C.O.
Abbreviation for Entry Control Officer.

Economic Factor
Includes expenses caused by the loss of tools, apparatus, equipment, manpower, property, and systems, in addition to legal expenses.

Ectopic Pregnancy
Pregnancy in which the fetus is implanted elsewhere than in the uterus such as in the fallopian tube or abdominal cavity.

Edema
Condition in which fluid escapes into the body tissues and causes local or generalized swelling.

Eductor
(1) Portable proportioning device that injects a liquid, such as foam concentrate, into the water flowing through a hoseline. (2) Syphon used to remove water from flooded basements.

EEBSS
Abbreviation for Emergency Escape Breathing Support System.

EEO
Abbreviation for Equal Employment Opportunity.

Efflorescence
Crystals of salt appearing as white powder on the surface.

Effluent
Any fluid that flows from a pipe or similar outlet. The term is most commonly used to describe waste products from industrial processes.

Egress
Place or means of exiting a structure.

Ejection Seat
Aircraft seat capable of being ejected in an emergency to catapult the occupant clear of the aircraft.

EKG
Abbreviation for Electrocardiogram.

Elastomer
Generic term for the rubber, neoprene, silicone, or plastic resin material of the facepiece seal, low-pressure hose, and similar SCBA components.

Electrical Heat Energy
Resistance heating, dielectric heating, heat from arcing, heat from static electricity. Poorly maintained electrical appliances, exposed wiring, and lightning are sources of electrical heat energy.

Electrical Service
Conductor and equipment for delivering energy from the electrical supply system to the wiring system of the premises.

Electrical Systems
Those wiring systems designed to distribute electricity throughout a building or vehicle.

Electric Arc
Sustained, visible discharge of electricity across a gap or between electrodes.

Electric Fence
Livestock-retaining fence with a low-voltage, high-amperage current flowing through it. The shock from the fence is intended to discourage animals from trying to escape.

Electric Shock
Injury caused by electricity passing through the body. Severity of injury depends upon the path the current takes through the body, the amount of current, and the resistance of the skin.

Electrocardiogram (EKG)
Test used to observe the function of the heart.

Electrode
Conductor used to establish electrical contact in a circuit.

Electrolysis
(1) Chemical change; especially decomposition produced in an electrolyte by an electric current. (2) Form of corrosion found in aluminum.

Electrolyte
(1) Substance that dissociates into ions in solution or when fused, thereby becoming electrically conducting. (2) Energy component within the human body that can be lost to sweating.

Electron
Minute component of an atom that possesses a negative charge.

Elevated Master Stream
Fire stream in excess of 350 gpm (1 400 L/min) that is deployed from the tip of an aerial device.

Elevated Storage
Water storage reservoir located above the level of the water supply system to take advantage of head pressure.

Elevating Platform
Work platform attached to the end of an articulating or telescoping aerial device.

Elevating Water Device
Articulating or telescoping aerial device added to a fire department pumper to enable the unit to deploy elevated master stream devices. These devices range from 30 to 75 feet (9 m to 23 m) in height.

Elevation
(1) Height of a point above sea level or some datum point. (2) Drawing or orthographic view of any of the vertical sides of a structure or vertical views of interior walls.

Elevation Cylinder
Hydraulic cylinders used to lift the aerial device from its bed to a working position. Also called Hoisting Cylinder.

Elevation Loss
See Elevation Pressure.

Elevation Pressure
Gain or loss of pressure in a hoseline due to a change in elevation. Also called Elevation Loss.

Elevation View
Architectural drawing used to show the number of floors of a building, ceiling heights, and the grade of surrounding ground.

Elevator
(1) Hinged, movable control surface at the rear of the horizontal stabilizer of an aircraft. It is attached to the control wheel or stick and is used to control the pitch up or down or to hold the aircraft in level flight. (2) Passenger-carrying car in a multistory building. (3) Tall structure used to store grain or feed at an agricultural site.

Elliptical
Describes a large cylindrical, oblong water tank that is used on tankers or tender.

ELT
Abbreviation for Emergency Locator Transmitter.

Embolism
Sudden blocking of an artery or vein by a clot or foreign material that has been carried by the blood.

Emergency Escape Breathing Support System (EEBSS)
Safety system on an SCBA that allows two units to be hooked together in the event that one fails.

Emergency Lighting System
(1) System of interior and exterior low-power incandescent and/or fluorescent lights that are designed to assist passengers in locating and using aircraft emergency exits but that are not bright enough to assist aircraft rescue and fire fighting personnel in carrying out search and rescue operations. (2) Battery-operated floodlights in a building that are designed to activate when normal power supply is interrupted.

Emergency Locator Transmitter (ELT)
Radio transmitter carried by most aircraft. The radio is activated by impact forces. Once activated, the ELT transmits a variable tone on the emergency frequencies as an aid in locating the accident site.

Emergency Medical Technician (EMT)
Professional-level provider of basic life support emergency medical care. Requires certification by some authority.

Emergency Response Guidebook (ERG)
Manual provided by the U.S. Department of Transportation that aids emergency response personnel in identifying hazardous materials placards. It also gives guidelines for initial actions to be taken at hazardous materials incidents.

Emergency Traffic
Urgent radio traffic; a request for other unit to clear the radio waves for an urgent message. Also called Priority Traffic.

Emergency Truck
Van or similar-type vehicle used to carry portable equipment and personnel.

Emergency Valve
Self-closing tank outlet valve.

Emergency Valve Operator
Device used to open and close emergency valves.

Emergency Valve Remote Control
Secondary means, remote from tank discharge openings, for operation in event of fire or other accident.

Emetic
Agent that causes vomiting.

Empennage
Aircraft tail assembly including the vertical and horizontal stabilizers, elevators, and rudders.

Emphysema
Dilation of the alveoli, resulting in labored breathing and increased susceptibility to infection; a chronic obstructive pulmonary disease.

Employee Assistance Program (EAP)
Any one of many programs that may be provided by an employer to employees and their families to aid in solving work or personal problems.

EMT
Abbreviation for Emergency Medical Technician.

Emulsifier
Compound that supports one insoluble liquid in suspension in another liquid.

Endothermic Heat Reaction
Chemical reaction in which a substance absorbs heat energy.

Energy-Absorbing Liner
Portion of the firefighter's helmet designed to cushion blows to the head.

Engine
Fire department pumper.

Engine Company
Group of firefighters assigned to a fire department pumper. They are responsible primarily for providing water supply and attack lines for fire extinguishment.

Engineer
(1) Fire apparatus driver/operator. (2) Fire protection or fire prevention person qualified by professional engineering credentials.

Engine House
Firehouse or fire station.

Engine Numbers
For identification, engines of multiengine aircraft are numbered consecutively 1, 2, 3, 4, etc., as seen from the pilot's seat. They are numbered left to right across the aircraft even though some may be mounted on the wings or on the tail of the aircraft; that is, in the L-1011 and DC-10, the tail-mounted engine is number 2.

Engine Pressure
See Net Pump Discharge Pressure.

Engulf
To flow over and enclose. In the fire service context it refers to being enclosed in flames.

Entry Clothing
Personal protective clothing that is designed for entering into total flame and for specialized work inside industrial furnaces and ovens. Also called Fire Entry Suit.

Entry Control Board
Record-keeping clipboard equipped with a clock, tables, and slots for tallies; used by entry control officers in the United Kingdom, Australia, and New Zealand to keep track of all firefighters wearing SCBA.

Entry Control Officer (E.C.O.)
Command position at a confined space rescue operation responsible for keeping account of rescuers who enter the hazard zone.

Entry Point
Ventilation opening through which replacement air enters the structure. This is usually the same opening that rescue or attack crews use to enter the structure. Also called Entry Opening.

Entry Suit
See Entry Clothing.

Envenomization
Poisonous effects caused by the bites, stings, or deposits of insects, spiders, snakes, or other poison-carrying animals.

Epidermis
Outer layers of the skin. It is made up of an outer dead portion and a deeper living portion.

Epiglottis
Elastic cartilage located at the roof of the tongue that folds over the glottis to prevent food from entering the trachea during swallowing.

Epilepsy
Chronic brain disorder marked by seizures; usually associated with alteration of consciousness, abnormal motor behavior, and psychic or sensory disturbances.

Epistaxis
See Nosebleed.

Equal
In terms of specifying apparatus, it means the same level of quality, standard, performance, or design but not necessarily identical.

Equal Employment Opportunity (EEO)
Personnel management responsibility to be sensitive to the social, economic, and political needs of a jurisdiction or labor market.

Equipment
Portable tools or appliances carried on the fire apparatus but that are not permanently attached to or part of the apparatus.

Equipment Strip
Removal of essential fire fighting tools and equipment at the fire scene before a pumper proceeds to the water source.

Equivalency
Alternative practices that are acceptable for meeting a minimum level of fire protection.

ERG
Abbreviation for Emergency Response Guidebook.

Esophagus
Portion of the digestive tract that lies between the throat and the stomach.

Etiologic Agents
Living microorganisms, like germs, that can cause human disease; a biologically hazardous material.

Eustress
Just enough stress to allow one to perform well; in other words, when the person controls the stress.

Evacuation Chute/Slide
Aircraft-door-connected escape slides that when deployed will inflate and extend to the ground. Pneumatic in operation, most are automatic by opening the door; some require manual activation, which is a short pull on a lanyard. Many may be disconnected from the aircraft and used for a flotation device in water crashes.

Evaluation
Systematic and thoughtful collection of information for decision making. It consists of criteria, evidence, and judgment.

Evaluation Report Form
Form used by supervisors to record their impressions of a subordinate's effectiveness.

Evaluation Step
Fourth step in conducting a lesson in which the student demonstrates that the required degree of proficiency has been achieved.

Evidence
One of three requirements of evaluation. The information, data, or observation that allows the instructor to compare what was expected to what actually occurred.

Evisceration
Protrusion of the intestines or other internal organs through an opening or wound.

Evolution
(1) Sequential operation. (2) Operation of fire service training or suppression covering one or several aspects of fire fighting.

EX
Rating symbol used on lift trucks that are safe for use in atmospheres containing flammable vapors or dusts.

Excelsior
Slender, curled wood shavings used for starting fires or packing fragile items.

Exclusionary Rule
Judicially established evidentiary rule that excludes from admission at trial evidence seized in a manner considered unreasonable within the meaning of the Fourth Amendment of the U.S. Constitution.

Exhalation
Act of breathing out; expiration.

Exhalation Valve
One-way valve that lets exhaled air out of the self-contained breathing apparatus facepiece.

Exhaust Area
Area behind a jet engine where hot exhaust gases present a danger to personnel.

Exhauster
Device that speeds the discharge of air from a dry-pipe sprinkler system.

Exhaust System
Ventilation system designed to remove stale air, smoke, vapors, or other airborne contaminants from an area.

Exit
That portion of a means of egress that is separated from all other spaces of the building structure by construction or equipment and provides a protected way of travel to the exit discharge.

Exit Access
Portion of a means of egress that leads to the exit. Hallways, corridors, and aisles are examples of exit access.

Exit Capacity
According to code requirements, the maximum number of people who can discharge through a particular exit.

Exit Device
See Panic Hardware.

Exit Discharge
That portion of a means of egress that is between the exit and a public way.

Exit Opening
In ventilation, the opening that is made or used to release heat, smoke, and other contaminants to the atmosphere.

Exit Stairs
Stairs that are used as part of a means of egress. The stairs may be part of either the exit access or the exit discharge when conforming to requirements in the Life Safety Code®.

Exothermic Heat Reaction
Chemical reaction in which a substance releases heat energy.

Expander
(1) Device that enlarges the expansion rings used for securing threaded couplings to fire hose. (2) Inner component of a screw-in expander coupling.

Expansion Joint
Flexible joint in concrete used to prevent cracking or breaking because of expansion and contraction due to temperature changes.

Expansion Ring
Malleable metal band that binds fire hose to a threaded coupling by compressing the hose tightly against the inner surface of the coupling.

Expansion Ring Method
Means of attaching a threaded coupling to a fire hose. A metal expansion ring is placed inside the end of the hose and then expanded to compress the hose tightly against the inner surface of the coupling.

Expellent Gas
Any of a number of inert gases that are compressed and used to force extinguishing agents from a portable fire extinguisher. Nitrogen is the most commonly used expellent gas.

Expert Witness
Person who has special knowledge in a particular field through specialized skill, expertise, training, and/or education and is adjudged qualified to render expert opinions in that field in court proceedings.

Explosive Atmosphere
Any atmosphere that contains a mixture of fuel to air that falls within the explosive limits for that particular material.

Explosive Breathing Technique
Individual emergency conditions breathing technique used by a firefighter wearing SCBA during accidental submersion; the firefighter holds his or her breath, rapidly inhales and exhales, and then holds breath again.

Explosive Limit
See Flammable Limit.

Explosives
Materials capable of burning or bursting suddenly and violently.

Exposure
(1) Structure or separate part of the fireground to which the fire could spread. (2) People, property, systems, or natural features that are or may be exposed to the harmful effects of a hazardous materials emergency.

Exposure Bag
Special neoprene bag into which a person is placed for field treatment of hypothermia.

Extend
(1) Line may be extended by adding hose, straightening, or rerouting the hose already laid. (2) To increase the reach of an extension ladder by raising the fly section.

Extension Cylinders
Hydraulic cylinders that control the extension and retraction of the fly sections of an aerial device.

Extension Fly Locks
Devices that prevent the fly sections of a ground or aerial ladder from retracting unexpectedly.

Extension Ladder
Sectional ladder of two or more parts that can be extended to various heights.

Extension Ram
Powered hydraulic tool designed especially for straight pushing operations that may extend as far as 63 inches (1 600 mm). Also called Ram.

Exterior Exposure
Building or other combustible object located close to the fire building that is in danger of becoming involved due to heat transfer from the fire building.

External Respiration
Inhalation and exhalation of air into and from the lungs.

External Water Supply
(1) Any water supply to a fire pump from a source other than the vehicle's own water tank. (2) Any water supply to an aerial device from a source other than the vehicle's own fire pump.

Extinguish
To put out a fire completely.

Extinguisher
Portable fire fighting appliance designed for use on specific types of fuel and classes of fire.

Extinguisher Hose
Braided, rubber-covered hose used on extinguishers that is made to withstand pressures up to 1,250 psi (8 619 kPa).

Extinguishing Agent
Any substance used for the purpose of controlling or extinguishing a fire.

Extremely Hazardous Substance
Chemicals determined by the Environmental Protection Agency (EPA) to be extremely hazardous to a community during an emergency spill or release as a result of their toxicities and physical/chemical properties. There are 402 chemicals listed under this category.

Extrication
Incidents involving the removal and treatment of victims who are trapped by some type of man-made machinery or equipment.

Extrication Group
The group within the incident command system that is responsible for extricating the victim(s).

Extrude
To shape heated plastics or metal by forcing them through dies.

Extruded Coupling
Coupling manufactured by the process of extrusion.

F

FAA
Abbreviation for Federal Aviation Administration.

Facepiece
That part of an SCBA that fits over the face and includes the head harness, facepiece lens, exhalation valve, and connection for either a regulator or a low-pressure hose. Also called Mask.

Faceshield
Protective shield attached to the front of a fire helmet. Also called Helmet Faceshield.

Facilities Unit
Functional unit within the support branch of the logistics section of an incident management system; provides fixed facilities for incident. These facilities may include incident base, feeding areas, sleeping areas, sanitary facilities, and a formal command post.

Factory Certified
Qualification of fire department personnel who attend special manufacturers' repair schools to become formally qualified in certain testing and maintenance procedures.

Factory Mutual System (FM)
Fire research and testing laboratory that provides loss control information for the Factory Mutual System and anyone else who may find it useful.

Factory Raise
See Hotel Raise.

Fahrenheit Scale
Temperature scale on which the freezing point is 32 degrees and the boiling point at sea level is 212 degrees.

Fainting
Momentary loss of consciousness caused by insufficient blood supply to the brain; syncope.

Fall Line
Term used for the portion of a rope used in a block and tackle system that runs between the standing block and the leading block (if so equipped) or the power source. Also called Pull Line, Pulling Line, and Weft Yarn.

Fallopian Tubes
Paired structures of the female reproductive system that conduct eggs from the ovaries to the uterus.

False Ceiling
Additional suspended ceiling below the true original ceiling forming a concealed space.

False Front
Additional facade on a building applied after the original construction for decoration; creates a concealed space.

False Roof
Fascia or facade added to some buildings with flat roofs to create the appearance of a mansard roof.

Family Education Rights and Privacy Act of 1974
Provides that an individual's records are confidential and that information contained in those records may not be released without the individual's prior written consent.

Fan
Generic term used interchangeably for both blowers and smoke ejectors.

Fan Light
Semicircular window, usually over a doorway, with muntins radiating like the ribs of a fan.

Farm Implement
General term used to describe farm machinery.

Fascia
Flat horizontal or vertical board located at the outer face of a cornice.

Fast Attack Mode
When the first-arriving unit at a fire makes a quick offensive attack on the fire.

FCC
Abbreviation for Federal Communication Commission.

FDC
Abbreviation for Fire Department Connection.

FDIC
Abbreviation for Fire Department Instructors Conference.

Febrile Convulsions
Convulsions brought on by fever; occurs most often in children.

Federal Aviation Administration (FAA)
Subdivision of the U.S. Department of Transportation that is involved with the regulation of civil aviation.

Federal Communications Commission (FCC)
Federal agency charged with the control of all radio and television communications.

Feedback
Student responses generated by questions, discussions, or opportunities to perform that demonstrate learning or understanding.

Feeder Line
See Relay-Supply Hose.

Feed Main
Pipe connecting the sprinkler system riser to the cross mains. The cross mains directly service a number of branch lines on which the sprinklers are installed.

Female Coupling
Threaded swivel device on a hose or appliance made to receive a male coupling of the same thread and diameter.

Femoral Artery
Principal artery of the thigh. Pulse may be felt in the groin area.

Femur
Bone that extends from the pelvis to the knee; the longest and largest bone of the body.

Fender
Exterior body portion of a vehicle adjacent to the front or rear wheels.

Fetus
Unborn child after the second month of pregnancy.

FFFP
Abbreviation for Film Forming Fluoroprotein Foam.

Fiberboard
Lightweight insulation board made of compressed cellulose fibers; often used in suspended ceilings.

Fibrillation
Rapid, ineffective contraction of the heart.

Fibula
Smaller of the two bones of the lower leg.

Field Sketch
Rough drawing of an occupancy that is made during an inspection. The field sketch is used to make a final inspection drawing.

Field Unit
See Brush Apparatus.

Fifth Wheel
Device used to connect a truck tractor or converter dolly to a semitrailer in order to permit articulation between the units. It is generally composed of a lower part consisting of a trunnion, plate, and latching mechanism mounted on the truck tractor (or dolly) and a kingpin assembly mounted on the semitrailer.

Fifth-Wheel Pickup Ramp
Steel plate designed to lift the front end of a semitrailer to facilitate the engagement of the kingpin into the fifth wheel.

Figure Eight
Forged metal device in the shape of an eight; used to help control the speed of a person descending a rope.

Figure Of Eight Knot
Knot used to form a loop in the end of a rope; should be used in place of the bowline knot when working with synthetic fiber rope.

Filler Yarn
Threads running crosswise in fabrics or woven hose.

Fillet Weld
Weld made in the interior angle of two pieces placed at right angles to each other.

Fill Hose
Short section of hose carried on apparatus equipped with booster tanks to fill the tank from a hydrant or another truck.

Fill Opening
Opening on top of a tank used for filling the tank; usually incorporated in manhole cover.

Fill Site
Location at which tankers/tenders will be loaded during a water shuttle operation.

Fill-The-Box
Slang for a request by a unit responding on a reduced assignment to send the balance of the assignment.

Film Forming Fluoroprotein Foam (FFFP)
Foam concentrate that is based on fluoroprotein foam technology with aqueous film forming foam (AFFF) capabilities.

Filter Breathing
Individual emergency conditions breathing technique used by a firefighter with a depleted air supply. The firefighter inserts the regulator end of the low-pressure hose into a pocket or glove or inside the turnout coat to help filter smoke particles and to protect the firefighter from inhaling superheated air.

Filter Canister
Filtration device containing chemicals to filter out harmful substances through adsorption or absorption on negative-pressure respirators. This should not be used for fire fighting or IDLH atmospheres.

Fin
Fixed or adjustable airfoil attached longitudinally to an aircraft to provide a stabilizing effect in flight.

Final Approach
That portion of the landing pattern in which the aircraft is lined up with the runway and is heading straight in to land.

Finance/Administrative Unit
Responsible for all costs and financial actions of the incident; includes the time unit, procurement unit, compensation/claims unit, and the cost unit.

Finger
Long, narrow extensions from the main body of a natural cover fire.

Finish
(1) Arrangement of hose usually placed on top of a hose load and connected to the end of the load. Also called Hose Load Finish. (2) Fine or decorative work required for a building or one of its parts. (3) Finishing material used in painting.

Finished Foam
Completed product after the foam solution reaches the nozzle and air is introduced into the solution (aeration).

Fire
Rapid oxidation of combustible materials accompanied by a release of energy in the form of heat and light.

Fire Alarm
(1) Call announcing a fire. (2) Bell or other device summoning a fire company to respond to a fire or other emergency.

Fire Alarm System
(1) System of alerting devices that takes a signal from fire detection or extinguishing equipment and alerts building occupants or proper authorities of a fire condition. (2) System used to dispatch fire department personnel and apparatus to emergency incidents.

Fire Apparatus
Any fire department emergency vehicle used in fire suppression or other emergency situation.

Fire Apparatus Driver/Operator
Firefighter who is charged with the responsibility of operating fire apparatus to, during, and from the scene of a fire operation or any other time the apparatus is in use. The driver/operator is also responsible for routine maintenance of the apparatus and any equipment carried on the apparatus. This is typically the first step in the fire department promotional chain. Also called Chauffeur and Driver/Operator.

Fire Behavior
Manner in which fuel ignites, flames develop, and heat and fire spread; sometimes used to refer to the characteristics of a particular fire.

Fire Blanket
Blanket stored in a case in a kitchen or similar location that is intended to be used to wrap around a victim whose clothing catches fire.

Fire Boat
Boat that carries large fire pumps and is capable of supplying boat-mounted master streams or water supply hoselines to land-based fire fighting apparatus. Also called Marine Unit.

Fire Bomb
Incendiary device used to start an arson fire.

Fire Break
Any natural or man-made barrier that stops or slows the advance of a wildland fire.

Fire Brigade
(1) Organization of industrial plant personnel trained to use fire fighting equipment within the plant and to carry out fire prevention activities. (2) Term used in some countries, outside the United States, in place of fire department.

Fire Broom
Broom used in wildland fire fighting.

Fire Bucket
Bucket with a round bottom usually painted red and marked with the word fire to discourage use for purposes other than fire fighting; frequently kept filled with water, sand, or other fire extinguishing material. Also called Fire Pail.

Fire Buff
One who is a fire department enthusiast.

Fire Bug
Common slang term to describe an arsonist or pyromaniac; also describes a person who does not only set fires but also enjoys watching them.

Fire Building
(1) Building in which a fire originated. (2) Building in which a fire is in progress. (3) Training building in which fire fighting is practiced. Also called Burn Building.

Fire Camp
Camp near a large natural cover fire for coordinating agencies, communications, logistics, and support.

Fire Cause
Agency or circumstance that started a fire or set the stage for one to start; source of a fire's ignition.

Fire Cause Determination
Process of establishing the cause of a fire through careful investigation and analysis of the available evidence.

Fire Cut
Angled cut made at the end of a joist or wood beam in a masonry wall.

Fire Damper
Device that automatically interrupts airflow through all or part of an air-handling system, thereby restricting the passage of heat and the spread of fire.

Fire Department Connection (FDC)
Point at which the fire department can connect into a sprinkler or standpipe system to boost the water flow in the system. This connection consists of a clappered siamese with two or more 2½-inch (65 mm) intakes or one large-diameter (4-inch [100 mm] or larger) intake. Also called Fire Department Sprinkler Connection.

Fire Department Instructors Conference (FDIC)
Annual meeting of fire department training officials sponsored by the International Society of Fire Service Instructors.

Fire Department Physician
Physician designated by a fire department to treat members of the department.

Fire Department Pumper
Piece of fire apparatus having a permanently mounted fire pump with a rated discharge capacity

of 750 gpm (3 000 L/min) or greater. This apparatus may also carry water, hose, and other portable equipment.

Fire Department Sprinkler Connection
See Fire Department Connection.

Fire Department Water Supply Officer
Officer in charge of all water supplies at the scene of a fire; duties include placing pumpers at the most advantageous hydrants or other water sources and directing supplementary water supplies, including water shuttles and relay pumping operations. This may also be a permanent, full-time staff position with responsibility for coordinating, with other local agencies, water supply projects of concern to the fire department.

Fire Detection Devices
Devices and connections installed in a building to detect heat, smoke, or flame.

Fire Detection System
System of detection devices, wiring, and supervisory equipment used for detecting fire or products of combustion and then signaling that these elements are present.

Fire Devil
Small cyclone or twister that forms when heated fire gases rise and cooler air rushes into the resulting low-pressure areas; most common in forest fires but can also be encountered in large structural fires.

Fire District
Designated geographic area where fire protection is provided (usually through a supporting tax) or an area where fire prevention codes are enforced.

Fire Door
Rated assembly designed to automatically close and cover a doorway in a fire wall during a fire.

Fire Drill
Training exercise to ensure that the occupants of a building can exit the building in a quick and orderly manner in case of fire.

Fire Entry Suit
See Entry Clothing.

Fire Escape
Means of escaping from a building in case of fire; usually an interior or exterior stairway or slide independently supported and made of fire-resistive material.

Fire Extinguisher
Portable fire fighting device designed to combat incipient fires.

Firefighter
Active member of the fire department; also spelled fire fighter.

Firefighter's Axe
See Axe.

Firefighter's Carry
One of several methods of lifting and carrying a disabled victim to safety.

Fire Flank
Sides of a natural cover fire.

Fire Flow
Quantity of water available for fire fighting in a given area. It is calculated in addition to the normal water consumption in the area.

Fire Flow Testing
Procedure used to determine the rate of water flow available for fire fighting at various points within the distribution system.

Fire Gases
Those gases produced as combustion occurs.

Fireground
Area around a fire and occupied by fire fighting forces.

Fireground Commander
See Incident Commander.

Fireground Perimeter
Work area surrounding the fire building.

Fire Guard
Person trained and assigned to watch for fires and life safety for specified periods or events.

Fire Hall
Term used in northwestern United States and Canada. *Also see* Fire Station.

Fire Hazard
Any material, condition, or act that contributes to the start of a fire or that increases the extent or severity of fire.

Fire Hose Float
Water-rescue flotation device made from inflated fire hose.

Fire House
See Fire Station.

Fire Hydrant
Upright metal casting that is connected to a water supply system and is equipped with one or more valved outlets to which a hoseline or pumper may be connected to supply water for fire fighting operations. Also called Hydrant.

Fire Hydraulics
Science that deals with water in motion as it applies to fire fighting operations.

Fire Inspector
Fire prevention specialist and/or fire or arson investigator.

Fire Lines
(1) Boundaries established around a fire area to prevent access except for emergency vehicles and persons having a right and need to be present. (2) In wildland fire fighting, a line scraped clean of combustibles around the fire perimeter to remove fuel and contain the fire.

Fire Line Tape
Plastic marking tape strung around an emergency scene to keep bystanders away from the action.

Fire Load
Maximum amount of heat that can be produced if all the combustible materials in a given area burn.

Fire Mark
Distinctive metal marker once produced by insurance companies for identifying their policyholders' buildings.

Fire Marshal
Highest fire prevention officer of a state, province, county, or municipality.

Fire Pail
See Fire Bucket.

Fire Partition
Fire barrier that extends from one floor to the bottom of the floor above or to the underside of a fire-rated ceiling assembly. A fire partition provides a lower level of protection than a fire wall.

Fire Perimeter
Edge of a natural cover fire.

Fire Point
Temperature at which a liquid fuel produces sufficient vapors to support combustion once the fuel is ignited. The fire point is usually a few degrees above the flash point. Also called Burning Point.

Fire Police
Members, usually of a volunteer fire department, who respond with the fire department and assist the police with traffic control, crowd control, and scene preservation and security; common only in the mid-Atlantic states of the U.S. Also called Special Police.

Fire Prevention
Part of the science of fire protection that deals with preventing the outbreak of fire by eliminating fire hazards through inspection, code enforcement, education, and investigation programs.

Fire Prevention Bureau
Division of the fire department responsible for conducting fire prevention programs of inspection, code enforcement, education, and investigation.

Fire Prevention Code
Law enacted for the purpose of enforcing fire prevention and safety regulations.

Fire Prevention Week
Week proclaimed each year by the President of the United States to commemorate the anniversary of the great Chicago conflagration on October 9, 1871; takes place the week in which October 9 falls.

Fireproof
Resistance to fire. The term Fireproof is a misnomer because it means that something will not burn. All material, other than water, will burn at some point. Other terms, such as fire resistive or fire resistant, should be used to indicate the degree of resistance to fire.

Fire Protection Engineer
Graduate of an accredited institution of higher education who has specialized in engineering science related to fire protection.

Fire Pump
(1) Water pump used in private fire protection to provide water supply to installed fire protection systems. (2) Water pump on a piece of fire apparatus.

Fire Report
Official report on a fire kept as a permanent record; generally prepared by the officer in charge of the fire operation.

Fire Resistance Rating
Amount of time a material or assembly of materials will resist a typical fire as measured on a standard time-temperature curve.

Fire Resistive
Ability of a structure or a material to provide a predetermined degree of fire resistance; usually according to building and fire prevention codes and given in hour ratings.

Fire Retardant
Chemical that is applied to material or another substance and that is designed to retard ignition or the spread of fire.

Fire Risk
Probability that a fire will occur and the potential for harm it will create.

Fire Science
Study of the behavior, effects, and control of fire.

Fire Season
Time of year when natural cover fires are most likely to occur.

Fire Service
(1) Organized fire prevention, fire protection, and fire fighting services. (2) Members of fire prevention, suppression, and training organizations individually and collectively. (3) All allied organizations who assist in preventing and combating fires.

Fire Service Hose
Specially constructed hose designed to withstand the hazards of the fire scene.

Firesetter
Person who starts a fire deliberately.

Firesetting
Starting a fire, usually deliberately.

Fire Station
Building in which fire suppression forces are housed. Also called Fire House.

Fire Stop
Solid material, such as wood block, placed within a wall void to retard or prevent the spread of fire through the void.

Fire Storm
(1) Atmospheric disturbance caused by heat rising from a conflagration. (2) Violent conversion caused by a rising column of heated air that creates intense winds toward the fire center encompassing the entire fire area.

Fire Stream
Stream of water or other water-based extinguishing agent after it leaves the fire hose and nozzle until it reaches the desired point.

Fire Tetrahedron
Model of the four elements required to have a fire. The four sides represent fuel, heat, oxygen, and chemical chain reaction.

Fire Trap
Slang for an old structure in such a deteriorated state that it is highly susceptible to fire; inadequate protective equipment and exits; considered likely to contribute to major loss of life in case of fire.

Fire Triangle
Plane geometric figure in which the three sides of an equilateral triangle represent oxygen, heat, and fuel — the elements necessary to sustain combustion.

Fire Tube
See Heating Tube.

Fire Wall
(1) Rated separation wall, usually extending from the foundation up to and through the roof of a building, to limit the spread of a fire. (2) Bulkhead separating an aircraft engine from the aircraft fuselage or wing.

Fire Whirlwind
Revolving mass of air created by a fire, normally a forest fire.

Firing Out
To set backfires that will impede the growth of an uncontrolled natural cover fire.

First Aid
Immediate medical care given to a victim until he or she can be transported to a medical facility.

First Alarm
Initial fire department response to a report of an emergency.

First-Degree Burn
Burn affecting only the outer skin layers; characterized by redness and pain.

First-Due
Apparatus that should reach the scene of an emergency first.

First-In
First company or apparatus to arrive at a fire location.

First Responder (EMS)
(1) First person arriving at the scene of an accident or medical emergency who is trained to administer

first aid and basic life support. (2) Level of emergency medical training, between first aider and emergency medical technician levels, that is recognized by the authority having jurisdiction.

Five-Minute Escape Cylinder
Small air cylinder used as a backup air source with airline respirators.

Fixed-Temperature Device
Fire alarm initiating device that activates at a predetermined temperature.

Fixed Window
Window that is set in a fixed or immovable position and cannot be opened for ventilation.

Flail Chest
Condition in which several ribs are broken, each in at least two places.

Flame
Burning gas or vapor of a fire that is visible as light of various colors.

Flame Detector
Also called Light Detectors; these are used in some fire detection systems. There are two basic types: those that detect light in the ultraviolet wave spectrum (UV detectors) and those that detect light in the infrared wave spectrum (IR detectors).

Flame Front
Outermost edge or surface of the flame.

Flame Impingement
Points at which flames contact the surface of a container or other structure.

Flame Interface
Area or surface between the gases or vapors and the visible flame.

Flame Out
Unintended loss of combustion in turbojet engines resulting in the loss of engine power.

Flameover
See Rollover.

Flame Propagation Rate
Velocity at which combustion travels through a gas or over the surface of a liquid or solid.

Flame Resistant
Materials that are not susceptible to combustion to the point of propagating a flame AFTER the ignition source is removed.

Flame Spread
Movement of a flame away from the ignition source.

Flame Spread Rating
Numerical rating assigned to a material based on the speed and extent to which flame travels over its surface.

Flame Test
Test designed to determine the flame spread characteristics of structural components or interior finishes.

Flammable
Capable of burning and producing flames.

Flammable Gases
Gases that will burn.

Flammable Limit
Percentage of a substance in air that will burn once it is ignited. Most substances have an upper (too rich) and lower (too lean) flammable limit. Also called Explosive Limit and Flammable Range.

Flammable Liquid
Any liquid having a flash point below 100°F (37.8°C) and having a vapor pressure not exceeding 40 psi absolute (276 kPa).

Flammable Materials
Substances that ignite easily and burn rapidly.

Flammable Range
See Flammable Limit.

Flammable Solids
Solid materials other than explosives that are liable to cause fires through friction or retained heat from manufacturing or processing or that ignite readily and then burn vigorously and persistently, creating a serious transportation hazard.

Flank
Sides of a natural cover fire.

Flanking
Attacking the sides of the fire from a less active area or from an anchor point; the intent being to have the two crews attacking the flanks meet at the head of the fire.

Flaps
Adjustable airfoils attached to the leading or trailing edges of aircraft wings to improve aerodynamic performance during takeoff and landing. They are normally extended during takeoff, landing, and slow flight.

Flashback
Spontaneous reignition of fuel when the blanket of extinguishing agent breaks down or is compromised through physical disturbance.

Flash Fire
Type of fire that spreads rapidly through a vapor environment.

Flash Fuels
Ground cover fuels that are easily ignited and burn rapidly. Examples are grass, leaves, and pine needles.

Flashing
(1) Liquid-tight rail on top of a tank that contains water and spillage and directs it to suitable drains; may be combined with DOT overturn protection. (2) Sheet metal used in roof and wall construction to keep water out.

Flashing Drain
Metal or plastic tube that drains water and spillage from flashing to the ground.

Flashover
Stage of a fire at which all surfaces and objects within a space have been heated to their ignition temperature, and flame breaks out almost at once over the surface of all objects in the space.

Flash Point
Minimum temperature at which a liquid gives off enough vapors to form an ignitable mixture with air near the liquid's surface.

Flash Resistant
Aircraft materials that are not susceptible to burning violently when ignited.

Flat-Head Axe
Axe with a cutting edge on one side of the head and a blunt or flat head on the opposite side.

Flat Load
Arrangement of fire hose in a hose bed or compartment in which the hose lies flat with successive layers one upon the other.

Flat Raise
Raising a ladder with the heel of both beams touching the ground.

Flat Roof
Roof that has a pitch not exceeding 20 degrees. A slight pitch is required to facilitate water runoff.

Flat Slab
Type of concrete floor construction that provides a flat surface for the underside of the floor finish.

Flight
Series of steps between takeoff and landing of an aircraft.

Flight Controls
General term applied to devices that enable the pilot to control the direction of flight and attitude of the aircraft.

Flight Data Recorder
Recording device on large civilian aircraft to record aircraft airspeed, altitude, heading, acceleration, etc., to be used as an aid to accident investigation; commonly referred to as the "black box."

Flight Deck
Cockpit on a large aircraft that is separated from the rest of the cabin.

Flight Service Station
Facility from which aeronautical information and related aviation support services are provided to aircraft. This also includes airport and vehicle advisory services for designated uncontrolled airports.

Floating Dock Strainer
Strainer designed to float on top of the water; used for drafting operations. This eliminates the problem of drawing debris into the pump and reduces the required depth of water needed for drafting.

Floating Ribs
Two lowest pairs of ribs; so called because they are connected only to vertebrae in the back.

Floor Plan
Architectural drawing showing the layout of a floor within a building as seen from above. It outlines the location and function of each room.

Floor Runner
Heavy plastic or canvas placed on a floor to protect the floor's surface or covering from firefighter traffic; used during salvage operations.

Flow
Motion characteristic of water.

Flow Hydrant
Hydrant from which the water is discharged during a hydrant flow test.

Flowmeter
Mechanical device installed in a discharge line that senses the amount of water flowing and provides a readout in units of gallons per minute (liters per minute).

Flow Pressure
Pressure created by the rate of flow or velocity of water coming from a discharge opening. Also called Plug Pressure.

Flow Test
Tests conducted to establish the capabilities of water supply systems. The objective of a flow test is to establish quantity (gallons or liters per minute) and pressures available at a specific location on a particular water supply system.

Fluid
Any substance that can flow; a substance that has definite mass and volume at constant temperature and pressure but no definite shape and that is unable to sustain shear stresses.

Fluid Mechanics
Branch of physics dealing with the behavior of fluids, particularly with respect to their reaction to forces applied to them.

Fluoroprotein Foams
Foam concentrates fortified with fluorinated surfactants. These surfactants enable the foam to shed, or separate from, hydrocarbon fuels.

Flush Bolt
Locking bolt that is installed flush within a door.

Flush Hydrant
Hydrant installed in a pit below ground level, such as near the runway area of airports or other locations, where aboveground hydrants would be unsuitable.

Fly
Extendable section of ground extension or aerial ladder.

Flying Shore
Shore for vertical surfaces, such as a wall, that is braced against another vertical surface.

Fly Rope
See Halyard.

FM
See Factory Mutual System.

Foam
Extinguishing agent formed by mixing a foam concentrate with water and aerating the solution for expansion; for use on Class A and Class B fires. Foam may be protein, synthetic, aqueous film forming, high expansion, or alcohol type.

Foam Blanket
Covering of foam applied over a burning surface to produce a smothering effect; can be used on nonburning surfaces to prevent ignition.

Foam Concentrate
Raw chemical compound solution that is mixed with water and air to produce foam.

Foam Eductors
Type of foam proportioner used for mixing foam concentrate in proper proportions with a stream of water to produce foam solution.

Foam Proportioner
Device that injects the correct amount of foam concentrate into the water stream to make the foam solution.

Foam Solution
Mixture of foam concentrate and water after it leaves the proportioner but before it is discharged from the nozzle and air is added to it.

Fog Stream
Water stream of finely divided particles used for fire control.

Foil Back
Blanket or batt insulation with one surface faced with metal foil which serves as a vapor barrier and heat reflector.

Fold-A-Tank
See Portable Tank.

Folding Door
Door that opens and closes by folding.

Folding Jack
Common type of lifting jack. The frame of the folding jack is made of metal bars of equal lengths fastened in the center to form X's. This jack has limited use and is considered safe only for light loads.

Folding Ladder
Short, collapsible ladder easy to maneuver in tight places such as reaching through openings in attics and lofts.

Food Unit
Functional unit within the service branch of the logistics section of an incident management system; responsible for providing meals for personnel involved with incident.

Footing
(1) That part of the building that rests on the bearing soil and is wider than the foundation wall. (2) Base for a column.

Footplate
(1) A 4-inch (100 mm) metal plate that runs around the bottom edge of an elevating platform to prevent a firefighter's feet from slipping off the edge of the platform. (2) A 4-inch (100 mm) metal plate that runs around the bottom edge of any railing on a balcony or elevated walkway to prevent someone's foot from slipping off. Also called Kickplate.

Force
(1) To break open, into, or through. (2) Simple measure of weight, usually expressed in pounds or kilograms.

Forced Ventilation
Any means other than natural ventilation. This type of ventilation may involve the use of fans, blowers, smoke ejectors, and fire streams. Also called Mechanical Ventilation.

Forcible Entry
Techniques used by fire personnel to gain entry into buildings, vehicles, aircraft, or other areas of confinement when normal means of entry are locked or blocked.

Fording
Ability of an apparatus to traverse a body of standing water. Apparatus specifications should list the specific water depths through which trucks must be able to drive.

Fore
Front or nose section of an aircraft or toward that area. Also called Forward.

Foreman
Rank used for a company officer in some departments.

Forensic Science
Application of scientific procedures to the interpretation of physical events such as those that occur at a fire scene; the art of reconstructing past events and then explaining that process and one's findings to investigators and triers of fact; criminalistics.

Forensic Scientist
One who applies scientific procedures to the interpretation of physical events such as those that occur at fire scenes; one who is adept at reconstructing past events and then explaining that process and findings to investigators and triers of facts; a criminologist.

Foreseeability
Concept that instruction should be based not only on dangerous conditions that may exist in training but also on anticipating what firefighters might face on the job.

Forestry Hose
Single-jacket, small diameter hose used to combat fires in the forest and in other wildland settings.

Forged Couplings
Coupling formed by pounding a hot metal pellet into a forging die, which forms the metal into the desired shape.

Fork Pockets
Transverse structural apertures in the base of the container that permit entry of forklift devices.

Formaldehyde (HCHO)
Colorless gas with a characteristic pungent odor produced when wood, cotton, and newspaper burn; an eye, nose, and throat irritant.

Formative Evaluation
Ongoing, repeated assessment during course development and during or after instruction to determine the most effective instructional content, method, aids, and testing techniques.

Former
Frame of wood or metal that is attached to the truss of the fuselage or wing of an aircraft in order to provide the required aerodynamic shape.

Formula
Any variety of mathematical computations used in the fire service primarily to determine pressures, flows, and friction loss.

Forward
See Fore.

Forward Lay
Method of laying hose from the water supply to the fire scene.

Four-Step Teaching Method
Teaching method based upon four steps: preparation, presentation, application, and evaluation.

Four-Way Hydrant Valve
Device that permits a pumper to boost the pressure in a supply line connected to a hydrant without interrupting the water flow.

Fracture
Break or rupture in a bone.

Frame
Part of an opening that is constructed to support the component that closes and secures the opening such as a door or window.

Free-Burning Stage
Second stage of burning. The fire burns rapidly using up oxygen and building up heat that accumulates in upper areas at temperatures that may exceed 1,300°F (700°C).

Freeflow
Continuous flow of air from the regulator, usually venting into the atmosphere.

Freight Container
See Container.

Friction Burn
See Abrasion.

Friction Loss
Loss of pressure created by the turbulence of water moving against the interior walls of the hose or pipe.

Front Bumper Well
Hose or tool compartment built into the front bumper of a fire apparatus.

Front-Mount Pump
Fire pump mounted in front of the radiator of a vehicle and powered off the crankshaft.

Front Stringer
Stringer that supports the side of the stairs with a balustrade.

Frostbite
Local freezing and tissue damage due to prolonged exposure to extreme cold.

Frostnip
Superficial tissue damage caused by freezing; limited in scope and does not destroy the full thickness of skin.

Fuel
Flammable and combustible substances available for a fire to consume.

Fuel Break
Wide separation in vegetation that helps slow the spread of a wildland fire.

Fuel Siphoning
Unintentional release of fuel from an aircraft caused by overflow, puncture, loose cap, etc. Also called Fuel Venting.

Fuel Venting
See Fuel Siphoning.

Fulcrum
Support or point of support on which a lever turns in raising or moving something.

Full-Cycle Machine
Machine with a clutch that, when tripped, cannot be disengaged until the crankshaft has completed a full revolution and the press slide a full stroke.

Full Structural Protective Clothing
Protective clothing including helmets, self-contained breathing apparatus, coats and pants customarily worn by firefighters (turnout or bunker coats and pants), rubber boots, and gloves. It also includes covering for the neck, ears, and other parts of the head not protected by the helmet or breathing apparatus. For hazardous materials, bands or tape are added around the legs, arms, and waist.

Full Trailer
Truck trailer constructed so that all of its own weight and that of its load rests upon its own wheels; that is, it does not depend upon a truck tractor to support it. A semitrailer equipped with a dolly is considered a full trailer.

Fully Involved
When an entire area of a building is completely involved in heat and flame.

Fume Test
Qualitative test of a self-contained breathing apparatus facepiece fit in which a smoke tube is used to check for leakage around the facepiece.

Functional Fixity
Decision-making problem characterized by the tendency to use an object only for its designed purpose.

Furring
Wood strips fastened to a wall, floor, or ceiling for the purpose of covering material.

Fused Head
Automatic sprinkler head that has operated due to exposure to heat.

Fused Joint
Bones joined to form a rigid structure, as in the skull.

Fuselage
Main body of an aircraft to which the wings and tail are attached. The fuselage houses the crew, passengers, and cargo.

Fusible Link
Connecting link device that fuses or melts when exposed to heat. Used in sprinkler heads, fire doors, dampers, and ventilators.

G

Gabled Roof
Style of pitched roof with square ends in which the end walls of the building form triangular areas beneath the roof.

Gage
See Gauge.

Gage Lines
Term used in steel construction to describe lines parallel to the length of a member on which holes for fasteners are placed. The gage distance is the normal distance between the gage line and the edge or back of the member.

Gallbladder
Sac located just beneath the liver that concentrates and stores bile.

Galley
Food storage and preparation area of large aircraft.

Gallon
Unit of liquid measure. One U.S. gallon (3.785 L) has the volume of 231 cubic inches (3 785 cubic centimeters). One imperial gallon equals 1.201 U.S. gallons (4.546 L).

Gallons Per Minute (GPM)
Unit of volume measurement used in the fire service for water movement.

Gambrel Roof
Style of gabled roof on which each side slopes at two different angles; often used on barns and similar structures.

Gamma Rays
Electromagnetic radiation emitted from radioactive substances; similar to X-rays.

Gang Nail
Form of gusset plate. These thin steel plates are punched with acutely V-shaped holes that form sharp prongs on one side that penetrate wooden members to fasten them together.

Gangrene
Local tissue death as the result of an injury or inadequate blood supply; often caused by frostbite.

Gas
Compressible substance, with no specific volume, that tends to assume the shape of a container. Molecules move about most rapidly in this state.

Gas Chromatogram
Chart from a gas chromatograph tracing the results of analysis of volatile compounds by display in recorded peaks.

Gas Chromatograph
Device to detect and separate small quantities of volatile liquids or gases through instrument analysis.

Gas Chromatography
Characterizing volatilities and chemical properties of compounds that evaporate enough at low temperatures of about 50°C to provide detectable quantities in the air through the use of instrument analysis in a gas chromatograph.

Gaskets
(1) Rubber seals or packings used at joints in self-contained breathing apparatus to prevent the escape or inflow of gases. (2) Rubber seals used in fire hose couplings and pump intakes to prevent the leakage of water at connections.

Gas Mask
See Canister Apparatus.

Gated Wye
Hose appliance with one female inlet and two or more male outlets with a gate valve on each outlet.

Gate Valve
Control valve with a solid plate operated by a handle and screw mechanism. Rotating the handle moves the plate into or out of the waterway.

Gauge (Gage)
(1) Instrument used to show the operating conditions of an appliance or piece of equipment. (2) Measurement for wire diameter.

General Alarm
Larger than normal complement of firefighters and equipment assigned to an incident of large magnitude. In smaller departments this might mean that all available units are assigned to the incident.

General Aviation
All civil aviation operations other than scheduled air services and nonscheduled operations for remuneration or hire.

General Order
Standing order, usually written, that is communicated through channels to all units and remains in effect until further notice.

General Staff
Group of incident management personnel: the incident commander, operations section chief, planning section chief, logistics section chief, and finance/administrative section chief.

Generator
Auxiliary electrical power generating device. Portable generators are powered by small gasoline or diesel engines and generally have 110- and/or 220-volt capacities.

Genitourinary System
System that includes all the organs involved in reproduction and in the formation and voiding of urine.

Gibbs Cam
Ascender for rope climbing.

Gin Pole
Vertical lifting device that may be attached to the front or the rear of the apparatus. It consists of a single pole that is attached to the apparatus at one end and has a working pulley at the other. Guy wires also may be used to stabilize the pole.

Girder
(1) Large, horizontal structural member used to support joists and beams at isolated points along their length. (2) Steel frame members in a bus that run from front to rear to strengthen and shape the roof bows.

Gladhands
Fittings for connection of air brake lines between vehicles. Also called Hose Couplings, Hand Shakes, and Polarized Couplings.

Glare
Uncomfortably bright light, either direct or reflected.

Glass Door
Door consisting primarily of glass; usually set in a metal frame.

Glazier's Tool
Tool used for removing windows from their mountings.

Glazing
(1) Part of a window that allows light to pass. (2) Glass or thermoplastic panel in a window.

Gloves
Part of the firefighter's protective clothing ensemble necessary to protect the hands.

Glucose
Simple sugar.

Glue-Lam Beam
Wooden structural member composed of many relatively short pieces of lumber glued and laminated together under pressure to form a long, extremely strong beam.

Goals
Broad, general nonmeasurable statement of desired achievement.

Going Fire
Slang for a fire of such size and complexity as to be uncontrollable by initial attack units; commonly used term for large natural cover fires.

Governor
Built-in pressure-regulating device to control pump discharge pressure by limiting engine rpm.

GPM
Abbreviation for Gallons Per Minute.

Gradability
Ability of a piece of apparatus to traverse various terrain configurations.

Grade
Natural, unaltered ground level.

Grade Beam
Concrete wall foundation in the form of a strong reinforced beam that rests on footings or caissons spaced at intervals.

Grade D Breathing Air
Classification of allowable contamination levels in breathing air. The CGA Grade D allows no more than 20 ppm carbon monoxide, 1,000 ppm carbon dioxide, and 5 mg/m^3 oil vapor.

Gradient Wind
Wind caused by air movement from a high- or low-pressure system; sometimes covering as much as 300 miles (480 km), with speeds of 5 to 30 miles per hour (8 km/h to 48 km/h), and gradual shifts in direction.

Grading Schedule
Schedule of deficiency points by which insurance engineers grade the fire defenses of a community.

Grading System
System used to convert achievements to grades or class standing.

Grain Bin
Large, cylindrical tank used to store harvested grain, corn, or other similar commodities.

Grand Mal
See Tonic-Clonic Seizure.

Gravity System
Water supply system that relies entirely on the force of gravity to propel the water throughout the system. This type of system is generally used in conjunction with an elevated water storage source.

Gravity Tank
Elevated water storage tank for fire protection and community water service. A water level of 100 feet (30 m) provides a static pressure head of 43.4 psi (300 kPa) minus friction losses in piping when water is flowing.

Green Fuels
Vegetation that has a high moisture content and will not easily burn.

Grid
See Complex Loop.

Gridded Piping System
See Complex Loop.

Grid Map
Plan view of an area subdivided into a system of squares (numbered and lettered) to provide quick reference to any point.

Grid System Water Mains
Interconnecting system of water mains in a criss-cross or rectangular pattern.

Grommets
Reinforced eyelets in salvage covers through which fasteners may be passed; permit hanging of covers with ropes or pike poles over wall shelving and in other difficult areas.

Gross Weight
Weight of a vehicle or trailer together with the weight of its entire contents.

Ground Cover Fire
Fire involving any natural vegetation, particularly near or on the ground; a natural cover fire. Also called Ground Fire or Wildland Fire.

Ground Fault
Accidental grounding of an electrical conductor.

Ground Fault Circuit Interrupter
Electrical device designed to discontinue the flow of electricity when grounding occurs. In the event of a short circuit in the device it prevents electrocution of people in contact with the electrical device.

Ground Fire
See Ground Cover Fire.

Grounding
Reducing the difference in electrical potential between an object and the ground by the use of various conductors.

Ground Jack
See Stabilizer (1).

Ground Ladder
Ladders specifically designed for fire service use that are not mechanically or physically attached permanently to fire apparatus and do not require mechanical power from the apparatus for ladder use and operation.

Ground Support Unit
Functional unit within the support branch of the logistics section of an incident management system; responsible for fueling/maintaining/repairing vehicles and transporting of personnel and supplies.

Group
Subunit of the incident command system. It is composed of a number of individual units that are assigned to perform a particular function.

Grouping
Furniture, stock, and merchandise moved in a compact arrangement to facilitate protection by the least number of salvage covers.

Group Supervisor
Person in charge of a group within the incident command system.

Growth Ring
Layer of wood (as an annual ring) produced during a single period of growth.

Guards
Protective coverings over dangerous pieces of machinery.

Gusset Plates
Metal or wooden plates used to bind roof or floor components into a load-bearing unit.

Guy Ropes
Ropes attached between the tip of a raised aerial device and an object on the ground to stabilize the device during high wind conditions; should be used only if approved by the manufacturer of the aerial device.

Gypsum
Inorganic product from which plaster and plasterboard are constructed.

H

HAD
Abbreviation for Heat Actuating Devices.

Half Hitch
Knot that is always used in conjunction with another knot. The half hitch is particularly useful in stabilizing tall objects that are being hoisted.

Half-Life
(1) Time required for half of something to undergo a process. (2) Time required for half the amount of a substance in or introduced into a living system or ecosystem to be eliminated or disintegrated by natural processes. (2) Period of time required for any radioactive substance to lose half of its strength or reduce by one-half its total present energy.

Halligan Tool
Prying tool with a claw at one end and a spike or point at a right angle to a wedge at the other end. Also called Hooligan Tool.

Halogenated Agents
Chemical compounds (halogenated hydrocarbons) that contain carbon plus one or more elements from the halogen series. Halon 1301 and Halon 1211 are most commonly used as extinguishing agents for Class B and Class C fires. Also called Halogenated Hydrocarbons.

Halogenated Hydrocarbons
See Halogenated Agents.

Halogens
Name given to the family of elements that includes fluorine, chlorine, bromine, and iodine.

Halon
Halogenated agent; extinguishes fire by inhibiting the chemical reaction between fuel and oxygen.

Halyard
Rope used on extension ladders to extend the fly sections. Also called Fly Rope.

Handi-Talki
See Portable Radio.

Handline
Small hoselines (2½ inch [65 mm] or less) that can be handled and maneuvered without mechanical assistance.

Handrail
Top piece of a balustrade that is grasped when ascending or descending a stairway. Handrails may be attached to the wall in closed stairways.

Handsaw
Manually operated saw that is useful on objects that require a controlled cut but are too big to fit in the jaws of a scissors-type cutter or unsuitable for cutting with a power saw.

Hand Shakes
See Gladhands.

Hand Tool
Tool that is manipulated and powered by human force.

Hard Line
See Booster Hose.

Hard Sleeve
See Hard Suction Hose.

Hard Suction Hose
Noncollapsible, rubberized length of hose with a steel core that connects a pump to a source of water and is used for drafting. Also called Hard Sleeve.

Hardware
(1) Refers to the computer, electronic components, keyboard, CRT, disk drives, and other physical items connected within the computer system. (2) Ancillary equipment, other than ropes and harnesses, used in rope systems.

Hardy Cross Method
Iterative technique used for solving the complicated problems involving gridded water supply systems.

Hasp
Fastening device consisting of a loop, eye, or staple and a slotted hinge or bar; commonly used with a padlock.

Hatch
Openings in the ceilings or roofs of buildings; fitted with removable covers for the purpose of providing access and ventilation to the cockloft or roof. Also called Scuttle.

Hay Hook
See Bale Hook.

Hazard Area
Established area from which bystanders and unneeded rescue workers are prohibited.

Hazard Class
Group of materials designated by the Department of Transportation (DOT) that share a major hazardous property such as radioactivity or flammability.

Hazardous Atmosphere
Any atmosphere that is not conducive to the support of human life. This includes atmospheres that contain toxic gases or vapors and atmospheres that are oxygen deficient or heated.

Hazardous Chemical
Defined by the Occupational Safety and Health Administration (OSHA) as any chemical that is a physical hazard or a health hazard to employees.

Hazardous Material
Any material that possesses an unreasonable risk to the health and safety of persons and/or the environment if it is not properly controlled during handling, storage, manufacture, processing, packaging, use, disposal, or transportation.

Hazardous Substance
Any substance designated under the Clean Water Act and the Comprehensive Environmental Response, Compensation and Liability Act (CERCLA) as posing a threat to waterways and the environment when released. (U.S. Environmental Protection Agency.)

Hazardous Wastes
Discarded materials regulated by the Environmental Protection Agency because of public health and safety concerns. Regulatory authority is granted under the Resource Conservation and Recovery Act. (U.S. Environmental Protection Agency.)

Hazen-Williams Formula
Empirical formula for calculating friction loss in water systems; fire protection industry standard. To comply with most nationally recognized standards, the Hazen-Williams formula must be used.

Head
(1) Front and rear closure of a tank shell. (2) Water pressure due to elevation. For every 1-foot increase in elevation, 0.434 psi is gained (for every 1-meter increase in elevation, 9.82 kPa is gained). Also called Head Pressure. (3) Top of a window or door frame. (4) Most active part of a ground cover fire; the forward advancing part.

Head-End Power
Power developed by generators in a train's locomotive to support the energy needs of the other cars in the train consist.

Header
(1) Gathering unit portion of a combine. (2) Term used to describe the looming up of smoke from a fire.

Head Harness
Straps that hold the self-contained breathing apparatus facepiece in place. Also called Spider Strap.

Head-On Collision
Collision occurring when the front of a vehicle strikes either another vehicle in the front or a stationary object.

Head Pressure
Pressure exerted by a stationary column of water, directly proportional to the height of the column. *Also see* Head (2).

Heart
Hollow muscular organ that receives the blood from the veins, sends it through the lungs to be oxygenated, and then pumps it to the arteries.

Heart Attack
See Acute Myocardial Infarction.

Heat
Form of energy that is proportional to molecular movement. To signify its intensity, it is measured in degrees of temperature.

Heat Actuating Devices
Thermostatically controlled detection devices used to activate fire equipment, alarms, or appliances.

Heat Cramps
Heat illness resulting from prolonged exposure to high temperatures; characterized by excessive sweating, muscle cramps in the abdomen and legs, faintness, dizziness, and exhaustion.

Heat Exhaustion
Heat illness caused by exposure to excessive heat; symptoms include weakness, cold and clammy skin, heavy perspiration, rapid and shallow breathing, weak pulse, dizziness, and sometimes unconsciousness.

Heat From Arcing
Type of electrical heating that occurs when the current flow is interrupted.

Heating Tube
Tube installed inside a tank to heat the contents. Also called Fire Tube.

Heating, Ventilating, And Air Conditioning (HVAC) System
Heating, ventilating, and air-conditioning system within a building and the equipment necessary to make it function; usually a single, integrated unit with a complex system of ducts throughout the building. Also called Air-Handling System.

Heat Of Combustion
Amount of heat generated by the combustion (oxidation) reaction.

Heat Of Decomposition
Release of heat from decomposing compounds, usually due to bacterial action.

Heat Of Friction
Heat created by the movement of two surfaces against each other.

Heat Of Solution
Heat released by the solution of matter in a liquid.

Heat Of Vaporization
Quantity of heat required to change a liquid into a vapor.

Heat Protective Shield
Reflective shield attached around an elevating platform to protect the firefighters in the platform from the effects of radiated heat.

Heat Sensor Label
Label affixed to the ladder beam near the tip to provide a warning that the ladder has been subjected to excessive heat.

Heat Stroke
Heat illness caused by heat exposure, resulting in failure of the body's heat regulating mechanism; symptoms include high fever of 105° to 106°F; dry, red, hot skin; rapid, strong pulse; and deep breaths, convulsions. May result in coma or possibly death. Also called Sunstroke.

Heat Transfer
Flow of heat from a hot substance to a cold substance. This may be accomplished by convection, conduction, or radiation.

Heat Treatment
Controlled cooling or quenching of heated metals, usually by immersion in a liquid quenching medium; its purpose is to harden the metal.

Heavy Content Fire Loading
Storing of combustible materials in high piles that are placed close together.

Heavy-Duty Appliances
Master stream equipment.

Heavy Fuels
Massive natural cover fuels such as logs, snags, and large limbs. Heavy fuels are not easy to ignite; once ignited, they burn slowly and hot.

Heavy Rescue Vehicle
Large rescue vehicle that may be constructed on a custom or commercial chassis. Additional equipment carried by the heavy rescue unit includes A-frames or gin poles, cascade systems, larger power plants, trench and storing equipment, small pumps and foam equipment, large winches, hydraulic booms, large quantities of rope and rigging equipment, air compressors, and ladders.

Heavy Stream
See Master Stream.

Heavy Timber Construction
Type of construction where the load-bearing structure is composed of large wooden beams and trusses.

Heel
(1) Base or butt end of a ground ladder. (2) To steady a ladder while it is being raised. (3) Rear portion of a natural cover fire.

Heelman
Firefighter who carries the butt end of the ladder and/or who subsequently heels or secures it from slipping during operations.

Heel Plate
Metal reinforcement at the heel or butt of a ladder; generally shaped to give the ladder more stability.

Heimlich Maneuver
Technique to clear an obstruction from a victim's airway.

Helmet
Protective headgear worn by firefighters that provides protection from falling objects, side blows, the fire environment elements, and eye injuries.

Helmet Faceshield
See Faceshield.

Helmet Identification Shield
Insignia or plaque fastened to the front of the firefighter's helmet that generally displays the name of the city, and the firefighter's initials, unit, and rank.

Hematoma
Localized collection of blood in an organ, tissue, or space as a result of injury or a broken blood vessel.

Hemispherical Head
Head that is half a sphere in shape; used on MC-331 high-pressure tanks.

Hemoglobin
Oxygen-carrying component of red blood cells.

Hemorrhage
Profuse discharge of blood.

Herbicides
Chemicals designed to control or eliminate all or certain kinds of plants.

Higbee Cut
Special cut at the beginning of the thread to provide positive identification of the first thread and to eliminate cross threading. Also called Blunt Start.

Higbee Indicators
Notches or grooves cut into coupling lugs to identify by touch or sight the exact location of the Higbee Cut.

High-Pressure Air
Air pressurized to 3,000 to 5,000 psi (21 000 kPa to 35 000 kPa); used to differentiate from older air cylinders using a pressure range from 1,800 to 2,200 psi (12 600 kPa to 15 400 kPa).

High-Pressure Fog
Fog stream operated at high pressures and discharged through small diameter hose.

High-Pressure Hose
Hose leading from the air cylinder to the regulator; may be at cylinder pressure or reduced to some lower pressure.

High-Pressure Nozzle
Fire stream nozzle that is designed to be operated in excess of the 100 psi (700 kPa) to which ordinary fog nozzles are designed.

High-Rack Storage
Warehousing storage of materials on high, open racks that may be as high as 100 feet (30 m).

High-Rise Building
Any building that requires fire fighting on levels above the reach of the department's equipment. Various building and fire codes will also have written definitions of what is to be considered a high rise.

High-Rise Pack
Special kit for high-rise operations containing hose, adapters, nozzle, and spanner wrenches.

High Speed Turnoff/Taxiway
Curved or angled taxiway designed to expedite aircraft turning off the runway after landing.

High-Value District
Section of a city in which valuable property is located and in which additional companies and apparatus are needed to combat a fire.

Hinged Door
See Swinging Door.

Hip
Junction of two sloping roof surfaces forming an exterior angle.

Hip Roof
Pitched roof that has no gables. All facets of the roof slope down from the peak to an outside wall.

Hitch
(1) Connecting device at the rear of a vehicle used to pull a full trailer with provision for easy coupling. (2) Loop of rope that secures the rope but that is not a part of a standard rope knot.

Hives
Red or white raised patches on the skin, often attended by severe itching; a characteristic reaction in allergy responses.

H-Jack
See Box Stabilizer.

Hoisting Cylinder
See Elevation Cylinder.

Hold-Down Locks
Locks that secure the aerial device in its cradle during road travel.

Holdfast
Constructed anchor for a guy line.

Hook
Curved metal devices installed on the tip end of roof ladders to secure the ladder to the highest point on the roof of a building.

Hook And Ladder
Old term for an aerial ladder truck.

Hooking Up
Slang for connecting a fire department pumper to a hydrant or connecting a discharge hose to the pumper.

Hooligan Tool
See Halligan Tool.

Hopcalite™
Catalytic chemical that converts carbon monoxide to carbon dioxide.

Hopper
(1) Any of various receptacles used for temporary storage of material. (2) Tank holding liquid and having a device for releasing its contents through a pipe. (3) Freight car with a floor sloping to one or more hinged doors for discharging bulk contents.

Hopper Window
Type of swinging window that is hinged at the bottom and swings inward.

Horizontal Motion
Side-to-side swaying motion.

Horizontal Split-Case Pump
Centrifugal pump with the impeller shaft installed horizontally and often referred to as a split-case pump. This is because the case in which the shaft and impeller rotates is split in the middle and can be separated exposing the shaft, bearings, and impeller.

Horizontal Ventilation
Any technique by which heat, smoke, and other products of combustion are channeled out of a structure by way of existing or created horizontal openings such as windows, doors, or other holes in walls.

Horseshoe Load
Arrangement of fire hose in a hose bed or compartment in which the hose lies on edge in the form of a horseshoe.

Hose Bed
Main hose-carrying area of a pumper or other piece of apparatus designed for carrying hose. Also called Hose Body.

Hose Belt
Leather belt or nylon strap used for securing and handling charged hoselines, tools, or tying off a ladder. *Also see* Rope Hose Tool or Hose Strap.

Hose Bin
Tray or compartment, often located on the running board or over a hose bed, for carrying extra hose.

Hose Body
See Hose Bed.

Hose Bridge
Device placed astride hose to prevent damage to hose from traffic passing over it. Also called Hose Ramp.

Hose Cabinet
Recessed wall cabinet that contains a wall hydrant and preconnected fire hose for incipient fire fighting. Also called Hose Rack.

Hose Cap
Threaded female fitting used to cap a hoseline or a pump outlet.

Hose Clamp
Mechanical or hydraulic device used to compress fire hose to stop the flow of water.

Hose Control Device
Device used to hold a charged hoseline in a stationary position for an extended period of time.

Hose Couplings
(1) Metal fasteners used to connect fire hose together. (2) *See* Gladhands.

Hose Dryer
Enclosed cabinet containing racks on which fire hose can be dried.

Hose Hoist
Metal device having a roller that can be placed over a windowsill or roof's edge to protect a hose and make it easier to hoist. Also called Hose Roller.

Hose Jacket
(1) Outer covering of a hose. (2) Device clamped over a hose to contain water at a rupture point or to join hose with damaged or dissimilar couplings.

Hose Lay
Layouts of hose from a fire pump to the place where the water needs to be.

Hose Layout, Complicated
Hose layout that includes the use of multiple lengths of unequal hoselines, unequal wyed or manifold lines, siamesed lines, or master stream devices. Such a layout requires the pump operator to perform complicated calculations in order to supply the lines properly.

Hose Layout, Simple
Hose layout that includes the use of single hoselines or multiple, wyed, siamesed, or manifold lines of equal length.

Hoseline
Section of flexible conduit that is connected to a water supply source for the purpose of delivering water onto a fire.

Hose Load Finish
See Finish.

Hose Pack
Compact bundle of hose, usually bound to facilitate moving.

Hose Plug
Threaded male fitting used to cap off a pump intake.

Hose Rack
See Hose Cabinet.

Hose Ramp
See Hose Bridge.

Hose Record
Individual history of a section of hose from the time it is purchased until it is taken out of service.

Hose Reel
Cylindrical device upon which fire hose is manually or mechanically rolled for later deployment.

Hose Roller
See Hose Hoist.

Hose Strap
Strap or chain with a handle suitable for placing over a ladder rung; used to carry and secure a hoseline. *Also see* Hose Belt or Rope Hose Tool.

Hose Test Gate Valve
Special valve designed to prevent injury caused by a burst hoseline during hose testing.

Hose Tool
See Hose Strap.

Hose Tower
Part of a fire station or building designed so that fire hose can be hung vertically to drain and dry.

Hose Trough
See Hose Tube.

Hose Tube
Housing used on tank and bulk commodity trailers for the storage of cargo handling hoses. Also called Hose Trough.

Hose Wringer
Device used to remove water and air from large diameter hose.

Hotel Raise
Method of raising a fire department extension ladder in line with several windows so that individuals can simultaneously escape from more than one floor. Also called Factory Raise.

Hotline
Telephone line and operation set up for the purpose of receiving information, often anonymously given.

Hot Refuel/Defuel (Rapid Refuel/Defuel)
Refueling or defueling of an aircraft while the engines are operating.

Hot Smoldering Phase
Phase of combustion when the level of oxygen in a confined space is below that needed for flaming combustion. The hot smoldering phase is characterized by glowing embers, high heat at all levels of the room, and heavy smoke and fire gas production.

House Lights
Lights throughout the fire station that are controlled from the alarm or watch desk, which makes it possible to illuminate the entire station in case of emergency.

House Line
Permanently fixed, private standpipe hoseline.

House Watch
Duty of maintaining the fire station alarm center for a prescribed period of time.

Human Factors
(1) Individual's attributes or characteristics that cause that individual to be involved in more accidents than others. (2) Natural desire to conserve our human resources as well as to prevent needless suffering from physical pain or emotional stress.

Humerus
Bone of the upper arm.

HVAC System
Abbreviation for Heating, Ventilating, and Air-Conditioning System.

Hydrant
See Fire Hydrant.

Hydrant Adapter
Adapter, fitting, or coupling to connect hose or pumper intake hose to a fire hydrant.

Hydrant Pressure
Amount of pressure being supplied by a hydrant without assistance.

Hydrant Wrench
Specially designed tool used to open or close a hydrant and to remove hydrant caps.

Hydration
(1) Act or process of combining with water. (2) Condition of having adequate fluid in body tissues. (3) Chemical process in which concrete changes to a solid state and gains strength.

Hydraulic Calculations
Process of using mathematics to solve problems involving fire hydraulics.

Hydraulic Jack
Lifting jack that uses hydraulic fluid power supplied from a manually operated hand lever.

Hydraulic Pump
Positive displacement-type pump that imparts pressure on hydraulic oil within the hydraulic system.

Hydraulics
(1) Operated, moved, or effected by means of water. (2) Of or relating to water or other liquid in motion. (3) Operated by the resistance offered or the pressure transmitted when a quantity of liquid is forced through a comparatively small orifice or through a tube. (4) Branch of fluid mechanics dealing with the mechanical properties of liquids and the application of these properties in engineering.

Hydraulic System
(1) Aircraft system that transmits power by means of a fluid under pressure. (2) Aerial apparatus system that provides power to the stabilizers and aerial device.

Hydraulic Ventilation
Method of ventilating a fire building by directing a fog stream of water out a window to increase air and smoke movement.

Hydrocarbons
Organic compound containing only hydrogen and carbon and found primarily in petroleum products and coal.

Hydrogen Chloride (HCl)
Gas produced by the combustion of polyvinyl chlorides. When inhaled, it mixes with the moisture in the respiratory tract and forms hydrochloric acid.

Hydrogen Cyanide (HCN)
Colorless, toxic gas with a faint odor similar to bitter almonds; produced by the combustion of nitrogen-bearing substances.

Hydrogen Sulfide (H_2S)
Colorless gas with a strong rotten-egg odor produced when rubber insulation, tires, and woolen materials burn and by the decomposition of sulfur-bearing organic material; dangerous because it quickly deactivates the sense of smell. It is commonly called silo gas, although it is actually one of several components of silo gas.

Hydrokinetics
Branch of hydraulics having to do with liquids (water) in motion, particularly in relation to forces created by or applied to the liquid in motion.

Hydroplaning
Condition in which moving tires are separated from pavement surfaces by steam and/or water or liquid rubber film, resulting in loss of mechanical braking effectiveness.

Hydrostatics
Branch of hydraulics dealing with the properties of liquids (water) at rest, particularly in relation to pressures resulting from or applied to the static liquid.

Hydrostatic Test
Testing method used to check the integrity of pressure vessels.

Hygroscopic
Ability of a substance to absorb moisture from the air.

Hyperglycemia
Excessive sugar in the blood due to lack of insulin to metabolize the sugar. Also known as Diabetic Ketoacidosis.

Hypergolic
Chemical reaction between a fuel and an oxidizer that causes immediate ignition on contact without the presence of air. An example is the contact of fuming nitric acid and UDMH (unsymmetrical dimethyl hydrazine).

Hypergolic Materials
Materials that ignite when they come in contact with each other. The chemical reactions of hypergolic substances vary from slow reactions that may barely be visible to reactions that occur with explosive force.

Hypertension
Abnormal elevation of blood pressure.

Hyperventilation
Rapid breathing that overoxygenates the blood.

Hypoglycemia
Condition in which the level of sugar in the blood is abnormally low; can be life-threatening.

Hypotension
Low blood pressure; blood pressure lower than normal.

Hypothermia
Abnormally low body temperature.

Hypovolemic Shock
Shock caused by loss of blood.

Hypoxia
Condition caused by a deficiency in the amount of oxygen reaching body tissues.

I

I Beam
Steel or wooden structural member with a cross section resembling a capital I.

IC
Abbreviation for Incident Commander.

ICC
Abbreviation for Interstate Commerce Commission; now the U.S. Department of Transportation.

ICS
Abbreviation for Incident Command System.

Idle Thrust/RPM
Aircraft engine running at the lowest possible speed.

IDLH
Abbreviation for Immediately Dangerous to Life and Health.

IFR
Abbreviation for Instrument Flight Rules.

IFSTA
Acronym for International Fire Service Training Association.

Ignition
Beginning of flame propagation or burning; the start of a fire.

Ignition Source
Method (either wanted or unwanted) that provides a means for the initiation of self-sustained combustion.

Ignition Temperature
Minimum temperature to which a fuel in air must be heated in order to start self-sustained combustion independent of the heating source.

Ike-O-Hook
Steel hook with an eyelet on one end; used for hanging salvage covers and other devices from pike poles or ropes.

Ilium
One of the two large bones that form the winged portion of the pelvic girdle.

Illustration
Method of teaching that uses the sense of sight. Showing by illustration includes the use of drawings, pictures, slides, transparencies, film, models, and other visual aids that may clarify details or processes.

ILS
Abbreviation for Instrument Landing System.

Immediately Dangerous To Life And Health (IDLH)
Any atmosphere that poses an immediate hazard to life or produces immediate irreversible, debili-

tating effects on health. A companion measurement to the PEL, IDLH concentrations represent concentrations above which respiratory protection should be required. IDLH is expressed in ppm or mg/m^3.

Immiscible
Incapable of being mixed or blended with another substance.

Immobilization
To hold a part firmly in place, as with a splint.

Immunity
Freedom from legal liability for an act or physical condition.

Impact Hammer
See Pneumatic Chisel/Hammer.

Impaled
(1) Condition resulting when a victim's head or other appendage pierces a stationary object such as a windshield. (2) Condition resulting from a foreign object becoming lodged in some portion of a victim's body.

Impaled Object
Object that has caused a puncture wound and remains embedded in the wound.

Impeller
Vaned, circulating member of the centrifugal pump that transmits motion to the water.

Impeller Eye
Intake orifice at the center of a centrifugal pump impeller.

Impinging Stream Nozzle
Nozzle that drives several jets of water together at a set angle in order to break water into finely divided particles.

Implosion
Rapid inward collapsing of the walls of a vessel or structure because the walls are unable to sustain a vacuum.

Impounded Water Supply
Generally used to describe an open, standing, manmade reservoir but can be used to describe any type of standing, static water supply.

Inappropriate Response
Effect of a decision-making problem. The person in charge and subordinates might try to hide their fear or revulsion by joking, getting angry, or rationalizing the problem away.

Inboard/Outboard
Refers to location with reference to the centerline of the fuselage (i.e., inboard engines are the ones closest to the fuselage; outboard engines are those farthest away).

Incendiarism
Deliberate setting of a fire or fires by a human being.

Incendiary
Fire believed to have been deliberately set; an incendiary agent such as a bomb.

Incendiary Device
Contrivance designed and used to start a fire.

Inches of Mercury
Scale used in measuring negative pressure; used to measure barometric pressure.

Incident
Emergency or nonemergency situation at which fire personnel operate.

Incident Action Plan
Strategic goals, tactical objectives, and support requirements for the incident. All incidents require an action plan. For simple incidents, the action plan is not usually in written form. Large or complex incidents will require that the action plan be documented in writing.

Incident Commander (IC)
Person in charge of the incident management system during an emergency.

Incident Command System (ICS)
Management system of procedures for controlling personnel, facilities, equipment, and communications so that different agencies can work together toward a common goal in an effective and efficient manner.

Incipient Phase
First phase of the burning process where the substance being oxidized is producing some heat, but the heat has not spread to other substances nearby. During this phase, the oxygen content of the air has not been significantly reduced.

Increaser
Adapter used to attach a larger hoseline to a smaller one. The increaser has female threads on the smaller side and male threads on the larger side.

Incrustation
Deposit on the inner wall of a water pipe creating additional friction and loss of pressure.

Index Gas
Any commonly encountered gas, such as carbon monoxide in fires, whose concentration can be measured.

Indicating Valve
Water main valve that visually shows the open or closed status of the valve.

Indicator
Visual remains at a fire scene revealing the fire's progress and action.

Indicator Action
Part of a behavioral objective that tells how a student will show a desired behavior so that it can be observed and measured.

Indictment
Formal written accusation charging the defendant with a crime.

Indirect Attack
Directing the fire stream at the ceiling level of a room or building in order to generate a large amount of steam. The steam helps darken the fire and cool the area enough so that firefighters may safely enter and make a direct attack to extinguish the fire.

Individual Container
Product container used to transport materials in small quantities; includes bags, boxes, and drums.

Individual Emergency Conditions Breathing
Procedures or techniques performed by an individual during emergencies where SCBA malfunctions, remaining air supply is inadequate for escape, or air supply is depleted.

Individualized Instruction
Process of matching instructional methods and media with learning objectives and students' learning styles.

Industrial Consumption
Water consumed from the water supply system by industrial facilities.

Industrial Fire Brigade
Team organized within a private company or plant to respond to fires and emergencies on that property.

Industrial Hose
Fire hose, usually of lighter construction than fire service hose, used by industrial fire brigades.

Inertia Lights
Light mounted in the aircraft structure so that a sharp deceleration, such as a crash situation, will activate the light. It can also be turned on manually and removed from the mounting to be used as a portable flashlight.

Inerting
Introducing a nonflammable gas (i.e., nitrogen or carbon dioxide) to a flammable atmosphere in order to remove the oxygen and prevent an explosion.

Inferior
Near the feet; below.

Inflow
Flow of grain toward the vortex of the discharge funnel in a grain bin.

Information Officer
Responsible for interface with the media or other appropriate agencies requiring information direct from the incident scene. Member of the command staff.

Information Presentation
Lesson plan format that addresses the cognitive objectives by introducing new information, facts, principles, and theories.

Information Sheet
Instructional sheet used to present ideas or information to the learner; used when desired information is not in printed form or otherwise available to the student.

Infrared Scanner
Device that detects radiant heat emitted by concealed materials by converting infrared energy to an electrical signal; used primarily by the fire service to detect hidden fires.

Ingestion
Taking in food or other substances through the mouth.

Inhalation
Taking in materials by breathing through the nose or mouth.

Inhalation Tube
See Low-Pressure Hose.

Inhalator
Mechanical device for administering breathing oxygen to an individual who is breathing.

Inhibitors
See Stabilizer (2).

Initial Attack
First attack when hoselines are employed to prevent further extension of fire and to safeguard life and property while additional lines are being laid and other forces put in motion.

Initiators
Cylinder-shaped explosive or gas pressure devices used to create gas or mechanical pressure to activate another device; usually found in the seat and canopy ejection mechanism of jet military fighter aircraft.

Injector Lines
Small tubes or hoselines that inject fuel into the combustion chamber of an engine at high pressures. These pressures may be in excess of 1,200 psi (8 400 kPa).

Injury
In general terms an injury is defined as a hurt, damage, or loss sustained as a result of an accident.

In-Line Eductor
Eductor that is placed along the length of a hoseline.

In-Line Relay Valve
Valve placed along the length of a supply hose that permits a pumper to connect to the valve to boost pressure in the hose.

Insecticides
Chemicals designed to control or eliminate certain kinds of insects.

In Service
(1) Operating. (2) Available for an assignment.

Insoluble
Incapable of being dissolved in a liquid (usually water).

Inspection
Formal examination of an occupancy and its associated uses or processes to determine its compliance with the fire and life safety codes and standards.

Instructional Development Process
Process of designing classroom instruction that consists of three major components: analysis, design, and evaluation.

Instruction Order
Organization of jobs or ideas according to learning difficulty so that learning proceeds from the simple to the complex.

Instructor
Person charged with the responsibility to conduct the class, direct the instructional process, teach skills, impart new information, lead discussions, and cause learning to take place.

Instrument Flight Rules (IFR)
Regulations governing the operation of an aircraft in weather conditions with visibility below the minimum required for flight under visual flight rules.

Instrument Landing
Landing an aircraft by relying only upon instrument data.

Instrument Landing System (ILS)
Electronic navigation system that allows aircraft to approach and land during inclement weather conditions.

Insulating Glass
Two panes of glass separated by an air space and sealed around the edge.

Insulin
Hormone produced by the pancreas. Its function is to regulate the level of sugar in the blood.

Insurance Services Office (ISO)
Formed January 1971; a national insurance organization licensed as a fire rating organization; an advisory organization to other property-liability insurance companies. Also called Rating Bureau.

In-Swinging Door
Door that swings away from someone who stands on the outside of the opening.

Intake
Inlet for water into the fire pump.

Intake Area
Area in front of and to the side of a jet engine that might be unsafe for personnel.

Intake Hose
Hose used to connect a fire department pumper or a portable pump to a nearby water source. It may be soft sleeve or hard suction hose.

Intake Pressure
Pressure coming into the fire pump.

Intake Relief Valve
Valve designed to prevent damage to a pump from water hammer or any sudden pressure surge.

Intake Screen
Screen used to prevent foreign objects from entering a pump.

Integral Construction
Method of construction used on all types of buses. The manufacturer assembles the vehicle starting with the frame and chassis assembly and proceeds item by item to the finished vehicle. Also called Bird Cage Construction.

Intercostal
Space between the ribs.

Intercostal Muscles
Muscles between the ribs.

Interior Exposure
Areas of a fire building that are not involved in fire but that are connected to the fire area in such a manner that may facilitate fire spread through any available openings.

Interlocking Deadbolt
See Jimmy-Resistant Lock.

Intermodal Container
See Container.

Internal Respiration
Exchange of oxygen and carbon dioxide in the bloodstream at the cellular level.

International Fire Service Training Association (IFSTA)
Nonprofit educational alliance organized to develop training materials for the fire service.

Interstate Commerce Commission
See U.S. Department of Transportation.

Interstitial Space
See Attic.

Intestine
Portion of the digestive tube that extends from the stomach to the anus.

Inversion
Atmospheric phenomenon that allows smoke to rise until its temperature equals the air temperature and then spreads laterally in a horizontal layer. Also called Night Inversion.

Inverter
Auxiliary electrical power generating device. The inverter is a step-up transformer that converts the vehicle's 12- or 24-volt DC current into 110- or 220-volt AC current.

Investigation
To conduct an official inquiry.

Investigation Mode
See Investigative Mode.

Investigative Mode
When the first-arriving companies go on standby because the cause of the alarm is not readily ascertainable. Also called Investigation Mode.

Involuntary Muscle
Muscle that acts without voluntary control.

Involved
Actual room, portion, or area of building involved in or affected by fire.

Ion
Unbalanced atom; any atom that has an electrical charge, either positive or negative.

Ionization
Process by which an object or substance gains or loses electrons, thus changing its electrical charge.

Ionization Detector
Type of smoke detector that uses a small amount of radioactive material to make the air within a sensing chamber conduct electricity.

Ipecac Syrup
Medication used to induce vomiting.

Iris
Colored portion of the eye that surrounds the pupil.

Ironing
Flattening deformation of aerial device base rails caused by the pressure exerted when the device is extended and retracted.

Irritating Materials
Liquids or solids that upon contact with fire or exposure to air give off dangerous or intensely irritating fumes.

Ischium
One of the two bones that form the lower portion of the pelvic girdle.

ISFSI
Acronym for International Society of Fire Service Instructors.

ISO
Abbreviation for Insurance Services Office.

Isoamyl Acetate
Banana oil; used for an odor test of facepiece fit.

J

Jack
Portable device used to lift heavy objects with force applied by a lever, screw, or hydraulic press.

Jacket
Metal cover that protects the tank insulation.

Jack(ing) Plates
Plates located on solid frame members on the undercarriage of a bus to facilitate the placement of jacks for lifting.

Jackknife
(1) Turning the tractor portion of a tractor-tiller aerial apparatus at an angle from the trailer to increase the stability when the aerial device is being used. (2) Condition of truck tractor/semi-trailer combination when their relative positions to each other form an angle of 90 degrees or less about the trailer kingpin.

Jack Pads
See Stabilizer Pad.

Jackplates
See Footplate.

Jalousie Window
Window consisting of narrow, frameless, glass panes set in metal brackets at each end that allow the panes a limited amount of axial rotation for ventilation.

Jamb
See Frame.

JATO
Acronym for Jet-Assisted Takeoff.

Jaws
See Powered Hydraulic Spreader.

Jet
Term used in England for a fire stream.

Jet-Assisted Takeoff (JATO)
Rocket or auxiliary jet used to augment normal thrust for takeoffs.

Jet Pump
Water-operated pump that creates a suction by using the venturi principle.

Jet Siphon
Section of pipe or hard suction hose with a 1½-inch (38 mm) discharge line inside that bolsters the flow of water through the tube. The jet siphon is used between portable tanks to maintain a maximum amount of water in the tank from which the pumper is drafting.

Jettison
To selectively discard aircraft components such as external fuel tanks or canopies.

Jetway
Enclosed ramp between a terminal and an aircraft for loading and unloading passengers.

Jib
Lever used with a block and tackle to lift or lower.

Jimmy
To pry apart, usually to separate the door from its frame to allow the latch or bolt to clear its strike.

Jimmy-Resistant Lock
Auxiliary lock having a bolt that interlocks with its strike and thus resists prying. Also called Vertical Deadbolt or Interlocking Deadbolt.

Job
(1) Organized segment of instruction designed to develop psychomotor skills or technical knowledge. (2) Slang used in the Eastern United States fire service to describe a working fire.

Job Breakdown Sheet
Instructional sheet listing step-by-step procedures and required knowledge. It is designed to assist in teaching and learning a psychomotor objective.

Job Safety Analysis
Method of analyzing occupational hazards and working toward their solution.

Jockey Pump
Small-capacity, high-pressure pump used to maintain constant pressures on the fire protection system. A jockey pump is often used to prevent the main pump from starting unnecessarily.

Joist
Horizontal supporting member in a roof, ceiling, or floor assembly.

Joule
Unit of work. It has taken the place of the calorie in the International System of Units for heat measurement (1 calorie = 4.19 J).

Journal
Book in which all activities of a fire shift are recorded. Also called Day Book, Log Book, or Record Book.

Judgment
One of three requirements of evaluation. The decision-making ability of the instructor to make comparisons, discernments, or conclusions about the instructional process and learner outcomes.

Jugular Vein
Large vein on either side of the neck.

Jumar
Ascender for rope climbing.

Jumpseat
Seats on a fire apparatus that are behind the front seats.

Junction Box
See Connection Box.

K

Kalamein Door
See Metal-Clad Door.

Kasch Step Test
Medical test used to measure cardiovascular fitness.

Kelly Day
Rotating off-duty shift in addition to the normal off-duty schedule of the firefighter.

Kelly Tool
Prying tool similar to a claw tool but with an adze blade at one end and a forked blade at the other end.

Kernmantle Rope
Rope that consists of a protective shield (mantle) over the load-bearing core strands (kern).

Key
Device that, when inserted into a key plug, causes the internal pins or disks to align in a manner that allows the plug to turn within the cylinder; a device that allows the operator to lock and unlock a locking mechanism.

Key Box
See Key Safe.

Key-In-Knob Lock
Lock in which the lock cylinder is within the knob.

Key Plug
See Cylinder Plug.

Key Points
Factors that condition or influence operations within an occupation; information that must be known to perform the operations in a job.

Key Safe
Boxlike container that holds keys to the building, usually mounted on or in the front wall; requires a master key to open. Also called Key Box or Knox Box (trade name).

Key Tool
Tool for manipulating an exposed lock mechanism so that the latch or deadbolt is retracted from its strike; used in conjunction with a K-Tool.

Keyway
Opening in a cylinder plug that receives the key.

Kickplate
See Footplate.

Kidneys
Paired organs located toward the rear wall of the abdominal cavity. Their function is to filter blood and produce urine.

Kiln Dried
Term applied to lumber that has been dried by artificially controlled heat and humidity to a prescribed moisture content.

Kilopascal (kPa)
Metric unit of measure for pressure; 1 psi = 6.895 kPa, 1 kPa = 0.1450 psi.

Kinematic Viscosity
Ratio of a fluid's absolute viscosity (lb sec/ft^2) to its mass density (lb sec^2/ft^4).

Kinetic Energy
Energy that a body possesses because of its motion.

Kingpin
Attaching pin on a semitrailer that connects with pivots within the lower coupler of a truck tractor or converter dolly while coupling the two units together.

Kink
Severe bend in a hoseline that increases friction loss and reduces the flow of water through the hose.

Kink Test
Test of hose under extreme conditions to ensure performance by folding the hose over on itself, securing it to maintain the kink, and pressurizing. Pressures used vary with the type of hose tested.

Kip
Unit of weight equal to 1,000 pounds; used to express deadweight load.

Kit
Collection of tools or equipment kept in one location for a specific purpose.

Knockdown
Reduction of most flame and heat generation by a fire, using an extinguishing agent such as water, in order to bring the fire to an overhaul stage.

Knox Box (Trade Name)
See Key Safe.

Knurled
Having a series of small ridges or beads, as on a metal surface, to aid in gripping.

Kraft Paper
Strong brown paper made of sulfate pulp.

K-Tool
V-blade tool that is designed to pull lock cylinders from a door with only minimal damage to the door itself.

Kussmaul's Respiration
Deep, rapid respirations characteristic of hyperglycemia (or diabetic ketoacidosis) that result as the body tries to eliminate excess carbon dioxide.

L

Labeled Assembly
See Rated Assembly.

Labels
Four-inch-square diamond markers required on individual shipping containers smaller than 640 cubic feet (18 m^3).

Labor
Muscular contractions of the uterus designed to expel the fetus from the mother.

Laceration
Jagged tear or wound.

Lactic Acid
Hygroscopic organic acid normally present in tissue.

Ladder
Two rails or beams with steps or rungs spaced at intervals; any fire department ladder of varying length, type, or construction.

Ladder Bed
Rack or racks in which ladders are carried on a ladder truck.

Ladder Belt
Belt with a hook that secures the firefighter to the ladder.

Ladder Carry
Any organized system for carrying ladders.

Ladder Company
Group of firefighters assigned to a fire department aerial apparatus who are primarily responsible for search and rescue, ventilation, salvage and overhaul, forcible entry, and other fireground support functions. Also called Truck Company.

Ladder Cribbing
Pieces of cribbing that have been attached to two lengths of webbing to form the appearance of a ladder.

Ladder Float
Inflated tire or inner tube fastened to a ladder and used to rescue persons from water or ice.

Ladder Gin Pole
Gin pole in which the load-supporting member is a straight ladder.

Ladder Locks
See Pawls.

Ladder Pipe
Master stream nozzle mounted on the fly of an aerial ladder.

Ladder Spur
Spiked device that is attached to the foot of a ladder to provide good traction on soft ground.

Ladder Stop
Blocks that limit the travel of the fly section(s) on an extension ladder to prevent the sections from being separated.

Lagging
Heavy sheathing used in underground work to withstand earth pressure.

Lag Screw
Large wood screw with a hexagonal or square head for turning with a wrench.

Laid Rope
Rope constructed by twisting several groups of individual strands together.

Lake Test
Method of testing a salvage cover for leaks by forming a catchall to hold a small "lake" of water and observing for leakage on the underside.

Laminar Flow
Fluid is in the state of laminar flow if its Reynolds number is 2,100 or less; laminar flow is related to very low liquid velocities.

Laminated Glass
See Safety Glass.

Laminated Plastic
Sheet material made of lamination cloth or other fiber impregnated with plastic and brought to the desired thickness or shape with heat and/or pressure.

Lamination
(1) Bonding or impregnating superposed layers with resin and compressing under heat. (2) One of several layers of lumber making up a laminated beam.

Landing
Floor on each story where a flight of stairs begins and ends.

Landing Roll
Distance from the point of touchdown to the point where the aircraft is brought to a stop or exits the runway.

Landing Site
Area in which a helicopter will land during air medical evacuations.

Land Line
Telephone.

Lantern Roof
Roof style consisting of a high gabled roof with a vertical wall above a downward-pitched shed roof section on either side.

Lapping
Means by which fire spreads vertically from floor to floor in a multistory building. Fire issuing from a window laps up the outside of the building and enters the floor(s) above, usually through the windows.

Large Diameter Hose (LDH)
Relay-supply hose of 3½ to 6 inches (90 mm to 150 mm); used to move large volumes of water quickly with a minimum number of pumpers and personnel.

Large Intestine
Hollow structure of the gastrointestinal tract located just below the stomach. Also called Colon.

Laryngectomee
Person who has undergone a total or partial surgical removal of the larynx.

Laryngectomy
Surgical removal of the larynx.

Larynx
Organ of voice production.

Latch
Spring-loaded part of a locking mechanism that extends into a strike within the door frame.

Latch Bolt
Latch with a shim or plunger that causes the latch to operate in a manner similar to a deadbolt. The latch plunger prevents "loiding" of the latch.

Latent Heat Of Vaporization
Quantity of heat absorbed by a substance when it changes from a liquid to a vapor.

Lateral
Toward the side of the human body.

Lath
(1) Narrow strips of wood over which plaster is applied to form wall and ceiling surfaces. (2) Used to hold salvage covers, sheeting, or tar paper in place when covering a building opening during overhaul.

Law
Rules of conduct that are adopted and enforced by an authority having jurisdiction.

Law Of Association
Principle that learning comes easier when new information is related to similar things already known.

Law Of Effect
Notion that learning is more effective when a feeling of satisfaction, pleasantness, or reward accompanies or is a result of the learning process.

Law Of Exercise
Idea that repetition is necessary for the proficient development of a mental or physical skill.

Law Of Heat Flow
Natural law that specifies that heat tends to flow from hot substances to cold substances. This phenomenon is based on the supposition that one substance can absorb heat from another.

Law Of Intensity
Premise that if the experience is real, there is more likely to be a change in behavior or learning.

Law Of Readiness
Principle that a person learns when physically and mentally adjusted or ready to receive instruction.

Law Of Recency
Principle that the more recently the reviews, warm-ups, and makeup exercises are practiced before using the skill, the more effective the performance will be.

Law Of Specific Heat
(1) Measure of the heat-absorbing quality of a substance as measured in Btu's or kilojoules. (2) Relative quantity of heat required to raise the temperature of substances or the quantity of heat that must be removed to cool a substance.

Lay
To lay out hose in a predetermined sequence for fire fighting.

Layout
Distribution of hose at the scene of a fire.

LDH
Abbreviation for Large Diameter Hose.

Leader
Individual responsible for command of a crew, task force, strike team, or functional unit.

Leading Block
Pulley or snatch block used to change the direction of the fall line in a block and tackle system. This does not affect the mechanical advantage of the system.

Leading Edge Devices
Forward edges of aircraft wings normally extended for takeoff and landings to provide additional lift at low speeds and to improve aircraft performance.

Lean-To Collapse
Structural collapse where floor supports fail and the floors and roof drop in large sections and form voids. These sections remain in one piece with support on one side but collapse on the other.

Learning
Relatively permanent change in behavior that occurs as a result of acquiring new information and putting it to use through practice.

L-E-A-S-T Method
Progressive discipline method used in the classroom; stands for Leave it alone, Eye contact, Action, Stop the class, and Terminate.

Lecture
Teaching method in which the instructor verbally relays information to teach a lesson.

Ledge Door
Door constructed of individual boards joined within a frame. Also called Batten Door.

Ledger
(1) Horizontal framework member, especially one attached to a beam side that supports the joists. (2) Book in which financial records are kept.

Lee
See Leeward.

Leeward
Protected side; the direction opposite from which the wind is blowing. Also called Lee.

Left-Hand Door
See Third Door (2).

Legend
Explanatory list of symbols on a map or diagram.

Leg Lock
Method of entwining a leg around a ladder rung to ensure that the individual cannot fall from the ladder and thereby freeing the climber's hands for working.

LEL
Abbreviation for Lower Explosive Limit.

Lens
(1) Portion of the eye that focuses light rays onto the retina. (2) Clear portion of the self-contained breathing apparatus mask.

Lens Fogging
Condensation on the inside of the facepiece lens caused by moisture in the wearer's exhalations.

Lesson Plan
Outlined plan for teaching, listing pertinent teaching information and using the four-step teaching method.

Lethal Concentration, 50 Percent Kill (LC50)
Concentration of an inhaled substance that results in the death of 50 percent of the test population. (The lower the value, the more toxic the substance.) LC50 is an inhalation exposure expressed in parts per million (ppm), mg/liter, or mg/m^3.

Lethal Dose, 50 Percent Kill (LD50)
Concentration of an ingested or injected substance that results in the death of 50 percent of the test

population. (The lower the dose, the more toxic the substance.) LD50 is an oral or dermal exposure expressed in mg/kg.

Level A Protection
Highest level of skin, respiratory, and eye protection that can be afforded by personal protective equipment. Consists of positive-pressure self-contained breathing apparatus, totally encapsulating chemical-protective suit, inner and outer gloves, and chemical-resistant boots.

Level B Protection
Personal protective equipment that affords the highest level of respiratory protection, but a lesser level of skin protection. Consists of positive-pressure self-contained breathing apparatus, hooded chemical-resistant suit, inner and outer gloves, and chemical-resistant boots.

Level I Staging
Used on all multiple-company emergency responses. The first-arriving vehicles of each type proceed directly to the scene, and the others stand by a block or two from the scene and await orders.

Level II Staging
Used on large-scale incidents where greater alarm companies are responding. These companies are sent to a specified location to await assignment.

Level Of Learning (Instruction)
Depth of instruction for a specific skill and/or technical information that enables the student to meet the minimal requirements of the occupation.

Lever
Device consisting of a bar turning about a fixed point (fulcrum), using power or force applied at a second point to lift or sustain an object at a third point.

Leverage
Action or mechanical power of a lever.

Lexan®
Polycarbonate plastic used for windows. It has one-half the weight of an equivalent-sized piece of glass, yet it is 30 times stronger than safety glass and 250 times stronger than ordinary glass. It cannot be broken using standard forcible entry techniques.

Liability
To be legally obligated or responsible for an act or physical condition.

Liaison Officer
Point of contact for assisting or coordinating agencies; member of the command staff.

Lieutenant
Rank used in some fire departments for company officers.

Life Belt
Used to secure the firefighter; wide, adjustable belt with a snap hook that can be fastened to the rungs of a ladder leaving the firefighter's hands free for working. Formally known as a Class I life safety harness.

Lifeline
See Life Safety Rope.

Life Net
Canvas device with a folding circular metal frame and spring action used to catch persons who jump from buildings; not considered safe or effective for jumps from above the fourth floor of a building.

Life Safety Code® (NFPA 101)
See Code for Safety to Life from Fire in Buildings and Structures.

Life Safety Harness
Any harness that meets the requirements of NFPA 1983, *Standard on Fire Service Life Safety Rope, Harness, and Hardware. Also see* Class I, Class II, and Class III Harness.

Life Safety Rope
Rope that meets the requirements of NFPA 1983, *Standard on Fire Service Life Safety Rope, Harness, and Hardware,* and is to be used for the raising and/or lowering of people. Also called Lifeline.

Lift
(1) Apparatus for raising an automobile. (2) Component of the total aerodynamic force acting on an airplane or airfoil that is perpendicular to the relative wind and that for an airplane constitutes the upward force that opposes the pull of gravity. (3) Dimension from the top of one pouring of concrete in a form to the top of the next pouring; for example, "Pour concrete in 8-inch (203 mm) lifts."

Lift, Dependable
Height a column of water may be lifted in sufficient quantity to provide a reliable fire flow. Lift may be raised through a hard suction hose to a pump, taking into consideration the atmospheric pressure and friction loss within the hard suction hose. Dependable lift is usually considered to be 14.7 feet (4.48 m).

Lift, Maximum
Maximum height to which any amount of water may be raised through a hard suction hose to a pump.

Lift Slabs
System of concrete construction in which the floor slabs are poured in place at the ground level and then lifted to their position by hydraulic jacks working simultaneously at each column.

Lift, Theoretical
Theoretical, scientific height that a column of water may be lifted by atmospheric pressure in a true vacuum. At sea level, this height is 33.8 feet (10 m). The height will decrease as elevation increases.

Ligament
Tough band of fibrous tissue that connects bone to bone or that supports any organ.

Light Attack Vehicle
See Minipumper.

Light Box
See Connection Box.

Light Detector
See Flame Detector.

Light Rescue Vehicle
Small rescue vehicle usually built on a 1-ton or 1½-ton chassis. It is designed to handle only basic extrication and life-support functions and carries only basic hand tools and small equipment.

Light Shaft
See Light Well.

Lightweight Steel Truss
Structural support made from a long steel bar that is bent at a 90-degree angle with flat or angular pieces welded to the top and bottom.

Lightweight Wood Truss
Structural supports constructed of 2- x 3-inch or 2- x 4-inch (50 mm by 75 mm or 50 mm by 100 mm) studs that are connected by gusset plates.

Light Well
Vertical shaft at or near the center of a building to provide natural light and/or ventilation to offices or apartments not located on an outside wall. Also called Light Shaft.

Limb Presentation
Birth delivery in which the presenting part of a fetus is an arm or a leg.

Limited Access Zone
Large geographical area between the Support Zone and the Restricted Zone. This zone should contain the decontamination area, the safe haven, and the haz mat control officer.

Line
(1) Hoseline. (2) Rope or lifeline.

Lined Hose
Fire hose composed of one or two woven outside jackets and an inside rubber lining.

Lineman's Gloves
Special gloves insulated for protection against electrical current.

Linen Hose
Fire hose made of linen or flax fabric without a rubber lining; used for standpipe cabinets and forestry operations.

Line-Of-Duty
During the performance of fire department duties.

Line Organization
Portion of the fire department directly involved in providing fire suppression and rescue services.

Lintel
Support for masonry over an opening; usually made of steel angles or other rolled shapes singularly or in combination.

Lipid Pneumonia
Pneumonia that may follow the aspiration of an oily substance such as mineral oil.

Liquefied Compressed Gases
Gases that under the charging pressure are partially liquid at 70°F (21°C). Also called Liquefied Gas.

Liquefied Gas
See Liquefied Compressed Gases.

Liquefied Petroleum Gas (LPG)
Any of several petroleum products, such as propane or butane, stored under pressure as a liquid.

Liquid
Incompressible substance that assumes the shape of its container. The molecules flow freely, but substantial cohesion prevents them from expanding as a gas would.

Liquid Propellants
Liquids used in rockets as fuels and oxidizers.

Listed
Usually refers to a device that has been tested by the Underwriters' Laboratories Inc. or Factory Mutual System and certified as having met minimum criteria for the device tested.

Litter
(1) Fallen leaves or needles on top of a duff layer. (2) Inappropriately discarded rubbish. (3) *See* Stretcher.

Live Load
Loads within a building that are movable. Merchandise, stock, furnishings, occupants, firefighters, and the water used for fire suppression are examples of live loads.

Liver
Large solid organ of the abdominal cavity located just below the diaphragm. It secretes bile and performs many important bodily functions.

Load-Bearing Frame Members
Vertical portions of the frame that provide direct support to attached members.

Load-Bearing Wall
Wall that is used for structural support.

Loading Site
In a tanker/tender shuttle operation, the location where apparatus tanks are filled from the water supply.

Load Testing
Aerial device test intended to determine whether or not the device is capable of safely carrying its rated weight capacity.

Lobby Control
Person responsible for, and the process of, taking and maintaining control of the lobby and elevators in a high-rise fire fighting situation. Lobby control also includes establishing internal communications, coordinating the flow of personnel and equipment to upper levels, and coordinating with building engineering personnel.

Local Alarm System
Combination of alarm components designed to detect a fire and transmit an alarm on the immediate premises.

Local Wind
Wind whose speed and direction is influenced by local conditions such as topography, fires, and weather fronts.

Location Marker
Device, such as a reflective marker or flag, used to mark the location of a fire hydrant for quicker identification during a fire response.

Lock
(1) Device for fastening, joining, or engaging two or more objects together such as a door and frame. (2) *Also see* Pawls.

Locking Out
Process of shutting off and securing any power switches on a machine to prevent accidental or otherwise undesirable reenergization of the machine.

Lock Mechanism
Moving parts of a lock, which include the latch or bolt, lock cylinder, and articulating components.

Log Book
See Journal.

Logistics Section
Section of the incident management system responsible for providing facilities, services, and materials; includes the communications unit, medical unit, and food units within the service branch and also includes the supply unit, facilities unit, and ground support units within the support branch.

Logroll
Method for placing a patient onto a backboard by turning the patient as a unit, first onto the side, then onto the back.

Loiding
Method of slipping or shimming a spring latch from its strike with a piece of celluloid such as a credit card.

Long-Duration Apparatus
Breathing apparatus that supplies the wearer with air for more than 30 minutes.

Longeron
Longitudinal members of the framing of an aircraft fuselage or nacelle; usually continuous across a number of bulkheads or other points of support.

Longitudinal Hose Bed
Hose bed located to the side of the main hose bed; designed to carry preconnected attack hose.

Lookout Tower
Tower and station, usually on a high place, from which natural cover fires can be detected; also used for pinpointing lightning strikes and frontal systems approaching a given area.

Loop System
Water main arranged in a complete circuit so that water will be supplied to a given point from more than one direction. Also called Circle System, Circulating System, or Belt System.

Loose End
See Working End.

Louver Cut Or Vent
Rectangular exit opening cut in a roof, allowing a section of roof deck (still nailed to a center rafter) to be tilted, thus creating an opening similar to a louver. Also called Rafter Cut.

Low-Density Combustible Fiberboard
Highly combustible building material.

Lower Airway
Portion of the respiratory system below the epiglottis.

Lower Explosive Limit (LEL)
Lowest percentage of fuel/oxygen mixture required to support combustion. Any mixture with a lower percentage would be considered "too lean."

Low-Pressure Alarm
Bell, whistle, or other audible alarm that warns the wearer when the SCBA air supply is low and needs replacement, usually 25 percent of full container pressure.

Low-Pressure Hose
Generally, the hose containing pressure slightly above atmospheric leading from the regulator to the facepiece. Also called Inhalation Tube.

Low-Rise Elevator
Elevator that serves only the lower floors of a high-rise building.

LPG
Abbreviation for Liquefied Petroleum Gas.

Lugging
Condition that occurs when the throttle application is greater than necessary for a given set of conditions. It may result in an excessive amount of carbon particles issuing from the exhaust, oil dilution, and additional fuel consumption. Lugging can be eliminated by using a lower gear and proper shifting techniques.

Lumbar Spine
Portion of the spinal column formed by the five vertebrae extending from just below the ribs to the pelvis; the lower back.

Lungs
Paired organs of respiration that lie in the chest.

M

Machine-Guarding
Use of gates, covers, housings, deflectors, or other guards on power machinery to prevent the user from contacting moving parts or being struck by flying objects.

Magazine
Storage facility approved by the Bureau of Alcohol, Tobacco, and Firearms (BATF) for the storage of explosives.

Magnetic Particle Inspection
Form of nondestructive steel aerial device testing where the aerial device is magnetized and metal particles are applied. Deviances in the coating of the particles indicate flaws in the metal aerial device.

Main Guideline
Special rope used in the United Kingdom, Australia, and New Zealand as a safety guideline to indicate a route between the entry control point and the scene of operations.

Mainline Valve
Valve that when opened lets air from the cylinder travel its normal route through the regulator to the facepiece.

Maintenance
Keeping equipment or apparatus in a state of usefulness or readiness.

Major
Rank used by some fire departments for company officers.

Make The Fire
Order given to a specific unit to respond to a fire.

Makeup
All actions involved in connecting fire hose or apparatus to other equipment.

Making A Hydrant
Procedure for connecting to and laying hose forward from a fire hydrant.

Male Coupling
Hose nipple with protruding threads that fits into the thread of a female coupling of the same pitch and appropriate diameter and thread count.

Malicious
Often an element of arson; state requirements may vary, but often this state of mind is in the nature of intending to injure, vex, or annoy another person, to commit an unlawful act, and occasionally a wish to defraud.

Maltese Cross
Symbol of the firefighter; worn on the uniform or the cap. The popular variety of the Maltese cross is actually a modification of the cross patee rather than the actual eight-point cross.

Mammalian Diving Reflex
Autonomous physiologic reaction to immersion in cold water in which the blood and oxygen supply is shunted to the brain to keep the animal alive although outward appearances may suggest death.

Mandible
Lower jaw bone.

Manhole
(1) Hole through which a person may go to gain access to an underground or enclosed structure. (2) Openings usually equipped with removable, lockable covers and large enough to admit a person into a tank trailer or dry bulk trailer.

Manifold
(1) Hose appliance that divides one larger hoseline into three or more small hoselines. Also called Portable Hydrant. (2) Hose appliance that combines three or more smaller hoselines into one large hoseline. (3) Top portion of the pump casing. (4) Used to join a number of discharge pipelines to a common outlet.

Manila Rope
Rope made from manila fiber grown in Manila in the Philippines. It is not suitable for life safety applications.

Manipulative Lesson
Another term for the practical demonstration portion of a lesson plan.

Manipulative-Performance Test
Practical competency-based tests that measure mastery of the psychomotor objectives as they are performed in a job or evolution.

Manipulative Skills
Skills that use the psychomotor domain of learning; refers to the ability to physically manipulate an object or move the body to accomplish a task.

Mansard Roof
Roof style with characteristics similar to both gambrel and hip roofs. Mansard roofs have slopes of two different angles, and all sides slope down to an outside wall.

Manual Stabilizer
Manually deployed stabilizing device for aerial apparatus that consists of an extension arm with a jack attached to the end of it.

Manufacturer's Tests
Fire pump or aerial device tests performed by the manufacturer prior to delivery of the apparatus.

Marine Company
Personnel assigned to work on a fire boat.

Marine Unit
See Fire Boat.

Mars Light
Single-beam, oscillating warning light.

Mask
See Facepiece.

Masonry
Bricks, blocks, stones, and unreinforced and reinforced concrete products.

Mass Casualty Incident
See Multi-Casualty Incident.

Mass Transportation
Any mode of transportation designed to carry large numbers of people at the same time.

MAST
Acronym for Medical Antishock Trousers or Military Antishock Trousers.

Master Stream
Any of a variety of heavy, large-caliber water streams; usually supplied by siamesing two or more hoselines into a manifold device delivering 350 gpm (1 400 L/min) or more. Also called Heavy Stream.

Master Stream Nozzle
Nozzle capable of flowing in excess of 350 gpm (1 400 L/min).

Mastery Learning
Element of criterion-referenced or competency-based learning. Outcomes of learning are expressed in minimum levels of performance for each competency.

Materials Needed
List of everything needed to teach a lesson: models, mock-ups, visual aids, equipment, handouts, quizzes, and so on.

Mattress Chains
Light chains with hooks or locking devices used to bind a mattress in a roll for removal from a building.

Mattydale Hose Bed
See Transverse Hose Bed.

Maxilla
Upper jaw bone.

Maximum Daily Consumption
Maximum total amount of water used during any 24-hour interval over a 3-year period.

May
Term used in NFPA standards that denotes voluntary or optional compliance.

Maze
Training facility with or without smoke, lighted or unlighted in which firefighters wearing SCBA must negotiate obstacles to perform certain tasks.

Means Of Egress
Safe and continuous path of travel from any point in a structure leading to a public way. The means of egress is composed of three parts: the exit access, the exit, and the exit discharge.

Mechanical Advantage
(1) Gain in force, when levering, by moving the fulcrum closer to the object. (2) Using a block and tackle when hoisting.

Mechanical Filter
Air-purification component that physically separates the greatest part of water, oil, and other contaminants from compressed air. May also refer to the filter on a negative-pressure respirator that performs the same task.

Mechanical Foam
Foam that requires the blending of water, foam concentrate, and air to be developed.

Mechanical Heat Energy
Friction heat and heat of compression. Moving parts on machines, such as belts and bearings, are a source of mechanical heating.

Mechanical Systems
Large equipment systems within a building that may include, but are not limited to, climate-control systems; smoke, dust, and vapor removal systems; trash collection systems; and automated mail systems. These do not include general utility systems such as electric, gas, and water.

Mechanical Ventilation
See Forced Ventilation.

Medial
Toward the midline of the body.

Medical Antishock Trousers (MAST)
Used to counteract the effects of heavy blood loss. Also called Military Antishock Trousers.

Medic-Alert® Bracelet or Necklace
See Medical Identification Bracelet (or Necklace).

Medical Identification Bracelet (Or Necklace)
Medical identification worn by individuals having an illness that requires certain care and treatment. Also called Medic-Alert® Bracelet or Necklace.

Medical Unit
Functional unit within the service branch of the logistics section of an incident management system; responsible for providing emergency medical treatment for emergency personnel. This unit does not provide treatment for civilians.

Medic Unit
(1) Also called Paramedic Unit. (2) Ambulance staffed by paramedics. (3) Nonpatient transport vehicle used by paramedics to respond to emergencies.

Medium Diameter Hose (MDH)
2½- or 3-inch (65 mm or 77 mm) hose that is used for both fire fighting attack and for relay-supply purposes.

Medium-Pressure Air
Air pressurized from 2,000 to 3,000 psi (14 000 kPa to 21 000 kPa); used to distinguish specific types of breathing-air cylinders.

Medium Rescue Vehicle
Rescue vehicle somewhat larger and better equipped than a light rescue vehicle. This vehicle may carry powered hydraulic spreading tools and cutters, air bag lifting systems, power saws, oxyacetylene cutting equipment, ropes and rigging equipment, as well as basic hand equipment.

Medulla Oblongata
Small posterior portion of the brain continuous with the spinal cord; contains the centers for respiratory control, heartbeat, and other major motor control centers.

Membrane
Thin sheath or layer of pliable tissue that covers an organ; the lining of a cavity.

Membrane Roof
Roof covering that consists of a single layer of waterproof synthetic membrane over one or more layers of insulation on a roof deck.

Mesothelioma
Cancer of the membranes of the lungs, heart, or stomach; has been linked to earlier contact with asbestos.

Metabolism
Conversion of food into energy and waste products.

Metacarpal Bones
Five bones of the hand extending from the wrist to the fingers.

Metal-Clad Door
Door with a metal exterior; may be flush type or panel type. Also called Kalamein Door.

Metatarsal Bones
Five bones of the foot extending from the ankles to the toes.

Method Of Instruction
Procedure, technique, or manner of instructing others that is determined by the type of learning to take place. Typical examples are lecture, demonstration, or group discussion.

Micron
Unit of length equal to one-millionth of a meter.

Midipumper
Apparatus sized between a minipumper and a full-sized fire department pumper, usually with a gross vehicle weight of 12,000 pounds (5 443 kg) or greater. The midipumper has a fire pump with a rated capacity generally not greater than 1,000 gpm (4 000 L/min).

Midship Pump
Fire pumps mounted at the center of the fire apparatus.

Mil
One thousandth of an inch (0.001 inch [0.0254 mm]).

Military Antishock Trousers (MAST)
See Medical Antishock Trousers.

Mine Rescue Drill
Special drill, operated by the Mine Emergency Division of the U.S. Mine Safety and Health Administration, that can drill a 24-inch diameter (0.6 m) shaft through 50 feet (15 m) of solid limestone in one day.

Mine Safety And Health Administration (MSHA)
United States government organization that regulates mine safety.

Minimum Acceptable Standard
Lowest acceptable level of student performance.

Minipumper
Small fire apparatus mounted on a pickup-truck-sized chassis, usually with a pump having a rated capacity less than 500 gpm (2 000 L/min). Its primary advantages are speed and mobility, which enable it to respond to fires more rapidly than larger apparatus. Also called Light Attack Vehicle.

Miscarriage
Lay term for a premature expulsion of a fetus from the uterus that occurs naturally.

Mobile Radio
Radio mounted on an apparatus.

Mobile Water Supply Apparatus (Tanker/Tender)
Fire apparatus with a water tank of 1,000 gallons (4 000 L) or larger whose primary purpose is transporting water. The truck may also carry a pump, some hose, and other equipment.

Mock Incident
Simulated emergency that allows responders to test their skills under realistic conditions. Also called Staged Incident.

Mock-Up
Training device; a working model for realistic training and drilling.

Mode
Phase, step, or progression of applying fireground strategy.

Modern Mansard Roof
Roof style having sides that slope at only one angle up to meet a flat deck in the center section.

Moisture Barrier
(1) Liner within a piece of protective clothing that is designed to keep water out. (2) Backing found on building insulation that prevents moisture from entering the structure.

Molecular Sieve
Air-purification component that chemically absorbs water from compressed air.

Molotov Cocktail
Crude bomb made of a bottle filled with a flammable liquid and usually fitted with a wick that is ignited just before the bottle is hurled.

Monitor
(1) To measure, with monitoring devices, radioactive emissions from a substance (2) To closely follow radio communication. (3) To record and police operations. (4) To observe and record the activities of an individual performing a function. (5) Also called Monitor Appliance.

Monitor Appliance
Master stream appliance whose stream direction can be changed while water is being discharged. It can be fixed, portable, or a combination. *See also* Monitor (5).

Monitor Roof
Roof style similar to an exaggerated lantern roof having a raised section along the ridge line, providing additional natural light and ventilation.

Monitor Valve
Multidirectional valve used to control the flow of hydraulic oil through a hydraulic system.

Monitor Vents
Rectangular projections through roofs with metal, glass, or louvered sides. The sides are counterweighted, hinged, and designed to stay in place when held shut with a fusible link. Monitors are designed to ventilate an area when heat fuses the link.

Moody Diagram
Diagram used with the Darcy-Weisbach friction loss computation technique to relate the Reynolds number, pipe size, and roughness to a friction factor.

Mop-Up
Overhaul of a fire or hazardous materials scene.

Mortise
(1) Notch, hole, or space cut into a door to receive a lock case, which contains the lock mechanism. (2) Hole, groove, or slot cut into a wooden ladder beam to receive a rung tenon.

Mortise Cylinder
Lock cylinder for a mortise lock.

Mortise Lock
Lock mortised into a door. Also called Box Lock.

Motivation
Internal process in which energy is produced by needs or expended in the direction of goals.

Motive Power Unit
Engine, locomotive, or other power unit that provides power to move a train.

Motor Nerves
Nerves that carry impulses from the brain to the muscles.

Motor Vehicle Accident (MVA)
When one vehicle hits a stationary object or another vehicle.

Mousing
Process of wrapping a strong piece of twine 8 to 10 times around the open end of a hook in a block and tackle system. Mousing the hook prevents the hook from accidentally slipping off its intended anchor point.

Mouth-To-Mouth Breathing
Form of resuscitation by placing one's mouth over the victim's mouth and breathing into the victim. Also called Mouth-To-Mouth Resuscitation.

Mouth-To-Mouth Resuscitation
See Mouth-To-Mouth Breathing.

Movement Area
Runways, taxiways, and other areas of an airport that are used for taxiing or hover taxiing, air taxiing, and takeoff and landing of aircraft exclusive of loading ramps and aircraft parking areas.

Move-Up
Procedure where uncommitted apparatus are relocated to stations emptied by apparatus committed to a long-term incident.

MSHA
Abbreviation for Mine Safety and Health Administration.

Mucous Membrane
Membrane that lines many organs of the body and contains mucus-secreting glands.

Mucus
Slippery secretion that lubricates and protects various body structures.

Mullion
Vertical division between multiple windows or a double door opening.

Multibolt Lock
High security lock that uses metal rods to secure the door on all sides.

Multi-Casualty Incident
Emergency incident involving the injury or death of a number of victims beyond what the jurisdiction is routinely capable of handling. Also called Mass Casualty Incident.

Multipara
Woman who has previously given birth.

Multiple Alarm
Additional alarm, such as second or third, that is a call for additional assistance or response.

Multiple Jacket Hose
Type of hose construction consisting of a combination of two separately woven jackets (double jackets), or two or more interwoven jackets, and lined with an inner rubber tube.

Multiple Points Of Origin
Two or more separate points of fire origin discovered at a fire scene giving a strong indication of arson.

Multipurpose Fire Extinguisher
Portable fire extinguisher that is rated for Class A, Class B, and Class C fires. Also known as ABC Extinguisher.

Multistage Pump
Any centrifugal fire pump having more than one impeller.

Muntin
Small members dividing the glass panes in a window sash.

Muscle
Tissue composed of elongated cells that has the ability to contract when stimulated, thus causing bones and joints to move.

Mushrooming
Tendency of heat, smoke, and other products of combustion to rise until they encounter a horizontal obstruction. At this point they will spread laterally until they encounter vertical obstructions and begin to bank downward.

Mutual Aid
Reciprocal assistance by organizations under a prearranged plan or contract that each will assist the other when needed.

Mutual Company
Insurance company that is run to benefit the insured and in which any revenue above operating expenses is returned to policyholders as dividends.

MVA
Abbreviation for Motor Vehicle Accident.

Mystery Nozzle
Older style variable gallonage adjustable fog stream nozzle.

N

Nacelle
Housing of an externally mounted aircraft engine.

Nader Safety Lock
Vehicle door safety lock; required by law on all passenger vehicles built since 1973.

Nasal Cannula
Small tubular prong that fits into the patient's nostril to provide supplemental oxygen. Usually there are two, one for each nostril.

National Cave Rescue Commission
Division of the National Speleological Society that specializes in cave rescue.

National Defense Area (NDA)
Temporary establishment within the United States of "federal areas" for the protection or security of Department of Defense (DOD) resources. Normally, NDAs are established for emergency situations such as accidents. NDAs may be established, discontinued, or their boundaries changed as necessary to provide protection or security of DOD resources.

National Electrical Code® (NEC)
NFPA 70, National Electrical Code®, is the standard for electrical activity that contains basic minimum provisions considered necessary to safeguard persons and buildings. It was prepared by the NFPA National Electrical Code Committee.

National Fire Codes (NFC)
Series of volumes published by the National Fire Protection Association containing the current standards prepared by various committees and adopted by the Association.

National Fire Protection Association (NFPA)
Nonprofit educational and technical association devoted to protecting life and property from fire by developing fire protection standards and educating the public.

National Institute For Occupational Safety And Health (NIOSH)
Government agency that helps ensure the safety of the workplace and associated equipment through investigation and recommendation.

National Response Center
Federal organization charged with coordinating the response of numerous agencies to emergency incidents involving the release of significant amounts of hazardous materials.

National Standard Thread (NST)
Screw thread of specific dimensions for fire service use as specified in NFPA 1963, *Standard for Screw Threads and Gaskets for Fire Hose Connections.*

Natural Cover Fire
Fire involving ground cover grass, brush, trees, and other vegetation. Also called Wildland Fire.

Natural Ventilation
Techniques that use the wind, convection currents, and other natural phenomena to ventilate a structure without the use of fans, blowers, or other mechanical devices.

Nausea
Unpleasant sensation that leads to the urge to vomit.

Neat Cement
Pure cement uncut by a sand mixture.

Negative
Clear text radio response for "no."

Negative Buoyancy
Tendency to sink.

Negative Pressure
Air pressure less than that of the surrounding atmosphere; a partial vacuum.

Negative-Pressure Ventilation
Technique using smoke ejectors to develop artificial circulation and to pull smoke out of a structure. Smoke ejectors are placed in windows, doors, or roof vent holes to pull the smoke, heat, and gases from inside the building and eject them to the exterior.

Nervous System
Brain, spinal cord, and nerve branches from the central, peripheral, and autonomic systems that start, oversee, and control all of the functions of the body.

Net Pressure
See Net Pump Discharge Pressure.

Net Pump Discharge Pressure (NPDP)
Actual amount of pressure being produced by the pump. When taking water from a hydrant, it is the difference between the intake pressure and the discharge pressure. When drafting, it is the sum of the intake pressure and the discharge pressure. (**NOTE:** Intake pressure is credited for lift and intake hose friction loss and is added to the discharge pressure.) Also called Net Pressure or Engine Pressure.

Neurogenic Shock
Injury to the nervous system that causes failure of the circulatory system to fill enlarged blood vessels.

Neutral Pressure Plane
That point within a building, especially a high rise, where the interior pressure equals the atmospheric pressure outside. This plane will move up or down, depending on variables of temperature and wind.

Neutron
Part of the nucleus of an atom that has a neutral electrical charge.

Newel
Outer posts of balustrades and the stiffening posts at the angle and platform of stairways.

NFC
Abbreviation for National Fire Codes.

NFPA
Abbreviation for National Fire Protection Association.

NFPA 704 Labeling System
Identifies hazardous materials in fixed facilities. The placard is divided into sections that identify the degree of hazard according to health, flammability, and reactivity as well as special hazards.

NFPA 704 Placard
Color-coded, symbol-specific placard affixed to a structure to inform of fire hazards, life hazards, special hazards, and reactivity potential.

Niells-Robertson Stretcher
Stretcher that immobilizes a victim, prevents further spinal damage, and protects the head. Excellent for cave and confined-space rescues.

Night Inversion
See Inversion.

Night Latch
Button on a rim lock that prevents retracting the latch from the outside.

NIOSH
Acronym for National Institute for Occupational Safety and Health (U.S.).

Nitrogen
Inert gas that is commonly used as a propellant in portable fire extinguishers.

Nitrogen-Bearing Substances
Substances that produce hydrogen cyanide. Nitrogen-bearing substances are found in synthetic fibers such as nylon and polyurethane foam; some plastics (particularly in aircraft); and natural fibers such as wool, rubber, and paper.

Nitrogen Oxides
Group of gases consisting of nitrogen and oxygen and commonly given off as a by-product of the combustion process.

Nitroglycerin
Drug used in the treatment of angina pectoris, usually taken under the tongue.

Nomex® Fire-Resistant Material
Flame-resistant fabric used to construct firefighter's personal protective equipment.

Nomex® Hood
See Protective Hood.

Nomograph
Special chart, based on the Hazen-Williams formula, that can be used to assist in the determination of fire flows.

Nonbearing Wall
Usually an interior wall that supports only its weight; can be removed without compromising the structural integrity of the building. Also called Nonload-Bearing Wall.

Noncombustible
Incapable of combustion under normal circumstances.

Nonconforming Apparatus
Apparatus that does not conform to the standards set forth by NFPA standards.

Nondestructive Testing
Method of testing metal objects that does not subject them to stress-related damage.

Nonflammable
Incapable of combustion under normal circumstances; normally used when referring to liquids or gases.

Nonflammable Gases
Compressed gases not classified as flammable.

Non-Lifeline Rope
Rope that does not meet the requirements set forth in NFPA 1983, *Standard on Fire Service Life Safety Rope, Harness, and Hardware.*

Nonliquefied Gases
Gas, other than a gas in a solution, that under the charging pressure is entirely gaseous at 70°F (21°C).

Nonload-Bearing Wall
See Nonbearing Wall.

Normal Operating Pressure
Pressure found in a water distribution system during normal consumption demands.

Norm-Referenced Testing
Measurement of student performance against other students, with an emphasis on discriminating among students and assigning grades.

Nosebleed
Hemorrhaging from the nasal cavity. Also called Epistaxis.

Nosecup
Device inside a facepiece that directs the wearer's exhalations away from the facepiece lens and thus prevents internal fogging of the lens.

Nosing
Usually rounded edge of a stair tread that projects over a riser.

Nozzle
Appliance on the discharge end of a hoseline that forms a fire stream of definite shape, volume, and direction.

Nozzleperson
See Nozzleman.

Nozzleman
Individual assigned to operate a fire department nozzle. Also called Nozzleperson.

Nozzle Pressure
Velocity pressure at which water is discharged from the nozzle.

Nozzle Reaction
Counterforce directed against a person holding a nozzle or a device holding a nozzle by the velocity of water being discharged.

NST
Abbreviation for National Standard Thread.

Nuclear Heat Energy
Generated when atoms are either split apart (fission) or combined (fusion).

Nurse Tanker
Very large water tanker (generally 4,000 gallons [16 000 L] or larger) that is stationed at the fire scene and serves as a portable reservoir rather than as a shuttle tanker. Also called Nurse Tender.

Nurse Tender
See Nurse Tanker.

Objective
Purpose to be achieved by tactical units at an emergency.

Objective Test
Test in which the results are scientifically accurate or correct and cannot be influenced by outside factors.

Obsession
Persistent idea or thought that appears irrational to the holder but nevertheless continues to interfere with the individual's everyday behavior.

Occlusive Dressing
Watertight dressing for a wound.

Occupancy
Classification of use to which owners or tenants put buildings or portions of buildings; regulated by the various building and fire codes. Also called Occupancy Classification.

Occupancy Classification
See Occupancy.

Occupant
Person who lives in, uses, occupies, or has other possession of an apartment, house, or other premise.

Occupant Load
Total number of people who may occupy a building or portion of a building at any given time.

Occupational Analysis
Method of gathering information about an occupation and to develop a description of qualifications, conditions for performance, and an orderly list of duties.

Occupational Safety And Health Administration (OSHA)
Federal agency that develops and enforces standards and regulations for occupational safety in the workplace.

Odor Test
Qualitative test of facepiece fit.

Offensive Fire Attack
Aggressive, usually interior, fire attack that is intended to stop the fire at its current location. Also called Offensive Mode Attack.

Offensive Mode Attack
See Offensive Fire Attack.

Officer
(1) Any member of the fire service with supervisory responsibilities, which is company officer level and above. (2) Within an incident management system, Officer is reserved for the command staff positions of Safety, Liaison, and Information.

Ohm
Unit of measurement of electrical resistance; the resistance through which a current of one ampere will flow when there is a potential difference of one volt across it.

OJT
Abbreviation for On-the-Job Training.

Olfactory Fatigue
Gradual inability of a person to detect odors after initial exposure; may be extremely rapid in the case of some toxins such as hydrogen sulfide.

On-The-Job Training (OJT)
System of training firefighters that makes full use of personal contact between firefighters and their immediate supervisor; trains firefighters both physically and psychologically for the position they will perform.

Opacity
Capacity to obstruct the transmission of radiant energylike heat.

Open-Circuit Airline Equipment
Airline breathing equipment that allows exhaled air to be discharged to the open atmosphere.

Open-Circuit Self-Contained Breathing Apparatus
Breathing apparatus in which the wearer's exhalations are vented to the atmosphere.

Open-Head System
See Deluge Sprinkler System.

Open Stringer
Stringer that is notched to follow the lines of the treads and risers.

Open Up
To ventilate a building or other confined space.

Operation
One step in performing a job skill within an occupation. Operations are listed in the order in which they are performed.

Operational Period
Time scheduled for execution of a given set of operations as specified in the incident action plan.

Operational Strategy
Overall plan for incident attack and control.

Operational Tactics
Methods of employing equipment and personnel to obtain optimum results in carrying out operational strategies.

Operational Tests
Tests designed to ensure that the aerial device controls operate the aerial device in the intended manner.

Operations Section
Incident management system section responsible for all tactical operations at the incident.

Oral Airway
Device inserted into the patient's upper airway to keep the tongue from blocking the airway.

Orbits
Bony cavities in the skull that hold the eyeballs.

Order
Specific rule, regulation, or authoritative direction.

Ordinance
Law set forth by a governmental agency, usually at the local municipal level.

Ordnance
Bombs, rockets, ammunition, and other explosive devices carried on most military aircraft.

Organic Peroxide
Organic derivative of the inorganic compound hydrogen peroxide.

Orientation
(1) Direction in which a building faces. (2) Relating blueprints to the actual structure with respect to direction.

Orifice
Opening through which water is discharged.

Orifice Plate Meter
Device used for measuring water flow and is similar in principle to a venturi meter. The change of water velocity is accomplished by using a plate with an orifice that is smaller than the diameter of the pipe in which it is placed.

O-Ring
Circular gasket with rounded edges used for sealing between two machined surfaces; usually made of rubber or silicone.

ORMs
Acronym for Other Regulated Materials.

OSHA
Acronym for Occupational Health and Safety Administration (U.S.).

OS&Y Valve
Outside screw and yolk valve; a type of control valve for a sprinkler system in which the position of the center screw indicates whether the valve is open or closed.

Other Regulated Materials
ORM-A, -B, and -C are materials that do not meet the definitions of hazardous materials but possess enough hazardous characteristics that they require some regulation. ORM-D materials are hazardous materials transported in small quantities. ORM-E materials are those not included in any other hazard class.

Outer Shell
Outer fabric of protective clothing.

Outlet Valve
Valve that is farthest downstream in a tank piping system to which the discharge hose is attached.

Out-Of-Service
Unit that is not available for assignment to a response.

Out-Of-Service Resources
Resources, such as companies or crews, assigned to an incident but unable to respond for mechanical, rest, or personnel reasons.

Outrigger
See Stabilizer (1) and (4).

Outside Sprinkler
System with open heads, automatically or manually operated, to protect a structure or window openings against a severe exposure hazard.

Outside Standpipe
Standpipe riser on the exterior of a building and equipped with a fire department siamese connection.

Out-Swinging Door
Swings toward someone who stands on the outside of an opening.

Ovaries
Paired female reproductive organs located in the lower portion of the abdominal cavity.

Overburden
Loose earth covering a building site.

Overhand Safety Knot
Knot used in conjunction with other knots to eliminate the danger of the running end of the rope slipping back through a knot, causing the knot to fail.

Overhaul
Searching for and extinguishing any hidden or remaining fire once the main body of fire has been extinguished.

Overhead Door
Door that opens and closes above a large opening, such as in a warehouse or garage, and is usually of the rolling, hinged-panel, or slab type.

Overrun Area
See Stopway Area.

Overthrottling
Process of injecting or supplying the diesel engine with more fuel than can be burned.

Overturn Protection
Protection for fittings on top of a tank in case of rollover. May be combined with flashing rail or flashing box.

Oxidation
Chemical reaction in which oxygen combines with other substances. Fire, explosions, and rusting are examples of oxidation.

Oxides Of Nitrogen
Nitrogen oxide (NO_2) and nitric oxide (NO); can mix with moisture in the air and respiratory tract and form nitric and nitrous acids that can burn the lungs.

Oxidizer
Substance that yields oxygen readily and may stimulate the combustion of organic and inorganic matter.

Oxyacetylene Cutting Torch
Common forcible entry tool that cuts by burning. It is useful for penetrating heavy metal enclosures that are resistant to more conventional forcible entry equipment.

Oxygen (O_2)
Colorless, odorless, tasteless gas constituting 21 percent of the atmosphere.

Oxygenator
Simplified, convenient oxygen administration system for home use when prolonged administration is necessary.

Oxygen Deficiency
Insufficient oxygen to support life or flame; 16 percent oxygen is needed for flame production and human life.

Oxygen-Deficient Atmosphere
Any atmosphere containing less than the normal 21 percent oxygen found in atmospheric air.

Oxygen-Generating Apparatus
SCBA that chemically generates oxygen for breathing by the wearer. This apparatus is no longer acceptable by the fire service.

Oxygen Mask
Device that fits over a patient's nose and mouth; used to administer supplemental oxygen.

Oxyhemoglobin
Combination of oxygen and hemoglobin.

P

Package Markings
Descriptive name, instructions, cautions, weight, and specification marks required on the outside of hazardous materials containers.

Packaging
(1) Broad term the Department of Transportation uses to describe shipping containers and their markings, labels, and/or placards. (2) Readying a victim for transport.

Padlock
Detachable, portable lock with a hinged or sliding shackle.

Paid-On-Call Firefighter
Firefighter who receives reimbursement for each call that he or she attends. Also called Call Firefighter.

Pallor
Paleness of the skin.

Palpate
To examine by feeling and pressing with the palms and the fingers.

Pancake Collapse
Situation where the weakening or destruction of bearing walls cause the floors or the roof to collapse, which allows the debris to fall as far as the lower floor or basement. Typically, there will be little void space with these types of collapse.

Pancreas
Digestive organ of the abdominal cavity; secretes insulin and other important digestive juices.

Panel Cutter
Chisel-like tool used with a mallet or hammer to cut through sheet metal.

Panel Door
Door inset with panels, which are usually of wood, metal, glass, or plastic.

Panel Points
Points where the load of roof panels are transferred to trusses.

Panic Hardware
Locking assembly designed for panic exiting that unlocks from the inside when a release mechanism is pushed. Also called Exit Device.

Paradoxical Movement
Motion of an injured section of a flail chest; opposite to the normal movement of the chest wall.

Parallel Method
Constructing with hand tools a fire line parallel to a natural cover fire's edge. After the line is constructed, the fuel inside the line is burned out.

Parallel Operation
Operation of a multistage pump when each of its impellers receives water from a common source and contributes volume directly to the discharge. Also called Volume Operation.

Paralysis
Loss of muscle use or the loss of feeling, or both.

Paramedic
Professional level of certification for emergency medical personnel who are trained in advanced life support procedures.

Paramedic Engine
Fire engine company that carries firefighter/paramedics and paramedic equipment.

Paramedic Unit
See Medic Unit (1).

Parapet
(1) Extension of the exterior walls above the roof. (2) Any required fire walls surrounding or dividing a roof or surrounding roof openings such as light/ventilation shafts.

Parquet Flooring
Usually of wood, laid in an alternating or inlaid pattern to form various designs. The flooring strips may be glued together to make square units.

Particulate
Very small solid, such as dust, suspended in the atmosphere.

Partition
Interior wall that separates a space into rooms.

Part-Paid Firefighter
Firefighters paid on the basis of time that they are used.

Parts Per Million (ppm)
Ratio of the volume of contaminants (parts) compared to the volume of air (million parts).

Party Wall
Wall common to two buildings.

Pascal's Law
Points out that pressure acts in all directions and not simply downward.

PASS
Acronym for Personal Alert Safety System.

Patella
"Floating" bone supported by the tendon of the quadriceps muscle; kneecap.

Patio Door
Sliding glass door that is commonly placed in an opening that accesses the patio or rear of a residence.

Pattern
(1) Shape of the water stream as it is discharged from a fog nozzle. (2) Distinctive markings left on a structure or contents after a fire.

Pawls
Devices attached to the inside of the beams on fly sections used to hold the fly section in place after it has been extended. Also called Dogs or Ladder Locks.

PC
Abbreviation for Personal Computer.

PDP
Abbreviation for Pump Discharge Pressure.

Peak Hourly Consumption
Maximum amount of water used during any hour of a day.

Pedestal
See Control Pedestal.

Peer Pressure
Decision-making problem; the tendency of a decision maker to bow to the will of the group rather than to lead the group.

PEL
Abbreviation for Permissible Exposure Limit.

Pelvic Cavity
Lowermost portion of the abdominal cavity containing the rectum, the urinary bladder, and in the female, the internal sex organs.

Pelvis
Large bony ring formed by the sacrum and the two hip bones.

Pendant Sprinkler
Automatic sprinkler head designed for placement and operation with the head pointing downward from the piping.

Penis
Male organ of urinary discharge and copulation.

Penthouse
Room or building built on the roof, which usually covers stairways or houses elevator machinery, and contains water tanks and/or heating and cooling equipment.

Performance-Based Learning
See Competency-Based Learning.

Performance Bond
Binding financial agreement that ensures that the manufacturer will build the apparatus to the desired specifications. Usually, the amount of the bond is equal to the difference that would be required to have another manufacturer build the apparatus specified.

Performance Levels
Desired level of ability required to perform a particular job as specified in a behavioral objective.

Performance Requirements
Written list of expected capabilities for new apparatus. The list is produced by the purchaser and presented to the manufacturer as a guide for what is expected.

Performance Standards
Benchmarks for judging progress toward goals and objectives.

Performance Tests
Tests given in the middle or at the end of instruction to measure final performance.

Perfusion
(1) Fluid passing through an organ or a part of the body. (2) Method for giving a drug meant for a remote part of the body by sending it through the blood.

Perimeter
Perimeter of a wildland fire is the boundary of the fire. It is the total length of the outside edge of the burning or burned area.

Peripheral Nervous System
Portion of the nervous system consisting of the nerves outside of the brain and the spinal column.

Periphery-Deflected Fire Streams
Fire streams produced by deflecting water from the periphery of an inside circular stem in a fog nozzle against the exterior barrel of the nozzle.

Permanent Deformation
Deformation remaining in any part of a ladder or its components after all test loads have been removed.

Permissible Exposure Limit (PEL)
Maximum time-weighted concentration at which 95 percent of exposed, healthy adults suffer no adverse effects over a 40-hour work week; an 8-hour time-weighted average unless otherwise noted. PELs are expressed in either ppm or mg/m^3. They are commonly used by OSHA and are found in the NIOSH Pocket Guide to Chemical Hazards.

Personal Alert Device (PAD)
See Personal Alert Safety System.

Personal Alert Safety System (PASS)
Electronic lack-of-motion sensor that sounds a loud tone when a firefighter becomes motionless. It can also be manually triggered to operate. Also called Personal Alert Device.

Personal Computer (PC)
Computer designed to be used as a single workstation.

Personal Line
Short 20-foot (6 m) rope used in the United Kingdom, Australia, and New Zealand by an SCBA team member to maintain contact with another team member or the main guideline.

Personal Protective Equipment (PPE)
General term for the equipment worn by firefighters and rescuers; includes helmets, coats, pants, boots, eye protection, gloves, protective hoods, self-contained breathing apparatus, and personal alert safety systems (PASS devices). Also called Bunker Clothes, Protective Clothing, Turnout Clothing, or Turnout Gear.

Pesticides
Chemicals designed to control or eliminate undesirable forms of life.

Petit Mal Seizure
Term formerly used to describe Absence Seizure.

Phalanx
One of the digital bones of the hand or foot of a vertebrate.

Phantom Box
Predetermined fire department response assignment to a given location that is not equipped with a fire alarm box.

Pharynx
Portion of the airway between the nasal cavity and the larynx.

Phobia
Abnormal and persistent fear of a specific object or situation.

Phonetic Alphabet
Alphabet devised by the International Civil Aviation Organization for use in radio-telephone conversations in which a word is used phonetically in place of letters; for example, A is alpha, B is bravo, etc.

Phosgene ($COCl_2$)
Toxic gas produced when refrigerants, such as freon, plastics containing polyvinyl chloride (PVC), or electrical wiring insulation, contact flames; may be absorbed through the skin as well as through the lungs.

Photoelectric Detector
Type of smoke detector that uses a small light source, either an incandescent bulb or a light-emitting diode (LED), that shines its light into a dark sensing chamber.

Physical Properties
Those properties that do not involve a change in the chemical identity of the substance. However, they affect the physical behavior of the material inside and outside the container, which involves the change of the state of the material; for example, the Boiling Point, the Specific Gravity, the Vapor Density, and Water Solubility.

Physiological Stress
Stress caused by physical exertion.

Picket
Stake driven into the ground to anchor a guy line.

Pick-Head Axe
Forcible entry tool that has a chopping blade on one side of the head and a sharp pick on the other side.

Pick-Up Plate
Sloped plate and structure of a trailer, which is located forward of the kingpin and designed to facilitate engagement of fifth wheel to kingpin.

Pier
(1) Supporting section of a wall between two openings. (2) Short masonry column. (3) Elevated working platform that extends into a standing body of water.

Piercing Applicator Nozzle
Nozzle with an angled, case-hardened steel tip that can be driven through a wall, roof, or ceiling to extinguish hidden fire. Also called Puncture Nozzle.

Piezometer Tube
Device that uses the heights of liquid columns to illustrate the pressures existing in hydraulic systems.

Piggyback Transport
See Trailer-On-Flatcar (TOFC).

Pike Pole
Sharp prong and hook of steel on a wood, metal, fiberglass, or plastic handle used for pulling, dragging, and probing.

Pilaster
Rectangular masonry column built into a wall.

Pinch Point
Any point, other than the point of operation, at which it is possible for a part of the body to be caught between the moving parts of the machine or between a moving part and a stationary part.

Pin Lug Couplings
Hose couplings with round lugs in the shape of a pin.

Pipe Chase
Concealed vertical channel in which pipes and other utility conduits are housed. Pipe chases that are not properly protected can be major contributors to the vertical spread of smoke and fire in a building.

Pipe Plugs And Caps
Devices used to stop broken water lines in order to minimize water damage.

Piston Pump
Positive-displacement pump using one or more reciprocating pistons to force water from the pump chambers.

Piston Valve
Valve with an internal piston that moves within a cylinder to control the flow of water through the valve.

Pitch
(1) Spacing between rivet centers. (2) Slope of a roof expressed as a ratio of rise to span. (3) Resin present in certain woods. (4) Asphaltic, tarlike liquid used to repair blacktopped streets.

Pitched Roof
Roof, other than a flat or arched roof, that has one or more pitched or sloping surfaces.

Pitot Tube
Instrument containing a Bourdon tube that is inserted into a stream of water to measure the velocity pressure of the stream. The gauge reads in units of pounds per square inch (psi) or kilopascals (kPa).

PIV
Abbreviation for Post Indicator Valve.

PIVA
Abbreviation for Post Indicator Valve Assembly.

Pivoting Deadbolt
Lock having a deadbolt that pivots 90 degrees, designed to fit a narrow-entry, stiled door.

Pivoting Window
Window that opens and closes either horizontally or vertically on pivoting hardware.

Placard
Diamond-shaped sign that is affixed to each side of a vehicle transporting hazardous materials. The placard indicates the primary class of the material and, in some cases, the exact material being transported; required on containers that are 640 cubic feet (18 m^3) or larger.

Placenta
Temporary blood-rich structure in the uterus through which the fetus takes in oxygen, food, and other substances and gets rid of carbon dioxide and other wastes.

Placenta Previa
Condition in which the placenta is buried abnormally in the uterus so that it either partly or completely covers the opening of the cervix.

Plagiarism
To present as an original idea without crediting the source.

Plancier
Board that forms the underside of an eave or cornice.

Planning Meeting
Meeting held, as needed, throughout the duration of an incident to select specific strategies and tactics for incident control operations and for service and support planning.

Planning Section
Incident management system section responsible for collection, evaluation, dissemination, and use of information about the development of the incident and the status of resources. These units include the situation status, resource status, documentation, and demobilization as well as technical specialists.

Plans Review
Process of reviewing building plans and specifications to determine the safety characteristics of the proposed building. This is generally done before permission is granted to begin construction.

Plan View
Drawing containing the two-dimensional view of a building as seen from directly above the area.

Plasma
Fluid portion of the blood.

Plasterboard
See Wallboard.

Plaster Hook
Barbed collapsible hook on a pole used to puncture and pull down materials.

Plat
Drawing of a parcel of land giving its legal description.

Plate
Top or bottom horizontal structural member of a frame wall or partition.

Plate Glass
Sheet glass that is ground, polished, and clear.

Platelets
Cellular components of the blood that promote clotting.

Platform
(1) Intermediate landing between floors to change the direction of a stairway or to break up excessively long flights. (2) Main deck of an offshore drilling rig.

Platform Frame Construction
Type of framing in which each floor is built as a separate platform, and the studs are not continuous beyond each floor. Also called Western Frame Construction.

Platoon
Entire shift of a fire department; may indicate only those who are on or off duty.

Play A Stream
To direct a stream of water at the fire.

Playpipe
Base part of a three-part nozzle that extends from the hose coupling to the shutoff.

Pleura
Continuous membrane that lines the outer surface of the lungs and the internal surface of the thoracic cavity.

Plot Plan
Architectural drawing showing the layout of buildings and landscape features for a given plot of land. The view is from directly above.

Plug
(1) Fire hydrant. (2) Wooden peg used to stop a hole in a container.

Plug Pressure
See Flow Pressure.

Pneumatic Chisel/Hammer
Pneumatic chisel is useful for extrication work; designed to operate at air pressures between 100 and 150 psi (700 kPa and 1 050 kPa). During periods of normal consumption, it will use about 4 to 5 cubic feet (113 L to 142 L) of air per minute. Also called Air Chisels, Pneumatic Hammers, or Impact Hammers.

Pneumatic Power
Power derived by using the properties of compressed air at rest or in motion; generally used with a pressure regulator.

Pneumatic Tools
Tools that receive their operating energy from compressed air.

Pneumoconiosis
Lung disease resulting from habitual inhalation of irritant particles.

Pneumonia
Acute infectious disease of the lungs.

Pneumothorax
Accumulation of air in the pleural cavity, usually after a wound or injury that penetrates the chest wall or lacerates the lungs.

Point Of No Return
That time at which the remaining operation time of the SCBA is equal to the time necessary to return safely to a nonhazardous atmosphere.

Point Of Operation
Point at which the intended work is being done.

Point Of Origin
Exact location at which a particular fire started.

Poke-Through
Opening in a floor, ceiling, or wall through which ducting, plumbing, or electrical conduits pass. If these openings are not properly caulked or sealed, they can contribute significantly to the spread of smoke and fire in a building.

Polarized Couplings
See Gladhands.

Polar Solvents
Flammable liquids that have an attraction for water, much like a positive magnetic pole attracts a negative pole; examples include alcohols, ketones, and lacquers.

Pole
(1) Sliding pole from upper stories to the apparatus area of a fire station. (2) Ladder poles to assist in raising large ground ladders. (3) Pike pole.

Pole Ladder
Large extension ladder that requires tormentor poles to steady the ladder as it is raised and lowered. Also called Bangor Ladder.

Police Power
Authority that may be given to an inspector to arrest, issue summons, or issue citations for fire code violations.

Polyethylene Membrane
Type of plastic sheet used for waterproofing.

Polyvinyl Chloride (PVC)
Synthetic chemical used in the manufacture of plastics.

Pompier Belt
See Class I Harness.

Pompier Ladder
Scaling ladder with a single beam and a large curved metal hook that can be put over windowsills for climbing.

Popliteal Artery
Continuation of the femoral artery in the area behind the knee joint.

Porcelainize
To coat with a ceramic material.

Portable
See Portable Radio.

Portable Basin
See Portable Tank.

Portable Equipment
Those items carried on the fire apparatus that are not permanently attached to or a part of the apparatus.

Portable Fire Extinguisher
See Fire Extinguisher.

Portable Hydrant
See Manifold (1).

Portable Ladder Pipe
Portable, elevated master stream device clamped to the top two rungs of the aerial ladder when needed and supplied by a 3- or 3½-inch (77 mm or 90 mm) fire hose.

Portable Pump
Small fire pump available in several volume and pressure ratings that can be removed from the apparatus and taken to a water supply inaccessible to the main pumper.

Portable Radio
Hand-held radio used by personnel to communicate with each other when away from the vehicle radio. Also called Handi-Talki or Portable.

Portable Source
Water that is mobile and may be taken directly to the location where it is needed. This may be a fire department tanker or some other vehicle that is capable of hauling a large quantity of water.

Portable Tank
Collapsible storage tank used during a relay or shuttle operation to hold water from water tanks or hydrants. This water can then be used to supply attack apparatus. Also called Catch Basin, Fold-a-Tank, Portable Basin, or Porta-Tank.

Porta-Power
Manually operated hydraulic tool that has been adapted from the auto body business to the rescue service. This device has a variety of tool accessories that allows it to be used in numerous applications.

Porta-Tank
See Portable Tank.

Position
(1) Specific assignment during a fire operation. (2) To spot an apparatus for maximum use.

Positive Buoyancy
Tendency to float.

Positive Displacement Pumps
Self-priming pump that moves a given amount of water or hydraulic oil through the pump chamber with each stroke or rotation. These pumps are used for hydraulic pumps on aerial device hydraulic systems and for priming pumps on centrifugal fire pumps.

Positive Pressure
Air pressure greater than that of the surrounding atmosphere.

Positive-Pressure SCBA
Protective breathing apparatus that maintains a slight positive pressure inside the mask.

Positive-Pressure Test
Test to verify that there is positive pressure within a facepiece. After donning the facepiece, the wearer pulls the sealing surface of the facepiece away from the skin, allowing air to escape.

Positive-Pressure Ventilation (PPV)
Method of ventilating a confined space by mechanically blowing fresh air into the space in sufficient volume to create a slight positive pressure within and thereby forcing the contaminated atmosphere out the exit opening.

Posterior
At or toward the back.

Post-Fire Operations
Overhaul after knockdown that includes: searching for and extinguishing hidden fire, determining the fire cause, identifying and preserving evidence of arson, and making the building and area safe for occupation; may also include returning to quarters, preparing equipment for future response, and writing incident reports.

Post-Incident Trauma
Psychological stress that affects emergency responders after returning from a stressful emergency incident.

Post Indicator Valve (PIV)
Valve that provides a visual means for indicating "open" or "shut" position; found on the supply main of installed fire protection systems.

Post Indicator Valve Assembly (PIVA)
Similar to a PIV except that the valve used is of the butterfly type, while the PIV and the WPIV use a gate valve.

Post-Traumatic Incident Debriefing
Counseling designed to minimize the effects of post-incident trauma. Also called Critical Incident Stress Debriefing.

Potential Energy
Stored energy that has the ability to perform work once released.

Pound Per Square Inch — Absolute (psia)
Absolute pressure equals atmospheric pressure (14.7 psi) plus the gauge pressure. At 100 psig, absolute pressure equals 114.7 psia.

Pounds Per Square Inch (psi)
U.S. unit for measuring pressure. Its metric equivalent is kilopascals.

Pounds Per Square Inch — Gauge (psig)
Pressure above atmospheric pressure. At sea level, 0 psig is equal to 14.7 psia.

Powered Hydraulic Shears
Large rescue tool whose two blades open and close by the use of hydraulic power supplied through hose from a power unit.

Powered Hydraulic Spreaders
Large rescue tool whose two arms open and close by the use of hydraulic power supplied through hose from a power unit. This device is capable of exerting in excess of 20,000 pounds (900 kg) of force at its tips. Also called Jaws.

Power Plant
See Apparatus Engine.

Power Take-Off (PTO)
Rotating shaft that transfers power from the engine to auxiliary equipment. All farm tractors are designed to operate the PTO shaft at either 540 or 1,000 revolutions per minute.

Power Tool
Tool that acquires its power from a mechanical device such as a motor or pump.

Power Train
Means of transferring power from an engine to a pump; includes all power-transmitting components.

PPE
Abbreviation for Personal Protective Equipment.

PPM (ppm)
Abbreviation for Parts Per Million.

PPV
Abbreviation for Positive-Pressure Ventilation.

Practical Demonstration
Part of the lesson plan that addresses psychomotor objectives with a prepared job breakdown sheet.

Pre-Action System
Type of automatic sprinkler system in which thermostatic devices charge the system with water before individual sprinkler heads are fused.

Preassembled Lock
Designed to be installed as a complete unit (requiring no assembly) within a door. Also called Unit Lock.

Preconnect
(1) Attack hose connected to a discharge when the hose is loaded; this shortens the time it takes to deploy the hose for fire fighting. (2) Soft-sleeve intake hose that is carried connected to the pump intake.

Predischarge Alarm
Alarm that sounds before a total flooding fire extinguishing system is about to discharge. This gives occupants the opportunity to leave the area.

Pre-eclampsia
Abnormal condition with very high blood pressure after the sixth month of pregnancy. Other symptoms are protein in the urine and swollen ankles (edema). Also called Toxemia of Pregnancy.

Prefire Inspection
See Pre-Incident Planning.

Prefire Planning
See Pre-Incident Planning.

Pre-Incident Inspection
See Pre-Incident Planning.

Pre-Incident Plan
Document containing set procedures for possible incidents at a given location developed during pre-incident planning.

Pre-Incident Planning
Act of preparing to handle an incident at a particular location or a particular type of incident before an incident occurs. Also called Prefire Planning, Preplanning, Prefire Inspection, or Pre-Incident Inspection.

Preparation Step
First step in conducting a lesson in which the job or topic to be taught is identified, a teaching base is developed, and students are motivated to learn.

Preplanning
See Pre-Incident Planning.

Prescriptive Tests
Tests given at the beginning of instruction to determine what the student already knows.

Prescriptive Training
Instructional approach that uses the four-step teaching method in a different order: evaluation, preparation, presentation, application, and reevaluation.

Presentation Step
Second step in conducting a lesson; new information and skills are presented to the learners.

Presenting Part
Part of the baby that emerges first during delivery.

Preservice Tests
Tests performed on fire pumps or aerial devices before they are placed into service. These tests are broken down into manufacturer's tests, certification tests, and acceptance tests.

Pressure
Force per unit area measured in pounds per square inch (psi) or kilopascals (kPa).

Pressure-Demand Device
SCBA that may be operated in either positive-pressure or demand mode. This type of SCBA is presently being phased out and replaced with positive-pressure-only apparatus.

Pressure Differential
Effect of altering the atmospheric pressure within a confined space by mechanical means. When air is exhausted from within the space, a low-pressure environment is created and replacement air will be drawn in. When air is blown into the space, a high-pressure environment is created and air within will move to the outside.

Pressure Gauge
Registers the pump discharge pressure.

Pressure Governor
Pressure control device that controls engine speed and therefore eliminates hazardous conditions that result from excessive pressures.

Pressure Operation
Operation of a two- (or more) stage centrifugal pump in which water passes consecutively through each impeller to provide high pressures at a reduced volume. Also called Series Operation.

Pressure Point
Point over an artery where the pulse may be felt. Pressure on the point often helps to stop the flow of blood from a wound past that point.

Pressure-Reducing Valve
Valve installed at standpipe connections that is designed to reduce the amount of water pressure at that discharge to a specific pressure, usually 100 psi (700 kPa).

Pressure Regulator
Device used to maintain a constant pressure within a pump while operating.

Pressure-Relief Device
Automatic device designed to release excess pressure from a container.

Pressure Tank
Water storage receptacle that uses compressed-air pressure to propel the water into the distribution system. Pressure tanks are generally small and provide only a limited amount of water for fire protection.

Prestressing
Means whereby the reinforcing bars in concrete beams are placed in tension before the concrete is poured so that the member will develop greater strength after the concrete has set.

Preventive Maintenance
Ongoing inspection and upkeep intended to prolong the life and to prevent breakdown of apparatus, equipment, and facilities.

Priapism
Problem with the penis remaining erect too long. It may be caused by a urinary stone or a sore inside the penis or the central nervous system. Sometimes occurs in men who have sickle-cell anemia or severe leukemia.

Primary Feeder
Large pipes (mains), with relatively widespread spacing, that convey large quantities of water to various points of the system for local distribution to the smaller mains.

Prime
To remove all air from a pump in preparation for receiving water under pressure.

Primer
See Priming Pump.

Primer Oil Tank
Tank of oil used to seal and lubricate the priming pump.

Priming Pump
Small positive-displacement pump used to evacuate air from a centrifugal pump housing and hard suction hose. Evacuating air allows the centrifugal pump to receive water from a static water supply source. Also called Primer.

Primipara
Woman who has given birth to one healthy infant.

Priority Traffic
See Emergency Traffic.

Private Connection
Connections to water supplies other than the standard municipal water supply system; may include connection within a large industrial facility, a farm, or a private housing development.

Private Hydrant
Hydrant provided on private property or on private water systems to protect private property. Also called Yard Hydrant.

Proceed With Caution
Order for incoming units to discontinue responding at an emergency rate. Units should turn off warning devices and follow routine traffic regulations. Also called Reduce Speed.

Procurement Unit
Functional unit within the finance section of an incident management system; responsible for financial matters involving vendors.

Production Order
Order in which jobs must be done. The more difficult jobs may have to be done first.

Products Of Combustion
Materials produced and released during burning.

Progress Chart
Chart designed to record the progress of an individual or group during a course of study.

Progressive Hose Lay
Method used when fire apparatus cannot drive along a natural cover fire's edge. The operation consists of laying hose from a fire pump to the fire's edge, extinguishing fire in that area, connecting another section, advancing, and extinguishing more fire.

Progressive Method
Progressive method of constructing a fire line. Each member of a hand crew takes a few strokes to clear fuel or widen the break, advances a specified distance, takes a few strokes, advances, and so on.

Progress Tests
Given during instruction to measure improvement and to diagnose learning difficulties.

Projected Window
Type of swinging window that is hinged at the top and swings either outward or inward.

Prolapsed Cord
Delivery in which the umbilical cord appears at the vaginal opening before the head of the infant.

Prone
Position of lying face downward.

Propagation
Spread of combustion through a solid, gas, or vapor or the spread of fire from one combustible to another.

Proper Seal
Result of the facepiece fitting snugly against the bare skin and preventing entry of smoke, fumes, or gases.

Proportional Directional Control Valve
Controls the flow of hydraulic fluid through a hydraulic system.

Proportioner
Device used to introduce the correct amount of agent, especially foam and wetting agents, into streams of water.

Proportioning Valve
Valve used to balance or divide the air supply between the aeration system and the discharge manifold of a foam system.

Proprietary System
Fire protection system owned and operated by the property owner.

Protection Factor
Ratio of contaminants in the atmosphere outside the facepiece to the contaminants inside the facepiece; determined by quantitative fit testing from the manufacturer.

Protection Plates
Plates fastened to a ladder to prevent wear at points where it comes in contact with mounting brackets.

Protective Clothing
See Personal Protective Equipment.

Protective Coat
Coat worn during fire fighting operations.

Protective Hood
Designed to protect the firefighter's ears, neck, and face from exposure to extreme heat. Hoods are typically made of Nomex®, Kevlar®, or PBI® and are available in long or short styles.

Protective Trousers
Pants worn during fire fighting operations.

Protein Foam
Protein foams are chemically broken down (hydrolyzed) protein solids. The end product of this chemical digestion is protein liquid concentrate.

Proton
Part of an atom that possesses a positive charge.

Proximal
Located near the trunk of the body.

Proximate Cause
One that in a naturally, continuous sequence produces the injury, and without which, the result would not have occurred.

Proximity Clothing
Special personal protective equipment with a reflective exterior that is designed to protect the firefighter from conductive, convective, and radiant heat while working in close proximity to the fire. Also called Proximity Suit.

Proximity Suit
See Proximity Clothing.

Prussik Knot
Special knot used to assist a person climbing a rope.

Pry
To raise, move, or force with a prying tool.

Prying Tools
Hand tools that use the principle of leverage to allow the rescuer to exert more force than would be possible without the tool. These tools are characterized by their long, slender shape and are constructed of hardened steel.

PSI
Abbreviation for Pounds Per Square Inch.

PSIG
Abbreviation for Pounds Per Square Inch—Gauge.

Psychological Stress
Mental stress.

Psychomotor Learning
Learning that relates to physical or manipulative skills.

Psychomotor Seizure
Characterized by an altered personality state. In some patients, psychomotor seizures result in unexplained attacks of rage or stereotyped behavior.

PTO
Abbreviation for Power Take-Off.

Pubis
One of the bones that form the hip.

Public Service
(1) Slang used over the radio to have someone make a call by telephone. (2) Service rendered in the public interest.

Public Way
Parcel of land, such as a street or sidewalk, that is essentially open to the outside and is used by the public for moving from one location to another.

Pull Box
Manual fire alarm activator.

Pulley
(1) Small, grooved wheel through which the halyard is drawn on an extension ladder. (2) Wheel used to transmit power by means of a band, belt, cord, rope, or chain passing over its rim.

Pulling Line
See Fall Line.

Pull-In Point
Rotating portion of the machine that is capable of entangling a victim if a body part or piece of clothing comes in contact with that portion of the machine.

Pull Line
See Fall Line.

Pulmonary Artery
Major artery leading from the right ventricle to the lungs.

Pulmonary Edema
Accumulation of fluids in the lungs.

Pulmonary Embolism
Obstruction of the pulmonary arteries by foreign substance or blood clot.

Pulmonary Resuscitation
See Artificial Respiration.

Pulmonary Veins
Carry oxygenated blood from the lungs to the left atrium.

Pulse
Rhythmic throbbing caused by expansion and contraction of arterial walls as blood passes through them.

Pump
(1) To supply water to hoselines. (2) Device on the apparatus that imparts pressure on water for hoselines. (3) Apparatus that positions as the attack apparatus at the fire scene in a two-piece engine company.

Pump And Roll
Ability of an apparatus to pump water while the vehicle is in motion.

Pump Apparatus
Fire department apparatus that has the primary responsibility to pump water.

Pump Can
Water-filled pump-type extinguisher. Also called Pump Tank.

Pump Capacity Rating
Maximum amount of water a pump will deliver at the indicated pressure.

Pump Charts
Charts carried on a fire apparatus to aid the pump operator in determining the proper pump discharge pressure to use when supplying hoselines.

Pump Discharge Pressure (PDP)
Actual velocity pressure (measured in pounds per square inch) of the water as it leaves the pump and enters the hoseline.

Pump Drain
Drain located at the lowest part of the pump to help remove all water from the pump. This eliminates the danger of damage due to freezing.

Pumper, Class A
Pumper that delivers its rated capacity of at least 750 gpm (3 000 L/min) at 150 psi (1 000 kPa) net pump pressure at a lift of not more than 10 feet (3 m) with a motor speed of not more than 80 percent of the certified peak of the brake horsepower curve; will deliver 70 percent of rated capacity at 200 psi (1 350 kPa) and 50 percent of rated capacity at 250 psi (1 700 kPa).

Pumper, Class B
Pumper that delivers its rated capacity at 120 psi (800 kPa) net pump pressure at a lift of not more than 10 feet (3 m) with a motor speed of not more than 80 percent of the certified peak of the brake horsepower curve; will deliver 50 percent of its rated capacity at 200 psi (1 350 kPa) and 33⅓ percent of its rated capacity at 250 psi (1 700 kPa). Class B pumps have not been manufactured since the mid-1950s.

Pumping Apparatus
Fire department apparatus that has the primary responsibility to pump water.

Pump-Off Line
Pipeline that usually runs from the tank discharge openings to the front of the trailer. Most pumps are mounted on the tractor.

Pump Operator
Firefighter charged with operating the pump and determining the pressures required to operate it efficiently.

Pump Panel
Instrument and control panel located on the pumper.

Pump Tank
See Pump Can.

Punch Press
Large, heavy piece of industrial machinery used to cold-form sheet metal.

Puncture Nozzle
See Piercing Applicator Nozzle.

Puncture Wound
Open wound caused when an ice pick, knife, or other pointed object pierces the skin.

Pupil
Small opening in the center of the iris.

Purging
Freeing from impurities, such as ventilating a contaminated space, by introducing fresh air.

Purification System
Series of mechanical and chemical filters through which compressed breathing air is passed to remove moisture, oil, carbon monoxide, and other contaminants.

Purlin
Horizontal member between trusses that support the roof.

PVC
Abbreviation for Polyvinyl Chloride.

Pyro
See Pyromaniac.

Pyrolysis
Chemical decomposition caused by heat that generally results in the lowered ignition temperature of the material.

Pyromania
Uncontrollable impulse to set fires.

Pyromaniac
Person afflicted with pyromania.

Pyrometer
Device used to measure temperatures by wavelength or electrical generation. Pyrometers connected to thermocouples record the heat at various points.

Pyrophoric
A material that ignites spontaneously when exposed to air.

Pyrophoric Liquids
Ignite spontaneously in dry or moist air at or below 130°F (54°C).

Pyrophoric Materials
These elements react and ignite on contact with air.

Pyrotechnics
Fireworks.

Pyroxylin Plastic
Nitrocellulose plastic that is extremely combustible and susceptible to deterioration and self-ignition; produces toxic fumes when burned.

Q

Q
Slang for a Federal Q2B Mechanical Coaster Siren.

Quad
Four-way combination fire apparatus; sometimes referred to as quadruple combination. A quad combines the water tank, pump, and hose of a pumper with the ground ladder complement of a truck company.

Quadrant
One of the four regions into which the abdomen may be divided for purposes of physical diagnosis.

Qualitative Test (Facepiece Fit)
Test in which the wearer's sense of smell or taste is used to determine whether a facepiece fits properly. Examples are the irritant fume test, odor test, and taste test.

Quantitative Test (Facepiece Fit)
Test in which instruments determine the amount of contaminants inside the facepiece.

Quarterpanel
See Fender.

Quarters
Fire station or office.

Quarter-Turn Coupling
Sexless coupling with two hooklike lugs that slip over a ring on the opposite coupling and then rotate 90 degrees clockwise to lock.

Quench
To extinguish a fire by cooling.

Quick-Fill™ System
Mine Safety Appliances Company (MSA) system that can be used as an emergency breathing system connection or that can be used to refill SCBA cylinders during nonemergency conditions.

Quint
Fire apparatus equipped with a fire pump, water tank, ground ladders, and hose bed in addition to the aerial device.

R

Rabbet
Groove cut in the surface or on the edge of a board to receive another member.

Rabbeted Jamb
Jamb into which a shoulder has been milled to permit the door to close against the provided shoulder.

Rabbit Tool
Hydraulic spreading tool that is specially designed to open doors that swing inward.

Races
(1) Sliding channels between two sections of the aerial device. (2) Interior of a box-beam construction aerial device.

Rack
(1) Framework used to support ladders while being carried on fire apparatus. (2) Act of placing a ladder on apparatus.

Radial Artery
One of the major arteries of the forearm; located where the pulse can be felt at the base of the thumb.

Radial Engines
Internal-combustion, piston-driven aircraft engines with cylinders arranged in a circle.

Radiated Heat
See Radiation.

Radiation
Transfer of heat energy through light by electromagnetic waves. Also called Radiated Heat.

Radiation, Nuclear
Product of a process known as radioactivity; the emission of alpha, beta, and gamma radiation.

Radiative Feedback
Radiant heat providing energy for continued vaporization.

Radiator Fill Line
Small waterline leading from the fire pump to the radiator of the apparatus; used to refill the radiator during pumping at a fire scene.

Radioactive Material
Material whose atomic nucleus spontaneously decays or disintegrates, emitting radiation.

Radioactive Particles
Particles emitted during the process of radioactive decay. There are three types of radioactive particles: alpha, beta, and gamma.

Radio Systems Regulations
FCC rules that govern the operation of radio systems.

Radius
(1) Bone on the thumb side of the forearm. (2) One-half the diameter of a circle.

Rafter
Beam that supports a roof.

Rafter Cut
See Louver Cut.

Rail
(1) Horizontal member of a window sash. (2) Metal portion of a railroad track upon which the car wheels ride.

Raise
Any of several accepted methods of raising and placing ground ladders into service.

Raker
Angled timber bearing the load exerted on a raking shore.

Raking Shore
Shore footed on a horizontal surface used to brace a vertical surface.

Ram
See Extension Ram.

Ramp
(1) Area at airports intended to accommodate aircraft for purposes of loading or unloading passengers or cargo, refueling, parking, or maintenance. (2) Parking space between the fire station garage doors and the street.

Rape
Sexual intercourse by force.

Rapid Intervention Vehicle (RIV)
Small, quick-response fire fighting vehicle carrying at least 600 gallons (2 400 L) of water for producing AFFF, in addition to at least 500 pounds (225 kg) of either dry chemical or Halon 1211.

Rappel
Method of descending a rope and using some sort of friction device to control the descent speed. Also called Sliding Rope.

Ratchet-Lever Jack
Type of lifting jack that uses the principles of leverage to operate. It is capable of lifting moderately heavy loads but tends to be unstable. It is generally recognized as the most dangerous of all jacks.

Rated Assembly
Refers to doors, walls, roofs, and other structural features that may be, because of the occupancy, required by code to have a minimum fire-resistance rating from an independent testing agency.

Rate Meter
Nuclear radiation detection device.

Rate-Of-Rise Alarm System
One of the systems installed to detect fire by an abnormal rate of heat increase; operates when a normal amount of air in a pneumatic tube or chamber expands rapidly when heated and exerts pressure on a diaphragm.

Rating Bureau
See Insurance Services Office.

Razor Ribbon
Coil of lightweight, flexible metallic ribbon with extremely sharp edges; often installed on parapet walls and on fence tops to discourage trespassers.

Reaction, Chemical
Any change in the composition of matter that involves a conversion of one substance into another.

Reactive Materials
Substances capable of or tending to react chemically with other substances.

Reactivity
Ability of two or more chemicals to react and release energy and the ease with which this reaction takes place.

Reading A Roof
Process of observing important features of a roof from a point of safety in order to assess the roof's condition before stepping onto it.

Rear
Part of a natural cover fire opposite the head; the slowest burning part of the fire.

Rear-End Collision
Type of collision in which a vehicle is struck from behind.

Rebreather
Closed-circuit breathing apparatus.

Recall
(1) To call off-duty firefighters back to duty. (2) To order units responding to or on the scene of an emergency to return to their quarters.

Reciprocating Engines
Internal-combustion, piston-driven aircraft engines with cylinders arranged in opposition.

Reciprocating Saw
Electric saw that uses a short, straight blade that moves back and forth.

Record Book
See Journal.

Recovery
Situation where the victim is most probably dead, and the goal of the operation is to recover the body.

Red Blood Cells
Cellular components of the blood that transport oxygen from the lungs to body tissues and carbon dioxide from the tissues to the lungs.

Red Line
See Booster Hose.

Reducer
Adapter used to attach a smaller hose to a larger hose. The female end has the larger threads, while the male end has the smaller threads.

Reduce Speed
See Proceed With Caution.

Reducing Wye
Wye that has two outlets smaller in diameter than the inlet valve.

Reel Load
Arrangement of fire hose, especially large diameter hose, on a reel.

Reeving
Threading rope or cable through a block.

Refrigerant
Substance used within a refrigeration system to provide the cooling action.

Refrigerated Liquids
See Cryogens.

Refrigeration Unit
Cargo space cooling equipment.

Refuse Chute
Vertical shaft with a self-closing access door on every floor; usually extending from the basement or ground floor to the top floor of multistory buildings.

Reglet
Flat, narrow molding that forms a water seal for roofing in a parapet wall.

Regulator
Device between the facepiece and air cylinder of the SCBA that reduces the pressure of the air coming from the cylinder.

Regulator Breathing
Emergency procedure in which the firefighter breathes directly from the regulator outlet if the low-pressure hose or facepiece is damaged.

Regulator Gauge
Gauge connected to the regulator of an SCBA that indicates the pressure of the air reaching the regulator; used as an indication of the air pressure in the air cylinder.

Rehab
Term for a rehabilitation station at a fire or other incident where personnel can rest, rehydrate, and recover from the stresses of the incident.

Reinforced Concrete
Concrete that is internally fortified with steel reinforcement bars or mesh.

Rekindle
Reignition of a fire because of latent heat, sparks, or smoldering embers; can be prevented by proper overhaul.

Relative Humidity
Percentage of moisture in the air compared with the maximum amount of moisture that air will hold at a given temperature.

Relay
(1) Use of two or more pumpers to move water distances that would require excessive pressures if only one pumper was employed. (2) To shuttle water between a source and an emergency scene utilizing mobile water supply apparatus.

Relay Emergency Valve
Combination valve in an air brake system that controls brake application and also provides for automatic emergency brake application should the trailer become disconnected from the towing vehicle.

Relay Operation
Using two or more pumpers to move water over a long distance by operating them in series. Water discharged from one pumper flows through hoses to the inlet of the next pumper, and so on. Also called Relay Pumping.

Relay Pumping
See Relay Operation.

Relay-Supply Hose
Hose between the water source and the attack pumper, laid to provide large volumes of water at low pressure. Also called Feeder Line or Supply Hose.

Relay Valve
Pressure-relief device on the supply side of the pump designed to protect the hose and pump from damaging pressure surges common in relay pumping operations.

Relay Valve, In-Line
Special valve that is inserted in the middle of a long relay hose. This valve allows an additional pumper to connect to the line to boost pressure without having to interrupt the current flow of water.

Reliability
Consistency and accuracy of measurement in a test; a condition of validity.

Relief Cut
Cut made to reduce resistance and to facilitate the bending of a portion of a car or other object.

Relief Valve
Pressure control device designed to eliminate hazardous conditions resulting from excessive pressures by allowing this pressure to bypass to the intake side of the pump.

Remote Pressure Gauge
Pressure gauge that is not mounted on the regulator but can be seen by the SCBA wearer; commonly found on SCBA that have facepiece-mounted regulators.

Repair
To restore or put together that which has become inoperable or out of place.

Reporting Locations
Any one of six facilities/locations where incident-assigned resources may check in. The locations are: incident command post — resources status unit (RESTAT), base, camp, staging area, helibase, and division supervisor for direct line assignments.

Reproductive System
Body system that includes all the organs necessary for reproduction.

Rescue
Saving a life from fire or accident; removing a victim from an untenable or unhealthy atmosphere.

Rescue Breathing
See Cardiopulmonary Resuscitation.

Rescue Company
Specialized unit of people and equipment dedicated to performing rescue and extrication operations at the scene of an emergency. Also called Rescue Squad or Rescue Truck.

Rescue Officer
Officer in charge of the rescue company.

Rescue Pumper
Specially designed apparatus that combines the functions of both a rescue vehicle and a fire department pumper.

Rescue Squad
See Rescue Company.

Rescue Truck
See Rescue Company.

Reserve Apparatus
Apparatus not scheduled to respond to fires in normal or first-line duty but available for emergencies or replacing first-line equipment.

Reset
(1) To restore fire protection or detection equipment to original standby condition after operation. (2) To reactivate an inoperable fire alarm box or sprinkler system.

Residual Pressure
(1) Pressure at the test hydrant while water is flowing. It represents the pressure remaining in the system while the test water is flowing. (2) Pressure remaining at a given point in a water supply system while water is flowing.

Resistance Heating
Heat generated by passing an electrical current through a conductor such as a wire or an appliance.

Resources
All of the immediate or supportive assistance available to help control an incident including personnel, equipment, control agents, agencies, and printed emergency guides.

Resource Status Unit (RESTAT)
Functional unit within the planning section of an incident management system; responsible for recording and evaluating the status of resources committed to the incident, the impact that additional responding resources will have on the incident, and the anticipated resource needs.

Respiration
Act of breathing; the exchange of oxygen and carbon dioxide in the body tissues and lungs.

Respiratory Arrest
Cessation of breathing.

Respiratory Hazards
Gases and by-products of combustion that are hazardous to firefighters and rescue workers when inhaled.

Respiratory System
System of organs subserving the function of respiration consisting typically of the lungs and their nervous and circulatory supply and the channels by which these are continuous with the outer air.

Responder Unit
Emergency medical unit that carries first aid and/or advanced life support equipment but is not equipped for patient transport.

Responding
Clear text radio term given when a unit is en route to an assignment.

Response
Call to respond.

Response District
Geographical area to which a particular apparatus is assigned to be first due on a fire or other emergency incident. Also called District.

Response Time
Time between when a fire company is dispatched and when it arrives at the scene of an emergency.

Responsibility
Act or duty for which someone is clearly accountable.

Restricted Zone
Area of the incident including the product, its container, and the immediate area exposed to gases, vapors, mist, dust, smoke, or runoff.

Resuscitation
Act of reviving an unconscious patient. *Also see* Artificial Respiration.

Retard Chamber
Chamber that catches excess water that may be sent through the alarm valve during momentary water pressure surges. This reduces the chance of a false alarm activation. The retarding chamber is installed between the alarm check valve and alarm signaling equipment.

Retina
Lining of the back of the eye that receives visual images and transmits them to the brain.

Returning
Clear text radio term used when a company is leaving the scene of an incident.

Reverse Lay
Method of laying hose from the fire scene to the water supply.

Revolving Door
Door made of three or four sections, or wings, arranged on a central pivot that operates by rotating within a cylindrical housing.

Reynolds Number (R_E)
Mathematically calculated factor that determines the state of flow (laminar or turbulent) of a fluid.

Rhythm
Handling and climbing ladders with smooth motion.

Ribbon
Narrow strip of board cut to fit into the edge of studding to help support joists.

Rib Cage
Skeletal framework of the chest; composed of the sternum, ribs, and thoracic vertebrae.

Ridge
Peak or sharp edge along the very top of the roof of a building. Also called a Ridge Board, Ridge Beam, or Ridgepole.

Ridge Beam
See Ridge.

Ridge Board
See Ridge.

Ridgepole
See Ridge.

Rig
Any piece of fire apparatus.

Rigging
Ropes or cables used with lifting or pulling devices such as block and tackle.

Right Heart Failure
Failure of the right ventricle to pump blood effectively, causing backup of blood into the veins.

Right Of Entry
Rights set forth by the administrative powers that allow the inspector to inspect buildings to ensure compliance with applicable codes.

Right Of Privacy
Concept that means that an individual's records are confidential. *Also see* Family Education Rights and Privacy Act of 1974.

Rigid Conduit
Nonflexible steel tubing used for the passage of electrical conductors.

Rim Cylinder
Lock cylinder for a rim lock.

Rim Lock
Type of auxiliary lock mounted on the surface of a door.

Ring Stiffener
Circumferential tank shell stiffener that helps to maintain the tank cross section.

Rise
Vertical distance between treads or of the entire stairs.

Riser
(1) Vertical part of a stair step. (2) Vertical water pipe used to carry water for above ground fire protection systems such as a standpipe riser or sprinkler riser.

Rivet Construction
Multipiece metal structure (aerial device) fastened together by rivets.

Road Performance Test
Series of tests required to determine the performance ability of fire apparatus.

Roadside
Side of the trailer farthest from the curb when trailer is traveling in a normal forward direction (left-hand side); opposite to "curbside."

Road Tests
Preservice apparatus maneuverability tests designed to determine the road worthiness of a new vehicle.

Rocker Panel
Term used to describe the bottom portion of the door frame in an automobile.

Rolled Shape
Structural steel member made by passing a hot steel billet between shaped rollers until it reaches the required shape and dimensions.

Rollover
Unburned combustible gases released during the incipient or early steady-state phase accumulate at the ceiling level. These superheated gases are pushed, under pressure, away from the fire area and into uninvolved areas where they mix with oxygen. When their flammable range is reached, they ignite and a fire front develops, expanding very rapidly and rolling over the ceiling.

Romax
Trade name for nonmetallic-shielded cable.

Roof
Outside top covering of a building.

Roof Bows
Steel frame members that run horizontally from side to side.

Roof Covering
Final outside cover that is placed on top of a roof deck assembly. Common roof coverings include composition or wood shake shingles, tile, slate, tin, or asphaltic tar paper.

Roof Deck
Bottom components of the roof assembly that support the roof covering. The roof deck may be constructed of such components as plywood, wood studs (2 inches x 4 inches [50 mm by 100 mm] or larger), lath strips, and other materials.

Roof Ladder
Straight ladder with folding hooks at the top end. The hooks anchor the ladder over the roof ridge.

Rookie Academy
Special school to indoctrinate newly appointed firefighters in the rudiments of all fire service subjects.

Rope Hose Tool
Piece of rope spliced to form a loop through the eye of a metal hook; used to secure hose to ladders or other objects. *Also see* Hose Strap and Hose Belt.

Rotary Gauge
Gauge for determining the liquid level in a pressurized tank.

Rotary Gear Positive Displacement Pump
Type of positive displacement pump commonly used in hydraulic systems. The pump imparts pressure on the hydraulic fluid by having two intermeshing rotary gears that force the supply of hydraulic oil into the pump casing chamber.

Rotary Rescue Saw
See Circular Saw.

Rotary Vane Pump
Type of positive displacement pump used commonly in hydraulic systems. A rotor with attached vanes is mounted off-center inside the pump housing. Pressure is imparted on the water as the space between the rotor and the pump housing wall decreases.

Rotational Locks
Locking mechanisms that prevent the aerial device turntable from rotating unexpectedly.

Rotor
Rotating airfoil assemblies that provide lift for helicopters and other rotary-wing aircraft.

Round Turn
Element of a knot that consists of further bending one side of a loop.

RPM (rpm)
Abbreviation for Revolutions Per Minute.

Rub Rail
Sixteen-gauge steel W-shaped rails placed the full length of the sidewalls on a bus. They are intended to minimize penetration during collision.

Rudder
Upright movable part of the aircraft tail assembly that assists in the directional control of the aircraft. Also known as Vertical Stabilizer.

Run
Response to a fire or alarm.

Rung
Step portion of a ladder running from beam to beam.

Rung Block
See Truss Block.

Running Block
In a block and tackle system, the block attached to the load that is to be moved.

Running Fire
Natural cover fire that spreads rapidly.

Running Part
Part of the rope that is to be used for work such as hoisting, pulling, or belaying.

Runway
Defined rectangular area on airports prepared for the takeoff or landing of aircraft along its length.

Runway Threshold
Beginning or end of a runway that is usable for landing or takeoff.

Rupture Disk
Safety device that fails at a predetermined pressure and thus protects a pressure vessel from being overpressurized.

S

Sacrum
Portion of the spinal column just below the lumbar spine formed by five vertebrae fused with the pelvis.

SAE
Abbreviation for the Society of Automotive Engineers.

Safety
(1) Extra hitch tied in the end of a knot to prevent the end from being pulled through the knot. (2) Device designed to prevent inadvertent or hazardous operation. (3) To insert locking pins into appropriate openings on ejection seats in military aircraft to render the seats safe to work on or around.

Safety Bar
Hinged bar designed to protect firefighters from falling out of the open jump seat area of a fire apparatus.

Safety Belt
Life safety harness.

Safety Can
Flammable liquid container that has been approved by a suitable testing agency.

Safety Chain
Chain connecting two vehicles to prevent separation in the event the primary towing connection breaks.

Safety Gates
Protective guards that are placed over the apparatus jump seat opening to prevent firefighters from falling off the apparatus.

Safety Glass
Special glass prepared by laminating a sheet of transparent plastic between sheets of clear glass; primarily used in automobiles. Also called Laminated Glass.

Safety Glasses
See Safety Goggles.

Safety Goggles
Enclosed, but adequately ventilated, goggles that have impact- and shatter-resistant lens to protect the eyes from dusts, chips, and other small particles; should be OSHA approved. Also called Safety Glasses.

Safety Line
Extra rope tied to the main hauling rope in a rope rescue operation.

Safety Net
Used to protect firefighters in the event of a fall during aboveground rope training evolutions.

Safety Officer
(1) Fire officer whose primary function is to administrate safety within the entire scope of fire department operations. (2) Member of the Incident Command System command staff.

Safety Policy
Written policy that is designed to promote safety to departmental members.

Safety Program
Program that sets standards, policies, procedures, and precautions to safely purchase, operate, and maintain the department's equipment and to educate employees on how to protect themselves from personal injury.

Safety Relief Valve
Device on cargo tanks with an operating part held in place by a spring. The valve opens at preset pressures to relieve excess pressure and prevent failure of the vessel.

Safety Shoes
(1) Rubber or neoprene foot plates, usually of the swivel type, attached to the butt end of the beams of a ground ladder. (2) Protective footwear meeting OSHA requirements.

Salamander
Portable heating device; generally found on construction sites.

Salvage
Process by which firefighters attempt to save property from further damage by water, smoke, and heat by removing property from a fire area or by covering it.

Salvage Cover
Waterproof cover made of cotton duck, plastic, or other material used by fire departments to protect unaffected furniture and building areas from heat, smoke, and water damage; a tarpaulin. Also called Tarp.

Salvage Kit
Assortment of tools and appliances used for a specific purpose during salvage.

Sanction
Notice or punishment attached to a violation for the purpose of enforcing a law or regulation.

Sandshoe
Flat, steel plate that serves as ground contact on the supports of a trailer; used instead of wheels, particularly where the ground surface is expected to be soft.

Sanitary Sewer
Underground pipe used to carry waste from toilets and from other drains.

Sanitary Tee
Soil pipe fitting with a side outlet to form a tee shape. The side outlet has a smooth radius to permit unhampered flow in the fitting.

Sanitize
To make free from dirt or microorganisms that endanger health.

Sash
Framework in which panes of glass are set in a window or door.

Sash Cord
Used for tiebacks, for guy lines, or for securing salvage covers by lacing through grommets.

Sawtooth Roof
Roof style characterized by a series of alternating vertical walls and sloping roofs; resembles the teeth of a saw. This type of roof is most often found on industrial buildings.

Scapula
Shoulder blade.

SCBA
Abbreviation for Self-Contained Breathing Apparatus.

SCF (scf)
Abbreviation for Standard Cubic Foot.

SCFM (scfm)
Abbreviation for Standard Cubic Feet Per Minute.

School Bus
As defined by Federal Motor Vehicle Safety Standards, a passenger motor vehicle designed to carry more than 10 passengers, in addition to the driver, and which the Secretary of Transportation determines is to be used for the purpose of transporting preschool, primary, and secondary school students to or from such schools or school-related events.

Scissor Stairs
Two sets of crisscrossing stairs in a common shaft; each set serves every floor but on alternately opposite sides of the stair shaft. For example, one set would serve the west wing on even-numbered floors and the east wing odd-numbered floors, while the other set would serve floors opposite to the first set.

Sclera
White portion of the eyeball.

Screed
Two or more strips set at a desired elevation so that concrete may be leveled by drawing a leveling device over their surface; also the straightedge.

Screw-In Expander Method
Method of attaching threaded couplings to rubber-jacket booster hose with expanders that are screwed into place.

Screw Jacks
Long, nonhydraulic jacks that can be extended or retracted by turning a collar on a threaded shaft.

Scrub Area
Area within the span of reach of an aerial device.

SCUBA
Acronym for Self-Contained Underwater Breathing Apparatus.

Scupper
Form of drain opening provided in outer walls at floor or roof level to remove water to the exterior of a building in order to reduce water damage.

Scuttle
See Hatch.

Search And Rescue Operation
Organized search for the occupants of a building or for those lost in the outdoors and the rescue of those in need.

Search Warrant
Written order, in the name of the People, State, Province, Territory, or Commonwealth, signed by a magistrate, commanding a peace officer to search for personal property or other evidence and return it to the magistrate.

Seat Catapult
Device for catapulting the seat from an aircraft in case of emergency.

Seat Of Fire
Area in which the main body of fire is located.

Secondary Duties
Actions required to restore the emergency scene to a safe condition.

Secondary Feeder
Network of intermediate-sized pipes that reinforce the grid within the various loops of the primary feeder system and aid the concentration of the required fire flow at any point.

Second-Degree Burn
Burn penetrating beneath the superficial skin layers, producing edema and blisters.

Section
Organizational level of an incident management system having functional responsibility for primary segments of incident operations such as Operations, Planning, Logistics, and Finance/Administrative. The section level is organizationally between branch and incident commander.

Sectional View
Vertical view of a building as if it were cut into two parts. The purpose of a sectional view is to show the internal construction of each assembly.

Sector
Geographic or task-based subdivision within the Fireground Command System or National Fire Service Incident Management System.

Security Window
Window designed to prevent illegal entrance to a building.

Sediment
Dirt and other foreign debris that may fall out of a fluid and collect in fluid-moving equipment.

Seizures
Intense, involuntary muscular contractions caused by abnormal electrical impulses in the brain.

Selector Valve
Three-way valve on a fire department aerial apparatus that directs oil to either stabilizer control valves or the aerial device control valves. Also called Diverter Valve.

Self-Contained Breathing Apparatus (SCBA)
Protective breathing device worn in hazardous atmospheres. Also called Air Mask or Air Pack.

Self-Contained Underwater Breathing Apparatus (SCUBA)
Protective breathing apparatus designed to be used underwater.

Semiconductor
Material that is neither a good conductor nor a good insulator, and therefore may be used as either in some applications.

Seminal Vesicles
Storage area for sperm and seminal fluid in the male reproductive system.

Semitrailer
(1) Freight trailer that when attached is supported at its forward end by the fifth wheel device of the truck tractor. (2) Trucking rig made up of a tractor and a semitrailer.

Sensory Nerves
Nerves that conduct impulses from the skin and other sensory organs to the brain.

Sequential Training
Preferred training method in which the student is taken step by step from simple to complex exercises when learning to use equipment such as an SCBA.

Sergeant
Rank used by some fire departments for company officers or fire apparatus driver/operators.

Series Operation
See Pressure Operation.

Serrated
Notched or toothed edge.

Service Branch
Branch within the logistics section of an incident management system; responsible for service activities at an incident. Components include the communications unit, medical unit, and foods unit.

Service Records
Detailed description of maintenance and repair work for a particular apparatus or piece of equipment.

Service Test
Series of tests performed on apparatus and equipment in order to ensure operational readiness of the unit. These tests should be performed at least yearly or whenever a piece of apparatus or equipment has undergone extensive repair.

Session Guide
Plan for using a group of lesson plans or instructional materials during a predetermined period of instruction.

Set
See Deformation (1).

Setback
Distance from the street line to the front of a building.

Sewer Drain Guard
Strainer to prevent debris from getting into the sewer system; used when utilizing soil pipes to remove water during salvage operations.

Sexless Coupling
Coupling with no distinct male or female components.

Shackle
Hinged part of a padlock.

Shaft
Any vertical enclosure within a building; for example, a stairwell, elevator hoistway, etc.

Shall
Term used in NFPA standards denoting compulsory compliance.

Shank
Portion of a coupling that serves as a point of attachment to the hose.

Shear Line
Space between the shell and the plug of a lock cylinder; obstructed by tumblers in the lock position.

Shear Point
Hazard created by a reciprocal (sliding) movement of a mechanical component past a stationary point on a machine.

Shears
Powered hydraulic cutting tool that will cut most metals, other than case-hardened steel.

Shear Strength
Ability of a building component or assembly to resist lateral or shear forces.

Shear Stress
Stress resulting when two forces act on a body in opposite directions in parallel adjacent planes.

Sheathing
(1) Covering applied to the framing of a building to which siding is applied. (2) First layer of roof covering laid directly over the rafters or other roof supports. Sheathing may be plywood, chipboard sheets, or planks that are butted together or spaced about 1 inch (25 mm) apart. Also called Decking.

Shed Roof
Pitched roof with a single sloping aspect, resembling half of a gabled roof.

Sheet Bend
See Becket Bend.

Sheetrock®
See Wallboard.

Shelf Angles
Brackets fastened to the face of a building at or near floor levels to support masonry or wall facing materials.

Shell
(1) Outer component of a screw-in expander coupling. (2) Outer layer of fabric on personal protective clothing.

Shipping Papers
Shipping order, bill of lading, manifest, waybill, or other shipping document issued by the carrier.

Shock
Failure of the circulatory system to produce sufficient blood to all parts of the body; results in depression of bodily functions and eventually death if not controlled.

Shock Loading
See Dynamic Load.

Shoe
Metal plate used at the bottom of heavy timber columns.

S-Hook
S-shaped steel hook placed through salvage cover grommet holes when hanging covers during salvage operations; also used to hang covers for drying after cleanup.

Shop
Fire department maintenance or repair area.

Shoring
(1) Temporary support for formwork. (2) *Also see* Cribbing (2).

Shoring Block
Shim for a jack.

Short-Term Exposure Limit (STEL)
Fifteen-minute time-weighted average that should not be exceeded at any time during a work day. Exposures to substances at the STEL should not last longer than 15 minutes and should not be repeated more than four times per day with at least 60 minutes between exposures.

Shoulder Carry
Procedure of carrying fire hose or a ground ladder on the shoulder.

Shove Knife
Tool for loiding a latch on a lock.

Shutoff Nozzle
Type of nozzle that has a valve or other device for controlling the water supply. Firefighters use it to control water supply at the nozzle rather than at the source of supply.

Siamese
Hose appliance used to combine two or more hoselines into one. The siamese generally has female inlets and a male outlet and is commonly used to supply the hose leading to a ladder pipe.

Side Rails
Upper Side Rails: Main longitudinal frame members of a tank used to connect the upper corner fittings. Lower Side Rails: Main longitudinal frame members of a tank used to connect the lower corner fittings.

Sidewall Sprinkler
Sprinkler that extends from the side of a pipe and is used in small rooms where the branch line runs along a wall. It has a special deflector that creates a fan-shaped pattern of water. Also called Wall Sprinkler.

SIDS
Acronym for Sudden Infant Death Syndrome.

Sign
Evidence of illness or injury that can be observed by others.

Silage
Contents of a silo.

Silent Alarm
See Still Alarm.

Sill
(1) Bottom rough structural member that rests on the foundation. (2) Bottom exterior member of a window or door or the masonry below.

Silo
Tall, round structure found on farms; used to store feed for livestock.

Silo Gas
Collection of gases produced during the spoilage of crops in a silo. These gases include methane, carbon dioxide, nitrogen dioxide, and hydrogen sulfide.

Simple Fracture
Fracture in which the skin overlaying the broken bone is intact.

Simple Loop
Loop in which there are exactly one inflow point and one outflow point and exactly two paths between the inflow and outflow points.

Simple Tackle
One or more blocks reeved with a single rope.

Single-Acting Hydraulic Cylinder
Hydraulic cylinder capable of transmitting force in only one direction.

Single-Edge Snap Throw
Method of spreading a salvage cover with a snap action; intended for spreading covers in narrow spaces.

Single-Jacket Hose
Type of hose construction consisting of one woven jacket; usually lined with an inner rubber tube.

Single Ladder
See Straight Ladder.

Single-Ply Roof
See Membrane Roof.

Single Resource
Individual company or crew.

Single-Stage Centrifugal Pump
Centrifugal pump with only one impeller.

Siphon
Section of hard suction hose or piece of pipe used to maintain an equal level of water in two or more portable tanks.

Siphon Eductor
Water removal device that utilizes venturi action to evacuate water from basements, sumps, or low areas.

Siren
Audible warning device that makes a high-pitched or an alternating high- and low-pitched wailing sound when used by emergency vehicles.

Sisal Rope
Rope made from sisal fiber; most common substitute for manila. Sisal is a hard fiber with about three-fourths the tensile strength of manila. Its most common use is in binder's twine, but it is sometimes used in larger ropes.

Site
(1) Location of a building or construction. (2) Location of an incident.

Site Plan
Drawing that provides a view of the proposed construction in relation to existing conditions. It is generally the first sheet in a set of drawings.

Situation Status Unit (SITSTAT)
Functional unit within the planning section of an incident management system; responsible for analysis of situation as it progresses; reports to planning section chief.

Size-Up
Mental evaluation made by the operational officer in charge that enables him or her to determine a course of action to accomplish the mission; a mental process of evaluating all influencing factors before committing personnel and equipment to a course of action. Size-up includes such factors as time, location, nature of occupancy, life hazard, exposures, property involved, nature and extent of fire, weather, and fire fighting facilities.

Skeleton
Hard, bony structure that forms the main support of the body.

Skeleton Key
Key for a warded lock.

Skid Load
System of loading fire hose such that the top layer can be pulled off at the fire.

Skin
(1) Outer covering of the body, and the largest organ of the body; consisting of the dermis and the epidermis; contains various sensory and regulatory mechanisms. (2) Outer covering of an aircraft, which includes the covering of wings, fuselage, and control surfaces.

Skin Penetrating Agent Applicator Tool® (SPAAT)
Penetrating nozzle used on aircraft fires.

Skip Breathing
Emergency procedure in which the firefighter inhales normally, holds the inhalation for as long as it would take to exhale, takes another breath, and then exhales; used only when the firefighter is stationary and must wait for help.

Skull
Bony structure surrounding the brain; consists of the cranial bones, the facial bones, and the teeth.

Skylights
Glazed openings, often removable, on roofs over stairways and other vertical shafts that extend to the roof.

Slab
(1) Heavy steel plate used under a steel column. (2) Reinforced concrete floor. (3) Reinforced wall section in tilt-slab construction.

Slab Door
Door that has the appearance of being made of a single piece, or slab, of wood; may be of two types — either hollow core or solid core.

Sleeve
Tube or pipe extending through a floor slab to provide openings for the passage of plumbing and heating pipes to be installed later.

Slide Pole
Brass or stainless steel pole that allows firefighters to quickly slide down to the apparatus bay from the floor above.

Sliding Door
Door that opens and closes by sliding across its opening; usually on rollers.

Sliding Fifth Wheel
Fifth-wheel assembly capable of being moved forward or backward on the truck tractor to vary load distribution on the tractor and to adjust the overall length of combination.

Sliding Rope
See Rappel.

Sling Psychrometer
Meteorological instrument used to determine relative humidity.

Slip Hook
Hook used on a chain that is designed to be fastened by slipping it over a link in the chain.

Small Diameter Hose (SDH)
Hose of ¾ to 2 inches (20 mm to 50 mm) in diameter; used for fire fighting purposes. Also called Small Line.

Small Intestine
Portion of the intestine between the stomach and the colon.

Small Line
See Small Diameter Hose.

Smoke
Visible products of combustion, which vary in color and density depending on the types of material burning and the amount of oxygen present.

Smoke Curtains
Salvage covers placed in stairways, halls, or doors to prevent movement of smoke into clear areas.

Smoke Damper
Device that restricts the flow of smoke through an air-handling system.

Smoke Diver
Highly trained user of an SCBA.

Smoke Diver School
School that provides the firefighter with 25 to 30 hours of sequential training in SCBA use.

Smoke Ejector
Gasoline, electrically, or hydraulically driven blower device used to eject smoke from burning buildings; sometimes used to blow fresh air into a building to assist in purging smoke or other contaminants.

Smokehouse
Specially designed fire training building that is filled with smoke to simulate working under live fire conditions; used for SCBA and search and rescue training.

Smoke Jumpers
Wildland firefighters who are deployed into fire situations by parachuting from aircraft.

Smokeproof Enclosures
Stairways that are designed to limit the penetration of smoke, heat, and toxic gases and that serve as part of a means of egress.

Smoke Room
Enclosed area into which mechanically generated smoke is introduced and in which firefighters perform training exercises while wearing SCBA.

Smoke Shaft
Fireproof tower, equipped with an exhaust fan at the top, that is built into some newer buildings for the purpose of removing smoke directly to the outer air from any of the floors served that may become involved in a fire.

Smoke Tower
See Smokeproof Enclosure.

Smoke Tube

Device containing stannic or titanium tetrachloride used to produce nontoxic smoke for testing a facepiece seal.

Smoldering Phase

See Hot Smoldering Phase.

Smothering

Act of excluding oxygen from a fuel.

Snag

Standing dead tree.

Snap Coupling

Coupling set with nonthreaded male and female components. When a connection is made, two spring-loaded hooks on the female coupling engage a raised ring around the shank of the male coupling.

Society Of Automotive Engineers (SAE)

The initials SAE coupled with a number indicate the viscosity of motor oil.

Sodium Saccharin

Chemical substance used in qualitative facepiece fit taste tests.

Soffit

Lower horizontal surface such as the undersurface of eaves or cornices.

Soft Sleeve Hose

Large diameter, collapsible piece of hose used to connect a fire pump to a pressurized water supply source; sometimes incorrectly referred to as "soft suction hose."

Software

Computer program that performs a specific function or set of functions.

Soil Stack

Vertical pipe which runs from the horizontal soil pipe to the house drain to carry waste, including that from water closets.

Solar Heat Energy

Energy transmitted from the sun in the form of electromagnetic radiation.

Sole

Horizontal wooden member that rests upon the top of a foundation wall of a building. The vertical framing of the exterior walls and the first-floor wooden floor joists are supported by these members. Also called a Sill (1).

Sole Plate

Member against which the vertical load of a shore is ultimately exerted.

Solid

Substance that has a definite shape and size. The molecules of a solid generally have very little mobility.

Solid Core Door

Door whose entire core is filled with solid material.

Solid Stream

Hose stream that stays together as a solid mass as opposed to a fog or spray stream.

Solubility

Degree to which a solid, liquid, or gas dissolves in a solvent (usually water).

Soluble

Capable of being dissolved in a liquid (usually water).

SOP

Abbreviation for Standard Operating Procedure.

Sounding

Process of testing structural integrity of a roof or floor of a building, or of locating underlying supporting members, by striking the surface of the assembly with the blunt end of a hand tool.

SPAAT

Acronym for Skin Penetrating Agent Applicator Tool®.

Spacer

Length of timber that keeps a breast timber from shifting vertically.

Spalling

Occurs when excess moisture trapped within the cement or concrete expands. This expansion of the moisture results in tensile forces within the concrete, causing it to break apart.

Spandrel

That part of a wall between the head of a window and the sill of the window above it.

Spanish Windlass

Tool, such as a stick or dowel, used for post-tensioning lines by twisting.

Spanner Wrench

Small tool primarily used to tighten or loosen hose couplings; can also be used as a prying tool or a gas key.

Spar
Principal, span-wide aircraft structural member of an airfoil or control surface.

Spark
Slang term for buff. *See* Buff.

Speaking Diaphragm
Device on some self-contained breathing apparatus facepieces that aids oral communication.

Special Fire Hazard
Fire hazard arising from the processes or operations that are peculiar to the individual occupancy.

Special Police
See Fire Police.

Special Protective Clothing
(1) Chemical protective clothing specially designed to protect against a specific hazard or corrosive substance. (2) High-temperature protective clothing including approach, proximity, and fire entry suits.

Special Service
Fire company's assignment to a special detail such as removing water from a basement or directing traffic.

Special Service Unit
See Emergency Truck.

Specifications
(1) Detailed information provided by a manufacturer on the function, care, and maintenance of equipment or apparatus. (2) Detailed list of requirements prepared by a purchaser and presented to a manufacturer or distributor when purchasing equipment or apparatus.

Specific Gravity
Weight of a substance compared to the weight of an equal volume of water at a given temperature.

Specific Heat
Ratio between the amount of heat required to raise the temperature of a specified quantity of a material and the amount of heat necessary to raise the temperature of an identical amount of water by the same number of degrees.

Spectrochemical Analysis
Test method by which contaminants suspended in oil can be detected. A typical spectrochemical analysis will show contaminants in parts per million (ppm).

Speed Brakes
See Spoilers.

Speedometer
Dashboard gauge that measures the speed at which the vehicle is traveling.

Sphygmomanometer
Device for measuring blood pressure; blood pressure cuff.

Spider Strap
See Head Harness.

Spinal Column
Flexible bony structure that supports the central part of the body and encloses the spinal cord.

Spinal Cord
Part of the central nervous system contained within the spinal column, extending from the base of the brain to the coccyx.

Spirometer Test
Medical test used to measure pulmonary capacity.

Splash Guard
Deflecting shield sometimes installed on tank trailers to protect meters, valves, etc.

Splash Pattern
Characteristic pattern left on a wall by an accelerant splashed there; usually in the shape of an inverted "V".

Spleen
Solid organ of the abdominal cavity.

Splice
(1) To join two ropes or cables by weaving the strands together. (2) Process of joining two covers into a larger or longer one with a leakproof seal.

Splint
Any support used to immobilize a fracture or restrict movement of a part.

Split Lay
Hose lay deployed by two pumpers, one making a forward lay and one making a reverse lay from the same point.

Split-Sash
Two-piece window split horizontally in the middle.

Splitter Valve
Valve installed to divide the pipeline manifold.

Spoilage
Decomposition of grain or other perishable items.

Spoilers
Movable aerodynamic devices or plates on aircraft that extend into the airstream to break up the smoothness of flow and thus increase drag and decrease lift. This process results in reduced airspeed during descent and assists in slowing the aircraft after landing.

Sponges
Used for drying furniture and contents or for removing small amounts of water.

Spontaneous Combustion
See Spontaneous Ignition.

Spontaneous Heating
Heating resulting from chemical or bacterial action in combustible materials that may lead to spontaneous ignition.

Spontaneous Ignition
Combustion of a material initiated by an internal chemical or biological reaction producing enough heat to cause the material to ignite. Also called Spontaneous Combustion.

Spores
Reproductive particles produced by plants that may or may not be airborne.

Spot Fire
Natural cover fire caused by flying sparks or embers landing outside the main fire area.

Spotter
(1) Experienced firefighter who guides and directs bulldozer operations for wildland fire fighting operations. (2) Firefighter who walks behind a backing apparatus to provide guidance for the driver/operator. Also called Swamper.

Spotting
(1) Positioning the apparatus in a location that provides the utmost efficiency for operating on the fireground. (2) Positioning a ladder to reach an object or person. (3) When a wildland fire is producing spot fires.

Spray
Application of water through specially designed nozzles in the form of finely divided particles.

Spray Curtain Nozzle
Fog nozzle mounted to the underside of an elevating platform to provide a protective shield against convected heat for firefighters operating in the platform.

Sprinkler
Waterflow device in a sprinkler system. The sprinkler consists of a threaded nipple that connects to the water pipe, a discharge orifice, a heat-actuated plug that drops out when a certain temperature is reached, and a deflector that creates a stream pattern that is suitable for fire control. Also called Sprinkler Head.

Sprinkler Block
See Sprinkler Wedge.

Sprinkler Connection
See Fire Department Connection.

Sprinkler Head
See Sprinkler.

Sprinkler Kit
Collection of sprinklers, wedges, tongs, and wrenches used to close or replace open sprinklers.

Sprinkler Riser
Vertical pipe used to carry water to the sprinkler system.

Sprinkler System
See Automatic Sprinkler System.

Sprinkler Tongs
Tool used to stop the flow of water from a sprinkler head.

Sprinkler Wedge
Piece of wood in the shape of a wedge used to stop the flow of water from individual sprinklers. Also called Sprinkler Block.

Sprinkler Wrench
Special wrench designed for tightening or loosening sprinklers.

Spurs
Metal points at the end of a ladder or staypoles.

Squad
See Rescue Company.

Squeegee
Rubber-edged broomlike device used in salvage to assist in the removal of water from floors; used by pushing the water to a drain, disposal area, or collection place.

Stabilization
(1) Process of providing additional support to key places between an object of entrapment and the ground or other solid anchor points to prevent

unwanted movement. (2) Stage of an incident when the immediate problem or emergency has been controlled, contained, or extinguished.

Stabilizer
(1) Devices that transfer the center of gravity of the apparatus and prevent it from tipping as the aerial device is extended away from the center line of the chassis. Also called Outrigger (2) Chemicals added to unstable substances to prevent a violent reaction. Also called Inhibitors. (3) Airfoil on an airplane used to provide stability; for example, the aft horizontal surface to which the elevators are hinged (horizontal stabilizer) and the fixed vertical surface to which the rudder is hinged (vertical stabilizer). (4) Devices used to stabilize a rescue vehicle when a hydraulic lifting boom, gin pole, or A-frame is in use.

Stabilizer Foot
Flat metal plate attached to the bottom on the aerial apparatus stabilizer to provide firm footing on the stabilizing surface.

Stabilizer Pad
Unattached flat, metal plate that is larger in area than the stabilizer foot. The stabilizer pad is placed on the ground beneath the intended resting point of the stabilizer foot to provide better weight distribution. Also called Jack Pad.

Stack Action (Stack Effect)
(1) Air or smoke movement through a building. Simply stated, cool air enters the lower levels of a building, and warm air within the building rises to the upper levels. (2) Tendency of any vertical shaft within a tall building to act as a chimney or "smokestack" by channeling heat, smoke, and other products of combustion upward due to convection.

Stack Valve
Type of multidirectional valve used in an aerial device hydraulic system.

Staff Organization
Portion of the fire department that supports the line organization.

Staged Incident
See Mock Incident.

Staging
Process by which noncommitted units responding to a fire or other emergency incident are stopped at a location away from the fire scene to await their assignment.

Staging Area
(1) Location away from the emergency scene where units assemble and wait until they are assigned a position on the emergency scene. (2) Location on the emergency scene where tools and personnel are assembled before being used or assigned.

Stair Nosing
Plate that wraps around the front edge of the stair.

Stair Pressurization System
System that enables the stairwell to be subjected to separate air-handling controls that may, if desired, be adjusted to increase the air pressure in the stairway so that the smoke, heat, and other products of combustion on the fire floor will be confined therein.

Standard
Criterion documents that are developed to serve as models or examples of desired performance or behaviors. No one is required to meet the requirements set forth in standards unless those standards are legally adopted by the authority having jurisdiction, in which case they become law.

Standard Apparatus
Apparatus that conforms to the standards set forth by the National Fire Protection Association standards on fire apparatus design.

Standard Cubic Feet Per Minute (SCFM or scfm)
Volume of material based on the Standard Cubic Foot flowing past or through a specified measuring point.

Standard Cubic Foot (SCF or scf)
Amount of air in a cubic foot at sea level and at 70°F.

Standard Deviation
Average of the degree to which the scores in a test deviate from the mean.

Standard Operating Procedure (SOP)
Standard method in which a fire department carries out routine functions. Usually these procedures are written, and all firefighters should be well-versed in their content.

Standard Response
Predetermined amount of resources that will be dispatched to the report of an emergency.

Standard Thread
National Standard hose threads.

Standard Time-Temperature Curve
Graph that shows the rise and fall in temperature at a given time in a test fire. Also called Time-Temperature Curve.

Standard Transportion Commodity Code (STCC Number)
Numerical code used by the rail industry on the waybill to identify the commodity.

Stand By
(1) To remain immediately available. (2) To relocate to another fire station and cover that district for additional emergencies in the area. (3) To clear the airwaves for a broadcast.

Standing Block
Block, in a block and tackle system, that is attached to a solid support and from which the fall line leads.

Standing Part
That part of a rope between the working end and the running part.

Standpipe Hose
Single-jacket hose, lined or unlined, that is preconnected to a standpipe; used primarily by building occupants to mount a quick attack on an incipient fire.

Standpipe System
Wet or dry system of pipes in a large single-story or multistory building with fire hose outlets connected to them. The system is used to provide for quick deployment of hoselines during fire fighting operations.

Static
Stationary; without movement.

Static Electricity
Accumulation of electrical charges on opposing surfaces created by the separation of unlike materials or by the movement of surfaces.

Static Load
Motionless load.

Static Pressure
(1) Stored or potential energy that is available to force water through pipes and fittings, fire hose, and adapters. (2) Pressure at a given point in a water system when no water is flowing.

Static Rope
Rope that will stretch a relatively short distance under load.

Static Source
Body of water that is not under pressure or in a supply piping system and must be drafted from in order to be used. Static sources include ponds, lakes, rivers, wells, and so on.

Static Stress
Stress imposed on the aerial device when it is at rest.

Status Asthmaticus
Severe, prolonged asthmatic attack that cannot be broken with epinephrine.

Status Epilepticus
Occurrence of two or more seizures without a period of complete consciousness between them.

Staypoles
Poles attached to long extension ladders to assist in raising and steadying the ladder. Some poles are permanently attached, and some are removable. Also called Tormentor Poles.

Steady-State Phase
Generally considered the phase of the fire where sufficient oxygen and fuel are available for fire growth and open burning to a point where total involvement is possible.

Steam Conversion
Physical changing of water from a liquid to a gaseous form; water expands in size 1,700 times when it converts to steam.

Steamer Connection
Large-diameter outlet, usually 4½ inches (115 mm), at a hydrant or the base of an elevated water storage container.

Steeple Raise
See Auditorium Raise.

Steiner Tunnel
Horizontal test furnace 25 feet (7.6 m) long, 17½ inches (445 mm) wide, and 12 inches (305 mm) high used to observe flame travel. A 5,000 Btu (5 270 kJ) flame is produced in the tunnel, and the extent of flame travel across the surface of the test material is observed through ports in the side of the furnace.

Steiner Tunnel Test
Test used to determine the flame spread ratings of various materials.

STEL
Abbreviation for Short-Term Exposure Limit.

Stem
(1) Part of a lock cylinder that activates the bolt or latch as the key is turned. Also called Tailpiece. (2) Rod-type portion of a hydrant between the operating nut and the valve. (3) Introductory statement in a multiple-choice test item.

Stem Light
Elevating floodlighting tower.

Stem Wall
In platform frame construction, that exterior wall between the foundation and the first floor of a building.

Step Block
Piece of cribbing with a tapered end specially designed for stabilization of automobiles.

Sternum
Breast bone.

Stile
Vertical member of a window sash.

Still Alarm
Response to an emergency in which no audible alarm is sounded at dispatch. Usually a one- or two-company response. Also called a Silent Alarm.

Stillbirth
Birth of a dead fetus.

Stinger
Bright, one-directional, moving warning light.

Stokes Basket
Basket-type litter suitable for transporting victims from locations where a standard litter would not be easily secured.

Stoma
Small opening, especially an artificially created opening.

Stomach
Hollow digestive organ of the abdominal cavity.

Stop
To halt the progress of a fire.

Stops
Wood or metal pieces that prevent the fly section of a ladder from being extended too far.

Stopway/Overrun Area
Area beyond the runway end capable of supporting aircraft that overshoot the runway on aborted take-off or landing without causing structural damage to the aircraft.

Storage Tanks
Storage vessels that are larger than 60 gallons (227 L) and are located in a fixed location.

Story
Space in a building between two adjacent floor levels or between a floor and the roof.

Storz Coupling
Sexless coupling commonly found on large diameter hose.

Straight Jack
Stabilizing device that extends straight down from the chassis.

Straight Ladder
One-section ladder. Also called Single Ladder.

Straight Lay
Hose laid from the hydrant or water source to the fire.

Strainers
Wire or other metal guards used to prevent debris from clogging the intake hose of fire pumps.

Straining Piece
Length of timber that keeps pressure on the breast timbers of a flying shore.

Strap
Metal piece used to hold together joints in heavy timber construction.

Strategic Goals
Overall plan that will be used to control the incident. Strategic goals are broad in nature and are achieved by the completion of tactical objectives.

Strategy
Overall plan for incident attack and control.

Stratification
Settling of smoke at various vertical levels of accumulations or layers according to density of weight, the heaviest on the bottom.

Stratum
Sheetlike mass of rock or earth of one kind found in layers between layers of other kinds of material.

Stress
(1) Factors that work against the strength of any piece of apparatus or equipment. (2) State of tension put on a shipping container by internal or external chemical, mechanical, or thermal change. (3) Any condition requiring an adjustment or causing bodily or mental tension.

Stressed Skin
Outer surface of a structure when it provides lateral support.

Stress Test
Test in which a person's vital functions are monitored while the person labors.

Stretcher
Portable device that allows two or more persons to move the sick or injured by carrying or rolling while keeping the patient immobile.

Stretch Hose
To lay out hose as a line or advance it into a building.

Strike
Metal plate mounted in the door frame that receives the latch or deadbolt.

Strike Team
Group formed of five similar units meeting established manpower and equipment requirements with a strike team leader.

Striking Tools
Tools characterized by large, weighted heads on handles. This category of tools includes axes, battering rams, ram bars, punches, mallets, hammers, sledgehammers or mauls, chisels, automatic center punches, and picks.

Stringer
(1) Reinforced concrete construction: horizontal structural member supporting joists and resting on vertical supports. (2) General construction: the member on each side of a stair which supports the treads and risers. *Also see* Longeron.

Stripped Territory
Area that has been completely depleted of fire protection apparatus and staffing.

Strip Ventilation
See Trenching (2).

Strobe
Stationary flashing light.

Stroke
See Cerebrovascular Accident.

Structural Abuse
Using or changing a building beyond its originally designed capabilities.

Structure
Constructed object; usually a building standing free and aboveground.

Strut
(1) Aircraft structural components, such as the landing gear forces, designed to absorb or distribute abrupt compression or tension. (2) In a shore, any member that holds either a vertical or horizontal compression load.

Stud
Vertical structure uprights that make up the walls and partitions in a frame building.

Student
Most important member of any class in that all the activities and efforts are directed toward enabling him or her to learn.

Study Sheet
Instructional sheet designed to arouse interest in the assignment and to provide instructions for additional or outside study by the student.

Subbasement
Basement below the level of a first basement.

Subcutaneous Layer
Bottom layer of skin consisting of fatty tissues that insulate the body and store excess calories.

Subjective Test
Test in which the results may be influenced by the subject being tested, by the test itself, by the tester, or by other outside factors.

Sublimation
Vaporization of a material from the solid to vapor state without passing through the liquid state.

Submersible Pump
Pump capable of operating while placed underwater.

Substance Abuse
Uncontrolled use of a drug.

Substrate
Layer of material between a roof deck and the roof covering that may or may not be bonded to the roof covering. The most common substrate is roofing felt or tar paper.

Subsurface Injection
Pumping foam into the bottom of a container that is on fire. The foam rises to the top and forms a blanket that extinguishes the fire.

Sucking Chest Wound
Wound in which the chest wall is penetrated, causing air to accumulate in the pleural cavity.

Suction
(1) Misnomer used to describe the drafting process. (2) Inlet side of the pump that is better referred to as the intake. (3) *Also see* Hard Suction Hose.

Sudden Infant Death Syndrome (SIDS)
Sudden, unexplained death of an infant within the first six months of life. Also called crib death.

Sulfur Dioxide (SO_2)
Colorless gas with a highly irritating rotten-egg odor produced when sulfur-containing materials burn. Its pervasive odor makes it detectable below its IDLH level of 100 ppm.

Summative Evaluation
Comprehensive approach to evaluation by using test results, instructor observations, and the course critique to determine total course effectiveness.

Sump
(1) Low point of a tank at which the emergency valve or outlet valve is attached. (2) Area in the air-purification system that receives drainage.

Sump Basin
Pit or reservoir, often connected to a drain, that serves as a receptacle for water; can be improvised from salvage covers, ladders, and pike poles.

Sunstroke
See Heat Stroke.

Super Bus
School bus with an extra-large carrying capacity. These buses may carry up to 84 people seated and over 100 people if standing is permissible.

Superior
Near the head; above.

Supervisor
Individual responsible for command of a division/group/sector.

Supervisory Circuit
Electronic circuit within a fire protection system that monitors the system's readiness and transmits a signal when there is a problem with the system.

Supine
Lying horizontal in a face upward position.

Supine Hypotensive Syndrome
Condition during pregnancy or delivery in which the weight of the uterus pressing the inferior vena cava against the spine diminshes the flow of blood returning to the heart. To remedy, turn the woman on her side.

Supplemental Pumping
Pumping water from a stronger point in the water system to the units at the fire or pumping it back into the water system where it is weak. Used when a large fire overwhelms the water supply system.

Supply Hose
See Relay-Supply Hose.

Supply Unit
Functional unit within the support branch of the logistics section of an incident management system; responsible for ordering equipment/supplies required for incident operations.

Support Branch
Branch within the logistics section of an incident management system; responsible for providing the personnel, equipment, and supplies to support incident operations. Components include the supply unit, facilities unit, and ground support units.

Supported Tip
Operation of an aerial device with the tip of the device or the platform, if so equipped, resting on another object such as a window ledge or roofline.

Supports
Devices generally adjustable in height that are used to support the front end of a semitrailer in an approximately level position when disconnected from the towing vehicle. Formerly called landing gears, props, dollies, and legs.

Support Zone
Area encompassing the Limited Access Zone and restricted to emergency response personnel.

Surface Bolt
Sliding bolt installed on the surface of a door.

Surface Fire
Ground cover fire burning surface fuels such as fallen leaves and needles, duff, stubble, and grass.

Survey Meter
Nuclear-radiation detection instrument.

Suspended Ceiling
Very common ceiling system composed of a metal framework suspended from the underside of the roof or the floor above by wires. The framework supports fiberboard panels that constitute the finish of the ceiling. Common applications are in office buildings and in common areas of apartment buildings and hotels.

Suspension Harness
Web suspension network that supports the helmet on the firefighter's head and prevents the shell from striking the head when hit.

Swale
A low-lying or depressed stretch of land.

Swamper
See Spotter (2).

Sweep Pattern
Effective lateral range of an elevated master stream nozzle.

Sweetener
Component (generally charcoal) in an air-purification system that removes odors and tastes from the compressed breathing air.

Swinging Door
Door that opens and closes by swinging from one side of its opening, usually on hinges. Also called Hinged Door.

Swiss Seat
Harness that keeps a person's center of gravity near normal while rappelling.

Switchable Regulator
Positive-pressure breathing apparatus regulator that has a switch to accommodate donning.

Switch List
List of cars on a track and instructions as to where those cars go within the yard.

Symphysis Pubis
Juncture of the two pubic bones.

Symptom
Sensation or awareness of a disturbance of a bodily function as reported by the patient.

Syncope
Fainting; a brief period of unconsciousness.

Synergistic Effect
Phenomenon in which the combined properties of substances have an effect greater than their simple arithmetical sum of effects.

Synthesis
Process of combining elements to make a compound.

Systole
Rhythmic contraction of the heart by which blood is pumped throughout the body.

T

Tachometer
Dashboard or pump panel gauge that measures the engine speed in revolutions per minute (rpm).

Tactical Box
Reduced assignment to a fire alarm.

Tactical Objectives
Specific operations that must be accomplished to achieve strategic goals. Objectives must be both specific and measurable.

Tactics
Methods of employing equipment and personnel to accomplish specific tactical objectives in order to achieve established strategic goals.

Tag Line
Nonload-bearing rope attached to an object to help steer it in a desired direction.

Tailboard
Back step of fire apparatus.

Tailpiece
Part of a lock cylinder that activates the bolt or latch as the key is turned. Also called Stem.

Tally
Rectangular plastic identification tag used for entry control; used in the United Kingdom, Australia, and New Zealand.

Tandem
Two-axle suspension.

Tandem Pumping
Short relay operation in which the pumper taking water from the supply source pumps into the intake of the second pumper. The second pumper boosts the pressure of the water even higher. This method is used when pressures higher than the capability of a single pump are required.

Tanker
(1) Mobile water supply fire apparatus that carries at least 1,500 gallons (6 000 L) of water and is used to

supply water to fire scenes that lack fire hydrants. It is called a Tender in ICS terms. (2) In the ICS, tanker refers to a water-transporting fixed-wing aircraft.

Tanker Shuttle Operation
Tankers deliver water to a fire scene, generally in a rotating order.

Tape
(1) Tape recording of calls received and dispatched during communications center operations. (2) Code signals received on some types of alarm systems.

Tapped Out
See Under Control.

Target Hazard
Facilities in which there is a great potential likelihood of life or property loss.

Tarp
See Salvage Cover.

Tarsals
Seven bones of the ankle.

Task
Combination of duties and jobs in an occupation that are performed regularly and require psychomotor skills and technical information to meet occupational requirements.

Task Force
(1) Group of individuals convened to analyze, investigate, or solve a particular problem. (2) Group of resources with common communications and a leader temporarily assembled for a specific mission. An example would be a group of firefighters and equipment assigned to a special task such as backfiring; consists of three engines, a dozer, a hand crew, and task force leader. (3) Southern California term for a crew made up of two engines and a ladder company.

Taxiway
Specially designated and prepared surface on an airport for aircraft to taxi to and from runways, hangars, etc.

T-Bone Collision
See Broadside Collision.

Team Emergency Conditions Breathing (Buddy Breathing)
Procedures or techniques performed by a team of two individuals during emergencies when the SCBA of one person malfunctions or it does not have adequate air supply.

Technical Assistance
Personnel, agencies, or printed materials that provide technical information on handling hazardous materials or other special problems.

Technical Lesson
Another term for the information presentation portion of a lesson plan.

Technical Skills
Skills involving manipulative aptitude.

Technical Specialists
Personnel with special skills that are activated only when needed. Technical specialists may be needed in the areas of fire behavior, water resources, environmental concerns, resource use, and training. Technical specialists report initially to the planning section of an incident management system but may be assigned anywhere within the organizational structure as needed.

Telephone Alarm Box
Public fire alarm station that includes a telephone that gives a direct line on which the caller can talk to the complaint taker/dispatcher. Also called Call Box.

Telescoping Aerial Platform Apparatus
Type of aerial apparatus equipped with an elevating platform; also equipped with piping systems and nozzles for elevated master stream operations. These apparatus are not meant to be climbed and are equipped with a small ladder that is to be used only for escape from the platform in emergency situations.

Telescoping Boom
Aerial device raised and extended via sections that slide within each other.

Temperature
Measurement of the intensity of heat.

Temperature Bar
Reinforcing bar within concrete used to counteract stress caused by temperature changes.

Tempered Glass
Type of glass specially treated to become harder and more break-resistant than plate glass or a single sheet of laminated glass.

Temporal Artery
Any one of three arteries located on each side of the head above and in front of the upper portion of the ear; supplies blood to the scalp.

Tender
Term used within the incident command system for a mobile piece of apparatus that has the primary function of supporting another operation. Examples include a water tender that supplies water to pumpers, a fuel tender that supplies fuel to other vehicles, etc. *Also see* Tanker (1).

Tendons
Tough bands of inelastic tissue that connect muscles to bones.

Tenon
A projecting member in a piece of wood or other material for insertion into a mortise to make a joint.

Tensile Stress
Stress in a structural member that tends to stretch the member or pull it apart.

Tension
Those vertical or horizontal stresses that tend to pull things apart; for example, the force exerted on the bottom chord of a truss.

Tension Ring Method
Method used to attach a coupling to large diameter hose using a tension ring and contractual sleeve.

Territory
Specific geographical area to be covered by a responding company.

Test Item Analysis
Process that shows how difficult a test is, how much it discriminates between high and low scorers, and whether the alternative used for distracters truly work.

Test Planning
Steps to determine the purpose and type of test, identify and define learning objectives, prepare test specifications, and construct test items.

Tetrahedron
(1) Four-sided solid geometric figure that resembles a pyramid; used to represent the flaming mode of combustion consisting of fuel, heat, oxygen, and the uninhibited chain reaction. (2) Hollow four-sided object mounted on a central pivot; used to indicate wind direction at some airports.

Thermal Barrier
Heat protective barrier within protective clothing.

Thermal Column
Updraft of heated air, fire gases, and smoke directly above the involved fire area. Also known as Convection Column.

Thermal Layering
(1) Tendency of gases to form into layers, according to temperature. (2) Process of burning in a confined space in which the hottest air is found at the ceiling and the coolest air at floor level.

Thermal Protective Performance (TPP)
Rating given to protective clothing to indicate the level of heat protection it affords the wearer.

Thermocouple
Device for measuring temperature in which two electrical conductors of dissimilar metals, such as copper and iron, are joined at the point where the heat is to be applied.

Thermoplastic
Plastic that softens with an increase of temperature and hardens with a decrease of temperature but does not undergo any chemical change.

Thermoplastic Glazing
Plastic glazing made of acrylic, butyrate, or polycarbonate plastic; known for its resistance to breakage.

Third-Degree Burn
Full-thickness burn that destroys all skin layers and underlying tissue; it has a charred or white, leathery appearance, and there is a loss of pain or sensation to the area initially.

Third Door
(1) Automobile extrication technique used to free people who are trapped in the rear seat of a two-door vehicle. (2) Depending on local requirements, an additional emergency exit door may be found on the left side of some school buses. Also called Left-Hand Door.

Third-Party Testing Agency
Independent agency hired to perform nonbiased testing on a specific piece of apparatus.

Third Rail
Electrically charged rail found between the two rails that are designed to carry the wheels of a train. The third rail provides electrical energy for electric motor power units.

Thoracic Spine
Portion of the spinal column to which the ribs are attached.

Thorax
Portion of the body between the neck and the diaphragm; the chest.

Threaded Coupling
Male or female coupling with a spiral thread.

Thread Gauge Device
Device that is screwed onto the discharge of a hydrant to check the condition of the threads and ensure that they are not damaged.

Thready Pulse
Pulse that is very weak; characteristic of a person in shock.

Three-Ply Process
Process of producing rubber-covered hose in which a nitrile rubber is vulcanized to the interior surface of a woven polyester tube.

Threshold Limit Value (TLV)
Concentration of a given material that may be tolerated for an 8-hour exposure during a regular workweek without ill effects.

Threshold Limit Value/Ceiling (TLV/C)
Maximum concentration that should not be exceeded, even instantaneously.

Threshold Limit Value/Short-Term Exposure Limit (TLV/STEL)
Fifteen-minute time-weighted average exposure. It should not be exceeded at any time nor repeated more than four times daily, with a 60-minute rest period required between each STEL exposure. These short-term exposures can be tolerated without suffering from irritation, chronic or irreversible tissue damage, or narcosis of a sufficient degree to increase the likelihood of accidental injury, impair self-rescue, or materially reduce worker efficiency. TLV/STELs are expressed in ppm and mg/m^3.

Threshold Limit Value/Time-Weighted Average (TLV/TWA)
Maximum airborne concentration of a material to which an average, healthy person may be exposed repeatedly for 8 hours each day, 40 hours per week without suffering adverse effects. It is based upon current available data and is adjusted on an annual basis.

Throttle Control
Device that controls the engine speed.

Through The Roof
Fire that has gained sufficient headway and vented itself by burning a hole through the roof.

Throw A Ladder
Raise a ladder quickly.

Throwing Salvage Covers
To spread salvage covers by throwing them.

Thrust
Pushing or pulling force developed by an aircraft engine.

Thrust Reverser
Device or apparatus for diverting jet engine thrust for slowing or stopping the aircraft.

Thumbturn
Part of the lock, other than the key or knob, used to lock and unlock the door.

Tibia
Larger bone of the lower leg; shin bone.

Tie
(1) Metal strip used to tie masonry wall to the wood sheathing. (2) Device used to tie the two sides of a form together.

Tie In
(1) Securing oneself to a ladder; accomplished by using a rope hose tool or belt or by inserting one leg between the rungs. (2) Securing a ladder to a building or object.

Tier
(1) Horizontal division of a multistory building, usually the stories in a steel-frame building. (2) Layer of hose loaded in the hose bed of a fire apparatus.

Tie Rods
Metal rods running from one beam to the other.

Tiller
Rear steering mechanism on a tractor-trailer aerial ladder truck.

Tillerman
See Tiller Operator.

Tiller Operator
Driver/operator of the trailer section of a tractor-tiller aerial ladder apparatus. Also called Tillerman.

Tilting Joint
Joint that allows movement in a tilt steering wheel.

Tilt-Slab Construction
Type of construction in which concrete wall sections (slabs) are cast on the concrete floor of the building and are then tilted up into the vertical position.

Tilt-Up Wall
Precast concrete wall that is raised or tipped up into position with a crane.

Time-Temperature Curve
See Standard Time-Temperature Curve.

Time Unit
Functional unit within the finance/administrative section; responsible for record keeping of time for personnel working at an incident.

Tin-Clad Door
Similar to a metal-clad door, except covered with a lighter-gauge metal.

Tip
(1) Extreme top of a ladder. Also called Top. (2) Slang for a nozzle.

Title Block
Small information section on the face of every plan drawing. The title block contains such information as name of project, title of the particular drawing, scale used, and date of drawing and/or revisions.

TLV
Abbreviation for Threshold Limit Value.

TOFC
Abbreviation for Trailer-on-Flatcar. Also referred to as Piggyback Transport.

Toggle
(1) Hinge device by which a staypole is attached to a ladder. (2) Piece or device for holding or securing.

Tone Out
To dispatch by activating pagers or station-alerting equipment using radio tones.

Tones
Radio signals that activate pagers or station-alerting systems.

Tongue
Rib on the edge of a ladder beam that fits into a corresponding groove or channel attached to the edge of another ladder beam. Its purpose is to hold the two sections together while allowing the sections to move up and down.

Tongue And Groove
Projection on the edge of a board that fits into a recess in an adjacent board.

Tonic-Clonic Seizure
Generalized seizure characterized by loss of consciousness; severe muscle contractions; and sometimes, tongue biting, loss of bladder control, and mental confusion. Also known as Grand Mal Seizure.

Top
See Tip (1).

Top Ventilation
See Vertical Ventilation.

Torch
Professional firesetter, often for hire, that deliberately and maliciously sets fire to property.

Torching
Burning of fuel at the end of the exhaust pipe or stacks of an aircraft engine due to excessive richness of the fuel/air mixture.

Tormentor Poles
See Staypoles.

Torque
(1) Force that tends to create a rotational or twisting motion. (2) Measurement of usable engine power at the shaft.

Torque Box
Structural housing that contains the rotational system for the aerial device between the apparatus chassis frame rails and the turntable.

Torque Wrench
Specially designed wrench that may be set to produce a particular amount of torque on a bolt.

Tort
Wrongful act (except for breach of contract) for which a civil action will lie.

Total Energy
Total energy at any point in a system; the sum of the potential energy and kinetic energy at that point.

Total Flooding System
Fixed, special agent fire suppression system that is designed to flood an entire area with agent to extinguish a fire. Halon and carbon dioxide are the two most common agents used for this purpose.

Total Pressure
Total amount of pressure loss in a hose assembly due to friction loss in the hose and appliances, elevation losses, or any other factors.

Total Stopping Distance
Sum of the driver/operator reaction distance and the vehicle braking distance.

Touch Off
Term for setting a fire or for describing a fire that firefighters believe has been purposely set.

Touring Bus
See Commercial Motor Coach.

Tourniquet
Any wide, flat material wrapped tightly around a limb to stop bleeding; used only for severe, life-threatening hemorrhage that cannot be controlled by other means.

Tow Bar
Beam structure used to maintain the distance between a towed vehicle and the towing vehicle.

Tower
See Drill Tower.

Tower Ladder
Term used to describe a telescoping aerial platform fire apparatus.

Toxemia Of Pregnancy
See Eclampsia.

Toxic Atmosphere
Any area, inside or outside a structure, where the air contains substances harmful to human life or health when inhaled.

Toxic Gas
(1) Product of combustion that is poisonous; a gas given off from toxic materials by exposure to an intense heat environment. (2) Any gas that contains poisons or toxins that are hazardous to life.

Toxicity
Ability of a substance to do harm within the body.

Toxic Material
Substances that can be poisonous if inhaled, swallowed, absorbed, or introduced into the body through cuts or breaks in the skin.

Toxin
Substance that has the property of being poisonous.

TPP
Abbreviation for Thermal Protective Performance.

Trachea
Tubular structure of the respiratory system descending from the pharynx to the bronchi.

Traction
Act of exerting a pulling force.

Tractor-Tiller Aerial Ladder
Aerial ladder apparatus that consists of a tractor power unit and trailer (tiller) section that contains the aerial ladder, ground ladders, and equipment storage areas. The trailer section is steered independently of the tractor by a person called the tiller operator.

Traffic Control Device
Mechanical device that automatically changes traffic signal lights to favor the path of responding emergency apparatus.

Traffic Pattern
Traffic flow that is prescribed for aircraft landing or taking off from an airport.

Trailer
(1) Combustible material, such as rolled rags, blankets, newspapers, or flammable liquid, used to spread fire from one point or area to other points or areas, often used in conjunction with an incendiary device. (2) Highway or industrial-plant vehicle designed to be hauled by a tractor.

Trailer-On-Flatcar (TOFC)
Rail flatcar used to transport highway trailers. Also called Piggyback Transport.

Trailing Edge Devices
Rear edges of aircraft wings normally extended for takeoff and landings to provide additional lift at low speeds and to improve aircraft performance.

Train Consist
See Consist.

Training Aids
Teaching aids such as films, pictures, charts, maps, drawings, and posters.

Transfer
To move a firefighter to a different unit; the movement of companies or apparatus.

Transfer Of Learning
Opportunity to apply what has been learned in one situation to a new situation.

Transfer Valve
Valve used for placing multistage centrifugal pumps in volume or pressure operation.

Transfilling System
SCBA designed so that two SCBAs can be connected by a hose, allowing the air pressure of the

two SCBA cylinders to equalize; used as an EEBSS to equalize air pressure of one cylinder with an adequate air supply and another cylinder with depleted or inadequate air supply.

Transient Ischematic Attack (TIA)
Temporary blockage of an artery in the brain.

Transit Bus
Vehicle designed to move a large number of people over relatively short distances; most commonly found in urban or metropolitan areas that operate a mass transit system.

Transition
(1) Passage from one state, stage, subject, or place to another. (2) Section of a tank that joins two unequal cross sections.

Transmission Of Heat
Law of heat flow: conduction, convection, and radiation.

Transmit
To send out an alarm by vocal, visual, or audible means.

Transmitter
Device for sending codes or signals over alarm circuits or for sending voice communications over the air.

Transportation Area
Location where accident casualties are held after receiving medical care or triage before being transported to medical facilities.

Transportation Group
Group within the incident command system responsible for seeing that all victims are transported to the appropriate medical facility.

Transport Index
Number placed on the label of a package expressing the maximum allowable radiation level in millirem per hour at 1 meter (3.3 feet) from the external surface of the package.

Transverse Hose Bed
Hose bed that lies across the pumper body at a right angle to the main hose bed; designed to deploy preconnected attack hose to the sides of the pumper. Also called Mattydale Hose Bed.

Trash Line
Small diameter, preconnected hoseline intended to be used for trash or other small, exterior fires.

Trauma Kit
Well-stocked medical first-aid kit.

Travel Distance
Distance from any given area in a structure to the nearest exit or to a fire extinguisher.

Tread
Horizontal face of a step.

Treatment Group
Group within the incident command system responsible for triage and the initial treatment of victims.

Tree System
Water supply piping system that uses a single, central feeder main to supply branches on either side of the main.

Tremie
Chute used to deliver concrete to the bottom of a caisson.

Trenching
(1) Digging a trench in a slope to catch any burning, rolling material that could cross the control line. (2) Strip or trench ventilation is the process of opening a roof area the width of the building with an opening 2 foot (0.6 m) wide to channel out fire and heat.

Trench Jack
Any jack used to keep sheeting or wales apart for the insertion of a breast timber; also, a jack that is used as a breast timber.

Trench Ventilation
See Trenching (2).

Triage
System used for sorting patients to determine the order in which they will receive medical attention.

Triage Tagging
Method used to identify accident casualties as to extent of injury.

Triple-Combination Pumper
Fire department pumper that carries a fire pump, hose, and a water tank.

Triple Hydrant
Fire hydrant having three outlets, usually two 2½-inch (65 mm) outlets and one 4½-inch (115 mm) outlet.

Trouble Signal
Signal given by a fixed fire protection alerting system when a power failure or other system malfunction occurs.

Truck
(1) Self-propelled vehicle carrying its load on its wheels; primarily designed for transportation of property rather than passengers. (2) Slang term for an aerial apparatus. (3) Ladder truck.

Truck Company
See Ladder Company.

Truck Tractor
Powered motor vehicle designed to pull a truck trailer.

Truck Trailer
Vehicle without motor power; primarily designed for transportation of property rather than passengers and is drawn by a truck or truck tractor.

Trumpets
Symbolic insignia of rank used throughout the fire service that dates back to the time when fire officers gave commands through speaking trumpets.

Trunnion
In a hydraulic cylinder, the end of the piston rod that is connected to the anchor ear by the heel pin.

Truss
Construction member used to form a roof or floor framework. Trusses form triangles or combinations of triangles to provide maximum load-bearing capacity; often rendered dangerous by exposure to intense heat, which weakens gusset plate attachment.

Truss Block
Used to separate the beams of a truss beam ladder. Also called Beam Block and Run Block.

Truss Construction Ladder
Aerial device boom or ladder sections are constructed by trussed metal pieces.

Trussed Rafter
Roof truss that serves to support the roof and ceiling construction.

Tubular Deadbolt
Deadbolting bored lock. Also called Auxiliary Deadbolt.

Tubular Truss-Beam Construction
Similar in design to the truss construction of aerial ladders. Tubular steel is welded to form a box shape, using cantilever or triangular truss design.

Tumbler
Pin in the tumbler-type of lock cylinder.

Turbojet
Jet engine employing a turbine-driven compressor to compress the intake air, or an aircraft with this type of engine.

Turbulent State
Fluid flow is in the turbulent state at higher velocities where there is no definite pattern to the direction of the water particles. Turbulent flow is reflected by a calculated Reynolds number in excess of 2,100.

Turnaround Maintenance Tag
Tag attached to the valve on the oxygen tank of closed-circuit self-contained breathing apparatus that tells when the unit was last serviced, lists what services were performed, and indicates that the unit is ready to perform.

Turn Out
Alerting of a fire company for a response.

Turnout Clothing
See Personal Protective Equipment.

Turnout Gear
See Personal Protective Equipment.

Turntable
Rotational structural component of the aerial device. Its primary function is to provide continuous rotation on a horizontal plane.

Turret Pipe
Large master stream appliance mounted on a pumper or trailer and connected directly to a pump. Also called Deck Gun or Deck Pipe.

Twist Lock
(1) Mechanically operated device located on the corners of a container chassis and on automatic lifting spreaders; used for restraining a container during transport or transfer. (2) Type of positive connector used on most fire service extension cords; may be a two- or three-prong connector.

Two-Stage Centrifugal Pump
Centrifugal pump with two impellers.

Tying In
See Tie In (1) and (2).

Type A School Bus
Van conversion-type school bus with a gross vehicle-weight rating of less than 10,000 pounds.

Type B School Bus
Minibus-type vehicle with a gross vehicle-weight rating in excess of 10,000 pounds.

Type C School Bus
Conventional school bus vehicle with a gross vehicle-weight rating well in excess of 10,000 pounds. The engine is found ahead of the cab.

Type D School Bus
Cab-forward style school bus with a gross vehicle-weight rating well in excess of 10,000 pounds. The engine is found in the front, rear, or midship of the vehicle.

Type I Construction
Type I construction has structural members, including walls, columns, beams, floors, and roofs, that are made of noncombustible or limited combustible materials. Known in some codes as fire-resistive construction.

Type II Construction
Similar to Type I except that the degree of fire resistance is lower. Also known as noncombustible or noncombustible/limited combustible construction.

Type III Construction
It features exterior walls and structural members that are noncombustible or limited combustible materials. Interior structural members, including walls, columns, beams, floors, and roofs, are completely or partially constructed of wood. Commonly referred to as ordinary construction.

Type IV Construction
Heavy timber construction features exterior and interior walls and their associated structural members that are of noncombustible or limited combustible materials.

Type V Construction
It has exterior walls, bearing walls, floors, roofs, and supports that are made completely or partially of wood or other approved materials of smaller dimensions than those used for Type IV construction. Also called wood-frame construction.

U

UBC
Abbreviation for Uniform Building Code.

UL
Abbreviation for Underwriters Laboratories, Inc.

Ultimate Capacity
Total capacity of a water supply system, including residential and industrial consumption, available fire flow, and all other taxes on the system.

Ultrasonic Inspection
Nondestructive method of aerial device testing in which ultrasonic vibrations are injected into the aerial device. Deviance in the return of the waves is an indication that flaws exist.

Umbilical Cord
Flexible cord connecting the fetus to the placenta.

Uncontrolled Airport
Airport having no control tower in operation.

Undercarriage
(1) Portion of a vehicle's frame that is located beneath the vehicle. (2) Landing gear of an aircraft.

Under Control
Term used to describe the point in a fire incident when the fire's progress has been stopped. Final extinguishment and overhaul can begin at this time. Also called Tapped Out.

Underlayment
Floor covering of plywood or fiberboard to provide a level surface for carpet or other resilient flooring.

Underwriters Laboratories, Inc. (UL)
Independent fire research and testing laboratory.

Unibody Construction
Method of automobile construction used for most modern cars in which the frame and body of a vehicle is all one integral unit. Also called Unitized Construction.

Uniform
Official dress uniform or work uniform different from protective clothing.

United States Department Of Transportation (DOT)
Federal organization that regulates the transportation of hazardous materials. Formerly known as Interstate Commerce Commission.

Unitized Construction
See Unibody Construction.

Unit Lock
Lock designed to be installed in a cutout within the door without requiring disassembly and reassembly of the lock.

Unit Vents
Vents normally constructed of metal frames and walls and operated by a hinged damper that is controlled either manually or automatically.

Universal Coupling
Coupling device that permits unlike couplings to be connected.

Universal Joint
Multidirectional hinged joint used in the steering system and drivetrain of an automobile.

Unlined Hose
Fire hose without a rubber lining; most frequently used in interior standpipe systems and in wildland fire fighting.

Unloading Site
Place in the tanker shuttle operation where tankers unload their water into portable tanks.

Unprotected Openings
Openings in floors, walls, or partitions that are not protected against the passage of smoke, flame, and heat; generally used to refer to such openings in fire walls.

Unprotected Steel
Steel structural members that are not protected against exposure to heat.

Unstable Material
Material that is capable of undergoing chemical changes or decomposition with or without a catalyst.

Unsupported Tip
Operation of an aerial device with the tip of the device, or the platform if so equipped, in the air and not resting on another object. Also called Cantilever Operation.

Upper Airway
Portion of the respiratory system above the epiglottis.

Upper Coupler Assembly
Consists of upper coupler plate, reinforcement framing, and fifth-wheel kingpin mounted on a semitrailer. Formerly called Upper Fifth Wheel Assembly.

Upper Explosive Limit (UEL)
Maximum concentration of vapor or gas in air that will allow combustion to occur. Concentrations above this are called "too rich" to burn.

Upright Sprinkler
Sprinkler that sits on top of the piping and sprays water against a solid deflector that breaks up the spray into a hemispherical pattern that is redirected toward the floor.

Upstream
(1) Direction opposite the airflow. For example, the regulator is upstream from the facepiece. (2) Direction opposite to the flow of a stream.

Ureters
Paired tubes that conduct urine from the kidneys to the bladder.

Urgency
Decision-making problem. The necessity of making quick decisions at an emergency scene may tempt the inexperienced leader to make forced decisions too quickly.

Urinary Bladder
Hollow organ of the urinary system that serves as a storage place for urine until it is discharged from the body.

Uterus
Muscular, pear-shaped organ of the female reproductive system.

Utilities
Services, such as gas, electric, and water, provided to the public.

Utility Rope
Rope to be used in any situation that requires a rope — except life safety applications. Utility ropes can be used for hoisting equipment, securing unstable objects, and cordoning off an area.

V

Vacuum
Space completely devoid of matter or pressure. In fire service terms, it is more commonly used to describe a pressure that is somewhat less than atmospheric pressure. A vacuum is needed to facilitate drafting of water from a static source.

Vagina
Muscular, tubular structure of the female reproductive system that extends from the uterus to the vulva.

Validity
Extent to which a test measures what it says it will measure.

Valve
Mechanical device with a passageway that controls the flow of a liquid or gas.

Vapor Barrier
(1) Watertight material used to prevent the passage of moisture or water vapor into and through walls. (2) Special material used in the construction of personal protective equipment that prevents water from penetrating the clothing.

Vapor Density
Weight of a given volume of pure vapor or gas compared to the weight of an equal volume of dry air at the same temperature and pressure. A vapor density less than one indicates a vapor lighter than air; a vapor density greater than one indicates a vapor heavier than air.

Vaporization
Passage from a liquid to a gaseous state. Rate of vaporization depends on the substance involved, heat, and pressure.

Vaporizing Liquid Agent
(1) Any liquid that evaporates at elevated temperatures. (2) One of several agents used on Class B or Class C fires. (3) Extinguishing agent that produces vapors heavier than air; a smothering vapor agent.

Vapor Pressure
Measure of the tendency of a substance to evaporate.

Vapor Recovery System (VRS)
System that recovers gasoline vapors emitted from a vehicle's gasoline tank during product dispensing.

Vas Deferens
Seminal duct extending from the testicles to the seminal vesicle in the male reproductive system.

Vegetation Fire
See Natural Cover Fire.

Vehicle Rescue Technician (VRT)
Firefighter who is specially trained and certified to perform automobile extrications.

Vein
Any blood vessel that carries blood from the tissues to the heart.

Velocity
Speed; the rate of motion in a given direction. It is measured in feet per second (meters per second), miles per hour (kilometers per hour), and so on.

Vena Cava
Largest vein in the body through which blood is returned to the right atrium of the heart.

Veneer
Surface layer of attractive material laid over a base of common material; for example, a veneered wall (faced with brick) or a veneered door (faced with a thin layer of hardwood).

Vent
To release enclosed smoke and heat through an opening in the structure; opening is made by chopping a hole in the roof.

Vent Group
Incident command system term for those firefighters assigned to ventilate a structure.

Ventilation
Systematic removal of heated air, smoke, and/or gases from a structure and replacing them with cooler and/or fresher air to reduce damage and to facilitate fire fighting operations.

Ventricle
Lower chamber of the left or right side of the heart.

Venturi Meter
When coupled with a differential manometer, a venturi meter may be used to measure water velocity. The device consists essentially of a piece of pipe in which the cross-sectional area has been constricted.

Venturi Principle
When a fluid is forced under pressure through a restricted orifice, there is a decrease in the pressure exerted against the side of the constriction and a corresponding increase in the velocity of the fluid. Because the surrounding air is under greater pressure, it rushes into the area of lower pressure.

Vermiculite
Expanded mica used for loose fill insulation and as aggregate in concrete.

Vertebra
Any one of the 33 bones of the spinal column.

Vertical Deadbolt
See Jimmy-Resistant Lock.

Vertically Mounted Split-Case Pump
Centrifugal pump similar to the horizontal split-case, except that the shaft is oriented vertically and the driver is mounted on top of the pump.

Vertical Motion
Up-and-down, bouncing motion.

Vertical-Shaft Turbine Pump
Fire pump originally designed to pump water from wells. Presently, it still has application when the water supply is from a nonpressurized source. Vertical-shaft pumps ordinarily have more than one impeller and are therefore multistage pumps.

Vertical Shore
See Dead Shore.

Vertical Ventilation
Ventilating at the highest point of a building through existing or created openings and channeling the contaminated atmosphere vertically within the structure and out the top. Done with holes in the roof, skylights, roof vents, or roof doors. Also called Top Ventilation.

Vessel
Tank or container that may or may not be pressurized.

VFR
Abbreviation for Visual Flight Rules.

Vibrator
Mechanical device used in placing concrete to make certain that it fills all voids.

Violation
Infringement of existing rules, codes, or laws.

Visible
That which is clearly evident by visual inspection.

Visual Approach
Approach to landing made by visual reference to the surface.

Visual Flight Rules (VFR)
Rules that govern the operation of an aircraft during visual flight.

Vital Signs
Indicators of a patient's condition that reflect temperature, pulse, respirations, and blood pressure.

Vitreous Humor
Jellylike, transparent substance that fills the inside of the eyeball.

Vitrified Clay Tile
Ceramic tile baked to become very hard and waterproof.

Volatile
(1) Changing into vapor quite readily at a fairly low temperature. (2) Tending to erupt into violence; explosive. (3) Difficult to capture or hold permanently.

Voltage
Units of electrical potential.

Voltmeter
Device used for measuring the voltage existing on an electrical system.

Volume Operation
See Parallel Operation.

Volute
Spiral, divergent chamber of a centrifugal pump in which the velocity energy given to water by the impeller blades is converted into pressure.

V Pattern
Characteristic cone-shaped fire pattern left by fire on a wall at or near its point of origin.

VRT
Abbreviation for Vehicle Rescue Technician.

V-Type Collapse
Situation where the excess weight of heavy loads, such as furniture and equipment, concentrated near the center of the floor causes the floor to give way. A V-type collapse will result in void spaces near the walls.

Vulva
External female genitalia.

W

Wagon
(1) Water supply piece of apparatus in a two-piece engine company. (2) Special piece of fire apparatus that carries a large quantity of hose.

Wake Turbulence
Phenomena that result from the passage of an aircraft through the atmosphere; includes vortices, thrust stream turbulence, jet blast, jet wash, propeller wash, and rotor wash or downdraft.

Wale
Timber placed against sheeting planks to keep the planks in place.

Wallboard
Fire-resistive building material that consists of a layer of highly compacted gypsum material sandwiched between two layers of paper. Also called Drywall, Plasterboard, or Sheetrock®.

Wall Hydrant
Hydrant that protrudes through the wall of a building or pump house.

Wall Ladder
Straight, single-section ladder.

Wall Plate
In a raking shore or a flying shore, the continuous sheeting member placed immediately against the vertical surface that is shored.

Wall Post Indicator Valve (WPIV)
Similar to a PIV but mounted on the wall of the protected structure.

Wall Sprinkler
See Sidewall Sprinkler.

Warded Lock
Simple type of mortise lock that requires the use of a skeleton key to open.

Warm Gas Inhalator
Device that warms air for a hypothermia victim to breathe.

Warning Devices
Any audible or visual devices, such as flashing lights, sirens, horns, or bells, added to an emergency vehicle to gain the attention of drivers of other vehicles.

Warning Lights
Lights on the apparatus designed to attract the attention of other motorists.

Warp Yarn
Threads that run lengthwise in a fabric or woven hose.

Wash Down
To flush spilled liquids from the roadway.

Waste Line
Hoseline that is tied off or otherwise secured and is used to handle water in excess of that being used during a relay operation.

Watch
Period of time during which a firefighter is assigned to the communications center desk.

Watch Desk
Communications desk of a fire station.

Watch Line
Charged hoseline remaining at the scene of a fire with a detail of firefighters to stand guard against possible rekindling after the fire has been extinguished.

Watchman
Employee assigned to patrol and guard a property against fire or theft.

Water Curtain
Fan-shaped stream of water applied between a fire and an exposed surface to prevent the surface from igniting from radiated heat.

Water Department
Municipal authority responsible for the water supply system in a given community.

Water Distribution System
System designed to supply water for residential, commercial, industrial, and/or fire protection purposes. This water supply is delivered through a network of piping and pressure-developing equipment.

Waterflow Detector
Detector that recognizes movement of water within the sprinkler or standpipe system. Once movement is noted, the waterflow detector gives a local alarm and/or may transmit the alarm.

Water Hammer
Force created by the rapid deceleration of water. It generally results from closing a valve or nozzle too quickly.

Water Motor Gong
Audible alarm on an automatic sprinkler system that is powered by water flowing through the system.

Water-Reactive Materials
Substances, generally flammable solids, that react in varying degrees when mixed with water or exposed to humid air.

Water Solubility
Ability of a liquid or solid to mix with or dissolve in water.

Water Superintendent
Manager of the water department.

Water Supply
Any source of water available for use in fire fighting operations.

Water Supply Pumper
Pumper that takes water from a source and sends it to attack pumpers operating at the fire scene.

Water Tank
Water storage receptacle carried directly on the apparatus. NFPA 1901 specifies that Class A pumpers must carry at least 500 gallons (2 000 L). Also called Booster Tank.

Water Thief
This variation of a wye adapter has three gated outlets, usually two 1 ½-inch (38 mm) outlets and one 2½-inch (65 mm) outlet. There is a single inlet for 2½-inch (65 mm) or larger hose.

Water Tower
Aerial device primarily intended for deploying an elevated master stream. Not generally intended for climbing operations.

Water Vacuum
Appliance similar to a household vacuum cleaner designed to pick up water.

Waterway
Path through which water flows within a hose.

Waybill
Shipping paper used by a railroad to indicate origin, destination, route, and product. There is a waybill for each car, and it is carried by the conductor.

Web
Wide vertical part of a beam between the flanges.

Web Member
Secondary members of a truss that are contained between the chords.

Weep Hole
Small holes in masonry veneer wall that release water accumulation to the exterior.

Weeping
(1) Coupling leakage at the point of attachment. (2) Giving off or leaking fluid slowly.

Weft Yarn
See Filler Yarn.

Weld
Joint created between two metal surfaces when they are heated and the two metals run together.

Weldment
Structure formed by the welding together of two or more pieces.

Western Frame Construction
See Platform Frame Construction.

Wet-Barrel Hydrant
Fire hydrant that has water all the way up to the discharge outlets. The hydrant may have separate valves for each discharge or one valve for all the discharges. This type of hydrant is only used in areas where there is no danger of freezing weather conditions.

Wet Down
(1) To wet down or dampen debris after fire has been controlled but not completely extinguished. (2) Ceremony used in some departments to celebrate the acquisition of a new piece of apparatus.

Wet-Pipe Sprinkler System
Automatic sprinkler system in which the pipes are constantly filled with water under pressure.

Wet Standpipe System
Standpipe system that has water supply valves open and maintains water in the system at all times.

Wetting Agent
Chemical solution added to water to reduce its surface tension and improve its penetrating ability; detergent is a mild form of wetting agent.

Wet Water
Wetting agent that is introduced to water to reduce the surface tension and improve its penetration qualities.

Wheel Blocks
See Chocks.

Wheezing
Breathing noisily and with difficulty.

Wildland Fire
See Natural Cover Fire.

Wild Line
Uncontrolled hoseline and nozzle or butt that hrash about from the reaction of highly pressurized, flowing water.

Winch
Pulling tool that consists of a length of steel chain or cable wrapped around a motor-driven drum. These are most commonly attached to the front or rear of a vehicle.

Winders
Radiating or wedge-shaped treads at the turn of a stairway.

Windpipe
Trachea.

Wind Shakes
Damage done to timber by repeated flexing in the wind.

Wind Sock
Cone-shaped cloth sock located at airports to indicate wind direction and to some extent wind velocity.

Wind Tee
T-shaped indicator mounted horizontally on a pivot pole to swing freely in the wind; used as a wind direction indicator or landing direction indicator; may also be in the shape of a tetrahedron.

Windward Side
Side of the building the wind is striking.

Wire Cutters
Tool with approved, insulated handles to cut wire.

Wired Glass
Sheet glass containing wire netting, which increases resistance to breakage and penetration.

Wired Telegraph Circuit Box
Alarm system operated by pressing a lever in the alarm box that starts a wound-spring mechanism. The rotating mechanism transmits a code by opening and closing the circuit.

Womb
Uterus.

Wood Grain
Stratification of wood fibers in a piece of wood.

Wood Planer
Device commonly found in woodworking shops; used to smooth the surface of wooden boards.

Word Processor
Software program used with a personal computer, designed specifically for creating text documents.

Worker
See Working Fire.

Working End
Part of the rope that is to be used in forming the knot. Also called Bitter End or Loose End.

Working Fire
Term used to describe a fire at which considerable fire fighting activity will be required. Also called Worker.

Woven-Jacket Hose
Fire hose constructed with one or two outer jackets woven on looms from cotton or synthetic fibers.

WPIV
Abbreviation for Wall Post Indicator Valve.

Wrapped Hose
Nonwoven rubber hose manufactured by wrapping rubber-impregnated woven fabric around a rubber tube and encasing it in a rubber cover.

Wrecker
Tow truck.

Wristlet
Portion of the coat that prevents fire or water from entering the sleeve.

Wye
Hose appliance with one female inlet and two or more male outlets, usually gated.

X

Xiphoid Process
Flexible cartilage at the lower tip of the sternum.

Yard Hydrant
See Private Hydrant.

Y-Branch
Plumbing drainage fitting with a branch or branches that extend at an angle of 45 degrees.

Zero Mechanical State
State a machine is in when all power sources are neutralized and all parts of the machine are stabilized.

Index

IFSTA MANUALS AND FPP PRODUCTS

For a current catalog describing these and other products, call or write your local IFSTA distributor or Fire Protection Publications, IFSTA Headquarters, Oklahoma State University, Stillwater, OK 74078-0118. Phone: 1-800-654-4055

Awareness Level Training for Hazardous Materials

prepares fire, police, EMS, and public utilities to recognize and identify the presence of hazardous materials at an emergency scene. Addresses the requirements in NFPA 472, Chapter 2: Competencies for First Responders at the Awareness Level. Information found in the manual includes responsibilities of the first responder, identification systems, types of containers, and personal protective equipment. 1st Edition (1995), 152 pages.

Study Guide Awareness Level Training For Hazardous Materials

The companion study guide in question and answer format. (1995), 184 pages.

Fire Department AERIAL APPARATUS

includes information on the driver/operator's qualifications; vehicle operation; types of aerial apparatus; positioning, stabilizing, and operating aerial devices; tactics for aerial devices; and maintaining, testing, and purchasing aerial apparatus. Detailed appendices describe specific manufacturers' aerial devices. 1st Edition (1991), 386 pages, addresses NFPA 1002.

STUDY GUIDE FOR AERIAL APPARATUS

The companion study guide in question and answer format. 1991, 140 pages.

AIRCRAFT RESCUE AND FIRE FIGHTING

comprehensively covers commercial, military, and general aviation. All the information you need is in one place. Subjects covered include: personal protective equipment, apparatus and equipment, extinguishing agents, engines and systems, fire fighting procedures, hazardous materials, and fire prevention. Over 240 photographs and two-color illustrations. It also contains a glossary and review questions with answers. 3rd Edition (1992), 247 pages, addresses NFPA 1003.

BUILDING CONSTRUCTION RELATED TO THE FIRE SERVICE

helps firefighters become aware of the many construction designs and features of buildings found in a typical first alarm district and how these designs serve or hinder the suppression effort. Subjects include construction principles, assemblies and their resistance to fire, building services, door and window assemblies, and special types of structures. 1st Edition (1986), 166 pages, addresses NFPA 1001 and NFPA 1031, levels I & II.

CHIEF OFFICER

lists, explains, and illustrates the skills necessary to plan and maintain an efficient and cost-effective fire department. The combination of an ever-increasing fire problem, spiraling personnel and equipment costs, and the development of new technologies and methods for decision making requires far more than expertise in fire suppression. Today's chief officer must possess the ability to plan and administrate as well as have political expertise. 1st Edition (1985), 211 pages, addresses NFPA 1021, level VI.

SELF-INSTRUCTION FOR CHIEF OFFICER

The companion study guide in question and answer format. 1986, 142 pages.

FIRE DEPARTMENT COMPANY OFFICER

focuses on the basic principles of fire department organization, working relationships, and personnel management. For the firefighter aspiring to become a company officer, or a company officer wishing to improve management skills, this manual helps develop and improve the necessary traits to effectively manage the fire company. 2nd Edition (1990), 278 pages, addresses NFPA 1021, levels I, II, & III.

COMPANY OFFICER STUDY GUIDE

The companion study guide in question and answer format. Includes problem applications and case studies. 1991, 243 pages.

ESSENTIALS OF FIRE FIGHTING

is the "bible" on basic firefighter skills and is used throughout the world. The easy-to-read format is enhanced by 1,600 photographs and illustrations. Step-by-step instructions are provided for many fire fighting tasks. Topics covered include: personal protective equipment, building construction, firefighter safety, fire behavior, portable extinguishers, SCBA, ropes and knots, rescue, forcible entry, ventilation, communications, water supplies, fire streams, hose, fire cause determination, public fire education and prevention, fire suppression techniques, ladders, salvage and overhaul, and automatic sprinkler systems. 3rd Edition (1992), 590 pages, addresses NFPA 1001.

STUDY GUIDE FOR 3rd EDITION OF ESSENTIALS OF FIRE FIGHTING

The companion learning tool for the new 3rd edition of the manual. It contains questions and answers to help you learn the important information in the book. 1992, 322 pages.

PRINCIPLES OF EXTRICATION

leads you step-by-step through the procedures for disentangling victims from cars, buses, trains, farm equipment, and industrial situations. Fully illustrated with color diagrams and more than 500 photographs. It includes rescue company organization, protective clothing, and evaluating resources. Review questions with answers at the end of each chapter. 1st Edition (1990), 365 pages.

FIRE CAUSE DETERMINATION

gives you the information necessary to make on-scene fire cause determinations. You will know when to call for a trained investigator, and you will be able to help the investigator. It includes a profile of firesetters, finding origin and cause, documenting evidence, interviewing witnesses, and courtroom demeanor. 1st Edition (1982), 159 pages, addresses NFPA 1021, Fire Officer I, and NFPA 1031, levels I & II.

FIRE SERVICE FIRST RESPONDER

provides the information needed to evaluate and treat patients with serious injuries or illnesses. It familiarizes the reader with a wide variety of medical equipment and supplies. **First Responder** applies to safety, security, fire brigade, and law enforcement personnel, as well as fire service personnel, who are required to administer emergency medical care. 1st Edition (1987), 340 pages, addresses NFPA 1001, levels I & II, and DOT First Responder.

FORCIBLE ENTRY
reflects the growing concern for the reduction of property damage as well as firefighter safety. This comprehensive manual contains technical information about forcible entry tactics, tools, and methods, as well as door, window, and wall construction. Tactics discuss the degree of danger to the structure and leaving the building secure after entry. Includes a section on locks and through-the-lock entry. Review questions and answers at the end of each chapter. 7th Edition (1987), 270 pages, helpful for NFPA 1001.

GROUND COVER FIRE FIGHTING PRACTICES
explains the dramatic difference between structural fire fighting and wildland fire fighting. Ground cover fires include fires in weeds, grass, field crops, and brush. It discusses the apparatus, equipment, and extinguishing agents used to combat wildland fires. Outdoor fire behavior and how fuels, weather, and topography affect fire spread are explained. The text also covers personnel safety, management, and suppression methods. It contains a glossary, sample fire operation plan, fire control organization system, fire origin and cause determination, and water expansion pump systems. 2nd Edition (1982), 152 pages.

FIRE SERVICE GROUND LADDER PRACTICES
is a "how to" manual for learning how to handle, raise, and climb ground ladders; it also details maintenance and service testing. Basic information is presented with a variety of methods that allow the readers to select the best method for their locale. The chapter on Special Uses includes: ladders as a stretcher, a slide, a float drag, a water chute, and more. The manual contains a glossary, review questions and answers, and a sample testing and repair form. 8th Edition (1984), 388 pages, addresses NFPA 1001.

HAZARDOUS MATERIALS FOR FIRST RESPONDERS
prepares the reader to meet the objectives for First Responder at the Awareness and Operational levels contained in NFPA 472. The manual includes information on properties of hazardous materials, recognizing and identifying hazardous materials, personal protective equipment, emergency scene command and control, incident control tactics and strategies, and decontamination. Over 350 illustrations are used to reinforce the text. 2nd Edition (1994), 241 pages.

STUDY GUIDE FOR IFSTA HAZARDOUS MATERIALS FOR FIRST RESPONDERS
The companion study guide in question and answer format. 2nd Edition (1994), 253 pages.

HAZARDOUS MATERIALS: MANAGING THE INCIDENT
addresses OSHA 1910.120 and NFPA 472, *Standard for Professional Competence of Responders to Hazardous Materials Incidents.* Provides the reader with a logical, systematic process for responding to and managing hazardous materials emergencies. It is directed toward the haz mat technician, incident commander, the off-site specialty employee, and haz mat response team members. Includes numerous charts, diagrams, scan sheets, checklists, and reference information. Topics include haz mat management system, health and safety, ICS, politics of haz mat incident management, hazard and risk evaluation, decontamination, and more! 2nd Edition (1994)

STUDENT WORKBOOK FOR HAZARDOUS MATERIALS: MANAGING THE INCIDENT
The companion study guide in question and answer format. 2nd Edition (1994)

INSTRUCTOR'S GUIDE FOR HAZARDOUS MATERIALS: MANAGING THE INCIDENT
Provides lessons based on each chapter. 2nd Edition (1994)

HAZ MAT RESPONSE TEAM LEAK AND SPILL GUIDE
contains articles by Michael Hildebrand reprinted from *Speaking of Fire*'s popular Hazardous Materials Nuts and Bolts series. Two additional articles from *Speaking of Fire* and the hazardous material incident SOP from the Chicago Fire Department are also included. 1st Edition (1984), 57 pages.

EMERGENCY OPERATIONS IN HIGH-RACK STORAGE
is a concise summary of emergency operations in the high-rack storage area of a warehouse. It explains how to develop a pre-emergency plan, what equipment will be necessary to implement the plan, type and amount of training personnel will need to handle an emergency, and interfacing with various agencies. Includes consideration questions, points not to be overlooked, and trial scenarios. 1st Edition (1981), 97 pages.

HOSE PRACTICES
reflects the latest information on modern fire hose and couplings. It is the most comprehensive single source about hose and its use. The manual details basic methods of handling hose, including large diameter hose. It is fully illustrated with photographs showing loads, evolutions, and techniques. This complete and practical book explains the national standards for hose and couplings. 7th Edition (1988), 245 pages, addresses NFPA 1001.

FIRE PROTECTION HYDRAULICS AND WATER SUPPLY ANALYSIS
covers the quantity and pressure of water needed to provide adequate fire protection, the ability of existing water supply systems to provide fire protection, the adequacy of a water supply for a sprinkler system, and alternatives for deficient water supply systems. 1st Edition (1990), 340 pages.

INCIDENT COMMAND SYSTEM (ICS)
was developed by a multiagency task force. Using this system, fire, police, and other government groups can operate together effectively under a single command. The system is modular and can be used to meet the requirements of both day-to-day and large-incident operations. It is the approved basic command system taught at the National Fire Academy. 1st Edition (1983), 220 pages, helpful for NFPA 1021.

INDUSTRIAL FIRE BRIGADE TRAINING: INCIPIENT LEVEL
assists management in complying with applicable laws and regulations, primarily NFPA 600 and 29 CFR 1910, and to assist them in training those who provide incipient level fire protection for industrial occupancies. It is also intended to serve as a reference and training resource for individual emergency responders. 1st Edition (1995), 184 pages.

FIRE INSPECTION AND CODE ENFORCEMENT
provides a comprehensive, state-of-the-art reference and training manual for both uniformed and civilian inspectors. It is a comprehensive guide to the principles and techniques of inspection. Text includes information on how fire travels, electrical hazards, and fire resistance requirements. It covers storage, handling, and use of hazardous materials; fire protection systems; and building construction for fire and life safety. 5th Edition (1987), 316 pages, addresses NFPA 1001 and NFPA 1031, levels I & II.

STUDY GUIDE FOR FIRE INSPECTION AND CODE ENFORCEMENT

The companion study guide in question and answer format with case studies. 1989, 272 pages.

FIRE SERVICE INSTRUCTOR

explains the characteristics of a good instructor, shows you how to determine training requirements, and teach to the level of your class. It discusses the types, principles, and procedures of teaching and learning, and covers the use of effective training aids and devices. The purpose and principles of testing as well as test construction are covered. Included are chapters on safety, legal considerations, and computers. 5th Edition (1990), 326 pages, addresses NFPA 1041, levels I & II.

LEADERSHIP IN THE FIRE SERVICE

was created from the series of lectures given by Robert F. Hamm to assist in leadership development. It provides the foundation for getting along with others, explains how to gain the confidence of your personnel, and covers what is expected of an officer. Included is information on supervision, evaluations, delegating, and teaching. Some of the topics include: the successful leader today, a look into the past may reveal the future, and self-analysis for officers. 1st Edition (1967), 132 pages.

FIRE SERVICE ORIENTATION AND TERMINOLOGY

Fire Service Orientation and Indoctrination has been revised. It has a new name and a new look. Keeping the best of the old — traditions, history, and organization — this new manual provides a complete dictionary of fire service terms. To be used in conjunction with **Essentials of Fire Fighting** and the other IFSTA manuals. 3rd Edition (1993), addresses NFPA 1001.

PRIVATE FIRE PROTECTION AND DETECTION

provides a means by which fires may be prevented or attacked in their incipient phase and/or controlled until the fire brigade or public fire protection can arrive. This second edition covers information on automatic sprinkler systems, hose standpipe systems, fixed fire pump installations, portable fire extinguishers, fixed special agent extinguishing systems, and fire alarm and detection systems. Information on the design, operation, maintenance, and inspection of these systems and equipment is provided. 2nd Edition (1994).

PUBLIC FIRE EDUCATION

provides valuable information for ending public apathy and ignorance about fire. This manual gives you the knowledge to plan and implement fire prevention campaigns. It shows you how to tailor the individual programs to your audience as well as the time of year or specific problems. It includes working with the media, resource exchange, and smoke detectors. 1st Edition (1979), 169 pages, helpful for NFPA 1021 and 1031.

FIRE DEPARTMENT PUMPING APPARATUS

is the Driver/Operator's encyclopedia on operating fire pumps and pumping apparatus. It covers pumpers, tankers (tenders), brush apparatus, and aerials with pumps. This comprehensive volume explains safe driving techniques, getting maximum efficiency from the pump, and basic water supply. It includes specification writing, apparatus testing, and extensive appendices of pump manufacturers. 7th Edition (1989), 374 pages, addresses NFPA 1002.

STUDY GUIDE FOR PUMPING APPARATUS

The companion study guide in question and answer format. 1990, 100 pages.

FIRE SERVICE RESCUE PRACTICES

is a comprehensive training text for firefighters and fire brigade members that expands proficiency in moving and removing victims from hazardous situations. This extensively illustrated manual includes rescuer safety, effects of rescue work on victims, rescue from hazardous atmospheres, trenching, and outdoor searches. 5th Edition (1981), 262 pages, addresses NFPA 1001.

RESIDENTIAL SPRINKLERS A PRIMER

outlines United States residential fire experience, system components, engineering requirements, and issues concerning automatic and fixed residential sprinkler systems. Written by Gary Courtney and Scott Kerwood and reprinted from *Speaking of Fire*. An excellent reference source for any fire service library and an excellent supplement to **Private Fire Protection.** 1st Edition (1986), 16 pages.

FIRE DEPARTMENT OCCUPATIONAL SAFETY

addresses the basic responsibilities and qualifications for a safety officer and the minimum requirements and procedures for a safety and health program. Included in this manual is an overview of establishing and implementing a safety program, physical fitness and health considerations, safety in training, fire station safety, tool and equipment safety and maintenance, personal protective equipment, en- route hazards and response, emergency scene safety, and special hazards. 2nd Edition (1991), 366 pages, addresses NFPA 1500, 1501.

SALVAGE AND OVERHAUL

covers planning salvage operations, equipment selection and care, as well as describing methods and techniques for using salvage equipment to minimize fire damage caused by water, smoke, heat, and debris. The overhaul section includes methods for finding hidden fire, protection of fire cause evidence, safety during overhaul operations, and restoration of property and fire protection systems after a fire. 7th Edition (1985), 225 pages, addresses NFPA 1001.

SELF-CONTAINED BREATHING APPARATUS

contains all the basics of SCBA use, care, testing, and operation. Special attention is given to safety and training. The chapter on Emergency Conditions Breathing has been completely revised to incorporate safer emergency methods that can be used with newer models of SCBA. Also included are appendices describing regulatory agencies and donning and doffing procedures for nine types of SCBA. The manual has been thoroughly updated to cover NFPA, OSHA, ANSI, and NIOSH regulations and standards as they pertain to SCBA. 2nd Edition (1991), 360 pages, addresses NFPA 1001.

THE SOURCEBOOK FOR FIRE COMPANY TRAINING EVOLUTIONS

provides volunteer and career training officers and company officers with ideas for presenting weekly or monthly training sessions. The book contains plans for more than 50 different training sessions. Each session contains information on the standards that are covered, equipment that is needed, outlines for the presentations and practical exercises, and a listing of pertinent resources and training materials. The sessions cover basic fire fighting, apparatus operation, company evolutions, indoor sessions that can be used on rainy days, and competitive exercises with a practical training value. 1st Edition (1994) 238 pages.

STUDY GUIDE FOR SELF-CONTAINED BREATHING APPARATUS

The companion study guide in question and answer format. 1991, 131 pages.

FIRE STREAM PRACTICES

brings you an all new approach to calculating friction loss. This carefully written text covers the physics of fire and water; the characteristics, requirements, and principles of good streams; and fire fighting foams. **Streams** includes formulas for the application of fire fighting hydraulics, as well as actions and reactions created by applying streams under a variety of circumstances. The friction loss equations and answers are included, and review questions are located at the end of each chapter. 7th Edition (1989), 464 pages, addresses NFPA 1001 and NFPA 1002.

GASOLINE TANK TRUCK EMERGENCIES

provides emergency response personnel with background information, general procedures, and response guidelines to be followed when responding to and operating at incidents involving MC-306/DOT 406 cargo tank trucks. Specific topics include: incident management procedures, site safety considerations, methods of product transfer, and vehicle uprighting considerations. 1st Edition (1992), 51 pages, addresses NFPA 472.

FIRE SERVICE VENTILATION

presents the principles and practices of ventilation. The manual describes and illustrates the safe operations related to ventilation, products of combustion, elements and situations that influence the ventilation process, ventilation methods and procedures, and tools and mechanized equipment used in ventilation. The manual includes chapter reviews, a glossary, and applicable safety considerations. 7th Edition (1994), addresses NFPA 1001.

FIRE SERVICE PRACTICES FOR VOLUNTEER AND SMALL COMMUNITY FIRE DEPARTMENTS

presents those training practices that are most consistent with the activities of smaller fire departments. Consideration is given to the limitations of small community fire department resources. Techniques for performing basic skills are explained, accompanied by detailed illustrations and photographs. 6th Edition (1984), 311 pages.

WATER SUPPLIES FOR FIRE PROTECTION

acquaints you with the principles, requirements, and standards used to provide water for fire fighting. Rural water supplies as well as fixed systems are discussed. Abundant photographs, illustrations, tables, and diagrams make this the most complete text available. It includes requirements for size and carrying capacity of mains, hydrant specifications, maintenance procedures conducted by the fire department, and relevant maps and record-keeping procedures. Review questions at the end of each chapter. 4th Edition (1988), 268 pages, addresses NFPA 1001, NFPA 1002, and NFPA 1031, levels I & II.

CURRICULUM PACKAGES

COMPANY OFFICER

A competency-based teaching package with 17 lessons as well as classroom and practical activities to teach the student the information and skills needed to qualify for the position of Company Officer. Corresponds to **Fire Department Company Officer**, 2nd Edition.

The Package includes the Company Officer Instructor's Guide (the how, what, and when to teach); the Student Guide (a workbook for group instruction); and 143 full-color overhead transparencies.

ESSENTIALS CURRICULUM PACKAGE

A competency-based teaching package with 19 chapters and 22 lessons as well as classroom and practical activities to teach the student the information and skills needed to qualify for the position of Fire Fighter I or II. Corresponds to **Essentials of Fire Fighting**, 3rd Edition.

The Package includes the Essentials Instructor's Guide (the how, what, and when to teach); the Student Guide (a workbook for group instruction); and 445 full-color overhead transparencies.

LEADERSHIP

A complete teaching package that assist the instructor in teaching leadership and motivational skills at the Company Officer level. Each lesson gives an outline of the subject matter to be covered, approximate time required to teach the material, specific learning objectives, and references for the instructor's preparation. Sources for suggested films and videotapes are included.

TRANSLATIONS

LO ESENCIAL EN EL COMBATE DE INCENDIOS

is a direct translation of **Essentials of Fire Fighting**, 2nd edition. Please contact your distributor or FPP for shipping charges to addresses outside U.S. and Canada. 444 pages.

PRACTICAS Y TEORIA PARA BOMBEROS

is a direct translation of **Fire Service Practices for Volunteer and Small Community Fire Departments**, 6th edition. Please contact your distributor or FPP for shipping charges to addresses outside U.S. and Canada. 347 pages.

OTHER ITEMS

TRAINING AIDS

Fire Protection Publications carries a complete line of videos, overhead transparencies, and slides. Call for a current catalog.

NEWSLETTER

The nationally acclaimed and award-winning newsletter, *Speaking of Fire*, is published quarterly and available to you free. Call today for your free subscription.

COMMENT SHEET

DATE ____________________ NAME ____

ADDRESS ____

ORGANIZATION REPRESENTED ____

CHAPTER TITLE ______________________________________ NUMBER ___________

SECTION/PARAGRAPH/FIGURE __________________________ PAGE _____________

1. Proposal (include proposed wording or identification of wording to be deleted), OR PROPOSED FIGURE:

2. Statement of Problem and Substantiation for Proposal:

RETURN TO: IFSTA Editor
Fire Protection Publications
Oklahoma State University
Stillwater, OK 74078-0118

SIGNATURE ______________________________

Use this sheet to make any suggestions, recommendations, or comments. We need your input to make the manuals as up to date as possible. Your help is appreciated. Use additional pages if necessary.